# SMOKESCREEN

## ONE MAN AGAINST THE UNDERWORLD

### PAUL WILLIAM ROBERTS
### AND NORMAN SNIDER

Published in Canada in 2001 by
Stoddart Publishing Co. Limited
895 Don Mills Road, 400-2 Park Centre, Toronto, Canada M3C 1W3

Published in the United States in 2002 by
Stoddart Publishing Co. Limited
PMB 128, 4500 Witmer Estates, Niagara Falls, New York 14305-1386

**www.stoddartpub.com**

To order Stoddart books please contact General Distribution Services
*In Canada* Tel. (416) 213-1919     Fax (416) 213-1917
Email cservice@genpub.com
*In the United States* Toll-free tel. 1-800-805-1083 Toll-free fax 1-800-481-6207
Email gdsinc@genpub.com

10  9  8  7  6  5  4  3  2  1

**National Library of Canada Cataloguing in Publication Data**
Roberts, Paul William
Smokescreen: one man against the underworld
ISBN 0-7737-3323-X
1. Informers — Canada — Biography.  2. Undercover operations — Canada.  3.
Organized crime — Canada.  I. Snider, Norman, 1945–
II. Title.
PS8585.O299S46 2001     363.25'2     C2001-901988-2
PR9199.3.R529S46 2001

**U.S. Cataloging in Publication Data Available from the Library of Congress**
ISBN 0-7737-3323-X

Jacket Design: Angel Guerra
Text Design: Tannice Goddard

THE CANADA COUNCIL | LE CONSEIL DES ARTS
FOR THE ARTS | DU CANADA
SINCE 1957 | DEPUIS 1957

*We acknowledge for their financial support of our
publishing program the Canada Council, the Ontario Arts
Council, and the Government of Canada through the
Book Publishing Industry Development Program (BPIDP).*

Printed and bound in Canada

*Democracy don't rule the world,*
*you'd better get that through your head;*
*this world is ruled by violence —*
*but I guess that's better left unsaid . . .*
— *BOB DYLAN*

*For Tiziana, F.M., and Celine*

*Women and men, then, have the same nature in respect to guardianship of the state, save insofar as the one is weaker, the other stronger.*

— *PLATO*, THE REPUBLIC

# Contents

# Preface

*smokescreen (n.): a mass of smoke used to conceal the movements of troops; something intended to conceal or disguise one's activities.*
— OXFORD AMERICAN DICTIONARY

There are three main categories of police undercover workers: cops, informers, and paid agents. Cops do it as a part of their job; informers usually do it to save their own necks; and paid agents do it for cash. Supposedly. But it is the most difficult and dangerous job in law enforcement, and all things considered, it doesn't pay that well. For nearly seven years, C. Calvin Broeker has worked as both a Crown agent for the Royal Canadian Mounted Police and a paid agent for the United States Secret Service. During that time, he has infiltrated the Italian Mafia, the Hell's Angels and other biker gangs, the Russian Mafiya, Bulgarian government racketeers, and Native Indian smuggling rings operating out of reservations on the U.S.–Canada border. He has provided vital data on or been instrumental in apprehending drug smugglers, counterfeiters, illegal arms dealers, crooked bankers, and assassins. He has put dangerous men behind bars, and he has come closer than any outsider before him to looking on the new face of twenty-first-century crime: a nexus of highly organized criminal enterprises extending up from tobacco smuggling through narcotics and illegal arms deals into the highest levels of international business and politics. Many people want him dead. He ought to shut up and go quietly into the Witness Protection Program, grateful to still be alive. But he's not like that, and Canada doesn't really have a well-developed program anyway. If we live in the kind of society where he has to hide, he says, then we're in as much trouble as he is.

He's had plenty of threats, however, and not long ago an enforcer for one of the biker gangs was spotted inside the condominium complex where he lived. But Cal doesn't scare. He has never hidden, and he does not intend to hide now. The term "undercover," when applied to him, is even a misnomer, since Cal has never concealed his identity, just his motives and his loyalties. His possibly unequalled success as an undercover Crown agent relies partly on this lack of guile. He was never *behind* the smokescreen — he *was* the smokescreen.

Cal Broeker is a force of nature too. His story is unique, and so is he. It has much to say about the society in which we live, and about the nature of crime and criminals. It is writ large, like everything about Cal, who is a man with a mission, a knight on a quest in the age of the automobile and the anti-hero.

For those who live in Canada, particularly, it may come as something of a shock to discover what pullulates beneath the veneer of what *seems* to be the relatively tranquil surface of everyday life. And Cal's story begs the unpalatable question of what exactly it is that a person has to do before his right to human rights is revoked. Organized crime has declared war on the rest of us, and we're acting as if the criminals are errant schoolboys who can be made to see the error of their ways. They pour scorn on our rights, and we champion theirs.

A lot of the issues raised in this book merit close examination and extended debate, but we have chosen not to open the various cans of worms. This is the wrong place. That does not mean that no serious problems exist in the area of crime and policing, and within the law itself.

Organized crime has become as big a threat to our future peace and social stability as the Cold War ever was, but our misguided sense of fair play has left the police forces designed to combat it most encumbered when they need to be most free. There are some horrible realities in here, things few of us wish to face about the kind of society we've created. But this is not the principal reason why we wrote this book.

What interested us, as writers, was the story itself. It is not cunningly structured or ingeniously plotted. It can be baggy and repetitious. Character development is uneven or non-existent, and many of the supporting cast are mere stereotypes, monotonously predictable. There is no satisfying narrative arc. But it is utterly authentic, and the characters are real people in real situations. In a media-saturated, narcissistic culture, the stories we crave because they make sense of chaos increasingly come out of the chaos itself. News is entertainment. And reality is literally incredible. As we were prone to say on many occasions during the writing of this book, "You couldn't make this up. . . ."

This is real life. This is crime and punishment, war and peace — as they are, not as we would like them to be, not as myths. It's the thing itself. It's a slice. But we were increasingly impressed by how closely life was at times able to imitate art. It may not be as articulate, and it doesn't give a damn about plot, but we feel life more than compensates for these shortcomings by being shamelessly, rambunctiously real. Most of the dialogue in this book is taken from tapes or police transcripts of wire-tapped meetings, or from notes written immediately afterwards by Cal or one of his RCMP handlers. It's all unrevised and unrehearsed, lacking even the courtroom spin or gloss that would be added later to meet the needs of a Crown attorney.

Cal Broeker is also an obsessive and meticulous taker of notes. Along with his peeled honesty, this provides documents as relentlessly fascinating as any in social history. Few men have ever been more frank about their own strengths and weaknesses. His notes and musings are put on paper to help him understand himself, never to aggrandize himself, and they often reflect the complex pleasures offered by the examined life, especially when that life is staring into its own non-existence. He finds disgrace under pressure as compellingly interesting as grace. Unlike most philosophers and men of letters, Cal is unafraid of his own pettiness and triviality. It's all one big banquet of experience to him, and he treats a trite or clichéd thought the same as he does one of soaring profundity. It is only action he finds real, not ideas or thoughts. Not words. Ultimately, he is what he does, and what he does determines what he will next become. He tilts at real giants as well as windmills. This is what interested us — the warp and woof of complex character — and what also, so often, chilled and chastened us during the writing of this book; it's what made us continue with the project against sometimes daunting opposition, and

what allowed us to complete it the way we'd started out — as friends.

Although he operates within the law, Cal Broeker, as a Crown agent, is not a cop. The distinction is crucial on many levels, but most of all on the level of sensibility. As the reader will no doubt realize, Broeker could just as easily be committing the crimes he is endeavouring to prevent here. If money was ever the object, he would be rich indeed today. Merely by failing to report in, he could have driven away with hundreds of millions. But he's not about that. Like most of us, however, he's also not always entirely sure just what he *is* about. We liked this about his story too, liked the fact that he had turned his back on a white middle-class North American existence, only to be uncertain about exactly what it was he now faced.

Initially, we were somewhat troubled by the prospect of writing such an account from one person's perspective. But because of the nature of the story, we had little choice. Either the RCMP or the Secret Service, or both, we were cautioned, might try to issue an injunction against the book if they got wind of it, probably on the grounds that it endangered the lives of operatives still in the field or operations still under way. We have been very careful not to expose police operations or operatives, and have changed people's names wherever there was the slightest possibility of harm coming to them. But there would have been no point in stating our intentions to those concerned. There is little trust between the policeman and the writer — although we share certain similarities of purpose — and probably because the answer to that famous Socratic query is that *artists guard the guardians*. Although Cal did offer to arrange meetings with officers he felt could be trusted, we thought this would be placing too great a burden on all involved and could easily backfire. Besides, the risk was not worth its potential results, since it would have involved only a few officers who were peripherally involved with a couple of projects.

Naturally, we had no illusions about interviewing those whom Cal had sent to jail. And if we had had any, the shooting of a Montreal journalist delving into the activities of the Hell's Angels and the Russian Mafiya put paid to them. Yet we found, as we went through the transcripts and wiretaps and reports and taped conversations, that we got to know these "buddies" (as the Canadian police term them) as well as if we'd met them. They are probably not much like most people's notions of the professional criminal, though, and this too we found intriguing. We were less than enthralled, however, to find ourselves obliged, for legal reasons, to protect the identity of some of them. But only the Law knows what it is doing.

When you flip from zero to hero and back again as frequently as Cal Broeker has done over the past twenty years, you're going to leave a lot of confused people behind you. Cal doesn't understand that he moves too fast for many to comprehend what he's really about. He thinks he's a simple, straightforward guy because he approaches life simply and directly. Yet the life he views as humdrum would confound, exhaust, and terrify a dozen ordinary men, and it was difficult enough for two rather lazy and prevaricating writers to pin down its details so they made some kind of sense without bringing in external versions. Cal had enough of his own ad hominem variants and contrasting narrative styles for each story that the thought of sifting through anyone else's assaults on memory was a fearsome one.

Those few denizens of Cal's remote past who could be interviewed were, and extensive use was made of RCMP officers' notes from court briefs, which were exhilarating in their plodding banality and rank confusion when compared with Cal's analytic pincer attacks and strategic evasions. However, this is one man's story, told more often than not in his own words. We make no apologies for its being raw, even revolting at times. Policework is a dirty job, but no one *has* to do it. Writing this made us feel uncommonly grateful that many men and women choose to do it. Life would be unspeakably different if they did not.

Memory is a tricky thing. It's as much about what we choose to forget as it is about what we choose to remember. In putting this book together, we felt we were victims of Cal Broeker's memory just as often as we were beneficiaries of it. But the act of recalling, in detail, step by step, some of the incidents recounted here took its toll on Cal. He'd never done it before. Cathartic it certainly was, but catharsis isn't always a good thing. Not when you have no possible resolution for the trauma relived.

Sometimes it was palpable: the three of us felt drained, plugged into some low-grade anxiety, dispirited and depressed. Imagine how Cal must feel, we later thought.

This is the nature of crime, ultimately: low-grade anxiety and a feeling that something isn't right. The universe is out of joint. *Contra natura*, the ancients used to say. Against nature. Unnatural. People take their cue from the top, and criminals are no different. When the apex is rotten, the whole pyramid crumbles. If the polls are accurate, many people these days view the government as the biggest thief of all, and most sense that money has replaced morality. It may not buy you love, but it can buy you justice, revenge, the illusion of wisdom, a fair slice of peace, and an awful lot of luxury, gluttony, and lust. For the poor, as always, it's bread and circuses.

Since news is now a major form of entertainment — which is to say, life is recycled as entertainment — it is hardly surprising to find it resembling a permanent circus-cum-freakshow. Thus there is, we feel, some benefit to be had from reminding ourselves what reality is like in reality — even if we cannot bear too much of it. Although TV networks create programming designed to escort harmless and useful commercial messages into your home to help you better choose which is the optimum bar of soap or tampon, life is not about to do it. It's too unpredictable, too undomesticated, too uncivilized. And you couldn't make it up. It's God's novel, and He's never taken kindly to critics of any stripe. The shrieking bedlam only seems worse now than it ever was before because *now* is the bit you actually have to live in. *Before* was someone else's problem, and other people's problems are always a doddle to solve.

A glance at the whole history of kings and provosts and cannonballs, war and peace, tells us it was ever thus. It is frankly amazing that people of goodwill continue to will good in spite of the opposition. Yet if the world still worries you at our age, then you should worry — because you ain't gonna change it. But you've still got a shot at yourself.

In the adventures of C. Calvin Broeker, we humbly present a little parable or mystery play along the lines of *How to Find Fun and Profit in Hell Despite Yourself.* We hope you find it as entertaining and instructive to read as it was to write.

*Paul William Roberts and Norman Snider*
*Toronto, August 2001*

xiv |

# 1

## Leave Here Running

*Gonna leave here runnin', 'cause walkin's most too slow.*
— OLD BLUES SONG

In 1992, Big Cal Broeker was one of Chateaugay's leading citizens, a real straight arrow. The town was a tiny shoebox of a hamlet in upstate New York, on the edge of the Adirondack Mountains. Surrounded by sleepy farms, this hardscrabble jumble of red brick and white clapboard houses had changed little since the nineteenth century. Close to the larger community of Malone, Chateaugay was one village that time might well have forgotten. A visitor could easily imagine Rip Van Winkle, wrapped up in his beard, snoring away in the nearby woods.

Cal, however, had been anything but dozing in the ten years or so since he had arrived in town with his family and bought the local IGA from Jock Spokane. He had achieved the American dream. Loud, outgoing, energetic, more than a go-getter, Cal was a blazing veritable forest fire of enterprise. He had expanded the grocery store, added another in nearby Brainardsville, added an antique shop, added a restaurant called the Village Green opposite the Chateaugay store on the main street of town, added an apartment building, added a cozy little cabin on nearby Lake Chateaugay. Moreover, he had brashly amassed an entire motor pool of vehicles: two Chevy minivans and a green Chevy Suburban for the stores, and a sleek, customized 1990 red Cougar with a mock white ragtop for himself. Definitely a hot set of wheels.

Cal was a solid type. In addition to his business success, he was on the advisory board of the Citizens National Bank and the parish council of St. Patrick's Catholic Church, and he travelled around the state giving lectures in high schools on his extensive collection of historical uniforms, swords, and muskets, which he combined with a stern anti-drug message. He thought of himself first as a father, then as a husband, then as a businessman.

Cal Broeker, it had to be said, was no commonplace grocer.

Although he had dropped out of Alfred State College, in upstate New York, after just one disastrous semester, he had read deeply in history, especially military history. Ever since the teenage Cal had worked summers at Fort Niagara and dressed up in an eighteenth-century wool uniform, shot off muskets, and got a whiff of black powder, the past had been brilliantly alive for him. The American Revolution, the Civil War, the great European conflicts of the nineteenth century — all obsessed him, as did historical figures such as Napoleon and Frederick the Great. These great soldiers were animate to him in an almost hallucinatory way, just as they had been to Gen. George Patton, and he enjoyed applying the lessons of military strategy to his business activities on a daily basis.

If Chateaugay had only a tenuous hold on the modern world, Cal himself was decidedly a throwback to a more rugged time. In his own busy mind, he was the Napoleon of Franklin County. Or maybe, with his hair-trigger temper and outsized appetites for food, drink, adventure — hell, life itself — he was a marauding freebooter of a Viking. Or maybe the Spanish conquistador Pizarro. After all, he too wished to serve God and grow rich.

Cal had come to Chateaugay with his dark, pretty wife, Doris, and his two sons, Wesley and Mark. With them had come his troubled younger brother Keith, and his wife, Lorraine. Cal had looked out for Keith ever since they were kids back in Youngstown, New York, near Niagara Falls. Keith didn't have Cal's imposing height, but he lifted massive weights and took impressive care of himself. In the past, Cal had found Keith more than one job, and now he was working for his older brother part time at the store in Chateaugay, as well as holding down another gig as a guard at the Franklin Correctional Facility, near Malone. (Go-getting Cal, needless to say, had the contract to supply thirsty inmates with fruit juices and soft drinks.) Cal and Keith would show up at the store like two outlaw bikers on their black Yamaha 750cc Virago motorcycles, with the chrome-plated monkey-hanger handlebars. Then, like a quick-change artist, Cal would switch character, putting on a red apron and a shirt and tie, ready to go to work. Mr. Square Deal Grocer. In the future, this chameleonic ability would serve him well.

Cal had developed an intricate business plan that allowed each of his enterprises to feed into the others. He reduced his costs in the stores by using excess meat and produce in the restaurant. He doubled the size and inventory of the stores and offered some of the best prices in the area, undercutting the chains. A tiny village like Chateaugay was not an easy place to make good money, but Cal Broeker did. He was prosperous, respected; people in town looked up to him. It meant everything to him, his good reputation.

Five years after he came to Chateaugay, Cal split up with Doris. She had become too cautious and conservative in his eyes, while he seemed reckless and profligate in hers. She was always second-guessing his business manoeuvres, terrified they would end in disaster. Cal was a happy-go-lucky type, and Doris seemed to be forever bowed in thought, careworn, frowning. Finally, what he came to call her "über-caution" and she his "gambler's irresponsibility" brought the marriage to a grinding and permanent halt.

Divorced, he then married Amy. She had worked hard for him even back in the days when he was a meat manager for a grocery chain in a nearby town. His brother Keith hadn't liked Amy at first, and there were not a few tensions between Cal's sons and their new stepmom, but in general things were good. Evenings, he would walk hand in hand with Amy through the town, making sure everything was what it should be. People would smile and wave; Big Cal would laugh — HAHAHAHA — and wave back.

Then bad things started to happen to Cal Broeker.

Very bad things.

First, the IGA store in Brainardsville burned to the ground in just forty-five hellish minutes of apocalyptic destruction. The fire department said something about a compressor explosion. Cal was wildly super- stitious, and he had a keen eye for omens. He looked for numerical signs in nature, among the birds, and in the streets on licence plates and such. Threes were positive, sixes were bad, and nines were the worst. Nonetheless, he missed this one, just didn't see the fire coming. And it was one giant-sized omen, a two-storey billboard of doom. He was woefully underinsured, and he had a huge mortgage on the place. And he was still fighting out the terms of his divorce settlement with Doris. Then Ron Ong walked into Cal's life and changed it utterly.

The mysterious Ron Ong.

RON ONG'S REAL NAME was Ong Hean Soon. He favoured Savile Row suits and glittering Tag Heuer wristwatches. But Ong might as well have been sporting mandarin robes and a pigtail that day, because he opened a whole new world to Cal Broeker, a world of shadows and death.

Grey and balding, Ong specialized in "import-export." He was a ship- ping executive in his late forties out of Hong Kong — a landed immigrant living in Montreal, which was just one hour north of Chateaugay, across the Canadian border. There were many Montrealers with summer cot- tages or weekend houses on Lake Chateaugay, and Cal Broeker, that swarming forest fire of a go-getter, made some extra money by catering meals for them.

He was cleaning some fish for Ong by the lake one day when Ong began talking of his international business connections: shipping deals out of London, debentures out of Geneva. Cal was impressed. His gargantuan appetites were awakened.

Cal saw some major possibilities in Ron Ong.

Ron Ong saw some major possibilities in Cal.

Cal saw the opportunity, for instance, to expand his anarchic mini-empire outside Sleepy Hollowish Chateaugay. The big time was beckoning. Soon Ong was dropping into the IGA on a regular basis. He told Cal there were some people in Montreal he'd like him to meet. Good people, with valuable business connections. Cal made the short trip, and these good people turned out to be a pair of stocky Québécois brothers named Victor and James Leroy. They were wealthy grocery wholesalers with a company called Arroway Ltd., which had offices in old Montreal. Originally from Rimouski, on the south shore of the St. Lawrence, Victor had an MBA and James had worked for Xerox. They were educated types, smooth, the Leroys. They wore dark, well-cut suits, drove BMWs and Mercedes, and lived high, spending hours lunching at fine restaurants like the Anchor d'Or down by the port, drinking vintage wines and eating fabulous food. Montreal might not have been that far from Chateaugay, but for Cal Broeker it was a whole other world.

Soon, he was putting together a deal with the meat wholesalers who supplied IGA to export American tripe from Texas through Ron Ong and the Leroys' shipping connections to customers the Leroys had developed in Eastern Europe, especially Bulgaria. Cal was driving to Montreal every morning and returning to town in the evening. He was leaving the bulk of the work of running the grocery stores in Chateaugay to Amy and Keith, and charging across the border in his exuberant red Cougar to work with the Leroys, learning the ins and outs of international shipping and banking. Waybills, end-user certificates, freight-in-bond, debentures — the whole nine yards.

At this time, markets were exploding in Eastern Europe, and every import-export hustler worth his salt was packing up his laptop and his spare pair of red suspenders, and flying to the countries formerly associated with the Soviet Union to wheel and deal. As Cal would later discover, it was like trying to do business in frontier conditions, the Wild West of Mittel Europa.

Just now, however, Cal Broeker didn't have to go that far. He discovered something of a Wild West due south of Montreal. He soon learned that besides their legitimate grocery business, Victor and James Leroy were making literally millions of dollars dealing in contraband cigarettes with the Mohawk Indians who lived on the Kahnawake Reserve, just a few miles from downtown Montreal, and the nearby Akwesasne and Oka reserves. Through the Mohawks, the Leroys were connected to the Hell's Angels, the Colombians, the Mafia, all the big international players in organized crime. They worked a grey area between the strictly legal and the definitely illegal. With the global economy in eruption, the grey area expanded too, and Kahnawake had become a global free zone, a down-at-the-heels Casablanca right at the centre of the action. The Leroys desperately needed an American partner. A bright young guy like C. Calvin Broeker.

8 |

WITH SOME 35,000 MEMBERS, the Mohawks are the largest group of Iroquois people. Proud, with a glorious history, they are sufficiently independent to have fought the Wheeler-Howard Act of 1934, which granted American citizenship to all Native people living on U.S. soil. The majority of Mohawks are not criminals, of course, and work for a living. In fact, there was a group who famously worked high steel on the skyscrapers of Manhattan. There was also, however, as the confrontation at Oka in 1990 proved, a highly militant faction whose members didn't consider themselves citizens of either country, and who couldn't resist the opportunities for smuggling that their unique legal and geographical position gave them. Parts of Akwesasne, a reserve near Cornwall, Ontario, actually straddle the border between the United States and Canada. In places like these, with the co-operation of companies like Imperial Tobacco, legitimate businessmen like the Leroys worked a parallel market in the early 1990s. Mohawks on the Akwesasne Reserve had a dispensation from the U.S. government to strip taxes on tobacco for sale on the reserve. They then smuggled cigarettes back across the St. Lawrence, where they could undercut the legitimate price in Canada by hundreds of dollars per master case (fifty cartons).

For their smuggling activities, the Mohawks used ambulances, manure spreaders, school buses, milk tankers. They had a fleet of cars and a truckload of stolen licence plates that were switched from vehicle to vehicle five or six times a day. With cigarette taxes sky-high, the market was huge and they were reaping fortunes. Just immense profits. Millions.

These profits had to be laundered, and the Colombian cocaine cartels were good at that. Hijackings were frequent, so weapons had to be purchased for self-defence. Other criminal groups were all too eager to help out. Even more conveniently, Canadian and American police were not allowed on the reserves. The Mohawk police were often related to the smugglers, and enforcement was lax. The awesome profits from cigarette smuggling had been ploughed back into the reserves in the form of casinos, bingo palaces, speedways; they had become a kind of rural Las Vegas. But all these interlocking factors had also combined to make Akwesasne and Kahnawake focal points for international crime.

The meeting place for Montreal's disparate crime groups was a restaurant called, oddly enough, Matisse's. You could only wonder what had inspired the Greek owners to name their rambling ham-and-egg palace after one of the greatest painters of the twentieth century. Henri Matisse's elegance and flair had signally failed to rub off. The restaurant sat in a mall just across the river from the reserve, near the Mercier Bridge on rue St. Jacques. Matisse's attracted a strange mix of clientele. In the restaurant, frail senior citizens gobbled cheeseburgers. In the funky adjacent strip bar, the Mohawk runners in their turned-around ball caps and hockey sweaters made their deals and partied big time. The strip club opened at ten o'clock in the morning and carried on honky-tonkin' till 3 a.m. Cal had seen the Reeboks, wild-ass teenage Mohawk cigarette smugglers, blow $6,000 in a night on strippers and drinks for the house, leave penniless, then return days later with another wad to blow.

Party, party, party.

It was a crazy goddamn scene Cal encountered in Montreal among the Indian smugglers, a gold rush atmosphere peopled with outrageous characters. Sally and Roxanne, for instance. They were a devastatingly sexy pair of Mohawk sisters who had made a fortune smuggling cigarettes. First Nations poster girls of classic statuesque beauty, they had smouldering panther eyes, high cheekbones, and gleaming manes of thick black hair, and they moved like sultry pagan queens. Their sexuality was unabashed too, and they dressed in expensive, provocative kid-leather outfits with plunging necklines and skirts slit to the thigh, drum-tight. Their winkle-picker stilettos were so high they must have been walking on the tips of their toes. Their pockets and purses bulging with cash, they would go shop-shop-shopping in Montreal's best boutiques. Sally and Roxanne would snap up designer clothing cheek by jowl with the stuffy Westmount matrons at Holt Renfrew. Then they would stop off for drinks at the Ritz. When those two walked into a bar, you noticed. One time, they left a bag containing $20,000 cash on the roof of a cab, the driver of which drove off unknowingly, presumably dumping a windfall at someone's feet on the next sharp turn. But Sally and Roxanne didn't care, didn't even try to retrieve it — just laughed and laughed. Frequently, they snorted so much blow and knocked back so many cocktails on these shopping sorties that when the time came to pick up all the outfits they'd had altered, all the rarities specially ordered, all the customized accessories, they couldn't remember where they had been. They must have left hundreds of thousands in abandoned merchandise gathering dust in backrooms, attics, and cellars. They just laughed about this too, chopped out another line, ordered two more Negronis with a twist. But you never mistook them for fools. They were tough and smart, and they had made many, many millions on Tobacco Road from their base at Kahnawake.

Montreal in the 1940s and 1950s, in the time of Mayor Camillien Houde and the burlesque queen Lili St. Cyr, had been a notoriously wide-open city, with hookers and gambling freely available, quite the equal of Chicago in its Roaring Twenties heyday. Now, in the 1990s, just under the placid surface of conventional life in Montreal, Cal Broeker was encountering an update on that 1940s jamboree.

Meanwhile, back in dozing Chateaugay, something odd was going on with his marriage. Amy was complaining that he was spending too much time in Montreal. She was leaving suspiciously early in the morning to go and open the restaurant. His brother Keith always seemed to be around, and Amy was constantly going over to Keith's house to take a dip in the pool. Cal and Amy had always had an enviable sex life. Now it seemed to be dwindling into nothing.

Cal's sons, Wesley and Mark, had never liked Amy. They saw her as scheming and ambitious, interested only in their father's money. Now, they complained, she was locking them in their rooms when Cal was away in Montreal, generally acting the wicked stepmother. It didn't help matters when naughty Wesley — har, har — put bleach in Amy's cold cream.

The stores, left under Keith and Amy's supervision, had sunk into deplorable condition. Customers stopped coming in. The inventory was rundown, the bills were mounting. Cal owed plenty of money. A pile. By the spring of 1993, Keith and Amy had become sullenly resentful of Cal's activities in Montreal, accusing him of being mixed up with a bunch of unsavoury characters: criminals, Indians, Chinese. Small-towners had narrow, xenophobic ideas about outsiders, and Keith and Amy were not exempt. Of course, Cal did nothing to relieve their fears. He was sitting up all night, staring at a candle, meditating. They found that really weird. Keith's wife, Lorraine, stumbled across thousands of dollars in a Tupperware box stashed in the freezer. When she asked her husband about it, he said it was money Cal owed Amy.

Ron Ong was proving more troublesome than useful as well. In fact, he turned out to be one low-hustling sonofabitch. Ong was putting the finger on Cal for cash loans. He was sending him $8,000 invoices for airline tickets and $15,000 hotel bills. Ong's wife even phoned him up once and demanded $10,000 for their son's school tuition. Worse, Ong, promising magnificent returns on some nebulous investment, had wangled $20,000 from Emily Spokane, the widow of the man from whom Cal had bought the IGA. Then Ong and his entire family disappeared.

Cal had started taping Ong's phone calls, just in case the whole mess landed him in court. When Victor and James Leroy suggested that Cal involve himself in their cigarette-smuggling business, he started to tape them too. He wasn't just socializing with the wise guys any more — they were starting to drag him into business meetings with the Hell's Angels. Cal didn't want to go to jail. He was getting worried, though. It wasn't outside the realm of possibility.

Cal Broeker had always enjoyed good relations with the local detachment of the New York State police, however, so he went to them for advice. Don't do anything illegal, they counselled. That was some help. To bolster his credibility with the cops — in case that was the problem — he delivered an information package charting all he had heard and seen since he had started associating with the Leroys. Then he waited for a response.

Nothing happened.

The string finally came unravelled late in the summer. Cal had been travelling around with his collection of military artifacts when the financial crunch came. Suddenly, he had to raise $50,000 to pay the mortgages on the stores. Pushed to the wall, Cal went to Maine to auction off the cherished weapons and armour.

When he returned to Chateaugay, he realized things had changed irrevocably in his absence. Amy had moved out, for a start, just left him.

And coincidentally, Keith was now helping her move into a new apartment. Furthermore, Cal's wife and brother had emptied his bank account, leaving but thirteen cents. They had purloined the tapes he had made of Ong and the Leroys too, thinking them proof of Cal's transgressions. "When your sweetheart's lovin' your best friend, that's when your heartaches begin." Thus spake Elvis. But the King was oddly silent about what to expect when your own brother is putting the pork to your wife.

To make matters worse, if that were possible, Amy and Keith had tattled around Chateaugay about these new business connections in Montreal. People in small towns like to talk about the people in their small towns. The word around this town was that Cal Broeker had changed. He had become a schemer and a plotter; he had fallen in with bad company; he had gone crooked. Some were saying that he had set the fire in the store in Brainardsville himself for the insurance money; others maintained he had been sleeping with Amy long before the split with Doris and was now experiencing the wrath of God. Malicious gossip was nailing him to the cross, flaying him alive.

He finally confronted Keith down at the IGA, choosing his words carefully: "Get the fuck out here and never come back!" Cal said.

In all the years that followed, Cal Broeker never again laid eyes on his younger brother. Incredibly enough, when it came to the taking of sides, his own mother and father lined up with Keith and Amy. Now his money was gone, his reputation was trashed, his marriage was over. He was in business with thieves and killers! He was destitute! And his wife had just run off with his brother! He threw himself down on Mark's bed and cried till it hurt. He thought his heart was going to crack apart and fall out of his body into the dust. Had he been a dog, he would have howled.

CLARENCE CALVIN BROEKER, JR., was born in November 1953 in Niagara Falls, New York, the eldest of six children. His paternal grandfather had emigrated from Germany in 1915. The family put down roots among the German-Polish communities in Western New York, eager to push the First World War out of memory and find a new identity as thoroughgoing Americans. In Lockport, an old stop on the Erie Canal, Cal Senior worked as an accountant for his father-in-law, Cornelius Tothill, in his bakery.

Like Cal after him, Neil Tothill was an entrepreneur in the classic mode, running an amusement park, a bakery, a pizzeria, among other ventures. Cal's mother, Audrey, a large, severe woman, was a nurse.

Cal and his brothers and sisters grew up in a small ranch house on the rural outskirts. Cal and Keith shared a humble room in the basement. The parents were strict, methodical, Teutonic in their approach to child-raising. As the eldest, Cal had to care for the smaller children, cook for them, help out with the ironing. On Sundays, there was St. John's Lutheran and the youth group. In the summer, he helped pick the fruit crops of the Niagara Peninsula: cherries, peaches, pears.

He received mostly Cs and Bs in school. History was his favourite subject; there it was As all the way. At six, having been attracted to Homeric armour in a storybook, he fashioned breastplates and swords from construction scrap, then he and Keith acted out the siege of Troy in the woods. Soon he had squads of plastic toy soldiers; they became the main focus of his interest.

Nonetheless, once Cal was in high school, Audrey insisted that he take up a sport. Although he had the looming, powerful build of a defensive lineman, he had no interest in the jock thing, no interest in football or baseball. But it so happened that he had a natural gift for competitive swimming. In grade nine, he made the varsity team at Lewis and Porter Central School, and soon he was breaking school records, state records, winning medals left and right. When Cal graduated from high school, he won an athletic scholarship to Alfred State. His parents could never have afforded to send him to college, but his own abilities were taking him a long way. He was swimming at a national level; an Olympic tryout in Indiana wasn't out of the question.

His time at Alfred State turned out to be short. It was his first trip away from home, and he was only seventeen. Goddamn, it was time to party. He discovered beer, which he drank in Falstaffian quantities. He had to maintain a 2.5 or 3.0 grade point average to hang on to his swimming scholarship. At the December break, his average was 0.6. He had bought the books all right, but he hadn't bothered to open a single one of them.

Cal was abruptly hauled into the dean's office, where he was informed that the college wasn't going to continue paying for his hell-raising. He was told to go home and grow up. Humiliated, Cal was dragged back to

Lockport by his mom and dad. The instant he returned home, Audrey was on his back to find a job, any job. She belittled and berated him non-stop. Cal had blown his future. He would never make anything of his life. He was a disgrace to himself and his family.

His parents phoned their friends in the construction business, in Power and Gas. In the New Year, a pick-and-shovel job stared him in the face. Fuck that, thought Cal. Instead, he went to the recruiting office in Niagara Falls and joined the air force.

It was 1972, and the Vietnam War was still raging. Cal took to the service like he was born to it. Basic training was six weeks in Lackland, Texas. There were guys there from all over the States: surfers from California, mobsters from Brooklyn. In two weeks, Cal was a squad leader. Then he was sent to tech school in Chanute, Illinois, to learn flight engineering on heavy aircraft, jets with two or four engines. He specialized in tankers. Next thing he knew, he was ferrying fighters and bombers to Vietnam and Thailand on KC 135s out of the air base at Plattsburgh, New York. Soon, as a newly minted sergeant, he was flying support for bombing missions over Hanoi out of Utapao in Thailand and Clark Field in the Philippines. This, it then seemed, was what he had been born to do.

He was the crew chief. That meant he was responsible for the mechanical function of the aircraft while it was in the air. Fix the radar, fix the tack — he was an in-air jack of all trades. Except for the odd rocket attack, the combat missions were uneventful. It was life back at the base that could get you killed.

There were rough inter-service brawls on Guam — army, navy, and Marines duking it out on a Saturday night. Propeller-heads versus jarheads versus swabbies. Sometimes the blood flowed as plentifully as the beer. Once, he saw a guy get his face opened up with a broken beer pitcher over nothing by one of those grunts with the thousand-yard stare, just back from Nam. Cal quickly learned to either stand on his own two feet and duke it out or run like hell and duck under a strong table.

Bottom line, he liked to think his way out of a tough situation. After Alfred, Cal got his education where he found it, and he had learned a big lesson from *National Geographic*, from the story of the mountain gorilla. This creature would approach enemies with horripilating ferocity. More often than not, the foe turned tail and ran. Bluff, it seemed, went a long way. When you were Cal's size, you didn't have to fight at all if you got the other guy thinking an altercation might not be worth the trouble.

Then there were the racial tensions in barracks. You had some tough brothers working as flight drivers, mechanics, radar technicians; cats who had been weaned on broken glass and nitric acid. If you didn't stand up for yourself with these mothers, life could turn ten shades of nasty.

There were bars, clubs, whorehouses. But Cal didn't mess with the Thai girls. That wasn't his style. He didn't believe in casual sex, thought it was just trivial, a waste of time. Besides, not long before he left for the Far East, he had met and married Doris Sparks. Her parents had an antiques business for which Cal, on his leaves, was soon hauling back a bazaar of ivory carvings, bronze Buddhas, inlaid side tables, jewelled daggers, gilded door lintels, old firearms, and twenty-four-carat bracelets with enamelled earrings. He quickly learned what sold and what did not.

Meanwhile, there were terrorist attacks on the base. Air force personnel had been shot at, knifed, razored, macheted — you name it. Without permission, Cal decided to move downtown. He just moved right on in with a genial Thai family and lived, laughed, cried, slept, and ate with them — lizard, monkey, snake, fish soup, all that good stuff. But there were also attacks on GIs travelling alone downtown. Cal volunteered to ride the buses and act as bait. With his size and height, he was hard to miss beside the diminutive Thais. Nothing worth mentioning happened, but all the same it was Cal's very first exposure to undercover work. Adding another feather to his military cap, he won a medal at Clark for putting out a jet-fuel fire when a drive truck blew up. He was all over the place, making himself useful, doing far more than he had to. A good guy to have around, that's what he was.

Cal loved to serve, goddamnit. He wanted to help his country and was happiest when his country wanted his help. This life suited him to a T.

So when the war was over, he stayed on in the air force, based in Plattsburgh. However, peacetime duty just wasn't the same for him. There was too much emphasis on spit and polish, rules and reggies. Promotion had more to do with politics than merit. Big Cal by now had acquired many skills, but negotiating the twisting corridors of a bureaucracy was definitely not one of them. Nor was diplomacy. He began to chafe under the system, tired of being underused, sick of the verbal abuse. Thus, in 1976, he was given an honourable discharge.

While he was still in the air force, however, Cal had been working part time, busting shoplifters and walking the catwalks for the Golub Corporation in their Price Chopper stores at Plattsburgh. Now, cut loose from the service, he went full time. Bad-check collection, loss prevention, general security — they were all part of the job. If there was any trouble, it generally came from student drunks ambling in off the Plattsburgh State University campus. Compared with what had gone down in Thailand, dealing with these college kids was a cake walk.

But then he was transferred to a store in the black ghetto, on Hoosick Street in Troy, New York, just outside Albany. That was a different story. Pure horror. There were drugs, prostitution. Desperate homeless people would come into the store armed with pipes and knives. They were so hungry they had lost all shame and restraint. They would bite right through the plastic on wrapped floats of raw meat and chomp down on the bloody flesh right then and there. In America, with all its affluence. The other security men went armed, but Cal chose to work with just a billy club. He didn't want to go to jail for blowing away some guy trying to steal food.

All the same, shit happened.

There was the time a buddy of his, Jimmy Valik, handcuffed himself to a shoplifter who had tried to rabbit and run out the door. Both of them ended up hurtling through the store's plate-glass window. Just *craaash!*

Then there was the time Cal chased after a gang that had ripped off maybe twenty cartons of cigarettes, only to run into a bunch of their confederates lying in wait for him around the corner. He was gratified to find that he was being backed up by the store's cashiers, a bunch of feisty African-American women who started screaming at the gangbangers and beating them with broomsticks.

*Get da hell outta heah, you little mothafuckahs! Send y'all back to ya mommas!*

Cal worked for a year there, made seventy arrests. But it got to be the same old story as the air force: office politics, nepotism. Once again, he chafed under the constraints of wage-slave bureaucracy. Cal liked to run his own show, and that was impossible in a large organization. He remembered his grandfather used to say that a man should have a trade; no matter what happened, they couldn't take that away from you. The company needed butchers, so he learned how to work with meat. Learned how to butterfly, baste, fillet, debone, mince, and gut. And that's what he did for five years. Wesley was born in 1976, Mark in 1979. By 1982, after a few years working as the meat manager for Grand Union at Saranac Lake, he was ready to open his own grocery business. That's when the opportunity had come up to buy the IGA in Chateaugay.

NOW EVERYTHING WAS IN RUINS all around him. Cal's whole damn life was over, but he had to keep on living. Just like Napoleon, he planned to cut his losses, regroup, redefine, and reinvent himself. He determined that his first priority was to stay out of jail. To that end, he contacted Kellie Desmonde, an organized crime expert working with the New York State police. She in turn introduced him to a federal attorney working on an organized crime task force out of Syracuse. Cal was briefed and began working for the state police, unofficially, in an unpaid capacity. His life was trashed; this was the only direction he could see to go. There was a need to fight back against the evils that he felt had closed in on him.

There was also a need to right the tremendous wrongs that had been done to him, which included leaving the church that had abandoned him. Poisoned by Keith and Amy's bad-mouthing gossip, the ecclesiastical outpost he had loyally served looked the other way when his troubles came. So Cal turned to the ancient faith of his remote German forebears for solace and inspiration. He had always been drawn to the warrior cults of Odin and Thor, the Teutonic storm gods, with their austere code and the fanatic bravery they evoked in their followers. He was as alone now as any pagan knight fighting the good fight, and besides, the world had reduced itself to an elemental condition for him. Earth, water, fire, and air — these categories encompassed everything he now knew, and they spoke to his new stripped-down sensibility. The ancients, Cal felt, saw things more clearly than we do; they weren't afraid to call a spade a spade and evil what it was. Perhaps we had entered a new Dark Age, after all? It was in the spirit of a pagan warrior-monk that Cal set off into this uncertain new life. The idea consoled him deeply. And as he saw it, he was once again serving his country.

THE LEROYS, MEANWHILE, were still pushing for him to work the U.S. end of their parallel markets in cigarettes. Through them, he had met two Mohawk smugglers, Thomas Michaels, who was a warlord of the Mohawk Warrior Society and had been prominent at Oka (the 1990 confrontation between Indians and the police in Quebec), and Jamie Crow, as well as a biker named Armand Veilleux.

Jamie Crow was stocky, blue-eyed, with a beard. He looked like a lumberjack, or maybe somebody who worked at a car wash. He introduced Cal to a pretty, intelligent Mohawk woman named Elizabeth Dumas, whose brother, Nathan, had been one of the most successful and prominent cigarette smugglers on Kahnawake. Dumas was a crime lord who supposedly had had connections to several levels of the smuggling business. He had a reputation on the rez for firing an automatic rifle into the woods at the back of his house every night — *blurrrt-bllatt!* — just to let his neighbours, and everyone else out there, know that he was not the type of guy you'd want to mess with for too little.

With his cigarette-smuggling profits, Nathan had built Elizabeth a beautiful, secure house on the reserve. A miniature goddamn fortress, it was protected by a razor-wire fence and came complete with a remote-control electric gate, security cameras, guard dogs, and Chubb alarm systems. The house itself was a sprawling Gothic building with imported fireplaces, a massive safe, and an indoor gym. Elizabeth had designed the place herself and filled it with the best eighteenth- and nineteenth-century antiques money could buy. All around her, however, the Indians of Kahnawake continued to eke out a meagre, depressed, and depressing existence on the taxpayer's tab — with scant help from the crime lords.

Elizabeth and Nathan had also built a 5,000-square-foot warehouse with a large black-topped apron. No piddling small-timers, they were in the midst of building their own private helicopter pad when Nathan's sudden disappearance put an end to the flood of money. Maybe he was dead — a deal gone bad, an unpaid debt — Elizabeth never knew. There was a gas station near the highway fronting the property, and now it was her only source of income.

Elizabeth Dumas was a beautiful and intelligent woman. She took weekly lessons on the violin, and made frequent expeditions to the museums and art galleries of New York and Boston. There were shopping trips to Europe too. But she was also well versed in the traditional ways of | 19 the Six Nations: her father, a scholar and traditionalist, had compiled a dictionary of the Mohawk language. At the same time, the crime lord's sister was street smart and extremely tough. Although she was no smuggler herself, there was little she wouldn't do to protect what she viewed as hers. All in all, she was one interesting woman.

Jamie Crow, a former boyfriend of hers, thought Cal could help Elizabeth sell off three classic '59 E-type Jaguars. By now, she was running out of money. Crow had told Elizabeth of Cal's background in shipping and banking, and his interest in antiques, so she was keen to meet him. For all her sophistication, she found it hard to enlarge her circle of acquaintances beyond the reservation, which did not contain many people with whom she had much in common. They met for dinner at Matisse's with Crow and another man one day after Cal had finished wheeling and dealing at the Leroys' Arroway Ltd. Elizabeth was wearing designer jeans and an expensive cashmere sweater under a tan raincoat from Holt's. Cal was looking pretty good himself in suit and tie and dark green three-quarter-length leather coat. Sparks flew.

He was immediately struck by Elizabeth's direct stare and well-upholstered figure. He liked her take-no-prisoners attitude too. He liked it a lot. Elizabeth wanted a clean deal on the Jaguars. Given the crew she was accustomed to doing business with, it was no surprise to Cal that she was nervous about the autos being lost in some kind of back alley rip-off. She sure didn't want that to happen.

Now, the parking lot at Matisse's was a dangerous place for any woman at night, what with the overstimulated drunks from the strip club roaming around, revved up by hours of gazing at all that mouth-watering but unattainable flesh. So Cal walked Elizabeth out to her Pathfinder. She was suspicious and uncertain whether she wanted Cal to sell the cars for her. She wasn't in the habit of trusting anybody at first acquaintance; you didn't survive long in her world that way.

Elizabeth said, "I'm going to have to check you out before I make a decision."

Cal laughed hugely. He said, "Be my guest. I have nothing to hide."

They agreed to speak the following week. Jamie Crow wanted to party at the strip club, but Cal returned to Chateaugay to pick up his son Mark at the babysitter's. He wasn't going to abandon his kids — even if it meant putting up with Doris's I-told-you-so's. A week later, he called Elizabeth and they arranged to meet at her home on Kahnawake.

CAL DROVE ONTO THE RESERVATION and announced himself on the intercom at Elizabeth's front gate. Once he got the okay, he drove in and pulled up behind her house. He walked across the back patio and entered the home through the big French doors. He met Elizabeth's mother and her sister. Elizabeth's family members spoke Mohawk among themselves, and it just knocked him out. The language flowed like soft poetry; it called out to something profound in him, something that chimed harmonically with the ancient warrior he'd become. And something about Cal clearly struck a match in Elizabeth. She didn't meet too many upstanding citizens in her world, let alone any who appreciated the culture that meant so much to her. And Cal had checked out clean as a dream.

The Jaguars were soon sold. That was a blessing for Elizabeth too, because she was being forced to close the gas station, which left her with no source of income. One meeting led to another, and in the manner of such things, Cal and Elizabeth began an affair. After he finished work in Montreal, he would visit her on the rez. Often, he would spend the weekend. And Elizabeth had investigated him very thoroughly, he discovered; she had checked out his stores, talked to his sons, dug up the real story on his separation from his ex — and all of this before she had agreed to have any kind of dealings with him, business or personal. He admired that. He admired her thoroughness.

But finally, the long daily trip from Chateaugay to Montreal came to be too much for him. He wearied of balancing his new ventures in Montreal with the job of trying to clean up the mess left by his collapsed businesses in Chateaugay. Then there was little Mark's busy infant schedule. Cal had full custody of his sons, although he was in no position to exercise it — certainly not with both of them. Once he made six trips in one day. It was definitely too much, even though Elizabeth offered to let him and Mark live on the third floor of her house. But ultimately, no one wanted the little brothers to live apart.

Cal had been delving deep into the life of Kahnawake, and it was nothing like as poetic as the Mohawk language. Once he'd asked Thomas Michaels to help him cut up a deer he had killed. Thomas, who had taken Cal into his basement to show him a workout room he used for kick-boxing, pulled a new nine-millimetre Beretta out of the woodpile and fired several shots into the logs, inviting Cal to give it a try.

Thomas was a strange, haunted man. His brother had been shot to death in front of him when Thomas was just a boy. Like many of the Mohawks on Kahnawake, he drifted along from day to day, out of place in the white world. Their friendship, oddly, made Cal realize that the reservation was too unpredictable a place to raise his son.

He came to a decision. He asked his ex-wife Doris to care for Mark and take over the faltering IGA. (Keith and Amy kept the restaurant, without the stores. They soon drove it into the ground.) Meanwhile, Cal got the hell out of Chateaugay. He moved fully into his new self and onto the reservation with Elizabeth. In retrospect, it was like going from the frying pan and fire into the wok — but fire was one of the elements in which he felt comfortable then. It had burned down his store; now it was going to have to deal with him personally.

On the reservation, Cal's mission technically began. He soon made himself available for criminal offers. They weren't long in coming either.

HE FIRST MET RÉAL DUPONT through the Leroys, and he regretted it even back then. The man was redolent of extreme violence. Even his jangling, nerve-scraping Québécois accent was an assault. His dead black eyes were like a void in the soul, and his hair-trigger temper made you flinch every time he moved. He was not a good man, that much you could tell at a glance. You felt soiled and in mortal danger when you were anywhere near him. You felt anxious.

One day in the summer of 1994, Dupont handed Cal $10,000 in U.S.

counterfeit bills and said, "I don't want to see dis shit back." Evidently, he had plenty more of it — $120 million, to be exact.

Cal went to see his contacts in the New York State police's organized crime task force, Kellie Desmonde and her assistant, Craig Krauss, and asked them for help. Krauss went ballistic.

"I could fucking arrest you for having that right now! Are you crazy? You were told not to take any of that shit or you'd be committing a fucking crime! Give it back!"

"This is serious, Cal," said Kellie Desmonde. "Craig's right. You've gotta give it back. Immediately."

"I can't give it back," said Cal. "I give it back, Dupont's gonna hand me my ass."

Next day, he forced a meeting with Dupont.

"You're a little guy wid a grocery store," Dupont said. "You fuck wid me, I know where your kids live."

Dupont started that shit right away, the threats. Then he gave him half of the $10,000.

"Get rid of it," he said. "Or you dead, motherfucker!"

Cal went back to the bank in Chateaugay, plunked the fake bills down on the counter, and said, "This is counterfeit money and there's another hundred million where it came from. Deal with it!"

The bank manager called the Secret Service, which handles Treasury matters in the United States. Some agents were there in no time, and they soon asked Cal if he would work with them. The fact that he was living on Kahnawake didn't hurt either. The Secret Service set up a meeting for Cal with the RCMP.

Robert Hart, a special agent based in Syracuse, wrote a letter to Insp. Simon Spenser of the counterfeit section of the RCMP in Montreal. It read, in part:

**Dear Inspector Spenser,**

**Please consider this an official request to bring an individual to Canada for the purpose of becoming a confidential agent of the RCMP. . . . We believe this individual can provide assistance to your agency in our joint investigation of the C.19007 counter-**

**feit case. . . . This individual is described as a white/male, 6′4″, 260 lbs., brown hair, blue eyes . . . no known criminal record. . . .**

Cal signed a contract known as a letter of agreement (LOA). The LOA identified Réal Dupont and a couple of other buddies as the target of his mission. Cal wasn't an informer or a source. This distinction was impor- | 23 tant to him in his new life, his new direction.

He was now an RCMP undercover Crown agent.

# 2

# Outside the Law

*To live outside the law you must be honest.*
— BOB DYLAN

*There is no den in the wide world to hide a rogue. Commit a crime
and the earth is made of glass. Commit a crime, and it seems
as if a coat of snow fell on the ground, such as reveals in the
woods the track of every partridge, and fox, and squirrel.*
— RALPH WALDO EMERSON

The hour before dawn, the hour of the wolf, the time when death most
often comes. Mist sits low on the river, churning with the swift current,
rolling into still bays, spinning in backwater eddies. The forest is only
sounds: the humid breath of dense vegetation; an immeasurable pulsing
web of insects measuring time; pockets of birdsong, tuning pieces of the
mighty chorus and stately duets; lone, shrill animal complaints, urgent
warnings; a panicked beating of wings; branches creaking and crashing
into the swamp. With a sudden milky peace, dawn comes. The effulgent
vapours turn to steely cotton and simmer, the light there almost solid.

The crack of willow branches lashing wood, then the low tom-tom
beat of powerful turbines and the rippling gush of a foaming wake. The
barge appears as suddenly as a jet airplane, this intrusion of form within
the formless, this violation of antemorphic sanctity, heralded by cries of
horror and flight.

On its deck, protecting a mound of cargo beneath tarpaulins, stand fig-ures in camouflage combat fatigues, cradling M-16s and shotguns tenderly in their arms like thin dead babies. Occasionally, they sniff the parting mists, ears and minds cocked for trouble. In the half light, these military men could well be Asians, the scene upriver on the Mekong, where it winds through the jungle.

The barge is slowing as it meets indolent waters nearer the bank. The vast turbines are switched into reverse with a strained, deep, and hollow sound. Buildings suddenly appear, sucking the mist inside their concrete geometries: a row of houses; a road; a bridge, beneath which the barge takes shelter.

Snyegon. That's what they called this part of the rez.

The engines are cut; several men have jumped ashore with ropes and now pull until the beast is tamed. One of them, a good foot taller than the rest, walks away from the group, bidding farewell. He strolls up the embankment and onto the road that crosses this bridge. Reaching an old black Mercedes parked in a secluded laneway, he pops the trunk, then proceeds to peel off the army fatigues. Beneath them he wears a sober business suit and a tie. After his khakis are folded and locked in the trunk, Cal Broeker drives to Montreal.

EACH INDIAN'S NAME IS UNIQUE. Only he or she has it. These names sound beautiful, and they often *are* beautiful, translating to phrases such as "The Little Boat That Pulls the Bigger Ones" or "The Fire That Shows the Hunter His Home." Every conversation in the Mohawk language is also unique. You can't just come in on a meeting halfway through and expect to pick up the thread. Unless you've been there from the beginning, you won't know what anyone is talking about, for from the outset special terms are devised and attached to what is being discussed, to make the time being spent on it unique. It confers on each conversation a coded quality, and makes it utterly impossible for outsiders to understand what any Indian using his native tongue is talking about if he doesn't wish them to know. It accounts partly too for the lack of success governments have had in gathering intelligence on Indians believed to be engaged in subversive or criminal acts.

The white man has destroyed everything that was unique about the Indians, except their languages. It may suit us to believe that the original inhabitants of North and South America had no resistance to innocuous European diseases like the common cold, but in truth what they had no resistance to was something far more pernicious: our culture. In a failure to understand the great gift-giving ceremony of potlatch, where the gift is returned or given to someone else, colonists derived the term "Indian giver." Few of them realized that the sarcasm had been returned, however, for in the Native languages a person who accepts a gift but fails to return it or gift it to another is known as a "white taker."

LET'S CALL THE MAN HEADLIGHT.

Cal had been taken by a Mohawk contact — Dirty Frank — into an Indians-only bar on the edge of the Akwasasne Reserve to meet some people who wanted to do a little business. These people were a couple of runners — not just any runners, but supposedly the craziest and also the very best runners there were. Indians frequently go by English nicknames — which, taken together with their Native names and their regular English or French ones, gives many of them three names to use — and Headlight got his after an altercation with a boat propeller left him with a tasty scar on his cheek and only one eye (or headlight) that functioned. He was a big man among the runners. The bar was a dingy, desperate place, the kind of hard-drinking sty where alcohol pours like gasoline on fire. Fathers and sons, brothers, friends and acquaintances knifed each other here over a hostile word or dubious look. Thus Cal, a big gringo dressed in a suit and tie, felt like General Custer with a target painted on his back. It wasn't that the bar's denizens looked like they wanted to kill him — a number of them actually *offered* to kill him.

To diffuse this lethal atmosphere, Headlight, a small, slightly built man with a temper that was legendary, suggested the conversation might be better continued outside.

"Otherwise you gonna get scalped and beaten to pulp just for wearing that suit. Know what I'm saying?"

"Next time I'll come informal," Cal told him. His tone suggested he could take care of himself either way. You didn't show these guys weakness — they'd eat you.

Headlight and his partner, Stripe — so named because, during smuggling raids, he painted his face with camouflage tiger stripes — led Dirty Frank and Cal down to the river, where several small boats were moored. They talked in vague generalities around the subject of a tobacco-smuggling deal, then offered to take Cal over to an island that was the base of their operations.

"We'll show you what we do," Headlight explained. "And how we do it."

"I don't have time for no road trip," Cal replied, uncomfortable with this pair of clowns, but not about to show it.

"You ain't dressed for one, you mean." Headlight hissed out a laugh that blossomed into a bronchial coughing fit. Then he pointed across the river to a small tree-lined island a few hundred yards out. "It's just over there, guy. Even a white man can make that trip, yeah?"

"You might get a little mud on the soles of those shoes, though," Stripe added. Jokes weren't his forte.

"Okay, boys, I got the fuckin' point. Now let's have less yak about jokes and more about smokes, huh?" Cal knew it was important to re-establish his dignity, to make it clear that he wasn't rattled, and that he also wasn't the kind of person used to being the butt of jokes. "Let's go look at your island." Then, glancing down at Stripe's jeans, he added, "Those jeans look like shit when you buy them, or is it something you had to add yourself?"

Stripe scowled, but Headlight hissed another mirthless laugh.

Cal, followed by Dirty Frank, jumped into a small cargo boat as Headlight fired up a brace of big, powerful Mercury engines that raised the prow forty-five degrees and spewed out a churning wake as they shot across the brief stretch of brown water. It was like taking a Formula One racer to the corner store. Seconds later, Headlight threw the mighty engines into reverse to avoid crushing the small island dock.

The Indians escorted Cal down a well-worn, tree-lined path through the woods that obscured most of the small island beyond its shoreline. A casual observer might have assumed the place was deserted. A little beyond, past a bend in the path, lay a small house. Even this looked deserted. Shutters were hanging off, windows broken or missing entirely.

"This is our place," announced Headlight, as if he was presenting his guests the pleasure dome at Xanadu.

"Martha Stewart would blow your whole tribe for a night here," Cal said. "I want the number of your realtor, Headlight."

"Who's this Martha chick?" asked Stripe.

"That's the point," Headlight snapped, clearly embarrassed by his partner's stupidity. "No one's gonna give this shit-pile a second glance. But we fixed up the basement like Fort-fucking-Knox, see? And we hold all the product you're gonna buy down there — safe as fucking milk."

"In the age of lactose intolerance, man," Cal told him, "that's about as safe as shit."

"See for yourself." Headlight kicked open a rickety front door and flipped on a light switch.

A bare, dangling bulb came to life, revealing a steel-plated door almost immediately behind the dilapidated entrance hall. Headlight flung Stripe a bunch of unusually large keys. After several abortive attempts, the squat and somewhat flabby Indian found a key that opened a preposterously big padlock, freeing a pair of fat bolts that were securing the steel door.

"You don't believe me," Headlight said, "check it out." He made a mock courtly bow and swept his arm low to usher Cal through the creaking entrance.

The mottled sodium glow of the bulb behind revealed a narrow flight of worn stone stairs leading to a basement. Cal trod carefully, feeling the air around him turn much cooler, damp and musty. It was fungus climate, probably below the waterline. Soon he felt his shoes meet an uneven dirt floor, and as he turned to see who had followed him down, a weak bulb hanging alone in the centre of the small basement throbbed and glowed into coppery life, revealing dank stone walls that were stained with damp and patches of a thin, anemic moss that resembled mildew. The place was utterly bare of anything else. Cal told himself that he should have worn a miner's monkey suit and waders. No one had followed him down, he also quickly realized, but as he went to go back up the stairs and see what these clowns were up to, he heard Headlight's rasping voice.

"Make yourself comfortable, motherfucker!" he shouted. "'Cause this is your new home. We're gonna go find out just who the fuck you really are and what the fuck you're really up to. Bye!"

Cal ran at the stairs, but he wasn't even halfway up when he heard the sound of that heavy steel door creaking shut and its bolts sliding as the book-sized padlock's hook was snapped back into place.

The bastards then killed the dangling lightbulb.

"You motherfucking featherheads play this shit, it's gonna cost you!" Cal roared from behind the steel door.

"Send us an invoice," said Headlight. "To our secretary."

A chain or something was being fastened on the outside too, Cal could hear. He shouldered the door, then tried to find something to give him enough purchase to shake the thing. But there was nothing, and he knew for certain that his way out — if indeed there was a way out — did not lie in the way he'd entered his prison.

They were laughing outside as they walked away. Cal could hear Dirty Frank — whom he counted as a friend — trying the remonstrate with the runners.

"C'mon, guys! You're gonna fuck a good deal. Shit! Don't do this. He's okay! I promise you, man, he's a stand-up . . . He's . . . Shit, Heady, the guy's got fucking contacts, man! Contacts! You want the fucking Russians up your ass?"

But it wasn't having any effect on Cyclops and the Skunk. The voices faded away, and soon Cal heard the boat's outsized engines gargle into roaring life, then melt into the silence of river mists, until all he was left with were the creaks and drips and undefined scuttling sounds of the old cellar, whose form had vanished into an amorphous, pulsing black cloud.

Feeling his way around, Cal came to the first of two small barred windows that were reduced to vaguely glowing spectral forms. The bars were rusty, and he applied 280 pounds of leverage, attempting to shake one loose. Nothing moved, though. The second window was more promising: its middle bar started jiggling in the concrete sockets. Letting the full force of his rage at being imprisoned surge through his veins, Cal heaved and shook and battered at the bar, working it looser and looser. Suddenly the thing gave entirely, and with it stones, concrete, and the lower half of the window casing came cascading down, sending Cal reeling backwards into the darkness. Ever fastidious, he brushed himself off, then decided a good suit was a good suit: it would have to come off. Stripped down to his shorts, socks, and shoes, Cal rolled the suit and shirt up inside out, then secured the bundle with his necktie. Taking up the dislodged bar, he began digging and hacking away at the rest of the casing and the window, sending sparks and shards of stone and glass flying in all directions. It took him several minutes to clear a space large enough for himself to squeeze through. In the movies, it always looks easier. A sliver of glass dug into his stomach while he inched very slowly through the narrow opening and up towards the rectangle of twilight sky. To spare his legs, he hoisted himself up the final stretch and rolled out onto the cool, damp grass, where he lay gazing up at the early evening stars and laughing uncontrollably. So much for Fort-fucking-Knox! Brushing and picking the glass and stones from his flesh, he set off for the dock. All he needed now was a boat. . . .

There were plenty of them on the other side, moored around the Desolation Bar's dock, which now twinkled with lights in the distance. But there were none on this side. Shit!

Cal had been a championship swimmer in high school, after all, so the water held no fear for him. Not really. If he had to swim, he'd swim. Near the dock was a garbage bunker; he took a fairly clean black plastic sack from it, emptying out the cardboard boxes it contained. Then he neatly placed his clothes, along with his shoes and shorts, inside the bag and tied it tightly shut. As the cold water enveloped him, he flashed back to a childhood incident.

*Swimming in Lake Ontario, just off the mouth of the Niagara River, he is doing an easy breaststroke, just enjoying the water's cool embrace after the hot sun. Suddenly, he feels something like a slippery human arm coil around his chest. He instinctively pushes the thing away, and it slithers under his armpit. Ow! There's a sudden sharp pinch on his forearm, and then he sees the thing: freshwater eel. Big one too. Its looping charcoal form weaves through the dappled water around him, malevolent, alien, predatory, waiting for another opportunity. . . .*

The memory galvanized Cal into Olympic action. He shuddered mightily, striking out with legs and arms away from the reedy bank. The current was swift and strong farther out, and thrash as he might against it, he still felt himself being pushed downstream.

Considerably far downstream too, as he found when he scrambled ashore through the weeds and reeds of a swampy inlet. In his mind now: the Ulfheedin, an elite military unit in medieval Germany, the Wolf Warriors of Odin. They operated alone behind enemy lines, either gathering intelligence before a raid or assassinating leaders to sow chaos, terror, and confusion in the moments prior to an attack. They were good, but few lived to be very old. Still, the thought of these Stoic souls always consoled Cal when times were tough, and the river's smell of rotted fish and mown grass, mingled with faint woodsmoke, now seemed like the very essence of the European Middle Ages to him. Whatever it was that drove Cal Broeker, it was tied up with those distant times. Life then might have been nasty, brutish, and short, but it was also — or so he imagined — honourable, brave, and decent. The loneliness of UC work allowed him plenty of leeway in the area of imagination, true, but there were times when he felt himself simultaneously existing in the scarred flesh of some Ulfheedin warrior and the body known as Cal. It wasn't something he'd tell many people. They'd think he'd cracked, lost it. Except he didn't feel crazy: he felt sane. In a world he increasingly viewed as going headlong down to hell in a handcart — whatever *that* was — he felt whole, healed, and calm. If the price of that was strange thoughts, then what of it? Why the hell not?

The sense of aloneness, of being all one — as the term had been in Anglo-Saxon — persisted as he stumbled back along the riverbank towards the Indian bar and the dock where this little adventure had begun. By the time he reached it, he was dry and the cool night wind was sending chills up and down his spine. Stopping to dress, he spotted all the boats tied up beyond the platform, and putting his clothes aside, he crept over and prowled along until he spotted the craft with the big twin Mercury engines. Why not make the bastards pay for what they'd done? As he jumped into the boat, he felt blood from a cut foot squelch out the side of his wingtip Dexter shoe. It only strengthened his resolve. Reaching under the wooden transoms, he felt for the drainage plugs and ripped them out. Then he leapt into another vessel — the same kind of camouflaged smugglers' whaling barque with a giant engine — and did the same thing. Pushing the two boats away from their moorings, he tipped them over into the braided current to speed their fate. Moments later, they were fading from sight beneath the blackened sheen of the river.

Back in his clothes again, Cal felt a whole lot better, but he smelled bad. He smelled of river, gasoline, fish, and — the worst smell of all — fear. Many people would have hightailed it out of there, thinking themselves lucky to have escaped, but not Cal Broeker. He was heading straight back to the Desolation Bar to say hi to Headlight, Stripe, Dirty Frank, and . . . well, re-enact Little Big Horn, if that's what was required.

It was a scene right out of the movies: the sheriff, left for dead, shows up like a tattered ghost at the redskin stronghold, six-gun in hand. Cal stood in the doorway, dripping, stinking, bleeding, but dressed in dry clothes and in one big piece. The place went totally silent for several long seconds — the Indians were probably in shock — then, unbelievably, it erupted with good-natured mirth.

"How the hell did you do that?" a voice shouted.

Soon it was back-slapping, handshakes, and more laughter. Cal's stock had risen dramatically. Through Dirty Frank, he learned that Headlight had planned for him to sweat it out in the cellar overnight but had been having second thoughts because everyone he spoke to told him Cal would probably set fire to the house or something. Now he was relieved. Cal decided not to mention the *something* he had done until a little later on. What he needed most now was a beer and some Band-Aids for his bloody foot.

He was sucking on only his third beer when Dirty Frank asked if he wanted to leave. Cal wanted to leave all right. But the day hadn't been a total bust after all, since, as he shook hands with Headlight and a few others, each of them promised to get some sort of deal together with him.

He walked a couple of paces from the bar counter, then turned back dramatically, saying, "By the way, fuckweeds, I sank two of your boats out there so you'd have a little memento of our friendship. You'd better schedule their recovery into your Day-Timers for early tomorrow morning."

But the response was just more laughter, and then the Indians resumed their drinking.

"Did you really sink two boats?" asked Dirty Frank a little later on.

"Nawww," Cal replied convincingly. "Just kidding ya, that's all." He followed it up with one of his explosive laughs. *Har-har-har-har* . . .

INCIDENTS LIKE THIS built Cal's reputation on the reservation. At first it had been far from easy for him, an outsider living there. But as always, he persevered. Some nights in bed, he and Elizabeth would hear the crack-crack-crack of automatic gunfire in the woods surrounding the house or the high-pitched, angry roar of four-wheeler motorcycles buzzing the perimeter. The Mohawks were warriors with no war to fight and precious little territory to defend any more. Cal could understand their feelings: he was a big gringo living in their midst with one of their women. It had to be insulting. But that wasn't his problem, was it?

One night at around 3 a.m., the gunshots and the buzzing four-wheelers woke him from yet another sleep, and he decided he had to deal with the perpetrators, and deal with them in a way that they would understand. He jumped out of bed and strode through the house to the fireplace, where he'd hung the last remnant of his beloved collection of antique weapons: a vast two-handed Landskeneche broadsword. It had become his talisman, and he still owns it today. Taking the ancient sword down, he felt its weight and the cool corrugated steel of the handle charge his soul with the fortitude its original owners had needed before facing battle. Minutes later, he stood in the icy moonlight on Elizabeth's front lawn, wearing nothing but his jockey shorts and swinging eight feet of sword around his head like the blades of a helicopter. It must have been the first time the weapon had seen any action in 600 years.

Seeing him emerge from the house, the nocturnal visitors had retreated into the woods. "Come on out, you lily-livered fuckers. Kill me if you can!" Cal yelled into the darkness, which was now full of eyes and of silence. "Come on. You're so fuckin' brave — surely twenty of you can take me!" The only sound he heard in reply, though, was the swoosh of the mighty blade cutting circles in the frosty air.

Of course, he had no way of knowing if he would simply be shot from a distance. With a MAC-10 or a fully automatic AK-47, you didn't need to be a marksman, after all. Hell, Stevie Wonder and Ray Charles could go hunting with the kind of weaponry you could buy these days. And you could buy anything on the rez, thanks partly to the insane gun laws in the U.S. But despite the arsenal the Indians had at their disposal, no one took up Cal's challenge on that icy moonlit night, and no shots were fired. What those hiding in the woods made of the startling prospect before them is anyone's guess, but it's unlikely any of them forgot the sight of the huge white man with his spinning broadsword howling like a berserker out there in the moonlight on the frosted lawn.

The ploy worked, too. There was no more of the nighttime baiting, no more crack-crack-crack, no more buzzing four-wheelers to disturb the deep and ancient silence of the woods around Elizabeth's house. These woods had been home to her ancestors since a time when all the continent was legend, a magical extension of the Great Spirit. It had been sung into existence and was still interwoven with the invisible world, which contained the essences of all its various forms and was thus the real world. Like the mind of God.

Unlike, for the most part, the cities, the reservations still contained Indians who continued to follow the old ways — dignified and noble figures with faces straight out of scarred old sepia photographs from the nineteenth century. Mystical faces, the eyes redolent of atavistic powers, wisdom, and warriorhood, a oneness with nature, knowledge, and courage. Like the lined, majestic face of Crazy Horse, who still remembered what it was like when the Great Spirit held the deeds to his world. This was the kind of culture that spoke to Cal, the kind of society that fit him like a glove. He deeply respected those who still valued their prehistory; he felt at home with them, in a world that still had room for heroism, loyalty, and the kind of justice that knew right from wrong at first sight. He too instinctively believed that the golden age lay behind us, not ahead — thus atavism held no shame. He was a conservative inasmuch as he despised change for its own sake. Yet he also despised hypocrisy that posed as morality.

That's why he made a point of acquainting himself with the elders who controlled affairs on the rez. He presented various business propositions to them, propositions that would raise the standard of living for all of the reservation's inhabitants. He was never able to resolve the ancient Indian ways and their modern actions, and he was especially bothered by the social inequality of the rez, where children ran around barefoot and in rags alongside men who kept hundreds of millions of dollars mouldering on wooden skids in damp basements. Some of the elders clearly saw in him a good and decent man, someone who genuinely had their best interests at heart. But others were more hostile, suspicious of this white intruder. So ultimately, nothing came of Cal's philanthropic intentions. Although they were genuine enough, his attempts at doing good were also a consequence of his guilt: he'd deceived too many people he saw as decent human beings along with the ones who were clearly anything but decent.

Cal was not a man leading a double life, though, unlike most UC operatives. He was the same person when he was out drinking with his RCMP handlers as he was when sitting in Matisse's discussing a multi-million-dollar drug or weapons buy. A talented liar needs a very good memory to keep his lies straight, and thus Cal's success lay partly in the fact that he told very few lies. He was who he said he was. He checked out. He was on the square. And he really wasn't fooling anyone or using anyone. This is how he was able to live with Elizabeth so harmoniously. Besides her street smarts, she had her share of atavistic gifts too; her sixth sense was keenly developed. She could smell a rat or trouble, and in dreams, she saw shades of things to come just as clearly as she saw the scenes in her waking world. Her knowledge of medicinal plants and herbs was similarly not something learned in any school; she knew their seasons, their secret powers, and the subtle changes wrought by phases of the moon, eclipses, and equinoctial shifts. It was a talent every bit as natural as her cooking skills. You either had it or you didn't. You couldn't learn it — it had to be earned in other lives.

Many, many times, Cal found himself transfixed by the ancient beauty of the Indian world, a place in which the things white men scoffed at or pooh-poohed were embraced as realities, considered as normal as the setting sun, the day and the night, the turning wheel of the seasons, or the grandeur of the heavens in which unnumbered ancestors shone as stars. An apple-cheeked country boy at heart, Cal had never before felt so much a part of nature as he did on the rez. It was this sense of harmony and oneness that enabled him to see more clearly the wickedness and corruption that had lost us the paradise for which we still yearn. Criminals force us all to serve a life sentence in jail; he saw it so clearly now. The bad don't suffer because of the good, but the good suffer on account of the bad. Without criminals, there would be no walls or locks or wars or banks or suspicion or insurance or lawyers or endless nights. They fashion the hell our world has become, yet we are concerned about their rights, their comfort, their welfare. It doesn't make sense. There is a difference between crimes of poverty and organized crime, a big difference. Yet both are dealt with under the same law. But someone who steals in order to have enough is not the same as someone who steals in order to have too much. And an organization of individuals devoted to crime is very different from a lone thief.

The bad guys on the reservation were very busy too, Cal observed. Despite an antagonistic attitude towards the white man fostered by centuries of inequities and atrocities in the relationship, they were increasingly extending the scope of their criminal activities by forming alliances with various organized crime factions in the white world. The bikers, the Mafia, and the Russian mobsters had not the slightest jot of interest in the historical plight and current welfare of the Indians. But the unique legal position in which the reservations had been placed — as a result of treaties drawn up in the past by men who doubtless never imagined the nature of contemporary organized crime — must have seemed like paradise itself to the criminals. The Russians, reportedly, could scarcely believe their luck — or our stupidity — when they first found these autonomous, virtually cop-free zones right in North America, and right on the U.S.–Canada border, in some cases. You could stash one hundred kilos of cocaine, or one hundred cases of automatic weapons, or hundreds of millions in counterfeit money — anything, in fact — on these reservations, and the law of the land virtually guaranteed it would be protected from the nuisance of police investigation. Typically, police officers who are seeking someone believed to be on a reservation wait outside while the reservation's own police go in search of the suspect. Although the inhabitants of the reservations in general do not benefit from the criminal activities of the few, the bad guys are nonetheless shrewd enough to spread their wealth around among those few in authority able to do them some good.

To be granted a warrant for a full-scale bust on a reservation, the Canadian police were forced to make an application to the Ministry of Indian Affairs, stating among other things the identity of any agents involved. This was, to say the least, a far from satisfactory arrangement. All this bureaucratic red tape created the perfect circumstances for a little tobacco smuggling to burgeon into a massive and all-encompassing criminal enterprise that involved nearly every nefarious entity or faction in the underworld.

Because of the cunning way Cal was positioning himself on the rez, the Mohawks saw him as a corrupt businessman with connections to the Russian and Bulgarian mobs, while the Russians, the Italians, the bikers, and so on were given to believe he was a unique conduit into the reservations, a white man with exceptional contacts in the closed world of the Indians. The trick, in any of the projects Cal pursued during this period, was keeping each party away from the other. It wasn't easy. What most buddies lack in formal intelligence, they usually make up for with innate paranoia, irrational violence, and hair-trigger tempers. You'd be surprised how many people fall in line at the thought of getting beaten into blood pudding by a screaming psychopath who doesn't give a shit whether he lives or dies, and feels just the same about everyone else.

Then there were cases like Vic MacLoden. Vic was okay — at least, he wasn't the menace to society that some on the rez were. Not at first, anyway. Indeed, at first he was virtually a philanthropist, working his ass off at North Creek Enterprises, a misguided and mismanaged attempt to emulate the white man's entrepreneurial spirit. Vic was trying to put together a shipping company so that Indians could ship food at discounted rates up to Inuit communities in the Far North. Such communities had to pay outlandish prices for all their supplies, something many Indians viewed as yet another example of the exploitation of Canada's aboriginal peoples by the European oppressors. It was a noble and worthy venture, but Vic was not the ideal man for such an involved and complex enterprise. His organizational skills were minimal, as were his resources; even his imagination was on the verge of bankruptcy.

Big-hearted Cal — quite outside of his RCMP projects — worked extremely hard in an attempt to make some money connections for Vic, but his sources were invariably dubious in nature, and thus far more interested in the quick and easy profits available from tobacco smuggling than the slow and arduous, if noble, process of aiding the deprived and impoverished aboriginals in the Far North — even if they *were* distant cousins. All Cal was able to turn up for poor old Vic were empty promises.

But throughout the major undercover projects that Cal was soon to embark upon, Vic kept phoning him. The problem was that his calls went through to the central sting office — the RCMP command and control — where every telephone call was recorded. Cal had a soft spot for Vic, and he tried his damnedest to put him off. The trouble was that Cal had done such a great job of presenting himself as the very image of crooked afflu-ence that Vic, having finally found — or so he thought — his meal ticket, was not about to let it go. Abandoning his dream of shipping perfectly legitimate commodities to the Far North, Vic began grabbing at every straw that came his way — and there were an awful lot of straws passing through the rez. Soon his tape-recorded messages were babbling about "moving the big stuff across the water," importing "cases," "taking deliv-ery of the tea leaves," and countless other transparent euphemisms for smuggling illegal commodities that ranged from narcotics to automatic weapons. Even if Vic couldn't actually obtain *all* of these items, he could certainly obtain *some* of them. Anyone on the rez could. Cal was not supposed to make friends or exceptions among the Indian criminal community, so he could hardly continue to ignore Vic's increasingly des-perate sales pitches. Nor could his Montreal handlers. Eventually — after Vic's hundredth telephone offer — they instructed Cal to set up a buy.

Cal figured he would make one last attempt to scare Vic away, calling him on an untraceable pay phone. "Hey, Vic, buddy," he said. "You know what? You really don't want to deal with me. Honest, you fucking don't. The people I got around me are really dangerous sons of bitches, and they'll screw you over for sure once they catch you alone. You hear what I'm saying, Vic? You're too vulnerable. You don't want the kind of rip that takes your shit and then fucking sends you down too, do you? Take my advice, Vic, and don't fucking do it. Okay?"

Short of telling Vic that he was about to be busted by the cops — "Trust me, I know. I'm a fucking UC agent working for them . . ." — there was little more that Cal could say to help the man without endangering himself. But Vic was even stupider than Cal had bargained for.

"I'm not worried," he replied. "And I really want to do this, Cal. I really do."

42 |    The last time Cal saw Vic was at the meet he set up at Matisse's for a weapons buy. Around this stage of a project, Cal would typically be instructed to bring in an RCMP undercover officer and introduce him to the target as a client or end-user of some sort who would take over the deal from that point on. This was important, if not vital, to Cal, for it meant that he would almost certainly not have to testify in court. The moment he stepped into a witness box, his career undercover would be over. A real police officer was also essential for making arrests — civilians cannot actually arrest people, after all — but as it is with any bureaucracy, the introduction of a new element into an operation often meant gruelling delays, delays that sometimes cost the entire operation and at best only fuelled the fires of mistrust between Cal and his target. Unfortunately for Vic, however, this particular UC was swiftly in place. Cal turned Vic over to the "client" who, instead of making him rich, would soon be sending him to jail. But it wasn't exactly Cal's finest hour. The prisons had far too many Vics in them already; what they needed were bigger fish, the kind of people who kept the Vics of this world in business.

THE AMOUNT OF MONEY flowing through the rez was incredible, with tobacco smuggling, its base, providing a foundation of almost unlimited cash flow upon which the pyramid of all other criminal endeavours was constructed. If they were unsuccessful with the arms deals, drug deals, people-smuggling deals, counterfeit deals — or any of the many other illicit gateways to easy money — there was always tobacco and liquor to fall back on. The profit on a truckload of cigarettes was in the region of half a million bucks, and there was very little risk involved — for the Indians, at least. Even the public — the main beneficiaries of tax-free smuggled American liquor and cigarettes — seemed remarkably unconcerned about the apprehending and punishment of the smugglers. Indeed, the punishment was generally so light it amounted to a licence to continue. Where else could you clear $500,000 in six months? And when the Canadian government steeply raised the tax on tobacco during the early 1990s, the smugglers acquired a status akin to folk heroes.

There was scarcely a downtown bar or restaurant back then that was not visited during the course of an evening by a man with a large kit bag crammed with duty-free Marlboros that he would carry from table to table, booth to booth, for people to make their furtive purchases. Similarly, many a bartender could be viewed refilling, say, his Finlandia vodka dispensers from a DNP (duty not paid) gallon jug of Warsaw Velvet or some other "pure vodka" distilled and bottled not in Warsaw, but in New Jersey. In the U.S., such a jug of vodka would have cost about eight dollars, while in Canada, where only the government could peddle the booze it also taxed outrageously, it simply wasn't available (although 750 mL bottles of a similar vodka, manufactured in Montreal, were on the shelves and selling for precisely the same price as vodkas from Sweden, Poland, or Russia). If it had been available, it would have been priced in Canada at around eighty dollars.

What the government had to learn the hard way, the liquor control boards already knew: you can't rob the public too blatantly. And selling for eighty dollars something that many could buy for eight dollars a half-hour drive from where they lived was too blatant. The only way to control smuggling from the U.S. was to bring prices into alignment. But if the Americans were willing to budge on tobacco, they wouldn't on alcohol — and neither would the Canadians. The Canadian government made far too much money with its alcohol monopoly to consider lowering the tax, and since that monopoly in effect worked four ways — the government imported it, taxed it, distributed it, and sold it nearly exclusively — one hand was not about to petition the other for a tax reduction. What the government lost on tobacco revenues through a drastic decrease in smoking generally, however, it was happy to recoup from the remaining nicotine addicts by increasing the tax — never mind that it was already at several hundred percent in some cases. It wasn't that fewer people smoked than abstained — the statistics stand at somewhere around 50/50 — it was that fewer influential people smoked, and could thus impose their will more easily on the rest.

As Cal came to see as he delved deeper into the tobacco-smuggling activities on the rez, the smugglers could not have remained a thorn in the side of Canadian customs without the collusion of their suppliers. And their suppliers were the major multinational tobacco companies, though they would later plead innocent to this charge, blaming corrupt corporate executives.

Yet from a very early stage, Cal Broeker perceived that this argument could not hold water. Often, as much as 20 percent of a huge corporation's total sales of imported Canadian cigarettes came from reservations on the U.S.–Canada border, where the Indians, prodigious smokers though they may be, would have had to be puffing their way through 2,000 cigarettes each a day. Thus, Cal was to argue, no tobacco company could claim ignorance without also claiming to be breaking another law obliging them to register and monitor their tax-exempt sales. While it was legal for the Indians to buy tobacco products stripped of all revenue, it was not legal for them to resell these products untaxed themselves or pass them to anyone else intending to sell them off the reservations. Since, given the quantities involved, this was clearly what they were doing, then many senior tobacco company executives aware of their sales demographics — and few CEOs could plausibly exclude themselves from this group — were guilty of criminal collusion, or in other words, conspiracy to defraud the Canadian government of hundreds of millions of dollars in tax revenues. The Toronto *Globe and Mail* termed this alleged crime "the largest tax fraud in Canadian history."

Before he was able to penetrate to the stained heart of the tobacco-smuggling business, however, Cal discovered that another of the multiple projects he pursued simultaneously while on the rez interested his RCMP and Secret Service handlers more urgently.

WHENEVER CAL HAD considered taking a European vacation, Bulgaria wasn't high on his list of countries not to be missed. Yet to develop further his "Russian mob's frontman" image — and it had to be developed further if he was to survive much longer at the deadly locus of Canada's organized crime factions — it was becoming more than essential that he find some way of getting to the Eastern bloc in his other persona as an American businessman less concerned with ethics than with profits, and possessed of interesting connections in Canada. And Canada itself was now perceived as a land of golden opportunity in most of the world's poorer nations, especially by their criminal classes. Americans were a little too tough on crime, but Canadians . . . why, Canadians were such nice folk that they even seemed to realize criminals were just businessmen for whom jail was an occupational hazard. Therefore, why make jail sentences so long that they endangered a man's livelihood? No businessman minded getting two years less a day for an offence involving several million dollars if it really meant only two months of actual incarceration — and if, of course, he kept most of the money. Rumour had it, too, that some Canadian prisons were better than many country clubs in the old Eastern bloc: you could work on your golf game; your private room had a colour TV and its own phone; your choice of newspapers was delivered daily. Criminals were certainly treated better than the poor. It seemed to Cal, as it does to many, that only criminals could find this an exemplary situation — and they weren't even the ones whose taxes funded it.

# 3

# Parmakov's Castle

*Nothing is true; everything is permitted.*
— DOSTOEVSKY

While he was working with the Leroy brothers at Arroway Ltd. in Montreal, Cal Broeker met a Russian Bulgarian named Vulko Markov, who belonged to the vague world of international "trade consultants." In his forties, stocky and well-dressed, Markov wore his prematurely white hair combed straight back from a high forehead, Bela Lugosi–style. Like many Europeans, he spoke several languages well. If he sounds like a stereotype, it's because he basically was one — a familiar creature to those old enough to remember a notorious class of character from between the world wars, gentlemen of mysterious means who sprang from the deposed aristocracy of czarist Russia. After the fall of the Soviet Union, these men were themselves replaced by shadowy inheritors who were also deposed in their turn — the former Communist bosses of industry.

Markov had once been the CEO of one of the largest pharmaceutical distribution companies behind the Iron Curtain; his wife had even enjoyed celebrity status in Bulgaria. But that was then. Now, in Montreal, they were both having a hard time surviving, let alone crawling back up the money pile. The Leroys, on the other hand, had connections in all directions — there wasn't a pie worth sampling that hadn't seen one of their paws — and they used their connections, particularly the virtual corridor between their Montreal office and Eastern Europe, to pursue a novel approach to employment: they tried, where possible, to staff Arroway's stark rooms, its grim huts and joyless cubicles, with men and women who were "self-funding." This meant they didn't pay them much. The Leroys paid Markov, for example, $200 a week — good wages in Moscow; a pauper's insult in North America. Nights, he was forced to clean restrooms in nearby hotels to keep afloat while he worked on building up connections between Montreal and the concrete wastelands that sprawled beyond the tattered shreds of the old Iron Curtain.

All the same, Cal was impressed by Markov's stoicism. He kept up a meticulous front and never once complained about what God or history had done to him. Like one of those White Russians from the 1920s, he was always beautifully dressed in tailored suits, and he wore a $1,200 pair of Italian tortoiseshell spectacles. His manners remained gentlemanly and exquisite. Despite the narrow straits he was now sailing, Markov always comported himself as if he was still running that pharmaceutical corporation.

The way Cal saw it, Vulko Markov had nothing but class. From the Bulgarian, he learned that a patina of taste and education was easily acquired. Highly polished shoes, manicured nails, well-trimmed hair, and direct eye contact would run up a lot more mileage for Mr. Calvin Broeker than designer clothes and flashy jewellery.

THE IDEA BEHIND the Leroys' set-up was that the trade consultants in their office would make money by brokering deals with each other. Markov suggested to Cal that with the American's food connections and Markov's own Eastern European distribution network, they could do some profitable business.

Bulgaria was a poor, small country groaning under the burden of a weak and corrupt effort at post-Soviet democracy. In the early nineties, its prime minister, a Soviet-educated and trained apparatchik named Andrei Lukanov, realized that Communism was dying and turned his country's Marxist bureaucrats into businessmen. The change did little for their already doubtful ethics, and Bulgaria became a textbook example of the nightmare possibilities of reckless privatization. The country was soon dominated by semi-criminal oligarchies or groupings, economic networks such as Tron, Orion, and Multigroup. These groups engaged in legitimate commercial activities backed up by violent intimidation, assassination, and extortion. The new Bulgaria, with its lack of institutions, had created power vacuums that were filled by organized crime.

Some of these ugly new phenomena crossed the line over into the surreal. The wrestlers, for instance. The country had developed a vigorous Olympic wrestling tradition during the Communist era. When the wrestlers lost their funding after the fall of the Soviet empire, they moved into racketeering with help from friends in the security services. The wrestlers were the Bulgarian equivalent of the Hell's Angels: big, sullen thugs with a grudge against society yet an insatiable greed for its glittering prizes. They demanded respect, but they never returned it. There was one difference, though: instead of preying on the margins of society, they stood front and centre. Picture the WWF running America.

The wrestlers were huge and brutal; if crossed, they would beat the shit out of anybody right on the spot. Their loyalties were strictly temporary, offered on a per job basis, and there were always power plays within the group itself. All the Bulgarian criminals had tight connections to the Russian Mafiya — no surprise, given the closeness of the two countries' languages. Unlike the Hungarians and the Romanians, the Bulgarians liked the Russians. Just as their Russian counterparts did, the Bulgarian gangs had a vile reputation for torture and extreme violence that intimidated even other underworld players around the globe.

Markov brought to Montreal a man named Tudor Golubev. Golubev ran Omnigroup, which was a food-distribution network. Short, paunchy, tough, rugged, Golubev always carried a shotgun under the front seat of his car and a pistol in his belt. His company controlled grocery distribution on the Black Sea resorts and in the larger cities. In a characteristic bit of Bulgarian-style corporate diversification, he also owned a couple of discos and strip clubs. Cal was introduced to Golubev by Markov, and he in turn put him in contact with U.S. suppliers of tripe and beef products. Cal and his partners shipped lamb, meat products, tongue, cotton, and liquor. Cigarettes were their mainstay.

Of course, once he'd arrived in Sofia, Cal Broeker, gonzo capitalist, was unwilling to let it go at that.

JUST AS HE HAD IN CHATEAUGAY, Cal, before he'd been that long in the Eastern bloc, became an octopus of enterprise, a whirling dervish of a deal-maker, heading off in a half-dozen Bulgarian directions at once. And all this while he was tap dancing with Réal Dupont and dodging trouble on Kahnawake.

He had, through Markov, met a rep from a trading company out of New York City called Transcorp, Inc. This company was a larger, more street smart, better-established kind of operation than Arroway. Transcorp's reps had better connections than the Leroys in the infrastructure of various countries around the world — primarily because they had been doing it longer.

The CEO of Transcorp was a red-headed dynamo in her mid-thirties named Georgia Nelson. If the ex-Soviet boss was a familiar stereotype in the new global economy of the 1990s, so was the American amazon mini-tycoon represented by Georgia Nelson. Beautiful and brainy, ambitious beyond measure, she had smouldering brown eyes, long racehorse legs, and a passionate urge to dominate every single human being who came her way. Although Georgia had a steady boyfriend, she was instantaneously and overtly flirtatious with Cal. However, the Knight of the Baleful Countenance wasn't interested. Elizabeth was more than enough woman for any one man to handle. That was for certain.

The Transcorp reps were very interested in opening up the Balkans, and tin plate was what they had in mind, lots of it. They wanted to know if Cal would represent them or get into business with the Bulgarians on their behalf. He asked Markov if he thought he could make a deal. Vulko said, "For sure."

The idea had much to be said for it. Cal believed that if he acquired a background in the brutal business world of Eastern Europe, it would do a lot to help his RCMP undercover profile — and he was right.

Furthermore, Bulgaria was a good place to hide from Réal Dupont. The guy was now forcing, on his terms, that same $120-million counterfeit deal every time Cal saw him. Dupont tended to show up almost everywhere too.

Now, it was known to be very hard to get a steel contract out of Bulgaria. The quality of the product was good and the price cheap. The problem, however, with the steel mills in the ex-Soviet bloc was that they were very backward, and very backward in many ways too. Their smokestacks dated from the 1920s and were extravagantly unfiltered. And their smoke screened a multitude of sins. The Bulgarians generally liked to dump their waste untreated, and their workforce was so poorly paid it might as well have been slave labour. As a consequence, unsurprisingly, the plant in Kremikovtzi, near Sofia, was corrupt from top to bottom. Organized crime groups were all over the place, and many lesser schools of shark were also frenziedly feeding in the murky steelworks waters — largely owing to the extreme cheapness of what was produced there.

Acting for Transcorp, Cal agreed to negotiate a contract with the Kremikovtzi steelworks for 40,000 metric tons of tin plate, which was to be shipped to the auto manufacturer Daewoo. He was to be paid expenses, plus commissions on performance.

Cal formed his own trading company and named it Schwartz Adler (black eagle) to remind him of his Teutonic warrior's mission. He printed business cards featuring a rampant bird of prey: C. Calvin Broeker Ltd., International Trading Company. In addition, before he set out for Sofia, he armed himself with a small library of letters of recommendation. He had a letter from Grand Chief Joseph Tokwiro Norton, of the Mohawk Council of Kahnawake, saying that Calvin Broeker was authorized to obtain financing for a commercial centre "within the Territory of Kahnawake." Calvin Broeker, however, noted the cagey chief "has not been authorized to make any binding commitments on behalf of the Mohawk Council of Kahnawake." There was another letter of recommendation from Cal's local congressman in upstate New York, John H. McHugh. What's more, Cal got permission to establish a Hummer dealership in Bulgaria. He really liked these menacing paramilitary vehicles. He was also going to negotiate deals to ship wine, cement, and urea.

And by no means last or least, there was going to be a joint venture with Alitalia to promote ticket sales. Eastward ho!

Cal Broeker would be an international travelling medicine show of Yankee free enterprise, a walking statue of entrepreneurial liberty. Those ex-Commies wouldn't know what had hit them.

IN OCTOBER 1994, Cal flew to Sofia via Zurich. While in Switzerland, he attempted to pick up the trail of Ron Ong, who was rumoured to be there, still holding the $20,000 in debentures he had scammed out of Emily Spokane back in Chateaugay. But to no avail. The inexplicable Ong was nowhere to be found.

At the airport in Sofia, reality shone its searchlight through the cracks. Cal gawked at the Bulgarian guards in their full-length leather coats and the snarling German shepherd dogs straining at their leashes. It reminded him of a Second World War movie. The air was harsh and sullen with pollution; diesel fumes hung low on the horizon, and the tang of sewage mixed with cigarette smoke and cooking smells. It was nauseating. Decaying cement apartment blocks built in a monolithic, gloomy Stalin-era style were festooned with multicoloured laundry strung from one balcony to another; it was almost the only touch of gaiety in the grim cityscape — besides the twee gingerbread houses of the old part of town, which seemed purloined from a Lilliputian Vienna. Outside the lumbering apartments were parked Mercedes and BMWs loaded down with vulgar accessories: plastic flowers in gilded vases, huge furry dice, twitching phallic symbols. Right across the street were shops with pricey designer clothes from Italy, gourmet foods, CDs, cruise vacations, and computer software. Cal found that the players in the economic "groupings" dressed like peacocks, swaggered like lords, and drove big, flashy cars, but they lived in cramped, sordid apartments. Just like buddy back home.

True to form, Cal put up in style at the luxurious Vitosha Otani, a five-star, state-owned hostelry in the best part of town, at the foot of Mt. Vitosha, where no amount of Soviet concrete could conceal Bulgaria's eye-popping natural beauty. The hotel had been built in the 1980s by the Japanese, who were forging trade relations with the country at the time and needed somewhere to stay while doing it. Inside, there were several fancy restaurants, a nightclub with a lavish cabaret, and many stores stacked with Western merchandise, magazines, and newspapers. But just outside the front door, there were dancing bears, begging orphans, legless cripples with alms bowls, and fortune-telling gypsies. The bears had giant rings through their torn lips and noses; some of the cripples hauled them- selves around on hands as callused and mutilated as elephants' feet. The streets were jam-packed with rabid pariah dogs; there was always an urchin with pained eyes at your elbow, and someone was forever anxious to read your Tarot cards or tea leaves or palm.

After a couple days, Cal started making the rounds of the embassies, the government ministries, and the military, looking to put together his deals. It sure was a long way from Chateaugay and the IGA. But somehow, what with the gangs and the anarchic Prohibition-era atmosphere, it wasn't all that different from Kahnawake.

He soon found that getting around Sofia by taxi was going to be a problem. When you didn't know the correct price for the ride in from the airport to the city, the cabbies were happy to charge ten times the going rate, but they were decidedly less enthusiastic to have you haggling for an in-city trip like any other Sofian.

One time, he had a close call. He had gone to the German embassy to enquire about the location of a German company. A ratty taxi driver lounging in the foyer of the embassy said he would take him there. The man followed Cal out of the building, showing a conspicuous interest in his briefcase and its contents. Against his better judgement, Cal got into the guy's cab. The taxi started off in the right direction, but the driver soon stopped at a street market to pick up a pack of smokes. While the mangy cabby spoke to his pal at a stall, Cal was dismayed to note that the man kept turning his head to glance back at him. The market buddy then whispered something to a street kid, who promptly ran off down a back alley. The cabby came back to the car with a big smile but — guess what? — no smokes. Cal let him start off and travel a few miles, to avoid attracting the attention of the street vendor. As soon as the cab stopped for a light and a passing tram, however, he tossed the driver double the metered fare and leapt out. The cabby was right behind him.

"This not where you wantink," he said.

Cal kept walking.

"You get in big troubles." The cabby started kicking stones and cursing at him till he was bright red in the face.

Fuck you, asshole.

Cal kept walking. But it didn't take him long to realize that he was in the midst of Sofia's feared gypsy quarter — a forbidden zone to most Bulgarians, let alone Westerners, not to mention a big, conspicuous American wearing his best suit and toting his gleaming, prosperous executive briefcase. The sky seemed to be pressing down close on him now; it was an ominous leaden colour. You didn't want to be on the streets after dark anywhere in Sofia, and in the gypsy quarter, you didn't want to be on the streets, period. At night in his hotel room, Cal had heard the shouts, the screaming, the occasional gunfire drifting across Sofia. Employing all his *National Geographic* survival skills — and all his luck — Cal somehow made it back on foot to the Vitosha before the sun went down. Just aimed for the mountain and kept walking — head held high, eyes avoiding the hate-filled stares, ears closed to the jibes and catcalls. That hotel room never looked so good to Cal. He buried his face in his pillow for two hours, trembling and feeling very alone. The Vitosha would prove to be his fortress during the months ahead, his soaring white castle perched on a mountaintop in the midst of the Valley of the Shadow.

THE BULGARIAN ECONOMIC SYSTEM was crazy, loco; it was nuts — a weird patchwork of the remains of the Communist state and an inchoate, go-getting, free-market chaos. There might be only one shop for meat in this city of several hundred thousand souls, but there would be hundreds of stores selling liquor. Pharmacies were mostly still voodoo apothecaries' lairs from the nineteenth century, but you could buy a box of Tylenol from the man whose main trade was in bicycle repair and women's lingerie — he kept the space-age panacea behind a stack of brassieres that resembled canvas carrying cases for a brace of metronomes. The means of distributing consumer products — the supply-and-demand theory — was really confused; the most needed items were scarce, and the superfluous ones, the nonsense and frippery, were abundant. But there was little waste. Unlike the grocery stores Cal had known, the Bulgarian ones stocked nothing that got tossed into the garbage at week's end.

Sofia was tough, to be sure; a rough place to live, and a truly brutal place to do business. All in all, it was definitely Cal Broeker's cup of tea.

He rented an office and hired a secretary named Silvia for $150 a month. Since there were 3,200 Bulgarian leva to one American dollar, he instantly acquired the woman's undying loyalty, along with that of her entire family. He then hired a translator named William Parvanov. The guy was so precise and fast, Cal was amazed. William would typically finish his translation a split second after Cal had spoken the sentence in English.

Soon, he was meeting Vulko Markov's circle of friends — and each one had ideas about how he could use Cal Broeker. Characteristically, he started pretty much right at the top, with the former prime minister and chief mover of Multigroup, Andrei Lukanov, who himself had long been tight with Markov. The ex-boss of Bulgaria soon became Cal Broeker's good buddy too, and his generous patron.

He first met Lukanov at his mountain retreat near Borovicz, a spectacular location, for dinner with his wife, Urina, and their family. Vulko Markov had flown in especially to make the introduction in person. When he and Cal arrived, the former prime minister was down on his knees, at work in his garden. Lukanov was a short man with white hair that contrasted dramatically with his swarthy complexion. Beetle-browed, pot-bellied, given to wearing blue jeans and golf shirts, Lukanov was well-spoken, polite. A nice guy, in fact, with a big, toothy winner's smile. Yet it was still like meeting some warlord in ancient times.

"Many Bulgarian peoples get irritated vith you, Broeker," pronounced the former prime minister at that first meeting.

"Why?" asked Cal.

"Nobody in one grouping has share in your business. You spread everysink around."

Cal replied that this was intentional.

"One sink only keeps you alive."

"What's that?"

"These Indians. Nobody knows how powerful zey are. Everybody a leetle afraid."

When he left office in 1990, Lukanov had gone to prison for six months for economic crimes committed against the people during the Soviet era After his release, Lukanov became interested in international banking. He had connections to the Bulgarian National Bank, and he wanted Cal to help him move money into the United States and Canada — money laundering, not to put too fine a point on it. Dinner began. They ate fire-roasted mountain trout and traditional salad dishes prepared with goat cheese. What the former PM wanted to know was if Cal was the man for the job.

You bet he was.

His study of banking methods back home at the Citizens National in Chateaugay had revealed something called bridging accounts, which allowed one individual to set up an account in the name of somebody else. For instance, Andrei Lukanov could set up an anonymous account under the master account of C. Calvin Broeker, and the money could bounce happily from Bulgaria to the U.S. to the Cayman Islands, cha-cha-cha. It was laughably simple.

Lukanov also offered Broeker and Markov a continuing connection with Multigroup. They would be the grouping's Canadian and American representatives, its conduit to the United States.

"Let's see what happens with the tin plate first," said Cal.

He was hesitant to get in bed with Lukanov right away, all the way — at least not until he had concluded his affairs at Kremikovtzi.

"I am very interested in tobacco," said Lukanov. "If you get me right product, I pay cash right away."

Tobacco, Lukanov explained, would fit in well with his current activities. He was in the process of building up the disco and entertainment areas of his resort empire, and he needed to focus on that — but soon he would be able to turn his attention to matters financial. Soon.

He had his priorities straight. They loved disco, these Bulgarians, just adored every note that ABBA had ever stamped on vinyl or transferred to tape and then plastic. Bulgaria managed to combine the worst of East and West: Stalinist architecture and American disco. Ra-Ra-Rasputin . . . Here, Saturday night fever was more a 24/7 affair. If you had any money at all, you had a whole pile — and come nightfall, you plucked at a wardrobe bulging with broad lapels and white flared pants to go tripping the light (more often the heavy) fantastic across the pulsing strobe-lit floors of Zero's or the 007 Bar. "Stayin' alive, stayin' alive . . ." Of course, you didn't always manage to stay alive — the discos were notorious for vendetta slaughters, a bloodbath every week — but while you did live, you drank deeply from the well. If it's still 5000 B.C. in New Guinea, it's about 1975 in Sofia — at the apex, that is, because if you don't have any money, it's 1927. A time traveller in his own right, Cal was also not that averse to the disco floor — especially when it was redolent of such an intoxicating social climate and he was in such lofty company. No one said his new life couldn't be fun, did they?

| 59

Dinner with Lukanov ended with few hard commitments vis-à-vis business but lots of vodka-fuelled avowals of eternal friendship. When Cal and Markov reeled out of Lukanov's mountain lodge at about 2 a.m., Markov told him that the meeting had gone very, very well.

"I discussed you with the PM," he said. "He liked you very much."

This was good. Cal didn't want to think about what happened when the Bulgarian warlord took an instant dislike to someone.

"He said when you are ready," Markov added, "he will open the book for you. I'm going back to Montreal in a couple days, but when I return, we will set things up."

The old commissar's eyes were alight. He could see the days of cleaning hotel pissoirs blissfully receding into the past. In the meantime, he said, Lukanov was arranging things so Cal would be under the protection of Multigroup's muscle while he pursued the steel contract. Stayin' alive . . .

SEVERAL WEEKS AFTER CAL'S first meeting with the former prime minister, ten carloads of hitmen in BMWs pulled up in a convoy during a party at Lukanov's shimmering new nightspot. They walked in and sprayed the place with machine-gun fire, effectively closing it.

Cal's plans for moving Bulgarian funds to America came to a full stop in October 1996, however, the night Andrei Lukanov, on answering a knock at the door, had his head blown off. Some said it was rogue factions in Multigroup — which was not exactly structured like Proctor & Gamble or IBM. There were other theories involving the wrestlers, but nobody was ever charged, let alone brought to trial.

Back in November 1994, though, Cal had managed to get a meeting with the current president of Bulgaria, Zhelyu Zhelev. This pow-wow cost him $7,000, slipped into the pockets of several of the president's advisers. In the new Bulgaria, salaries were seldom paid — they were ceremonial, theoretical — so people made out the best they could. You typically had to pay a bribe to get your train tickets issued or your dry-cleaning back. You had to bribe the police to prevent the gypsies from stealing your shoes or your babies. You even had to pay a bribe to someone in order to bribe his boss (and he probably had to bribe the executive assistant to pull it off). So it was definitely not going to be a bargain to arrange a yak with the president. But Cal wasn't expecting it to come with such a vicious twist.

When he went to a meeting with the lawyer who was to set up the meeting with the president, the son of a bitch was full of threats. There the guy was, in his shithole of an office, with the secretary clacking away on a typewriter out of the 1940s, wearing his threadbare, double-breasted tent of suit with the nice egg stains on it, telling him, "If you cannot make successful deal after you meet president, I cannot guarantee your security. Mebbe you no leave my country."

Cal went ballistic.

"I don't need to meet the guy anyway. This was your fucking idea. Just call it off."

But the lawyer was desperate to be associated with any business deal that promised to ship so many metric tons of steel. Six million dollars was at stake, after all. He wanted the prestige and the exposure of the meeting with the president. He wanted. And of course, he backed down.

The lawyer and his friends tended to regard Cal as a prize catch, one to be displayed to all and sundry. It was no surprise, then, that the arrangements called for Cal to meet Zhelev in the White House — by sheer coincidence, no doubt, the name of the official residence of the Bulgarian leader — in the heart of Sofia.

It was a large, musty block-like structure, with a decidedly bureaucratic ambience. There was a small security room with a metal detector where guards did a quick body search and rifled through his briefcase. Cal noticed that there were odd, ugly patches on the walls and the floors. The stains of absence. Rugs and valuable paintings that had been there for decades — maybe centuries — had abruptly been removed to more private locations in the untamed, greasy kleptocracy that was now Eastern Europe. The interior of the hall was vast and empty, and there was a high-vaulted ceiling and a long stone staircase. The place felt desolate to him. According to William, his translator, the pillaging that took place in the confusion of the dissolution of the Soviet system had pretty much washed over everything in the country.

Cal and the translator were ushered into a small room by one of Zhelev's economic advisers. The floor had a worn oriental carpet, and there was a marble fireplace next to the couch where they sat. Cal presented the adviser with a set of flags: Bulgarian, Canadian, American. Soon Zhelev entered the room with his aides and secretaries, and they were told they had fifteen minutes. What followed was largely ceremonial: a lot of mutual stroking.

Nonetheless, out of this meeting with Zhelev came a wild proposal, a scintillating specimen of gonzo capitalism at its rabid finest. The Bulgarian government was interested in Cal Broeker's establishing an air corridor from Saudi Arabia to the U.S. via Bulgaria. State Department officials, when Cal contacted them, dryly replied that, generally speaking, air corridors were considered government-to-government issues, and were not usually found within the purview of individuals such as C. Calvin Broeker, no matter how enterprising. Although they were polite — unwilling to stomp the entrepreneurial spirit entirely to death — they were nonetheless firm about where business ended and politics began.

Next, Cal met with Maj. Gen. Oleg Bokov regarding the Hummers. Bokov, a leading figure in Bulgaria's military, was of course also involved in Multigroup. William the translator set up a meeting with representatives of two of Bulgaria's largest arms suppliers, companies improbably named Perrotex and Antimex. They too had some good ideas: moving arms from Canada into the U.S. through Cal's Mohawk connections on the rez, for example. The idea of Antimex operating in Akwesasne blew even Cal's mind — the sheer audacity of these people! Were there no limits to their predatory advance upon the rest of us?

Unfortunately, there were not. We were returning to the state of being settlers in an untamed land. He reported this particular nugget of intelligence to the military attaché at the U.S. embassy. However, the haughty old air force colonel in charge wasn't interested in the slightest. After ten creaking minutes, Mr. Broeker got the bum's rush. The problem was that he wasn't part of the official intelligence system, so he didn't exist. He was a nobody from nowhere. People — civilians, that is — were always walking into U.S. embassies with wild-eyed notions: aliens were about to invade; the Chinese had already invaded; the Russians were collaborating with aliens and the Chinese. A man named Lee Harvey Oswald had once walked into the Mexico City base with a ridiculous story concerning the Cubans and the Mafia. At the old Teheran bastion, visitors were always muttering about an imminent revolution steered by the clergy. The clergy! You get wise to alarmists and cranks in the diplomatic corps — it's an occupational hazard. Only a professional can accurately read the signs of mutiny, insurrection, or incipient turmoil in a foreign state. It takes years of training. It takes breeding.

So Cal then started to work on the contract for Daewoo: 10,000 metric tons of steel per month. It was all a game, he began to see, but a very tough one, nonetheless; a game no one could be assured of winning. It was even difficult to determine if you'd lost, sometimes. Thus it was no accident that few deals with foreigners got done in Bulgaria. Like the freshly minted MBAs who are dispatched to Sofia from Des Moines or Denver, laptops in hand, as someone's idea of an initiation — or maybe their idea of fun — Cal had his work cut out for him.

First, he would take one of the owner-grouping's principals out to dinner. The guy would invariably ask him for, say, $10,000 for the factory basketball team. Needless to say, the factory in question didn't have even a basketball, let alone a team! Then there were the bullshit artists who represented themselves as ex-KGB; they promised much and always had a lot of contacts, but in the end they could deliver nothing. You had to learn how to deflect them without arousing their hostility. Cal had to pay the lawyer for the steel company, though; he was the one who was going to make the introductions. His fee was $15,000 — and that was just for starters.

At the Kremikovtzi factory, he met people from every tier of the hierarchy, all the way down the line from the factory president to the head of the shipping department, his foreman, and the guys who actually pressed the steel. He had to have them all onside in order to put this deal together. He had to go to the factory and get to know everybody, including the Bulgarian military (which had an armed presence there and absolutely had to approve any sale of metals). You needed to know everybody because a foreman could be paid off by a competitor to torpedo your deal. If he wasn't in the loop, you were in trouble. And everybody assumed Cal was just as corrupt as they were. One man's meat is usually another man's meat too, after all.

One night, when he went out to dinner with a government official, there just happened be two unescorted single women at the restaurant. With their bouffant hair, grotesque makeup, and vacuous expressions, they weren't that tempting to him. Nor were they very subtle in their approach.

"You vant mebbe light my ceegie?" one woman said.

Cal made it clear he was there for business and that was all. He understood, in the circumstances, that sex was a barter item too, and he didn't want to be compromised. He didn't know who was talking to whom, either. Pillow talk, after all, was the common coin of industrial espionage. It was better to abstain. You just couldn't put everything out there to be totted up, priced, assessed, manipulated. Some things had to remain sacred, otherwise you'd end up negotiating with a dude in a red silk cape, horns on his head. The Bulgarians were always playing with him at these dinners too, trying to gross him out by offering dishes of brains or entrails, a beady-eyed goat's head, or a gristly stewed testicle. Sometimes they just tried to discover exactly how much he could drink. Whatever it was, they were always busy pumping him for personal details, looking for a chink in the armour, a weak link in the chain mail.

And they were all interested in cigarettes, legal or illegal. Deeply committed, impressively loyal smokers themselves — smoking was the national pastime, competitive, sincere, determined — when it came to nicotine, they wanted to do any kind of business. Representatives from Balkan Tabac made it clear, once they knew of Cal's tobacco connection, that they would make a deal any way he wanted a deal — up, down, sideways, or woven into a skein.

That other national pastime, the paying of bribes, wasn't as easy as it looked either, he came to see. If someone rips you, for instance, who's gonna go after him? The police? What if — as often was the case — it was the police you were bribing? He had to be extremely clear with everybody concerned that when the steel went on the boat and the letter of credit was paid, they'd get their $50, or their $10,000, commission. It wasn't going to happen a minute before, though. Clear?

Are you interested or not?

Cal's attitude did not necessarily sit well with everybody at the steel factory, however. Part of his order, it transpired, would have to be pried away from another order originally destined for Turkey. And the Turks, after all, understood how this bribery thing worked far better than the cursed Americans ever would.

One day, a representative of one of the groups he was meeting with pulled out a huge pistol and put it on the table.

"Tell me," the man said in a heavy accent, "vy should I not blow your fuckink head off?"

"Pick that fuckin' thing up," said Cal, "and pull the fuckin' trigger, right here." He tapped his forehead.

"You get nervous, I sink," observed the man.

"Put the fuckin' thing away," said Cal, "or I'm gonna pick it up and use it on you. Pop!"

The man obediently picked up his pistol and put it back in his coat.

Cal had been confident nothing would happen. Never in his life had he seen anybody go through with a showy threat like that one. People who are going to kill you don't warn you first — they kill you first. These assholes were just grandstanding. Occasionally, you might run into someone crazy enough to start shooting — he had met one or two of those types on the rez — but then you never called their bluff. You just stayed the fuck away.

In the new Bulgaria, you could get killed in the course of a *legitimate* business deal — if it didn't work out to everyone's satisfaction or taste. It was all a question of how gonzo you wanted to be, of how much slack head office cut you. There was also a little matter of U.S. law — not all free enterprise is legal, even in the home of the brave. Other American businessmen Cal met in Sofia claimed it was impossible to do business in Bulgaria. Totally impossible. But by the time he went back to New York in December, Cal Broeker had an office in the Kremikovtzi plant with his name on the door.

BACK IN NEW YORK, however, things had changed — or rather, the way he saw things had changed. It was as if he had never left Bulgaria.

When he returned to the States to work on the tin-plate deal from that end, he started to see how Transcorp, Inc. treated its other "trade consultants." When he began to notice what the company did to other people in the office, he got a trifle paranoid. The consultants were freelance people. The way he saw it, Transcorp fucked them out of deals they had worked years at.

"I know your commission's $50,000," they'd be told. "But we've put $100,000 of the company's money in and waited this long for the deal to come through, so this deal is going to come back to the company. See?"

The company's representatives could pull that on a guy because they'd have him working on three or four different projects at once — and they'd know he'd rather bite the bullet, and his tongue, than screw up his other deals. Cal began to take steps to ensure that this sort of garbage didn't happen to him.

The lovely Georgia was starting to get annoyed, meanwhile, because she wanted Cal in New York full time. He felt that she wanted to know every little bit there was to know about his life and his business, and he didn't like that. Worse, she wanted to control his commissions when they came in — wanted, for Chrissake, to deposit them in her own bank account. It was no surprise, then, that Georgia's eyebrows went all the way up when RCMP types started calling for him at the Transcorp office. They, however, only wanted to know what was happening with that one-man crime wave, Réal Dupont.

When Cal finally returned to Kahnawake, Elizabeth wanted him to reopen the gas station and get some business going through again. She also wanted him to come live with her and be a househusband — not retreat to Bulgaria again. He, after all, *had* set up house with Elizabeth. Meanwhile, he was still trying to liquidate those howling catastrophes that had once been businesses in Chateaugay, which his ex-wife Doris had been dutifully caretaking all this while. It wasn't so easy to walk away from a life when it kept pulling you back. In fact, life was more goddamn complicated when you turned your back on it than it was when you bent double and let it rip you another butt. Yet a warrior copes with this, manages the situation, and eventually he aspires to overcome — this was Cal's battle plan, anyway.

Then he got a call from Réal Dupont.

Who still wanted to do the counterfeiting deal.

Or fucking else.

DUPONT HAD HAD ART FRANKLIN, one of his henchmen, check Cal out in Bulgaria. He'd called the office in the Vitosha Hotel, claiming to have Bulgarian connections. He could have been lying, or maybe not. Now, though — and right now — Dupont wanted to meet and talk about counterfeit.

"I can't do it," said Cal. "I'm goin' back to Bulgaria."

"When you goin'?"

Cal told him.

"Where you leaving from?"

"New York."

And that was that.

Cal went to New York and had one day to spend in the office, giving Transcorp a pre-departure briefing. Next day, Georgia dropped him at Kennedy, and while he was standing in line at the Lufthansa check-in, he heard somebody say, "Hey, Broeker."

It was Réal Dupont. Again.

He had materialized from nowhere, the way he always did, like one of the angry, ungrateful undead. Now he stared balefully at Cal. He didn't really need to say anything — you knew what he had to say. The guy was a walking threat.

Cal said, "Hey, man. What you doin' here?"

Dupont said, "I'm comin' here to check you out. Can I see your ticket?"

"What for?"

"Just let me see da fuckin' thing!"

So Cal handed him the airline ticket. It was for a flight from New York to Frankfurt to Zurich to Sofia, and the return date was open.

"I want to see your passport too, motherfucker!"

Cal pulled it out and showed it to him.

"When you come back, I wanna do diss deal. Got it?"

Dupont was like something in a horror movie that won't die and won't go away. Cal wondered if he'd have to worry about him popping out of the can, jack-in-the-boxing up through the floorboards with his god-damn counterfeit deal for the next forty years.

"Wouldn't miss it for the world," he told Dupont. "Not for the world."

"You fucking right you won't, asshole."

But if he had persuaded Réal Dupont that he was an affluent interna-tional businessman, it was a small miracle. He was heading back to Sofia with exactly $1,800 in his pocket, money lent to him by Elizabeth. He didn't have a lot backing him up. He was going to cut the deals in his own name, though, using Transcorp as a credibility factor. The Transcorp reps were worried that he was going to move their deal over to somebody else. He wasn't passing their cards around. He wasn't their boy. He was grimly determined they weren't going to steal this deal from him, though — not this time, no way.

All things considered, Cal Broeker was nothing if not an optimist.

Luckily, he had made a good friend of Lubomir Parmakov, the manager of the Vitosha Hotel. Parmakov was six-foot-four, 240 pounds, with a big head, thinning grey hair, and a deep, sonorous Bulgarian voice — just a thundering, massive guy. Also one of the greatest guys he had ever met. This guy you didn't fuck with. This guy you treated right. Parmakov had declared his hotel off limits to the gangs, severely curtailing their operations there. He had cleverly set up the place with state employees, some of whom were connected to the different gangs, and he told them, knowing of their alliances, "When you're in here, you're loyal to me. When you're out there, you do your own thing."

The wrestlers had come anyhow, and had tried to take over the Vitosha's bar and the concessions. But Parmakov's security guys were tough too. They went to talk to them and told them to get the hell out, pushed them back on the street. It took balls to do that.

In the winter and spring of 1995, Parmakov allowed Cal Broeker to run up a tab for $20,000 in room fees, as well as faxes, phone calls back to the States, use of the office, and use of secretaries. Legitimate use. A room in the Vitosha didn't come cheap; it cost $500 a day. Transcorp kept saying, "Fine, we'll pay for it." But the money never came. It didn't seem to matter, though.

68 |     Every chance he had, Lubo would grab Cal and pick up his wife, and they'd all pour into his Range Rover and drive out of the cramped, old city into the fresh air and timeless beauty of the countryside to visit ancient boar-hunting lodges, towering monasteries, towns unchanged since the fifteenth century, and overgrown, crumbling medieval fortresses. Parmakov knew his American friend liked history.

In some ways, Bulgaria was the culmination of Cal's romantic quest for the past, the quest he had been pursuing since his teenage years at Fort Niagara. In the hard years ahead, he would often refer to it fondly as "the old country" — as if he himself were an immigrant, a stranger in this strange land of ours.

One fine day, now engraved in Cal's memory, he went for a trip with Stepan Rodonov, the man in charge of the military complex in the plant at Kremikovtzi. They went to Boncsko, in the Purin Mountains. It was a town that still had a curtain wall, a stone rampart with archers' steps behind it. The place hadn't changed much since the Turkish invasion in the sixteenth century. Sitting in the cupped palm of reddish ochre peaks, under a sky of deep, embattled clouds, the town reflected an ancient light, as if the very stones that built it viewed the passing parade with diffidence, knowing how ephemeral it all was in the eye of eternity. Time itself seemed cowed here, forced to slow its chariot in deference to the stately rhythms of a more humane pace that was the way of nature. The vines clung to rocks the same way as they clung to the works of man, restraining them, holding down the urge to gallop constantly towards a better future by revealing that it already existed, hidden beneath the surface complexities of a present that was always the sum of the past.

In Bulgaria, Cal felt the unfolding of that deep memory, as if the land was guiding him back to the origins of his own humanity. In Boncsko, he felt near the source, in the first chapter of the history of history. He wished the land would reach out and claim him the way it did the stones of civilization. The peace and certainty of a place that has deep roots were intoxicating. He remembered part of a poem he'd read in school:

*Bind me ye woodbines in your twines*
*Curl me about ye gadding vines*
*And O, so close your circles lace*
*That I may never leave this place . . .*

The banquet hall in the town had rough-hewn benches and a huge fireplace against one wall. In front of an enormous crackling fire, the sweaty villagers, half-drunk, salt tears flowing freely, sang a song that celebrated their town and its venerable past. Halfway through it, they all pulled out pistols and fired at the antique ceiling until shards of plaster showered down on the tables.

Cal fell in love with the scene; it was so elemental, so satisfyingly straightforward in its mix of human emotion and intellectual under-standing. History wasn't some dead study here; it lived, and not just in the stones and old wooden beams, but in the hearts of the men and women who were born and died here.

Later that evening, he lay in the cold upper rooms of a Tudor-style fourteenth-century burgher's mansion. It was remarkably like Elizabeth's house back on the rez, Cal thought. The same kind of throwback. And being an anachronism himself, an echo of simpler, more honest times, he could have moved right in to that house there and then. If he'd held on to them, most of his possessions — and definitely the weapons — would have fit right in as well. He slept on a rope bed covered with several itchy woollen blankets on a thin horsehair mattress. Cal loved the monastic austerity of the place; it seemed to evolve from the natural world around it rather than stand in defiance as modern structures usually did. He listened to the howl of wolves in the woods, and then heard the close growling and panting as they circled the walled compound outside, look-ing for their supper among the chicken runs and sheepfolds.

Next day, on the way up to one of the little villages in the mountains, across the snowy steppes and frozen valleys, Cal saw hunters with full beards that reached down to their bellies. Sunburned, windburned, they looked like Vikings lost in a time warp. With rifles slung over their backs and bandoliers crossed in an X, they made their way through the ancient forest in four feet of snow. They must have been in their sixties too — their faces creased with wrinkles, their expressions grave and solemn — though age comes more swiftly to those whose only roof is the sky. These ancient hunters wore what appeared to be ancient garments as well: swirling tunics made of fur or leather, cross-strapped boots, leggings, and small cone-shaped caps. They were accompanied by three boys wearing what were little more than rags, dragging sleds burdened with the great steaming cadavers of stags they had just killed. Tagging along beside them were four massive wolf-hunting dogs, wild-eyed, panting, their long sharp teeth flashing in the winter sunlight. The hunting party just materialized as if through the mists of time, silent, like a medieval dumb show, like a salutary omen or portent. Then they disappeared.

The intrusive sound of Lubo's SUV jerked Cal back into the late twentieth century, but the strange *tableau vivant* of hunters haunted him for days. They drove on. The mayor of the little mountain town they were visiting was a friend of Parmakov's, and the villagers decided to slaughter a pig in honour of the city slickers' visit. The pig, understandably, declined to co-operate. It didn't care who the guests were. And it got loose. Drunk on Bulgarian overproof vodka — something that took a little getting used to, even for him — Cal decided to help the hospitable villagers. He took off on his ten-league legs after the prodigal pig, slipped, fell in the mud, but dove as he did, and, reaching out, caught the squealing escapee by both its hind legs, hauled it high up for all to see, and with one deft stroke, cut its throat. The pig's contorted snout was now bubbling and screaming like a baby, while its neck pumped out blood.

They burned the pig's hair off with a blowtorch. In the process, one man also severely burned his leg. Killing has a way of coming back at you — which is probably why in Western society we've tried to cut it out, to sublimate it with extreme sports and war games. But — yee-haw! — ain't nothing like the real thing.

Cal was tripping. He was alive from hair to toes, all six-foot-four of the way. It sure beat the veil of illusion that was a butcher's counter, with its packaged chops and neat steak flanks in cling film and polystyrene. Reality let you know how it got the name, all right.

He helped gut the pig, cut him up the American way — his Price Chopper butcher's training, learned back in Albany, coming in handy. He even showed the crowd a better way to split the ribcage than the shattered mess that was the custom. These Bulgarian villagers were very impressed indeed. They thought it was great that an American could do something like this. The ones they'd seen till now generally behaved like babies when such bloody reality reared its head.

Another time, he went with William, his translator, to Stara Zagora, an old winery. With them were a government minister and Christo, the owner of the Sofia casino. They met the establishment's director, who showed them centuries-old cellars, even older barrels, and bottles that looked as if they'd been made at the dawn of viniculture itself. They talked, and of course they drank, late into the evening.

As they drove back in their Mercedes, however, Cal's friends got nervous. There had been frequent hijackings by gypsy gangs along the stretch of road they were travelling. William told him how the gypsies rolled up the telephone lines in the countryside at night, just so they could resell the copper. As a result, not surprisingly, the phones were often out. Once, these gypsies had even stolen the entire Eagle Bridge in Sofia; they simply tore it apart and shipped it to Germany, where it made someone quite a conversation piece. There's someone, somewhere in this world, who is prepared to steal you anything you want. Anything.

Cal remembered another trip on the way to a meeting when he saw a small convoy laden with cases of cigarettes being escorted through the twisting roads of the back country that led to Romania or Greece. Unsmiling gangsters in track suits herded the tobacco caravans from one country to another, brushing by small customs outposts as if they didn't exist. And they didn't, for all intents and purposes. Rules and regulations — laws — are not such a plague for others as they are for us.

Now, driving in the dark, guns came out, pistols were snatched from belts. Somebody had an AK-47. Or was it an M-16? The imagination runs riot in times like these. The Mercedes hit 140 kilometres. Then it hit a dirt berm, or a small hump spanning the road. Christo tried hitting the brakes, but they fought back and the car flew into the air. When it came down, all the passengers slammed their heads against the roof. Cal broke some teeth and cut his lip. William had opened the sunroof with his skull, and he was out cold. Who had blocked the road? Was it the gypsies or the gangs? It didn't matter. Christo and the government minister opened up with their weapons, firing wildly into the darkness. *Blat-blat-brrrrrrrrrrbbb!*

Their shots were answered by a gaping silence. There was no one out there, just phantoms of the mind.

Somehow, they made it back to Sofia. Next day, Cal had serious repairs done on his molars with some sort of surplus warhead pig iron or recycled lead. Later on, back in Canada, Jerry, Cal's dentist, marvelled at the state of Bulgarian medicine: the material his molars had been treated with was spectacularly poisonous, and would invade the whole body from the gums. It was a wonder he wasn't dead of toxic shock.

BUT THE CORE OF Cal's time was spent at Kremikovtzi, in the steel mill. He rode that horse, determined to tame the bucking bronco of bribes and intrigues that was business in Sofia. He stayed on in Bulgaria until it felt almost like home. He went out to the plant every day of the week, and then he went to his office to manage the progress of that deal. Defeat was not an option. Step by step by step, the tin-plate venture began to come together.

Then one day, Lubo Parmakov came to Cal and said, "I can't do it any more. Your company now owes the hotel $20,000."

The hotel's auditors had come in and told the manager to get the money now — today — or they would have Cal arrested. They wanted his passport too. Lubo wanted to deliver the bad news personally; he felt it was the least he could do for their friendship. So Cal called Georgia in New York and told her what was happening. She went scrambling immediately for the $20,000, with Cal on the other line. By now, there was a paddy wagon actually waiting for him outside the hotel. Needless to say, if Bulgaria's humbler dwellings were anything to go by, the nation's jail cells wouldn't much resemble their North American counterparts.

Lubo was upset about it all. He knew Cal was getting screwed on his deal, because he saw the work that was getting done and how far he had progressed into the Bulgarian infrastructure. But given the circumstances, there was really nothing Lubo could do. Cal toyed with flight, saw himself ducking out the back door of the Vitosha and walking over the mountains, anything to get the hell out of there. Just walk away and start hitchhiking to the border.

The next day, he had all his luggage hauled down to the lobby and placed by the front door. However, the police were in the lobby too, waiting for Cal to emerge. He was saying his goodbyes to Lubo in the back office when a woman from hotel accounting came in and delivered the reprieve. New York had wired $20,000 into Cal's bank account, which was down to a pitiful $5.78. He breathed a sigh of relief, but in truth he wasn't that relieved. The $20,000 paid the hotel bill and kept him out of jail, but that was it.

Mr. Broeker was broke.

He left the hotel and moved into his office downtown on Grdina Plitskaya. Lubo instructed his security goons to provide a little protection for his friend at the new location, but Cal was still strapped for cash. He slept on a mattress in the office now, and didn't even have money for laundry (not that laundry cost much in Sofia). In order to keep his suits pressed, he would go home early, hang them up immediately, and walk around the place in his underwear. If anybody was curious about his sleeping in the office, he told them he wanted to protect certain documents. Or alternatively, he'd say, "I work till I fall asleep."

The Bulgarians appreciated a hard-working guy, and Cal was nothing if not that. He worked hard to maintain the image of the rich businessman too, appearing once a day in the lobby of the Vitosha so, to anyone but Lubo, it looked like he was still shelling out the $500 a day for rooms. But it's not so easy to act rich if you don't feel rich.

He was hungry all the time now, forced to rely for his dinner on the banquet tables of the embassies and their eternal cocktail parties. Any night of the week, at least one major embassy is throwing a party in every capital city on earth with taxpayer money. Cal would walk into these parties and meet politicians and generals and princes and titans of industry, shooting the breeze with them, laughing at their jokes. Sometimes he bought cheap vegetables in the market — a pumpkin or potatoes — then he took them back to the office and cooked them up on a gas burner. He didn't go anywhere because he couldn't afford to get there. For close on eight weeks in the spring of 1995, he didn't have ten dollars on him. And what little he did have, he was saving for emergencies. The only thing that kept him going was the knowledge that the couple of hundred thousand dollars he stood to make on the deal would go a long way towards redeeming his reputation back home. He'd pay off all debts, meet all obligations, and spread the wealth around a little too.

74 |     Then a phone call came from Elizabeth, back on Kahnawake. She had always been blessed with the gift of being able to read the language of the unconscious, the ability to interpret dreams and other omens. And she had dreamed a dream that had warned of imminent danger. It was coming both from a woman with a skull-like mien and from other sources. The identity of the skull-like woman wasn't that difficult for Cal to dope out: Georgia wore her hair pulled tightly back on her head and braided behind, and treachery from that direction wasn't exactly unexpected. In her phone call, her voice sounding frail and very far away, Elizabeth emphasized that the danger was imminent. Like right now!

When he hung up the phone, Cal got the hell out of his office and kept watch from a nearby alley. The dream wasn't long in coming true. While Cal watched from his hiding place, a squad of thugs armed with baseball bats drove up in a big black car and broke into the office. Clearly, they were looking for him. When they couldn't find him, they simply smashed the place up a little, then left. He told Lubo Parmakov what had happened, and the hotelier told his own thugs to extend their watch over Cal's office 24/7 until the threat abated. Although he'd never really doubted Elizabeth before, after this incident Cal never questioned her sixth-sense pronouncements again.

Most improbably, the Bulgarian deals moved forward, growing step by step until they produced fruit. In June, a $6-million letter of credit moved from Daewoo's Hong Kong office to Chase Manhattan in New York, and from there to the Bulgarian National Bank and finally into Cal's hollow, famished account. Now everybody had to jump — it was just a question of how high. He'd done what he had said he would do.

"Where's your product?" asked Cal. "Let's rock 'n' roll!"

He went to the house of a merchant captain so that he could personally arrange the shipping of the tin plate. The impersonal approach didn't go far in Bulgaria. If you were out of sight, you were out of your mind as far as the biz community was concerned.

Thus, praising God — any god — for all His goodness, for all the good things He had provided (a little late, yet nonetheless provided), Cal ate *schema chorba*, tripe soup, roast venison with wildberries and bread-sausage stuffing, mashed red cabbage, and broiled potatoes, followed by a thick and creamy pudding. He drank vodka — the best much-filtered vodka, not the noxious, curdling jet fuel — and he cut a deal. The people from Daewoo flew over to gaze fondly at their tin plate sitting there in the factory, ready to be shipped; to shake the hands of those responsible for this miracle of trade; and to raise many a thimble of vodka in ceremonial toasts hailing the potential longevity and numerous offspring of such a fine, well-tempered deal.

Everything was sweet. Life itself looked good.

Then sweet Georgia Nelson arrived from New York and started royally fucking the deal. She thundered in like a herd of longhorns and began dismantling the careful structure of payoffs, bribes, and commissions that C. Calvin Broeker had so skilfully and arduously erected over so many long months. Life suddenly went from looking good to being extremely unpleasant and looking its age. Georgia didn't understand that there were people Cal had to pay simply to set up a meeting with somebody else, who would in turn want to be paid for his signature on a document. Whether the deal happened or not, the first guy did what you asked him to do and he expected the money. This wasn't America. These people were waiting in line to be paid. But in came Georgia, telling them: "You're not going to be paid because you're not part of the deal. Who the fuck are you?"

She had never done business outside the First World before, and there was what you might call some culture shock, some ethnic trauma, on both sides. The big-bellied Bulgarians, with their exaggerated masculinity and stolidly traditional views, weren't ready for the American amazon. In fact, they weren't ready for the female CEO in general, and wouldn't have been even if she wore a crinoline and cried a lot. As for Georgia, she definitely wasn't prepared for this world before time, or at least before Mrs. Pankhurst's time. Cal had to explain some nasty scenes and a lot of basic realities to her.

"You may be horrified by what you think of as corruption," he explained, "but it's what these people do to survive."

He was right about her being horrified. The two towering Americans started to argue. Before long, Georgia was talking about suing him for the expenses she'd already covered, and then some. In Bulgaria, women didn't threaten to sue men. They didn't threaten men, period. Cal had been there so long that he found it quaint.

"You've got to pick up the tab if you want me to continue," he told her.

He had to pay the hotel for a stack of incidentals. He had to pay the freight. He had to pay some tasty characters too, the kind to whom you don't relish trying to explain the reasons for your non-payment.

And he was getting squeezed at the factory. There were some tough meetings, ones that made anything in corporate America seem like kindergarten. Bulgarian law, evidently, was not conducive to the con man or the empty promise. Your word was your bond, and if it wasn't, you'd wish to God it had been. Cal was to be called out by the honchos at Kremikovtzi to perform financially on the letter of credit, which, after all, was what an LC was all about. It *guaranteed* payment.

Cal muttered about fixing everything tomorrow.

"You're not going to be around tomorrow if we don't have our money," his factory crew told him. "We want to be paid."

There were threats from the Bulgarians all the time now. It had become a nation of Réal Duponts. Cal constantly worried about being put in jail or otherwise forcibly kept from leaving the country. And these were the nicest things he faced.

He agonized over what course he should take, while Georgia played the bull in the china shop of his deal-making. He paced his office and the streets, often aware of men in alleyways watching him or cars that drove slowly twenty feet behind him. Fretting over every little noise, he stayed up the whole of one night, and just as an apocalyptic dawn sent rivers of blood streaming through the violet firmament, he hit upon a solution — indeed, the only possible solution.

Cal Broeker packed his bag, jumped on a plane, and returned to Canada, to Kahnawake and Elizabeth. It was summer and he needed a vacation in the worst way, so he took a month off. He wanted to collect his thoughts, and Elizabeth's telephone call about her dream had reminded him that he missed her. He left Sofia and the deal just to be with her — or so he persuaded himself — just to be home. To be back in the other world that had once seemed so far away, and that itself now seemed dreamlike.

It didn't seem dreamlike when he reached it, though. It was a world where everyone spoke his language, though few understood him. A world where no one fired guns at the ceiling in joy. And a world where, natu- | 77 rally, Réal Dupont was calling all the time, Cal's creditors in Chateaugay were losing patience, and all manner of minor irritants existed to show him that Bulgaria really wasn't such a bad place after all. Georgia called too, constantly asking when his vacation was due to finish, pushing him to go back and resurrect the deal. She dangled a pretty attractive carrot from her stick too, and it was covered in dollar signs.

Everything in Cal's life was maxed out: his credit card and his life. Cal Broeker was in a hole and digging deeper. Was this what happened when you tried to fight the good fight in a fallen world? Where the hell was this god of his, anyway? Having something to show for all this toil wouldn't be amiss, he told himself. Just to reassure me that I'm still divinely sanctioned. A little incentive . . .

Most men would have cracked under the strain, but not Cal. The strain made him stronger — it made him fight back. No strain, no gain.

Then, as we shall see, the Dupont counterfeit bust went down, and suddenly Calvin Broeker was golden again, much in demand. He was also in protective custody. He needed it too.

Georgia Nelson didn't know where he was when she placed the call. She didn't particularly care where he was, in fact, as long as he was on a plane to Sofia with her on August 22. But on August 20, Bulgaria exploded — or at least, Cal's bit of it did. It went up like a fireworks factory. He was getting calls from Sofia one after another, with people screaming their heads off. And when they weren't cursing or threatening, they implored him, "Get over here. Help us close. Help us finish."

The Dupont bust occurred on August 23. By then, Georgia was ripping his ass apart, just wreaking havoc. As Cal saw the situation, however, there was really no need for him to go back to Bulgaria. Transcorp already had its $6 million; the letter of credit was in the account. Daewoo, in a stirring display of trust and goodwill, had wired actual money. The company won't be doing that again in a hurry.

No steel was ever shipped, of course, but at least the Turks didn't get gypped out of their allotment. Presumably.

It all seemed so far off, it was hard to care.

Cal Broker was in a motel room in Vermont, under police protection night and day.

IT HAS TO BE SAID THAT CAL occasionally displays a genuine knack for screwing up, a talent for Olympic catastrophe as rich and fervid as his consummate genius for turbo-powered enterprise on a Brobdingnagian scale.

Still, although Sofia was now one destination he could erase from the world of possibilities, the Bulgarian connection would, as it was supposed to, prove invaluable for his future undercover activities. All the buddies back in Western civilization were now desperate to get into business with "the Russians," who had emerged as the global lords of crime. From evil empire to . . . well, evil empire.

Cal Broeker now had provable ties to the demon's lair that was Eastern Europe through his good pal President Andrei Lukanov. He was connected right to the very top, to the man himself. He had photographs to prove it too. Lots of them. Lukanov was still walking around then, of course, and would be for at least another year or so. And the Bulgarians' reputation for extreme and exotic violence, their aura of terror, would rub off on Cal by association. Guys on the street began to think he was dangerous. They weren't so wrong either. When the bad boys thought they were dealing with the Russians via Cal Broeker, they were actually dealing with the Royal Canadian Mounted Police.

The Mounties may not *always* get their man, but they are a police force with colour and the fizz of showbiz — why, they'd even sold their trademark image to the Walt Disney Company. They were made for C. Calvin Broeker, or so you'd think.

# 4

# The Rip Is
# Part of the Deal

*No graven images may be*
*Worshipped, except the currency.*
— ARTHUR HUGH CLOUGH

Cal Broeker met with his handlers at the Queen Elizabeth Hotel, on René Lévesque Boulevard, in downtown Montreal. They'd rented a room for the occasion. Gilles Chambertin, Serge Granier, and Luc Demaine were there representing the RCMP; the American Secret Service handlers were Lou Robinson and Rob Hart. They asked Cal to reiterate the entire story, from his initial concerns about doing business with the Leroys in Montreal right up to his first encounter with Réal Dupont.

"Would you recognize him again?" Cal was asked.

*Recognize him!* Forgetting him would be the problem.

Cal nodded.

"Is this the man? Here . . ." Demaine handed over an 8 x 10 photograph.

Cal found himself looking at a poker-faced man with the most complicated double-pate job imaginable: two mangy skeins of blond hair about the length of a horse's tail must have had to be wrapped around his head like a turban each morning, then glued into position so that they met in the middle as a small untidy haystack.

"Never seen *him* before . . . thank God!"

"How about this one?"

Cal took the next picture and found himself staring into Réal Dupont's soulless predator's eyes. The man was not photogenic.

"That's him, all right," said Cal.

"What do you know about this man?" he was asked.

"He's the man I've been meeting. The one who gave me the funny money."

"Do you know any more about him, what he is?"

"I just know he's underworld," said Cal. "Mafia or something."

"Or something . . ." Luc Demaine proceeded to recite an abbreviated version of Dupont's edifying biography. Somehow, none of the stages in Dupont's career came as a surprise — although you had to be impressed by his single-minded ambition. He never seemed to have doubted where his talents could best be employed, and from his late teens on, he began to climb the rungs of crime's ladder without looking back. His apprenticeship had been with the West End Gang — the so-called Irish Mafia — working the bars and strip clubs in Montreal. Then he'd transferred over to the bikers, who'd admired his work ethic, enthusiasm, and people skills, and set him to work as an enforcer, breaking heads, collecting debts, promoting their cause among business associates who mistook them for fools, and performing similar tasks requiring well-developed powers of persuasion. As he rose up the ranks from foot soldier, Dupont steadily acquired the kind of rewards and perks that go with hard work, loyalty, and dedication. Soon he was dealing drugs for himself as well as for the gang, and enhancing his reputation for extreme violence by adding to his repertoire a useful proficiency with weapons like baseball bats, lead pipes, chains, hammers, guns, and knives. If he hadn't killed anyone at that point — though he probably had — he'd certainly crippled, scarred, mutilated, mangled, tortured, and generally terrified dozens. Few were in any position to complain, however.

Demaine paused, looked searchingly at Cal, then asked, "Hearing all this, do you still want to go ahead with the project?"

He obviously didn't know Cal, who was, if anything, even more keen to pursue the counterfeit money trail after hearing the nature of the opposition.

"Absolutely!" he said.

"Okay," said Demaine, "then let's get down to business. Tell us, if you would, Calvin, what percentage of this deal you think is bullshit and what is real?"

"I think it's all real," replied Cal, a bit defensive. "He told me he can get his hands on $120 million, and I see no reason to doubt that's the kind of quantity involved here."

The Secret Service guys smiled and shook their heads. They saw reasons to doubt. In fact, as they now made plain, in the world of counterfeiting, a sum like $120 million was hard to accept. The Treasury boys back in the States openly scoffed at Cal's figures. No one would print up such a sum in one place, if only because the costs and risks of such an operation outweighed the potential profits. The price of paper, the time such a massive print run took, the problems of storage, the fact that the inks used were delicate and unstable, prone to discoloration and deterioration — all this, as well as the chances of so huge an operation getting busted while still in progress, made the sum Cal was suggesting highly improbable.

"No one prints those numbers," said Lou Robinson, with just the faintest trace of condescension in his voice. "They do a few million at the most. Tops."

"So why're you here then?" Cal asked him.

They were there, it turned out, because they'd already busted someone down south with several million in the same phony hundred-dollar bills. Some of them even had an M serial number, and there was no M series: it stood for Montreal. Réal Dupont's phone number was in this guy's address book, and Dupont clearly wasn't anyone's pal. You didn't phone Réal just to shoot the breeze or invite him for a picnic.

"So we're sure the guy's involved," explained Rob Hart, in case anyone couldn't follow the reasoning.

Gilles Chambertin, the soft-spoken, gentlemanly Québécois RCMP handler, then added that they were also sure there was a connection between Dupont and whoever was printing the counterfeit. Chambertin always treated Cal with great courtesy and respect, made him feel a part of the team instead of an intruder or worse. As incredible as it may seem, the cops in general rarely behaved towards Cal the way you'd imagine they might towards someone who was risking his life to help them do their job. But they were also used to dealing with snitches and informers, scum who'd been turned to save their own skins in some sort of plea bargain — and these days, plea bargains played a big part in most weighty criminal trials.

Cal had done a lot of thinking about "these days" since he'd left Chateaugay, a lot of thinking about what he considered to be the devolutionary changes North American society had been through during the last quarter of the twentieth century. If evolution is necessarily progress, why is the most powerful and technologically advanced nation in history in such a mess? It made you wonder. The public would howl if they knew the kind of backroom horse-trading that posed as justice these days, or so Cal was often forced to admit to himself when he watched the spectacle of some public prosecutor throwing back piranhas in the hope of landing a shark. But thanks to Hollywood, the public also had warped ideas about what criminals were really like, ideas as sentimental and romantic in their way as Dickens's views on poverty. There was no code of silence in real life, let alone honour. First thing buddy did when you read him his rights was finger everyone he'd ever known — and many he'd never known too — on the promise that the first-degree murder or armed robbery charge would be dropped to involuntary manslaughter or theft under. Criminals were rarely philanthropists; only Robin Hood was Robin Hood (although some historians even disputed this). Today's hoods like to steal from the rich, true, but not to give to the poor — in fact, they'll steal from the poor as well if they need to. Some of the counterfeit had already been used to swindle American senior citizens out of their social security checks.

The chief characteristics of the typical criminal, as Cal saw them, were greed and laziness, two mutually incompatible vices that could really be accommodated in a satisfactory manner only by a life of crime. Most crimes — the dope deal, the shooting or the kneecapping, the loansharking, the border hop, the firebombing — don't take very long to commit, so buddy's leisure time is expansive. But as everyone knows, leisure is also expensive. Work serves the dual purpose of financing life and reducing its costly leisure time. So the criminal's need for funding is far greater than that of most civilians. When you add in his need to impress his colleagues with a certain flair and largesse, along with his inherent greed, it is not difficult to imagine the irresistible attraction that literally printing one's own money must hold for the average bad guy.

The criminal's relationship with money is not the same as yours and mine, however. An efficient crime family or gang can often expect around a million dollars cash a week to come in, usually in smallish bills too. It has to be counted once, then recounted by someone else (there's no trust). Then much of it has to be banked. You cannot bank more than $10,000 cash at any one time in either the U.S. or Canada without obligating the bank to report the fact to a government body. Cash makes governments suspicious, uneasy. For one thing, the government can't tell if the money has been taxed or not. Where cash flows, there will money laundering be. The pet store, the variety store, and naturally the casino are among the most common cash-cleaning operations. In the U.S., where the Chase Manhattan Bank numbers operations with names like J.J.'s Money World or Ed's Credit Shack among its competitors, it is reportedly quite easy to find a friendly bank manager who has no problem with your hauling in garbage bags full of cash to make your weekly deposit, and who also sees no need to inform anyone you're a thousand times over the ten-grand limit (although for this courtesy, he will charge you a fee between 3 and 10 percent of your total deposit, something that both parties understand to be connected proportionately to the "difficulty" of the particular account). Anyone who's willing to forfeit $100,000 per week just to bank his million-dollar income is clearly grateful to have a banker willing to handle such a troublesome account.

The stately, plump Swiss banks, whose reputation for airtight discretion and dignified professionalism is exceeded only by their propensity for stealing everything from the long-unused accounts of those clients believed to have died or been murdered, charge a more or less standard 3 percent. That such deposit fees reveal complicity, if not outright conspiracy to defraud governments, that they reveal the bank benefiting from the proceeds of crime, and that they reveal numerous more arcane collaborations in crimes of money — all this goes without saying. It is undeniable. Yet you hardly ever hear it mentioned. There is only one reason for having a numbered or pseudonymous bank account, after all, and that reason is a criminal offence. No one should have such accounts, just as no one is permitted to have an unlicensed firearm. You don't need or want one unless you have committed, or intend to commit, a crime.

"What we want you to do," said Luc Demaine, having established Cal's willingness to continue, "is get involved with this group and try to draw out the money so we can take down Dupont in possession of the lot . . . as much as he has. Understand?"

Cal nodded.

"We can't pay you anything," Demaine then added matter-of-factly. "You're on your own."

Cal's face betrayed none of the thoughts or emotions seething within him. This was the first time that the subject of money had come up. He hadn't become an agent for money, though. In fact, he'd pumped his own money into the work of establishing a cover, of gaining Bulgarian credibility. Now the cash he'd salvaged from the wreck of his Chateaugay life had gone. Indeed, it was more than gone — he owed Elizabeth money. He didn't imagine this work would finance a James Bond lifestyle, but he had assumed he'd manage to cover his expenses. At least. But: "We can't pay you anything . . ." This he hadn't bargained for. He certainly hadn't budgeted for it either.

Demaine, aware of a slight narrowing in Gilles Chambertin's eyebrows, suddenly felt the need to elaborate. Economic crimes like counterfeiting, he explained, were not worth much. All they could do with the money, if and when they seized it, was to strike a match beneath it after the trial. There were probably no bank accounts full of real money to appropriate — or none they'd be able to reach. The crime wasn't even worth much as a jail sentence — a year or so before parole. Max. Although Dupont would get a good deal more, thanks to his opulent record, the numerous outstanding drug or assault charges, and the parole violations.

Demaine was sorry about the money, but that's the way it was. Then he sugared the pill: "If we get convictions and the takedown brings in what we're after, Cal, there'll be a suitable reward for you at the end."

Cal pictured a personalized RCMP coffee mug and an engraved maple leaf or beaver wall plaque: "To Cal, for services rendered."

"And of course, we will help with your expenses," Gilles Chambertin added, daring anyone to contradict his generosity.

Lou and Rob looked nervous.

"From our point of view," said Lou, "this is a Canadian project. So we can't get into any kind of reimbursement."

"Wouldn't fly down south," Rob Hart added, grimly inspecting his thumbnail. "No way."

Mixed messages, but Cal was appeased by the promise of expenses anyway. It shouldn't take long to set up Réal Dupont: the guy was champing at the bit to go.

"One thing I do need from you," Cal now said to the two Americans, "is some background. As you know, I don't have a criminal record. These fucking guys are gonna do diligence on me — if they haven't already done it. I need something, anything you can cook up. You know, I did a little time for this and that. Jeez! I know prisons, know what they're like on the inside. I used to deliver groceries to them in Malone, New York —" He stopped because the two Secret Service men were shaking their heads.

"Can't do it, sorry," said Lou Robinson, not sounding particularly sorry. "You're on your own. You'll have to manage. We can't help you."

"Wouldn't fly," Rob repeated. He looked to his colleague for any possibility of flight, then, receiving none, confirmed the verdict: "We can't give you any help, Calvin."

Maybe they'd just come up for the change of scenery?

Characteristically, Chambertin felt obliged to explain why his people couldn't fabricate a criminal record for Cal: he was an American, so the process would involve two governments and several different ministries. In other words, it was impossible. But, he implied, were it at all possible, he would have done it without hesitation.

Odd how one man's decency can make up for a legion of bureaucrats intent on covering their asses.

They didn't seem to realize, Cal thought, that behind Réal Dupont there was an organization. Although Dupont was the stereotypical bad guy, a walking argument against prisons as places of rehabilitation, maybe that was exactly what his bosses wanted him to be — so they could keep an illusion of distance between themselves and their foot soldiers. The suits and the jeans. Dupont wasn't the kind of guy to have lawyers, accountants, and notaries on retainer, yet his access to such people seemed effortless. And someone had already been checking out Cal's credentials. They'd called his friends, business associates, and even his family, generally with a bullshit reason, yet always with single-minded purpose. They would soon call his lawyer back in Chateaugay too, straightforwardly stating that Cal was doing some business with them and they were thus doing some diligence on him. No lawyer would find such a call surprising, and without needing to be told anything more, Cal's lawyer gave his callers the right answers, the answers they wanted to hear. There *was* nothing to hide.

But all the same, Cal would have felt more comfortable with some kind of record. Even a few traffic violations would have been better than nothing. Cops don't get tickets, but grocers don't necessarily get them either. Over the following weeks, Cal deliberately set out to get himself a criminal record — or a record, at least. It wasn't so easy. He would hurtle along highways doing twice the speed limit, only to find the OPP or highway patrol grunts already engaged in booking some unlucky soul for a broken tail light or violating the emissions standard. He'd turn onto one-way streets and, instead of ploughing into four lanes of oncoming traffic, find himself exceeding the speed limit on a deserted road. He shot red lights where cops were lurking in concealed driveways, only to find that the boys in blue were sleeping or too busy yakking to notice. Whenever a siren did sound behind him and he pulled over, ready to plead guilty to any charge, still fumbling with his unbuckled seat-belt clasp, the angry car and its pulsing red light would just continue straight on past him, more serious business on its mind.

Finally, one day when the air was high and blue and the leaves were a burning tapestry of carmine, amber, burnt sienna, and ochre, Cal saw a cruiser ahead in the middle lane. He overtook it doing 180, then, no signal, crossed three lanes and swerved off into the exit, which recommended using a speed one-tenth of the one he registered. Good advice too, since Cal found himself obliged to use most of a gravel shoulder to negotiate the exit's hairpin corner, and even then he had to thump and bump across thirty metres of rough pasture before rejoining the asphalt.

Oh, come on, boys! For a while he heard no siren. Surely no cop could overlook this apocalypse on wheels! Then — *weeyowww* — the siren and the cherry.

"Yessir," said Cal, when the officer asked him if he had any idea how fast he was going on that highway. "Over one-eighty. This baby can move when you want her to. And I'm in a real hurry. . . ."

He regretted the apology he tacked on to this, but being polite to men in uniform came naturally to Cal. The old Broeker charm worked its magic too, for by the time the officer returned to his cruiser, Cal had practically been invited home for dinner and was given a ticket for doing 110 in a 100. But at least it was a ticket. Cal had begun to think he'd die trying to get one.

With parking violations, though, he had better luck, acquiring three tickets in less than ninety minutes on the streets of Montreal. They'd be the first parking tickets that he didn't pay within twenty-four hours. It went against the grain too. He had to tear them up eventually to suppress the urge to settle the fines. It didn't exactly make him America's Most Wanted — not even Canada's — but at long last, C. Calvin Broeker had a record. If Réal Dupont had someone run Cal's driving licence — and it's not known whether he did — the unpaid tickets and the unattended court appearance for speeding would hardly have garnered respect, but they would have established two things that Dupont devoutly wished to know: Cal was definitely not a cop, and he was either a boy scout or a very shrewd, cautious, and clever operator. The latter profile was precisely how he presented himself, and also how many of Dupont's associates perceived him.

OUT OF THE MEETING at the Queen Elizabeth Hotel emerged Cal's first LOA with the RCMP; this outlined the details of his relationship with the police and the purpose of their mutual project. "Get Dupont," it might as well have been called. Among the many clauses, there was one that covered the responsibility the RCMP would accept for Cal if anything untoward happened to him during his work as a Crown agent. This responsibility could be quantified as "none whatsoever" — they wouldn't even cover medical costs for injuries arising from the project. Even if Cal hadn't known that Réal Dupont was capable of inflicting some pretty costly injuries, the clause still would have seemed unnecessarily harsh and callous.

The central issue, however, was one of legality. It is illegal for a foreign national to live and work in Canada without the appropriate visas and permits from the Canadian government. An American agent is not allowed to work within Canada without prior consent from the RCMP — that is, if he's working for U.S. law enforcement or security services. The CIA and other agencies continually violate this law, but Canada looks the other way, assuming that Washington and Ottawa share common goals. This (erroneous) assumption is behind numerous other courtesies extended to the global superpower. At Toronto's Pearson International Airport, for example, you can enter the United States of America before boarding an airplane. The terminal complex contains U.S. customs and immigration facilities, staffed by U.S. personnel who can deny or permit entry to their nation on the spot. If permitted entry, a traveller is technically in the U.S. before he even leaves Canada. The two countries also share the world's longest "undefended" border. But such demonstrations of amity are a one-way street: there are no Canadian customs facilities on U.S. soil. And while U.S. authorities are continually berating Canadian governments for their lax security at border crossings, there is very little co-operation from the FBI and other agencies over matters of Canadian security.

One thing that clearly emerges from Cal Broeker's story is that the U.S. is increasingly obliged to wage its war against organized crime and terrorism on Canadian soil, for the criminals and terrorists have made Canada their base — and for numerous reasons, one of which is the generosity of Canadian justice where the punishment of professional criminals is concerned, and another of which is the high quality of most Canadian prisons. But if the U.S. is keen to blame Canada for the ills that plague its society — and it has a tendency towards blame — it should recognize this works both ways. Canadians can equally blame the U.S., since there is also a cost to Canadian society for attracting criminal and terrorist organizations whose principal target is the wealth and power of America. It is now widely believed that Toronto, relatively small, clean, tranquil, and efficient though it may seem in comparison with other cities, is the global centre for organized crime. This assertion was made openly by members of the Italian Mafia to Canadian media on several occasions during the fall of 2000.

As Cal was beginning to learn, though, there was one activity that, in certain areas, genuinely could not be distinguished from organized crime: business, especially big business, and particularly international big business. Now, Cal was the last guy to suggest that the entrepreneurial spirit should be broken, that increased success should be punished by increased taxation, but he'd seen in Bulgaria that if those with wealth and power are allowed to influence politics, they will. And when that happens, the result is generally not as pretty as even those who engineered it might have imagined it to be.

As inhospitable and uncharitable as Cal's LOA most certainly was, however, it did contain one pleasant surprise: the "suitable reward" that had been mentioned at the Queen Elizabeth Hotel meeting was now specified as $50,000, to be paid upon the project's successful conclusion. Canadian dollars too. Thus for risking his life over an unspecified period of time — a "successful conclusion" could take months or years to achieve — Cal would earn around US$30,000, even if he spent twice that, over and above his expenses, achieving the "successful conclusion." But if the conclusion was not successful, he'd get nothing — no matter how much he'd spent in either time or money. And if the conclusion was Cal in a wheelchair for the rest of his days, too bad, because it wouldn't be a Canadian wheelchair. He'd have to crawl back to wherever his Blue Cross card was still valid, since the Canadian taxpayer wasn't going to spare a dime. Not that the Canadian taxpayer was ever consulted about this. Cal paid it little heed too. His desire was to be of service wherever and however he could. A warrior doesn't read the small print; a knight errant never inquires of the damsel if she will be grateful to be rescued from her distress.

All Cal now saw was the green light. His mission was a go. After months of prevarication, vacillation, and sheer miles of red tape preventing them from doing their job, the cops were suddenly all enthusiasm too. They wanted updates, reports on meetings, deadlines; they wanted progress.

—

RÉAL DUPONT — who had by now fronted Cal $60,000 in counterfeit to make the deal fly — was probably not someone to whom the term "coy" had ever been applied. Yet when he was faced with the deal he'd been seeking all this time — which, after all, was the biggest counterfeit money transaction in North American history — he backed off. Ever so slightly. He had his own bureaucratic squabbles to deal with.

92 |

Cal's first task, as he saw it, was to set up a bank account with Dupont or his "people." He would do this deal as if he were *really* doing this deal — that's the only way it would work. Yet if the cops had been hard enough to persuade, now the bad guys showed their own reluctance to give up old ways of thinking. At the numerous meetings Cal had with them during the fall of 1994, Dupont's "people" demanded the deal should be done in a variety of ways that all amounted to the same way in Cal's eyes: they'd bring their cash, he'd bring his cash, and they'd exchange counterfeit for real. They'd park a van in this driveway, he'd park a van in that driveway, and when or if the coast was clear, the vans would be driven away. Or a pickup truck would come to take the van. Or the deal would be done on the reserve, in Elizabeth's garage. Or Cal would fly down to the islands and put his money in their account while they did the same for him. It all involved cash for cash, and all too often it also involved being either too far from police jurisdiction or too close to civilian casualties for a SWAT raid to work. Everyone wanted people along for protection too — because the rip is always part of the deal. Every transaction in the criminal world involves the possibility of one or both parties attempting to get away with both cash and commodity. What's the loser going to do? Call the police?

Initially, the police settled for a plan that would have Cal drive with Dupont and the money to a bank, where Cal would transfer over his funds. Except he wouldn't, because the takedown would happen outside the bank, in a parking spot the cops would keep clear. Then they decided an alley beside the bank would be safer as far as civilian casualties went.

What Cal wanted was this: the RCMP would arrange for money to be in an account under Cal's name; he would then take Dupont to the bank and get its manager to confirm he was good for the funds. Dupont would then drive the money to a warehouse, which would be protected by the seal of an international government. Cal was careful not to say Bulgaria because he didn't want Dupont poking his nose into his other interests there — they hadn't yet been extinguished. That way, Dupont's people could keep an eye on the money while he and Cal went back to the bank and transferred over Cal's funds. Except they wouldn't, because the takedown would occur the moment the warehouse door was closed.

How much money did Cal need? This was the first question the cops wanted answered.

"Let's discuss price," Cal told Dupont during a meeting in a St-Hubert's Bar-B-Cue outlet on the south shore.

"I already fucking told you the price," Dupont said. "Fifty cents on da dollar."

"I don't buy *debts* for fifty cents on the dollar," Cal countered. "Don't fuck me around, Dupont, or there's no deal."

"So?" This had shut him up for once; he almost sounded meek. "What's your offer?"

"My people are willing to pay eight cents on the dollar." Cal had done his research on the subject, but as one might expect, there was far from a standard rate. It all depended on the quality of the counterfeit.

"Fucking bullshit!" Dupont spat. "You don't wipe your ass for eight cents, you motherfucker!"

They settled on fifteen cents. That day.


"OH, THIS IS BULLSHIT," Luc Demaine suddenly shouted, throwing down his pen.

Cal had met with the RCMP handlers to tell them he'd need around $10 million put into his account to make the deal work. Demaine didn't like it.

"There's no hundred and twenty million," he said. "They're just going to rip your money, that's all. They're playing you for a fucking idiot, and you're acting like one by believing them. We know Dupont, Cal. We *know* him. He doesn't have any hundred and twenty million in cash. No way!"

So Cal went back to Dupont. They met in another chicken barbecue joint on the outskirts of the Kahnawake Reserve.

"My people are nervous," Cal said. "They're not going to send any money until I physically see that you've got the amount you say you have. I don't care how I see it: you can blindfold me and drive me there; you can put me in the trunk of your fucking car, for all I care. But they're not going to wire a dime until I confirm you have your end in place, okay?"

Dupont shot across the table like liquid and grabbed Cal by the lapels. "Listen, motherfucker," he said, "I don't fucking trust you. I think you're a cop. But I am so sick of dis bullshit I'm gonna take the chance. I take you to see the money today, yeah? Okay? But I once suspect anyting — if I even smell a fucking cop — I blow off you fucking head. . . . And my people, they know where you children live. . . . Is that clear, motherfucker?"

"Same goes for me, Dupont," Cal told him calmly. "You don't have the cash or I can't fucking see it, I'm going to sit in that fucking bank until I know the money's wired back to the people it belongs to, okay? You got the money, you'll see I got mine. Right now, I don't fucking believe you got what you say you got — and I'm sick of your fucking threats. Is *that* clear, motherfucker?"

"Let's fucking go, *right now!*" Dupont threw a few bills on the table. His eyes were black with fury.

Inside Dupont's pickup, Cal began to feel the man's edginess in his own guts.

"Turn around," Dupont said, pulling a soiled handkerchief from the glove compartment. "I'm going to blindfold you."

Cal pushed his hands away and pulled a clean handkerchief from his own pocket, saying, "I'll put it on myself."

An elderly couple crossed in front of the pickup, glancing over at its occupants.

"Ah," Dupont said, sighing. "Forget it. I got a gun in my coat. First sign anyting is wrong, you a fucking dead man."

He took off like a bat out of hell, tires squealing, dust and gravel spewing in his wake. Dupont immediately slowed to a regular pace, however, peering into the rear-view mirror for signs of a tail. Turning onto the highway, he drove flat out for ten minutes, then suddenly pulled over on the hard shoulder and leapt out of the truck, scanning the mottled grey air above for helicopters or spotter planes. Then he sped off again. When

Cal switched on the radio, Dupont immediately killed it. A wild animal in danger, he wanted to hear as well as see. At the first of a series of underpasses, he pulled the truck over again.

"Get out!" As he said it, he was already halfway towards a parked dark blue sedan, pulling its keys out of his jeans.

Maybe this wasn't as spontaneous as it had seemed, Cal decided, slipping into the passenger seat next to Dupont. Were they being followed by a chopper, this little ploy would have thrown any airborne tail into confusion.

On the outskirts of Montreal, Dupont again pulled off the road, this time taking an exit and weaving through several side streets before pulling up in front of a suburban house. All the time he'd been looking around warily and leaning his head out the window to check the skies. He opened the garage and backed out another sedan — a brown one this time — slipping the blue one into its spot.

In this new vehicle, they took a circuitous route to the south shore area, pulling up in the alleyway between two low-rent houses and their gardens.

"Wait here," he told Cal. "I am going to fetch my brother."

It was hard to picture Dupont having such a thing as family.

He soon reappeared, accompanied by his brother, a stocky, beer-bellied man with a huge black beard.

Although the formalities of an introduction would have been absurd under the circumstances, Cal missed them. He was simply ordered out of the car and told to follow the two men to the end of the alley, where what looked like a homemade horsebox on wheels stood backed against some chain-link fencing. Dupont and his brother hauled the trailer away from the fencing. At the rear was a small door fastened shut by a tiny padlock. Dupont plucked out a key and opened it, motioning Cal to step inside the box.

There was barely enough room for one person. Around him in the cramped space Cal saw a stack of cardboard boxes, the same size as wine cases. Opening one, he found neat bundles of hundred-dollar bills banded together. He checked one bundle thoroughly: ten thousand American dollars. Then, methodically, he went through each of the boxes, counting the bundles and checking them at random to make sure it wasn't just paper. Before he'd finished, Dupont said: "There's eighty million there. We got the rest stashed somewhere else."

"Okay," Cal replied.

He began to examine a few of the bills carefully, taking them out of their bundles, again at random. Some had stains of dampness where the ink was slightly discoloured. "The quality ain't so hot," he told Dupont.

"Just bottom layers," said Dupont. "They got a bit wet." He seemed more annoyed than embarrassed.

The bills wouldn't pass in a bank, but they weren't bad on the whole.

"This is worth only twelve cents a dollar," Cal informed him all the same. "I told you quality was what mattered. Shit, you're selling me damaged goods here!"

This would buy him a little time, he thought. And he needed a little time to make sure that the money from the RCMP was in his account.

"I have to get back to you on that," said Dupont. "But now you know where the money is . . . anyting 'appens to it, you fucked! We going to go after you children and Elizabeth's children. We burn her fucking house down, motherfucker! Anyone try a rip on dis trailer, you fucked — you got me, pal? And we going to leave it 'ere. We ain't going to move it. So you the only one knows where it is, see?"

AS SOON AS HE COULD, Cal called his handlers with the news that the deal was on. It was a Thursday evening. On Friday, Dupont called Cal just after noon.

"Now I want to see what you fucking got."

Cal explained that the money was coming from Europe, that there was a seven-hour time difference, and that it would arrive soon. He explained this again to him on Saturday.

"Oh, you a fucking dead man," Dupont said the following day, when the money still hadn't come.

"Jesus Christ!" Cal replied. "It's fucking Sunday, man! The banks are *closed!*"

Trifles like this didn't concern Dupont, however. He cursed away all the same. He cursed all through Monday and Tuesday too. He would have cursed again on Wednesday, but Cal called Art Franklin at 11:15 a.m. to tell him the money had arrived, and to decide who should come to the bank to check it was there.

Cal met Franklin and another man later that day in Place Ville Marie, an underground shopping plaza. In his pressed jeans and tweed jacket, Franklin had the Ralph Lauren look of a well-built private-school teacher, bespectacled, benign. He had numerous legitimate business interests and was keen to get Cal involved in new projects he had going on over in China. The other man turned out to be a notary named Baultman. Clearly, Franklin didn't trust himself to ask the right questions in the bank.

The manager of the nearby Bank of Montreal had been briefed by the RCMP and knew the score. She was brisk and efficient — a little too brisk for Cal — and before long, the men were finally convinced that he indeed had the money. Seven million dollars in U.S. funds. Sitting with them in a bar minutes later, Cal thought to himself that the notary's time had been wasted — he hadn't said a word in the bank. But Baultman soon explained his own presence by outlining a new plan for how the money would be exchanged. Cal would hand it over, with proper documentation, as a loan to Franklin's company in China, AF Holdings. The loan would ostensibly be used for purchasing certain agricultural machinery, and he would receive invoices for it. Everything in order. Cal suddenly felt sick to his stomach. This would never fly with the handlers. He told Franklin that he'd have to consult his people and get back to him — and that he'd better keep Dupont off his fucking back or the deal was off.

"Fuck it, no!" said Luc Demaine, hearing this new twist. "There's always something with these guys, isn't there? We can't go through with this. I can't risk seven million dollars."

The sound of the money resonated between them, as if Demaine were realizing for the first time that he would never see such a sum in his bank account — not in this life.

"It isn't what we agreed."

"I know," said Cal. "Eleventh-hour bullshit is what it is."

"In court," said Demaine, "it'll get pissed on."

They'd wanted a straightforward transaction, but this wasn't one. If a judge was to ask Franklin if he'd received seven million from Cal Broeker in exchange for counterfeit money, Franklin could say, "No, your honour.

It was a loan to my company." And he'd have the paper that seemingly proved it.

After talking to Demaine, Cal arranged a meeting with Franklin to tell him the deal was off. He adopted an aggressive stance, all business.

"My people and me," he said, "we're sick of this monkeying around. Everything you wanted was done — you saw the money in the bank. All I've had from your people is threats and bullshit, and I'm sick of it. Then at the eleventh hour, you pull this stunt. Well, I'm sorry, Art, but I can't do business like this."

Franklin looked sad. He said, "We had to do it this way, Cal, because we don't know who you are. You got no background, know what I mean? We're uneasy."

"Listen," Cal told him, "I leave for Bulgaria in a week. I'm back around Christmas, then I'm over there again. So I'm away for about six months. You have your shit together by then and maybe we'll do business. Otherwise, so long. I don't deal like this. I'm a businessman!"

Réal Dupont went ballistic when he found out the deal was off. He demanded to meet immediately or said he'd go straight over to Elizabeth's house and trash it. He sounded as if someone had been rattling his cage.

"You don't do this fucking deal in six months' time exact," he told Cal, "you owe me sixty fucking grand, man! And I want every cent of it the same day, or you fucking dead."

Cal felt like yawning in his face. But he could tell by the way Dupont looked that if he did that, he wouldn't live long enough to close his mouth. "Okay," Cal said. "Catch you in six months."

"Where the fuck do you stay in Bulgaria? I want to keep in touch wid you there, motherfucker. I want to find out who the fuck you are."

Cal gave him the number of Parmakov's hotel, his castle. He even gave him the suite number just to keep him happy.

Dupont was at the airport to see him off, though.

CAL HAD SOWN CONFUSION in the ranks. With Art Franklin, he was careful to make sure that Dupont seemed primarily responsible for the collapse of the deal, and with Dupont, he blamed Franklin. With Armand Veilleux, the biker who'd introduced him to Art Franklin, he blamed Franklin. With the Mohawks on the reservation who'd made the original introduction to Veilleux, he blamed his distrust of Dupont. Thus when Cal left for Bulgaria, everyone was squabbling among themselves, blaming each other for lost opportunities. Again, it increased Cal's legend, made his front as a discriminating entrepreneur seem all the more believable.

# 5

# Real time

*This time tomorrow,*
*Reckon where I'll be?*
*In some lonesome valley*
*A-hanging on a white oak tree.*
— TOM DOOLEY

### April 1995

The day before the takedown on the $120-million counterfeit, Cal Broeker called Art Franklin at 9:45 a.m. from a pay phone in Westmount Square, on Greene Avenue in Montreal. Art was by now just the middleman in this deal. It had been taken over as a personal project by Réal Dupont.

"Have Dupont call me directly," Cal told Art.

A few minutes later the pay phone started to ring, but Cal instantly silenced it. The receiver looked like a toy in his big hand, and the phone booth itself barely contained his six-foot-four frame.

Dupont's voice bristled with suspicion. He made it clear, yet again, that he didn't trust Cal much — but then, he didn't trust anyone *much*.

"I'm setting the deal up for tomorrow," Cal told him. "I need to know who your banker — or your broker — is."

There was a pause. You could almost hear the wheels turning as Réal

Dupont's greed ground up against his caution. Finally, he told Cal to contact Justinian Sabot at Kestrel Investments on Maisonneuve. He rattled off a phone number, then he hung up.

Cal was put straight through to Sabot, who agreed to meet him at Place Ville Marie. Downtown Montreal's many underground shopping centres were a reminder on this fine, bright late-summer morning that the winters here were harsh.

"How will I know you?" asked Cal.

"Six-three, heavy set, blond hair, blue eyes." As if explaining this cop-like APB description, he added, "I'm an ex–federal prosecutor."

"You're American?"

"An import, yeah. Right. But I was a Crown attorney here too."

Cal smiled to himself. The guy was trying to impress him — or intimidate him. But the thing about Cal, as he'd often tell people, was that he didn't scare and he didn't care.

After hanging up the phone, he next checked in with his RCMP handlers, who okayed the meet. Cal hoped they'd keep out of the way. The more inconspicuous cops tried to be, the more they looked like cops trying to be inconspicuous. Any screw-ups now might prove fatal, and even if not precisely fatal, they'd certainly slam shut this narrow window of opportunity Cal had by now spent more than a year prying open.

Ninety minutes later, at noon, Cal met Justinian Sabot in the plaza. The man looked pretty much as he'd described himself, except he was more like six-one than six-three. They always give themselves an inch or two. He didn't mention the aura of sleaziness that hung over him, though. It was unmistakable, like the mark of Cain. It's what happens when straight guys go crooked, when right turns into wrong, when good goes bad. Cal knew all about good turning into bad — more than he'd ever wanted to know. Yet he still didn't understand it. It was a parallel universe, through the looking-glass; a place where when you reach the top, you're on the bottom.

After shaking hands, the two men walked over to the Bank of Montreal on St-Jacques, in the picturesque old part of the city. Cal had come to love Montreal. The city spoke to him, just poked its tongue in his ear and cooed to him some days. He'd never been to Paris, but he felt he didn't need to now that he'd seen Montreal. It seemed to be part Paris, part old

New York — the *West Side Story* New York, not the snarling, overcrowded steel-'n'-concrete city he saw today. But Montreal was small too. It had grace and charm and human proportions by day, yet by night it fizzed with clandestine excitement. It was sexy. It was manageable. It was about as modern as Cal wanted, yet it had a past not wanting in pomp and circumstance, far from devoid of great moments. There was blood in the soil, and that conferred a kind of sanctity on the place. Any other time, Cal would have enjoyed this walk through history — this indulgence of his great passion — but today too much weighed on his mind. Too much, he knew, might be about to go wrong. And if it did, *he'd* be history.

Sabot was a fast talker, a typical con man, schooled in the ways of making instant friendships, gaining instant trust. He did Cal's work for him, ironically. In no time at all, they were good ol' boys, two Americans out sucking on that oyster of theirs, the world. The pair of them were even laughing out loud at a shared joke as they filed through the bank's revolving doors. It was one of those grand old banks from another era that sought to impress customers and passers-by alike with its profligate opulence and overblown symbolism. A pair of nine-foot bronze angels held lamps here, a pride of burnished lions cavorted there. You couldn't decide whether this was rococo or art deco, but you knew the message was that money is power, and that this was money's temple.

Cal told a cashier that he wanted to see the manager, that she was expecting him. The two men were shown into a plain little office — quite out of character with money's high priestess, but a sign of the times. Banks were embarrassed by their own profits nowadays, and the Bank of Montreal — whose president had recently received a well-publicized $20-odd-million Christmas bonus — was more embarrassed than most. Even the manager seemed part of this attempt at image downsizing: she was somewhat matronly and wore the gabardine pinafore of a provincial French storekeeper. They were offered coffee but refused the refreshment — perhaps fearing it would stall the progress of business.

"Let me get straight down to business, ma'am," said Sabot, exuding a southern charm about as authentic as a cheap toupee. "Mr. Broeker and I are engaged in a — ah — business transaction involving a rather large sum of money, and I just need to know — 'scuse my bluntness — that he's good for it. You understand how it is."

"Indeed," said the bank manager, looking at Cal for confirmation.

He nodded at her. "It's okay. Show him the balance in the business account."

She tapped a few instructions on her keyboard and the computer began to hum and whirr portentously, then the printer came to life.

"We have done business with Mr. Broeker for a number of years," she told Sabot. "In fact, he's one of our preferred blue-chip customers. Here . . ." She tore a sheet of paper from the printer's tractor-feed and handed it to the former federal prosecutor.

Sabot scrutinized the sheet. It had the words "C. Calvin Broeker" and "General Account" spelled out in grey dot-matrix lettering across the top, then several columns of faded numbers. His eyes quickly gravitated to the credit memo and balance, which was $16,008,873.76. More than sixteen million dollars. The sum transfixed Sabot briefly. It must have influenced him profoundly, though, for his voice now came out greasy, unctuous.

"We-ell, everything seems to be in order," he said. "I thank you kindly for your time, ma'am."

Everyone stood.

"Sorry to trouble you like this," said Cal, and he winked at the manager. "I appreciate it. Thanks."

"Not at all," the manager told him, smiling broadly. "For a customer like you, we cannot do enough. Is there anything else we can help you with today?"

Don't go overboard, lady, Cal thought. It's just another day in money.

He'd been in the bank the previous day too, with his RCMP supervisor and handlers, who explained the situation to the manager. She'd agreed to co-operate fully. The money was really there, though, transferred short term from a police account. Very short term — it'd be gone by the morning. As he replied to the bank manager, Cal, like Demaine before him, wondered whether he'd ever see his own bank account with such a robustly healthy balance.

"No, that's all for today. Thanks very much. You can expect Mr. Sabot to be presenting my check tomorrow or the day after."

"I'll look after it personally, Mr. Broeker. Don't worry. Have a nice day."

"You too."

As they filed back through the revolving doors, Sabot said, "You see those two guys in the lobby there?"

"With the newspapers?" Cal *had* seen them, and his blood was running cold.

"Right," said Sabot. "They're cops."

"You think so?" Cal knew they were cops, although he didn't recognize them.

"Oh, yeah." Sabot didn't sound too worried. "Wanna play with them?"

"No, man. I don't want to play with no cops."

"No, just follow me — I'll prove it to you."

Sabot led the way back through the revolving doors. It was like a comedy routine. What they faced inside was laughable, all right: the two men who'd been sitting in the bank lobby were now on their feet, ready to follow Cal and Sabot. When they saw them coming back in, they froze and, for want of anything better to do, raised their newspapers and continued reading right where they stood — as if the news was so damn riveting they couldn't put it down. It was the worst give-up Cal had ever seen. The men might as well have been in their dress uniforms: the red coat, the breeches with the yellow stripe, Smokey the Bear hat. It was what he'd been dreading. He'd even elicited a promise from his handlers that they'd stay far away. They'd definitely broken that promise — and maybe they'd just broken everything else with it.

Yet Sabot, like many criminals, had no fear of cops. He thought they were stupid. He was the smart one, the genius. Besides, he knew when he was breaking the law — and right now, he knew he wasn't.

Faced with this ludicrous display, the ex–federal prosecutor simply laughed, waved at the two men, and went right back out through the revolving doors. See ya, assholes!

Cal joined him on the steps of the bank a second later, genuinely pained by what he'd seen.

"What do you want to do now?" he asked. "I mean, I'm not comfortable with cops hanging around. I'm not used to this shit."

"What do you mean?" said Sabot, still laughing. He was energized, revitalized by this brush with the law.

"I mean the deal's off."

"No, no . . ."

Now Sabot was concerned — his own bank balance would presumably be badly affected if the deal didn't go down. The extent of his involvement in the operation was anybody's guess, but involved he certainly was. Why else would he be here?

"It's crazy, isn't it? I mean, two guys sitting in a bank lobby reading newspapers! *Sitting!* Why aren't they in line like everybody else? That's just bullshit. It's *pathetic!*" Sabot said.

Cal wanted to play on Sabot's greed awhile longer. "Yeah. Well, it may be pathetic, but I don't like it," he said. "The deal's off."

The greed: it was a thing to behold. That's what always got the bad guys in the end — greed. An undercover cop would probably have tried to force the deal through, but not Cal. He knew these people.

*The best way to lure the enemy into a trap is to run away from him.*

"No, listen," Sabot urged him. "It's nothing! They probably just found out you got a lot of cash in the bank, so they're keeping their nose up your ass to see what you're all about, man. Don't worry about it. It's fucking nothing!"

"Tell that to Dupont," said Cal. "He finds out about this, he'll hit the fucking roof. It's off, man. I had enough trouble getting it this far. As it is, my people are beating me up over the money lying in my fucking bank for so long. I don't blame them either. Sixteen mill's a lot to lose — even for the Russians."

"I thought it was Bulgarians," said Sabot warily. "You said Bulgarians."

"Who d'you think the fucking Bulgarians are? *Jesus!*"

"Oh yeah, right." Sabot looked like he was processing this information for future use. "Come on, pal," he said. "Let's go back to my office and talk this over. It's okay. I promise you it's okay."

"It's Cal."

"What?"

"The name's Cal."

"Yeah, I know that."

"Not *pal.*"

"Whatever," Sabot muttered. "We'll go back to my office, okay? Call Dupont from there."

"And tell him we got cops up the wazzoo? Dream on."

"They can't do anythin' to us, man, we're Americans. Shit, what is it, a crime to have some cash in the bank in this fucking country? Let's talk it over. Maybe we don't tell Dupont?"

"Your fucking neck, pal." Sabot was hooked. "That client of yours looks like he could get pretty mean he finds out someone's been lyin' to him."

"Withholding information — it isn't lying," said Sabot confidently.

"Like I said, your fucking neck."

BACK AT KESTREL INVESTMENTS, Sabot had a quick conversation with one of his cronies, Pierre Maille. It didn't take long for them to decide that Réal Dupont had no need to know about the cops in the bank. It'd only make him nervous, and it wasn't good for him to be nervous because then everyone else got nervous, and *that* was counterproductive.

"So we'll call Dupont and tell him the deal's on, okay?" announced Sabot. "You want a Scotch? Something?"

"Little early for me," said Cal. "What you do is your business. Keep me out of it, 'kay?"

"Can we say the deal's on for tomorrow, then? It's fine . . . honest, it's fine."

"It's pathetic. Yeah, I heard you. You'd better be right, 'cause it ain't gonna be good for you if you're wrong. Understand?"

Sabot understood. Everyone knew about the Russians: they don't just kill you, they kill your whole fucking family, your dog, your cat — that's what the Russians do. They torture you for days with dental pliers and electric prods too. That's why no one fucks with the Russians. Buddy recited this mantra regularly, perhaps to ward off the evil it contained.

"You'll see," said Sabot. "I wouldn't fuck with you." He called Dupont, asking for a Mr. LaForest when his call was answered. It was a code, presumably. "Yeah," he told "LaForest." "We got a green light on the deal. It's on for 9 a.m. tomorrow, all right? Good. See you then."

They didn't really like dealing with Dupont any better than he did, Cal observed. It was interesting what greed would make men do. But if you lie down with dogs, don't be surprised to find shit on yourself. Let's hope it don't hit the fan first, though, Cal told himself, nodding.

"Great!" said Sabot. "Fucking great!"

———

CAL WENT BACK to the Kahnawake Reservation. At 6:45 p.m., he called Art Franklin on the cellphone while Elizabeth prepared dinner. Franklin told him to speak directly with Réal Dupont.

"Everything seems to be okay with your — er — banker," Cal told Dupont, but the man cut him off.

"Yeah, I 'ear," he snapped frostily. "I meet you at 9 a.m." Then he hung up.

Dupont had one of the ugliest accents Cal had ever heard, now he came to think of it. It was like a rat vomiting in a wind tunnel. Québécois French could be quite mellifluous, but it could also be a grating nasal twang pitched somewhere between Brooklyn and Marseilles. As he clicked off the phone, Cal had the distinct sensation he'd been chewing silver foil. Dupont always had that effect on him — the man exuded something unpleasant. Cal didn't dwell much on evil any more, though. He'd come to understand that darkness wasn't the opposite of light, but the absence of light — and an absence couldn't be a quality. Thus evil was not the opposite of good — this idea was a delusion, in fact — it was just the shortage of good. Yet, nonetheless, Réal Dupont made him think of evil. Dupont seemed both deluded and evil.

One thing Cal knew about him was especially sickening, especially telling — so much so that Cal ran it through his mind at least once a day to shore up the iron in his soul. Dupont had shipped some of the counterfeit to the U.S., where his people were using it for a special service they'd set up: a check-cashing service for old folks. They'd come to your apartment so you didn't have to go out in the dead of winter or hobble downtown if your legs had gone. They'd take your pension or welfare check and give you cash for it, on the spot. There was no charge for this service either; it was philanthropic. Nice men, you said to yourself. Kind men. It spared your old, aching bones one more trip. Then you went to spend the funny money and found out you'd been bilked. You probably got into a bit of trouble initially too. But a seventy-eight-year-old on welfare doesn't fit the specs of your usual counterfeiter, so you'd be okay — just out of pocket. These weren't the kind of people who could absorb a month's loss of income, though. They'd have to cut back on everything but the air they breathed. They really suffered. It was small-time stuff, but it was also truly repugnant. It stank. And it spoke volumes about the kind of guy who would do it with no conscience, no soul, no compassion. When you can't feel what others feel, Cal had always believed, you aren't fully human. You're something else.

He shook off the chill that had gripped his bones — these late-summer evenings in Eastern Canada never let you forget that King Winter would soon come again, that warmth and light were an illusion. Then he heard Elizabeth calling for him.

"Who were you talking to?" she asked.

"Just some business, sweetheart, that's all," he told her. She had no idea what he did for a living. She assumed he was just a smuggler and small-time buddy like many others she knew on the rez. Like her brother, though nowhere near as rich. She'd have been horrified to find out what he was really up to. She'd also be dead if any of the bad-ass warriors or their "business associates" ever suspected she was in on it. And that was the last thing Cal wanted. He liked Elizabeth a lot. True, their relationship and the opportunity it gave him to hang out on the rez with the sister of a big-shot Mohawk smuggler were superb cover for his job. But he also cared about her more than he'd cared for any woman since Doris. His second marriage didn't count; he'd deleted it from his catalogue. Sometimes he even wondered if he could make a real life for himself and Elizabeth. But he didn't wonder much. It was another life he'd be endangering. Being around Indians tended to make you a bit of a dreamer, though. All they had left were their dreams . . . and their nightmares. Why couldn't they find someone to interpret these? he wondered. Why could they not read the writing on the wall? The white man wasn't going anywhere. He was here to stay.

AT 7 A.M. THE FOLLOWING DAY, Cal met with his handlers to revise plans for the takedown. Everything was to go the way they'd decided nearly a year before. The Mounties would be tailing Cal all the way. A SWAT team would be waiting near the transaction site. He would not be exposed — or at least not for long. Providing everything went smoothly . . .

At 9 a.m. precisely, Cal Broeker shook hands with Justinian Sabot in the offices of Kestrel Investments. Then they sat down with cups of coffee to wait for Réal Dupont. Now Sabot looked like *he* had the taste of silver foil in his mouth, a result of the prospect of seeing Dupont, or Mr. LaForest, or whatever the hell else he called him. Or maybe it was just the day's business that preoccupied the ex–federal prosecutor. Whatever the case, he was not his usual garrulous self. And waiting drips bile into your guts. You're cocked and ready to fire, but there's nothing to shoot. Pierre Maille — the partner — was in and out of the room, so it was just Cal and Sabot there most of the time. They started exchanging war stories, and Sabot was curious about Bulgaria: Did the mob have the place sewn up? What's a country run by bad guys like? What do you eat? But the conversation quickly petered out.

By 9:30, Cal was wound as tight as a coil of Bulgarian telephone wire.

"Listen," he told Sabot, "I gotta go call my people, tell them Dupont hasn't showed yet."

"Huh?" said Sabot, some reverie shattered.

"We got trucks and people ready to move that shit straight to the docks. They don't wanna sit around waiting for the rip, you understand. I gotta let them know what's going on."

Cal always made sure everyone was used to his endless phone calls. Usually he carried a couple of cells — though not that day — and even chronically suspicious animals like Dupont soon came to accept that this was Cal. You do business with him, you accept he makes a lot of calls. And gets them too. You get used to it. But a cellphone is also a tracking device. If it's on, anyone who wants to and has the know-how can locate you to within a block. Everyone knew this, so Cal was acknowledging the fact by leaving his phones at home. Besides, in his experience, when a deal is going down, one wrong number calling in could screw everything up.

"Sure," Sabot said meekly. He didn't have to ask where the cells were — and he wasn't about to offer his office line.

"I'm gonna use the pay phone down in the street," Cal added. "In case you got heat."

"I'm gonna say, 'Fine, that's good,'" said Sabot. "But because *you* might have the heat." He guffawed. A regular comedy store, this guy was.

At the pay phone, Cal called his handlers and told them what the score was. They told him to hang in there; they'd notify all units there'd been a delay.

"Wonder what's keeping him?" wondered Sabot as 9:55 rolled around.

"I wonder if you wonder as much as I wonder," Cal said.

"More coffee?"

"Nah." Cal had drunk enough coffee for today. Possibly for the whole week. Maybe the year. It sat like a rippling lake of nitric acid in his stomach. Eating something you could swallow seemed like a good idea, yet he couldn't imagine trying to swallow something solid right now.

"Hey, I gotta call my people again," he told Sabot as Old Montreal's many and venerable bell-tower clocks began to strike ten.

"No prob," Sabot conceded.

"Oh, I'd say there was a prob," Cal returned. "In fact, I'd say there was a big fucking prob here."

"I'm gonna make some calls too, see what's going on," Sabot decided.

"Well, when you've heard the gossip, see if you can find out where Dupont is too," Cal said. "Y'know . . . while you're at it."

"That what I was gonna d—" Sabot started saying, only to glance up to see Cal flashing a very shit-eating grin at him.

"Sure you were."

Cal told the handlers what little he knew. Dupont still hadn't showed was all of it. No one seemed to know why. Had he got wind of the takedown? Was there a leak? A snitch? It was anybody's guess. Cal would just carry on hanging in there.

"Fucking guy," Cal cursed, narrowing his eyes into Sabot's for effect.

"Something must have come up," theorized Sabot, somewhat desperately.

"Oh, really," Cal threw back. "Like what? There's a hundred and twenty mill in the back of his truck, a certified check for sixteen mill waiting for him in my back pocket, and a crew of very jumpy Russkies waiting in a back alley for the deal to go down, and he — what? *what?* — he found something better to do? Something more lucrative?"

"Well, yeah . . . maybe . . . I dunno. I—"

"You what? You *think* so? Some piece of jailbait flagged him down and offered to blow him if he drove her to school is more like it. You think I don't know this is the biggest fucking piece of action you boys ever seen? You asshole!"

"Anything's possible."

"The fact that you think this worries me deeply, Sabot. It fucking worries me to the core, that's what it does."

"C'mon, Cal, relax," Sabot tried. "He'll show sooner or later. Yeah, he'll show. He's probably just being cautious, is all."

"Dupont doesn't even know how to spell 'cautious,'" Cal told him. "Like you." He enjoyed playing with Sabot. They should make the guy into an action toy.

BY 11:58 A.M., Cal had conducted five visits to the street pay phone and was about to make another. He was edgy. The handlers were edgy. And Sabot, he was beyond edgy. He'd run out of excuses and rationalizations for Dupont's no-show too.

"Cautious, eh?" said Cal, looking at his watch. "You must concede it's more like fucking paranoia than caution now, pal."

"Yeah, well . . . I, um . . . y'know, he . . . er—"

Cal cut him off. "Save it, Sabot. I'm gonna make one last call to my people, okay? Then if LaPont or DuForest or Forpont or whoever shitface really is don't show, I'm outta here and I'm outta your life for good. Got it?"

"Yeah. Got it. Listen, I don't blame you, man."

"I'm real glad about that, Sabot. 'Cause I blame you, and this better be all there is to blame you for too."

"Wha-whaddaya mean?"

"Think about it, okay?"

Cal told the handlers he was going to give it only one more hour. It'd look suspicious if he hung in any longer. They urged him to wait at least until he knew why Dupont hadn't showed. He'd think about it. No promises.

"DON'T ASK ME if I want another coffee, okay?" Cal told Sabot. "Ask me something else. Amuse me."

"Amuse you-fucking-self." This wasn't Sabot. It was Réal Dupont's jangling voice, swiftly followed by the rest of him. He flowed like liquid metal into the room, kicking the door shut behind him.

He was a state too, a mess. His black jeans and black T-shirt were smeared with dirt, his snakeskin cowboy boots were scuffed, he was unshaven, and his cold black eyes floated in pools of streaky crimson. He was supposed to be Métis — part Indian — but you couldn't see it in him. He was all white trash as far as Cal was concerned. Around five-seven with close-cropped brown hair, he had to be at least two hundred-odd pounds, but all muscle. He seemed permanently clenched too, fully cocked and ready to go off at any time. It had clearly been a hell of a night, though. Dupont was the kind of buddy who enjoyed the rough stuff — whether pitching or catching — and there were not a few cops who enjoyed dishing it out. There weren't many catchers, however. In Montreal, particularly on the south shore, a passive cop was a dead cop. Dupont didn't look like he'd done much pitching, but he had definitely done some. It had clearly been a meeting of minds — a hell of a night all round.

"Better late than never, eh?" he told Cal, one side of his thin mouth curling into what presumably was meant to be a smile. He had an arrogant way of tilting his head back and to one side when he spoke to you. In the body's language, this gesture said, "I'm gonna fuck you up, asshole." It was eloquent, this body language.

Evidently, he'd been picked up by the south shore cops late the previous night for a parole violation: he'd broken his curfew. Cal couldn't help smiling at the idea of Dupont even having a curfew. And then at the idea of him stuck in a jail cell for a bullshit charge with a hundred-million-dollar deal about to go down. Or go down the drain.

"What the fuck you grinnin' at, asshole?" Dupont glared at Cal.

"For a minute there, I thought you were gonna say sorry," Cal replied. "But I forgot it was you. Silly of me. So can we do business, or what?"

"I wanna use Maille's office, okay?" Dupont asked Sabot, though he was already halfway to the partner's office door. Turning when he reached the entrance, he told Cal, "Let's go in 'ere."

When Cal was inside, Dupont kicked the door shut, pushed him against the wall, and started to frisk him thoroughly, NYPD-style. "Listen, guy," he said in a throaty whisper as he worked, "I been inna fucking jail cell all night. I ham not in a good mood, 'kay? Now can we do some business today or not? I got no time to be fucked 'round."

When Dupont stood after finishing the pat-down, Cal roughly pushed him against the wall and began a pat-down of his own.

"I might as well convey that the distrust is mutual. Since we're leaving our manners at the door anyway."

Dupont let him finish, then shoved his arm away, saying, "Nothin' has gone the way I wanted with this deal, motherfucker. Nothin'! This deal fucking sucks, that's what I tink. It fuckin' stinks. And you know what? I tink that you are a fuckin' cop, that's what I tink."

Cal laughed at him, but it wasn't a good move. Dupont became very still, and he narrowed his black eyes until they looked like two gun barrels in a guard-tower window. "I tell you this," he said. "You fuck me an' it is the last person you ever gonna fuck. You hear me? I fuckin' know where you children are. I know where you living, where you friends living. See?"

"What'd you think I'm gonna do to you if there's a fuck-up?" Cal said, ready to take the guy if he had to. "Or if there's a rip, eh? You think I don't feel the same way, you crazy motherfucker?"

For all Cal knew, the place was wired. He had to be careful. He had to stay within the law — and offering to murder Dupont wasn't anywhere to be found in the Canadian legal code. It could be used to crack his credibility as a witness if he ever had to testify in this case. It could even be used by Dupont to plead entrapment or coercion. "Is it not true, Mr. Broeker, that you threatened to murder Mr. Dupont's children if he did not procure for you the counterfeit money?" That sort of thing. It didn't bear thinking about too closely, the legal stuff. If you dwelt on it too much, you ended up wondering who the law was there to protect.

"You wanna vendetta or you wanna do business?" Cal asked Dupont, reining himself in.

"Fuck you!"

"We gonna pursue this schoolyard shit all day? If we are, I'm outta here."

Dupont was clearly rattled. He'd checked Cal out sufficiently to know the guy had spent time in Bulgaria, and he knew he had Mafiosi and Russians around him. Like most operators, Dupont feared the Russians. He knew that whatever excess of violence he was capable of himself, the Russians could top it. So Dupont backed off.

"I'm fuckin hungry, man," he said. "First, we go eat lunch, 'kay?"

THEY WENT IN DUPONT's vehicle to Chi-Chi's on the south shore. It was a fast-food joint on Boulevarde Taschereau, a mall strip that stretched for miles, an anonymous wasteland of cheap motels, body shops, vacant lots, scrap yards, and every kind of junk-food outlet known to man. The diet went with the habitat. And it was in this suburban hell that buddy and co. pre-ferred to operate. Its anonymity helped make them invisible. "Land of the Three Ms," Cal had dubbed it: McDonalds, malls, and machine guns.

Cal pushed some nachos around a plate. What was this guy up to? If they didn't move it, the banks would be closed. Dupont silently worked his way through a couple of tortillas, a quesadilla, two burritos, and a bowl of guacamole — all of it washed down by three double bloody Marys. When he finished he belched loudly, then tipped about half a gram of coke onto the crook of his thumb and snorted it loudly, right there in the booth with the waitress hovering nearby. The dumb fuck.

"Wha-at?" snapped Dupont, glaring at Cal.

"Nothin'. I like to see a man enjoy a hearty breakfast."

"Fuck you!" Dupont flipped open his phone and called his brother, telling him, "*Amene tout le maudit paquet.*"

By now it was past 3:30 p.m.

Damn! Cal told himself. He definitely wouldn't be able to get the check today. What was Dupont playing at?

"I tell my brother to bring all the money," Dupont said. "One 'undred fifty mill." It was being brought to a location on the south shore. "He be there in fifteen minute."

"I thought it was one-twenty."

"What I just say?"

"Then the price stays the same — twelve. I ain't prepared to do more. And we can't do the bank till tomorrow now — thanks to breakfast here."

"And you," Dupont told him, "be prepared to spend the fuckin' night wid me, you ass taped to a fuckin' chair in my basement. You ain' leavin' till I got the fuckin' money in my 'ands and I am countin' it. I don't give a fuck about you Bulgarians, you Russians, you fuckin' Yankees, or any-ting. You gonna be wid me till I leave for the fuckin' islands, 'kay?"

"Okay," said Cal.

Leaving for the islands! It was such a buddies' cliché . . .

———

THEY LEFT CHI-CHI'S and drove to a house and compound not far away, across from a body shop, with a rear driveway concealed from view. Cal recognized the area as the same one he'd been brought to a year earlier, when he first saw the money. This time, though, it was half an hour before the money arrived, in that same do-it-yourself horsebox trailer, which was being pulled by Dupont's fat brother's pickup. There were sixty boxes, two rows of banded hundreds stacked in each. Cal started opening boxes and riffling the blocks of bills. This made Dupont laugh out loud — an unappealing sound, more like a goat cussing than a man amused.

"I ain't counting it," Cal told him. "I'm fucking checkin' to see it ain't paper — because it gets there and it's paper, my ass is fucking grass, man."

Cal noticed that some of the boxes were sodden and the bills inside damp. Probably stored in some leaky cellar. It seemed to epitomize the lack of respect these people had for money — for everything. They loved nothing sufficiently to respect it. But at least he knew for sure that the guy still had 150 million U.S. dollars in counterfeit. Clearly, it wasn't so easy to unload. Cal had been fairly certain he wasn't being led on a wild goose chase — *fairly* certain. After all, he'd seen it the previous year. But until now, he wasn't entirely convinced Dupont wouldn't try to make the rip *all* of this deal.

The money was next transferred to Dupont's white Ford Econoline van. As Dupont climbed into the driver's seat, he banged down a can of gasoline on the centre aisle, between him and Cal.

"I even smell cops," he said, "I fuckin' douse you and all the money and set fire to the whole fuckin' lot, man. Unnerstan'?" He unscrewed the cap on the gas can.

"Whoa!" Cal told him. "You can douse me, but don't fucking douse the money, man. Bad enough it's fucking damp. It gets to Bulgaria and it smells or there's discoloration 'cause the gas reacts with the ink, they're gonna have a shit fit, man! Don't do it."

Dupont weighed this information. He'd been snorting blow since they'd left the restaurant and looked wired enough to burst into flames himself. But clearly, coke or not, Cal's logic made sense to him. A moment later, Dupont replaced the cap, set the gas can behind him, then picked up a tire iron from the floor of the van and laid it in his lap.

"One fuckin' cop," he said, "or I even suspect a bad deal — or even I just fuckin' feel like it — I ham gonna stick this through the side of your head."

As they took off, Cal noticed a gas station with a pay phone and asked Dupont if he could call the Bulgarians: "Just to make sure the truck is gonna be there at the warehouse to pick up the fucking money."

The story he'd told Dupont was that they had diplomatic immunity on both the shipment and the warehouse itself. He didn't specify *whose* diplomatic immunity — Dupont's imagination would handle that. The place had an official seal on it.

"We can't get hit on there," he'd said. "Even when we unload or load, we're safe. We're fucking immune."

This way, the presence of Bulgarians served Dupont's purposes as much as it did Cal's. So he agreed to the call, telling Cal to make it quick. Or else.

Breathing a mental sigh of relief, Cal called the handlers and told them the shipment was on its way.

"How'd you get to a phone?"

"Never mind how I got to a fucking phone," said Cal. "The shipment's on its way to Candiac. We're at the corner of Route 87, okay?"

"What are you doing there? We're following you north in a white pickup."

Shit, thought Cal.

"No," he said, "that's Dupont's brother. I'm in a white van. You're following the wrong fucking truck."

They had all their air and ground surveillance on an empty truck.

"You'd better redirect because we're gonna be at the warehouse in fifteen minutes."

"What's the situation?"

"I haven't seen any guns," Cal told them. "He's got a tire iron and a can of gas, that's all."

Back in the van, Dupont was enjoying a typical buddies' fantasy. A classic. He was going to send the cherries a Christmas card from Barbados. He called them cherries because of the red flashing light on their police cars. "I'm gonna write, 'Fuck you,'" he was saying. "'Fuck you, I got away.'" He had a couple of outstanding charges that he was due in court for — small-time stuff, drug offences — and he saw himself lounging with a tall cocktail, little umbrella in it, the lot, in a deck chair by the turquoise ocean. It was a dream. Like any dream, though, like the Mohawks' dreams, it could alternate with a nightmare. Periodically, Dupont recalled what stood between him and a life of Caribbean ease, and to dispel this nightmare, it seemed, to exorcise it, he had to summon up the spectre of revenge. "Anyting go fuckin' wrong," he'd say, "then you fuckin' gonna be the first to die."

"Yeah, I got that," Cal told him.

"If they put me away, I got friends who fuckin' gonna chop up you kids an'—"

"Skull-fuck my mother — yeah, I got that too."

"Shut the fuck up!" Dupont gripped the wheel like a kamikaze pilot. His pupils had dilated so much from coke and adrenaline that his eyes resembled plugholes, drainpipes, sewer tunnels. Or maybe sighting tubes for the beast that squatted in the black hole of his mind.

What must it be like in there? Cal wondered. What made these guys tick? As long as he'd been around them, bad guys still puzzled him. What was it that told someone it was okay for him to prey on his fellow man? He'd seen guys who were multi-millionaires still get enthused about some hundred-dollar scam. No matter how much money they had, they couldn't stop being criminals. They *liked* it. It wasn't a poverty issue; it wasn't Robin-fucking-Hood. It was Hood fucking everyone else. Buddy liked being buddy. They got their rocks off breaking the law, and life just wasn't the same without it. Even if Dupont made it down to the Caribbean, he'd blow it sooner or later by perping some sort of scam — perping it just for the adrenaline, just for the *principle* of crime.

At the end of the day, criminals were . . . well, criminals. And jail wasn't any solution to it. The jails are full of criminals. Criminals feel at home in jail. They don't mind it. All their friends are there. Besides, they never stay in for long if they're connected. If they've got money and friends outside. If they've got a smart lawyer. If Dupont went down — and right then, it was a big if — he'd still be out soon enough. Was it likely he'd forget who sent him away? And this was if he couldn't reach out from jail itself — reach out and touch someone. *Someone.* Cal thought about his children. Was he really endangering them by doing this job? There were times when these thoughts plagued him. But there were other times when he told himself that if no one did the job, then they might as well announce that the bad guys had won. *Crime pays! Go ahead, boys, take whatever you want — we can't stop you.* This thought fed iron into his soul, sat him high in the saddle again. You couldn't think too generally about crime — it was too overwhelming. You had to stick with the specifics. Like a restaurateur, a police officer had to face every day like the first, and people remembered only your last triumph or fiasco.

WHEN HE AND CAL ARRIVED at the gates to the warehouse complex in Candiac, Réal Dupont was describing the villa he'd have down in the Caribbean. Security would be a priority: "Big fuckin' iron gates," he was saying. "And cameras, razor wires, fuckin' dogs, armed guards . . . no one gonna fuck with me there."

The dream house sounded more like a jail. Cal found the thought amusing, but he didn't feel amused right now. It was close to 9 p.m. The next hour would see the culmination of a year's work — or the culmination of something else. No more fuck-ups, he prayed as he tapped the code onto a plastic-covered keypad by the gates and watched them open. They drove over to his lock-up, opened up its sliding door, and started unloading the van. Through the right-hand wall, in the next unit, a surveillance group would be watching and videotaping. There'd be no move until all the boxes were unloaded, however. That was the way the legal boys wanted it, and you didn't argue with them or their reasons. Mopping his brow theatrically, Cal took off his jacket and hung it on the vehicle's side mirror. This was the code: when they saw the jacket from their vantage point nearby, the main SWAT team would then take one minute to throw open the adjacent lock-up's door, tear out, secure the area, and grab the target, the money, the lot. That was the theory.

Two minutes passed. No sign of them. Cal thought fast. He wasn't about to spend the night duct-taped to a chair in Réal Dupont's basement, *that* was for sure. Something told him that he'd never leave Dupont's place alive, no matter what else happened. The guy was just as likely to try a rip as he was to kill Cal for sheer amusement.

Dupont was in the back of the van now, straightening up a blanket he'd used to hide the boxes while they were driving. Light as a chipmunk despite his towering 280 pounds, Cal jumped onto the fender and swiftly but with great force pushed the lock-up door off its sliding track. It wasn't much, but it would buy him a little time. If it wasn't enough, he'd have to come up with something else. But what? With Dupont occupied, Cal now had time to survey the scene. Across the road from the warehouse complex in the parking lot of a St-Hubert's Bar-B-Cue — ironically, the exact same chicken spot where he'd first met Dupont a year ago — he saw the brown surveillance truck. It was unquestionably the right truck — he could even read the plates — and dimly through its blacked-out windows he made out the forms of people moving around. What the fuck were the cops doing? There had to be some kind of problem, he realized. Why else weren't they here? They *had* to have seen him.

"All right," said Dupont, jumping down from the van and slamming its door. "Let's get outta here."

Cal put his jacket back on and brushed himself off as Dupont reached up to slide the door shut. Finding it jammed, he tugged for a few seconds before calling Cal over.

"What da fuck is diss!" he said. "Fuckin' door is stuck. Come 'ere an' help me with it."

With exaggerated gestures, Cal took the jacket off again, this time laying it on the ground. If they didn't see that, they were blind. He joined Dupont tugging on the door handle for a few seconds, then he walked over to the van and took out the tire iron. Standing back on the fender, he started to lever the door's runner back into its track. They see me doing this, he told himself, they have to know I've got trouble. They *have* to. Feeling the cool, solid weight of the iron in his hand, Cal realized this might be the last chance he'd have to hold a weapon. He could see the claw on its curved end smacking into Dupont's skull, the dark, viscous blood welling up to fill the small crater of shattered bone, torn skin, and matted hair. He felt the anxious, expectant adrenaline surge tighten his arm muscles, readying them for the eruption of violence. He almost did it too. Every cell in his body pulsed on red alert, but he felt the tide crest, then ebb, saw the window of opportunity close.

Six minutes had passed by the time he'd got the door working again. It slid shut with a thump, $150 million in counterfeit behind it. There was no sign of any SWAT team. There wasn't even a traffic cop. Jee-zuss!

What the fuck was going on? Here they have the biggest sting of its kind in either U.S. *or* Canadian history, and all they have to do is move on in right now to get their man. *But they're nowhere to be seen.* This was *their* plan too! The rest — Bulgaria, the bank account, the warehouse — had all been Cal's idea, but this was their contribution. So where were they? There wasn't even a Plan B, nothing in reserve. If he got through the night ahead, Cal thought, the next opportunity wouldn't come until the bank tomorrow. Oh, Christ! He saw himself — the hostage! — being marched in through the revolving doors between Dupont and a bunch of his biker buddies, armed to the teeth. Your money or your life — *and* your life. Right now, the cops had it clear and easy — the only possible victim was Cal. Tomorrow there would be civilians everywhere — women, children, baby carriages . . . It was the kind of situation they hated. Justifying the loss of civilian life — even when what you were doing was safeguarding it — was next to impossible these days. People had forgotten what war was really like. They weren't prepared to make sacrifices, let alone *be* sacrifices. Cal couldn't see a happy ending to tomorrow, however he looked at it. They had to move today, *had* to . . . Or else what?

Briefly, he saw himself jumping from the moving van as they drove over to Dupont's place. Only briefly, though. That was Hollywood shit. It doesn't happen in real life. You jump from a truck, you break your fucking ankle is what happens. Then you end up getting dragged in chains behind the truck. Or something.

Its crippled fluorescent light throbbing like a lighthouse beacon, a pay phone sat across the road from the warehouse. Fortunately. Cal had been blessed by pay phones on this job. It wasn't always so easy, so convenient.

"Listen," he said as Dupont pulled out the van keys and opened the driver's door, "if the money's gonna stay here and I'm gonna be your fucking hostage, I gotta make sure the truck's gonna be here, my people are gonna get the money, it ain't gonna disappear, and I ain't gonna be fucked."

"Okay," said Dupont, slightly more relaxed now that he thought the worst part was over. "But make it fuckin' quick." Or else.

"I don't know what your fucking guys are doing," Cal told his supervisor, "but the truck's here, they aren't, and I'm on my way to a fucking basement somewhere."

"They had some battery problems. We lost contact . . ."

They'd also been locked in the unit since 8 a.m., with no food, nothing to drink, no washroom, no radio, and only visual contact with the others.

"Duracells," Cal said. "Haven't you seen the ads? They keep on going, know what I mean? Jesus H. Christ, what am I dealing with here? The fucking Mickey Mouse Club!"

"Shut up and listen," said the voice in Cal's ear. "We'll be with you in two minutes. Just do exactly as they say, and don't worry. Do we have a shooter yet?"

"No. It's just as it was."

When Cal emerged from the phone booth, Dupont had pulled the van up to the warehouse gates and was waiting with engine running. Two minutes. It might as well be two hours if they're not here in fifteen seconds, Cal told himself.

"Move it!" Dupont barked through the window. "Let's go."

Cal nodded at the front wheel, saying, "Your tire always like that?"

"What? Like what?" Dupont opened the door and slid out to take a look.

Before he'd even noticed nothing was wrong with the tire, they were surrounded by the SWAT team. Black masks, black everything, the men seemed to be spat out from the very ether. They were everywhere, flashlights tearing through the mottled night, voices yelling, screaming, arms shoving, grabbing, machine-gun barrels pointing. "Don't fucking move! . . . Hands above your head! . . . Move away from the vehicle! . . . Kneel down! . . . Keep those fuckin' hands where I can see 'em!"

Cal was pushed against the van and patted down roughly by a guy who discreetly whispered in his ear, "Nice work! Just stay down, shut up, and play dumb." Then he was handcuffed and marched away.

He saw Dupont glaring at him through those pitiless black eyes. Just glaring. Dupont's nightmare had torn its way through the fabric of reality and was here. Right now. Yet all the guy said throughout the entire takedown was, "I'm so fuckin' tired, man." He kept on saying it too. "So tired . . . I just wanna get into my bed an' sleep, that's all. . . . Can I just go to bed now?" Cal could still hear him when he was being driven away. "I just wanna sleep, is all. . . . It's been such a long day, man, such a long, long day. Cannot I go to my bed now? An' my sleep?"

But the woods were dark and deep, and Dupont had quite a ways to go before he got some sleep. Did he ever wonder, wondered Cal, that he ought to have taken the other road? There's usually a reason roads are less travelled.

AFTER THE COUNTERFEIT TAKEDOWN, in the late spring of 1995, Cal Broeker was sent with a bodyguard to a spa in the Eastern Townships of Quebec. It was the high-end version of a safe house. The word on the street was that Art Franklin, Réal Dupont's people, and the Indians were all trying to locate him. Since no disclosure had been made, no one was sure what exactly had happened during the arrest of Dupont. The law requires that all details of a case — including the identity of any agents — be made available to defence lawyers before the trial of the accused begins, even though this may expose, and thus endanger, any undercover operatives involved. But in this case, Dupont had been caught red-handed with the counterfeit bills — it was on video too — so unless he mounted an elaborate defence, no such disclosure was necessary. It was also hard to imagine any defence that would exonerate Dupont this time. He'd have to plead guilty. He did plead guilty. He *was* guilty.

After the arrest of Art Franklin and Armand Veilleux, the two of them did a private deal, with Franklin taking the fall for Veilleux, who ran a strip club for the bikers in Montreal and was thus less expendable. The prosecutor in this case let it be known that if Cal had to be called to testify, he would be asking the court for federal penitentiary time, instead of just provincial jail time. Since the bikers had a lot of control in Quebec jails, this meant the difference between hard time and an austere vacation. But it also meant that Cal was exposed in the prosecution's disclosures to defence attorneys. Before long, Armand Veilleux had faxed the information on C. Calvin Broeker, along with his photograph, over to the bikers' clubhouse in Sorelle, where it was reportedly pinned up on the dart board. It was also faxed to allied gangs around North America.

Cal's continued success as an agent depended entirely on his ability to deliver unequivocal arrests, like Dupont's — or rather, their consequent convictions. Although his identity has been revealed in numerous disclosures, he has yet to appear as a witness in court. This knife-edge of deniability was all that stood between him and forced retirement — or worse. Cal's reading of Tsun-tsu's *Art of War* — a sort of Zen and the art of self-preservation — and of Napoleonic military strategy had, how-ever, taught him the value of such techniques as "spreading smoke" across your trail or increasing your strength by creating the illusion that your forces are more numerous than they really are (Napoleon lit extra campfires at night), as well as various other psychological gimmicks of strategy. With no reliable news or information sources, criminals, Cal found, were particularly susceptible to such strategies.

He offered to go back to the reservation. He felt he owed it to Elizabeth; he didn't want to disappear from her life entirely. But the RCMP refused to allow it. The risk was too great. Nonetheless, by cellphone, Cal kept in touch. He put it out that Dupont had tried a rip. Since he'd seen Cal being arrested alongside him, even Dupont couldn't be certain what had really gone down. In the world of crime, no one trusts anyone much anyway. That and the greed fuelling every bad boy meant that Cal could keep up with most of the deals still being probed. The reserve was a jamboree of crime, and any one project opened up half a dozen others. The trick was for Cal to keep his distance yet still be reachable. It was a trick that he mastered utterly, thanks to new technology. To the world of electronic communications, in Marshall McLuhan's phrase, everywhere was any-where, and anywhere was everywhere. Although both felt like nowhere.

Using his cellphones in conjunction with such things as call forward-ing, call answering, and teleconferencing, Cal could make it seem as if he was in California — or indeed almost anywhere on earth. His story was that he'd escaped FBI custody and was on the run. He just had to make it believable. It all depended on a detailed working knowledge of local conditions. If he was supposed to be in, say, Los Angeles, he would have a second wristwatch set to Pacific Time. He would also keep track of the weather in L.A. and make sure he was up on any regional peculiarities, like festivals, strikes, wars, or holidays. Through contacts, he would have a few local numbers rigged to either teleconferencing or call forwarding. He could be more convincing than he even needed to be, and the result in this case was an offer of more smuggling deals that would eventually net one of the biggest operators in the history of con-traband — Larry Miller.

About two weeks after Dupont's arrest, Cal Broeker was taken to the U.S. border at Rouses Point, New York, and transferred to the protection of the Secret Service in Burlington, Vermont. He stayed in different hotels for the next six weeks, continuing to do phone business and feed misinformation to his targets. It was during this period that he received several phone calls from associates of Larry Miller, offering him deals that involved products ranging from hijacked cigarettes to pirate gasoline, although their main interest was in smuggling alcohol into Canada. This, naturally enough, piqued the interest of Cal's RCMP handlers, who agreed to initiate a probe after listening to recorded phone calls Cal had made while he was still in protective custody in Vermont.

| 127

Memories in crime are on the whole short — the prolonged revenge saga is more Hollywood mythmaking — so Cal eventually decided to move back to Canada and onto the rez. It was, he felt, essential to the new project. It underscored his innocence in the Dupont counterfeit deal by endorsing his new role as victim of a rip-off. It also allowed him time to sort the business from the pleasure — if not the romantic commitment — in his relationship with Elizabeth.

The Dupont takedown, as noted, proved to be the largest haul of counterfeit money in North American history. Because of this, Cal's "suitable reward," when it finally came through, was $120,000, not the promised $50,000. Hearing this, the U.S. Secret Service, who'd benefited as much as the Canadians from the successful capture of Dupont and his money, were shamed into coming up with another $20,000, which, they expected Cal to believe, was the highest award they had ever paid out. So C. Calvin Broeker was able to pay off his debts and tell himself that a new day had dawned. He was also able to keep up the front of being a semi-legitimate entrepreneur, a cover that was largely responsible for his ability to penetrate the world of organized crime. He felt vindicated, and he felt somewhat healed of the scars from his old life. He also felt like going back into the fray, for a warrior is defined by the calibre of his enemies and the bravery of his assaults upon them. He is what he does.

# 6

# Orienter

*You know there ain't no Devil,*
*just God when he's drunk.*

— TOM WAITS

"Why do you do this kind of work, Mr. Broeker?" asked the police psychiatrist.

"I don't have any reason *not* to do it," replied Cal. "I'm already in it up to my eyeballs. I've been exposed by name — who I am and *what* I am. My photo's pinned to the Hell's Angels clubhouse wall, or so I'm told. If I dropped out now, it wouldn't matter to the people after me, but it would matter to the people who still believe in me — and *that* would jeopardize what I believe to be some valuable pending operations. So I don't have any reason *not* to do it."

"In this work, there are many opportunities, are there not, Mr. Broeker?" the shrink pursued. "Opportunities to enrich yourself illegally. Opportunities to accept gifts — of sex, of property, of cash — all manner of things. Why do you not take these opportunities when they arise?"

"Money isn't an issue with me," said Cal. "And casual sex doesn't interest me at all."

"What does interest you?"

"My good name. Certain values that my grandparents instilled in me — values that I know seem old-fashioned, but they make me tick. It's important for me to serve on the right side, to serve a good master. That way, I know the work I do benefits others, helps promote the good cause. There's too much bad in the world for me to stand by and watch it thrive. I was taught to treasure a good name above all. Like I said, I know it's old-fashioned."

"You've told me a little about your personal life before you started this work," said the shrink. "Is it possible that through this work, you are getting revenge on those, like your wife and brother, whom you were unable or unwilling to punish before?"

"I don't think so. I like to think I can rise above that, but it's true that I am trying to show my children, by example, the sort of values I believe are worthwhile. Yes."

A PSYCHIATRIC EVALUATION is routine for undercover operatives who are either between jobs or about to embark an another assignment, because the work takes its toll. The stress of pretending to be someone else can manifest itself in different ways too. The UC is sometimes in danger of becoming what he's hunting, either by succumbing to the temptations that surround him or by growing genuinely fond of those he's leading to the slaughter. The constant fear of exposure also makes family life difficult. He rarely goes home during a project for fear of being tailed — and being tailed doesn't just mean exposure, it means the bad guys know where to find his wife and children, information that can be used to extort a confession or for revenge, or both. The UC can also start to feel alienated from his real life by the character he plays — the swearing, the smoking, and the drinking — and he becomes less willing to be around his loved ones. He feels both polluted and polluting. It is not as easy for him to change out of his work clothes as it is for other men. UC work is tough, and few are suited to it.

But Cal Broeker was a natural. He passed his psychiatric assessment in the spring of 1995 with flying colours. Although he generally cussed more than he would have dared do around his grandparents, Cal was hardly any different whether he was with the good, the bad, or those on an ugly hair-trigger. He didn't fear exposure, since he was not pretending to be someone else; he could run into an old friend while in the company of someone like Réal Dupont and not be at all fazed. At the end of the day, most UCs are cops, and it's pretty easy to find out if someone's a cop — thus the UC will use a false identity. But false identities are easily exposed too, either through bad luck or through a few phone calls. Cal didn't have to worry on that account. His wallet still contained its original ID; the only things he was careful to hide were his LOA and the copies he kept of his scrupulous notes on meetings and telephone conversations. Although most, if not all, cop UCs backed off at the slightest hint of trouble, of exposure — indeed, that's what the rules say they *must* do — Cal would take it as an opportunity to consolidate his cover.

An example. While once in Toronto, he received a call on one of his cellphones from Lenny and Stack, two members of an Ontario biker gang (which merged with the Hell's Angels in the wake of the Quebec gang wars, early in 2001). They controlled various sex and drugs angles in the province, originally either for or with the Italian Mafia, and more recently either for or with the Russians. The bikers had been suspicious of Cal ever since Armand Veilleux had linked him with the Dupont takedown, but they had little proof — and of course, Cal was busy playing on their greed and their fascination with well-run operations. Their own campaigns were all too often crude and violent affairs. But bikers get old like the rest of us, and many gang members had shed their biker image — the colours, the leather and denim — for Armani business suits. They preferred to think of themselves as businessmen too. Some even sent their children to private schools. If nothing else, the clean-cut image drew less heat, and now that they were doing bigger deals — hundreds of tons of cocaine or marijuana — they no longer wanted the attention and media coverage they had once courted so assiduously. But old ways die hard. What it came down to was that they needed people like Cal to teach them new tricks of the trade. Instead of a shotgun and a bag of cash, they were dealing with letters of credit and end-user certificates, and these items required expertise. A cargo of cocaine packed in cans of Colombian tuna has to be shipped impeccably; nothing must seem out of the ordinary because there's several hundred million dollars at stake. And because crooked experts in international shipping are not a dime a dozen, Cal knew he was needed, knew he was not as expendable as they tried to make him feel. So when he heard outright hostility in Lenny's voice, he was not particularly troubled.

"We wanna meet with you, Broeker," Lenny snarled. "Right fucking *now!*"

*When pursued by an enemy, retreat before you turn to attack and you will regain the element of surprise.*

"I'm busy," Cal told him. "I got a lot of stuff to do today." They had no idea where he was anyway.

"You better fucking get your ass down here right now, or we're gonna come after you and fucking drag you down here by the hair! You fucking hear me?"

"I'm on my fucking way," Cal snapped, hanging up with an angry *thwack!*

He marched into the bathroom to finish shaving, then had a better idea. Within five minutes, he'd shaved his head bald and formed his beard into a goatee. He ran down to the garage.

Not twenty minutes later, he arrived at the bar where Lenny and Stack waited, looking like Beelzebub in one hell of a bad mood.

"So! I'm fucking here, boys!" Cal said, towering over them. "And I don't have any fucking hair, so if you're gonna pull me by something, it's gonna have to be my fucking prick — and for that, you're gonna have to be fucking sure about what you're doing, because there'll be goddamn war before I go quietly. How 'bout that, motherfucker?"

Here are two bikers ready to hog-tie Cal and take him up north for a little ride, but inside a minute they're not just tame, they're actively trying to pacify *him.*

"We were kidding you," Lenny protested. "It was a joke."

"Am I laughing?" Cal asked.

The fact that he was there proved to the bikers that he couldn't be heat. They hadn't been joking, of course, and if Cal had been a cop UC, he would have terminated his cover, closed that particular operation. No UC in his right mind would have shown up alone after a call like that. It might have been foolhardy, but it achieved the dual objectives of increasing biker confidence in Cal and safeguarding the project he was working on. This project was to add as much information as possible to police data on the biker gangs in Canada, whose prominence in the underworld was becoming increasingly blatant as they helped the Russians take over more and more of the Italian Mafia's turf.

In March 2001, a series of coordinated dawn raids by 2,000 policemen in Quebec and Ontario had virtually every biker in the two provinces in jail. The main purpose of the raids was, however, to seize the gangs' records, download the C drives on their computers, and analyze these drives for details of biker business. Ironically, and as much as they liked to perpetuate their traditional outlaw image, the bikers did business like anybody else. They had to: organized crime is *organized*. Cal was assured that if anything relating to him showed up on the computer disks, it would be wiped off before they were handed back so his identity would remain secret. And there was one immediate payoff: the Daytimer of one clubhouse's computer showed a meeting scheduled with the gang's accountants, who were flying in from Amsterdam in a few days. Police were there at the airport to greet them.

THE PSYCHIATRIST GAVE Cal a clean bill of mental health for the next LOA. This time, the target was Larry Miller, who ran what was reckoned to be the biggest smuggling operation in the United States. Miller had been arrested only once, for armed bank robbery in Chicago back in the fifties. He'd done ten years for that. Since then, he had proved a slick operator, building a massive business empire, legitimate and otherwise, and amassing millions. He was well connected too. Part Indian, he had ties with reservations on both sides of the border, and he was linked to New York's Genovese crime family. Also, it was believed, he had a relationship going with the Russia Mafiya. The word was that no one fucked with Larry Miller — he was ruthless and didn't hesitate to order executions, kneecappings, leg-breakings, and the like. Both U.S. and Canadian police forces had been after him for years on numerous charges — tax evasion, smuggling, contravening customs-and-excise rules — but he was far too clever to be caught by normal methods. Even if he was caught, he had the best lawyers as well as people to take the fall for him — guys who would plead guilty and do time so he could walk. You don't catch that kind of criminal easily. No one had yet penetrated Miller's operation successfully. But the cops thought that Cal might just stand a chance.

Late winter in 1995 found C. Calvin Broeker working as an established antiques dealer in Montreal. He had leased one floor in a storefront property, Antiquaires Greene, at 1350 Greene Avenue in Westmount, from a business acquaintance, Mr. Gonzalez, another antiques dealer who still had a pair of chattering green parrots and two floors full of furniture and *objets d'art* there. Cal told him to leave the stuff where it was. He knew the guy well enough to confide in him that he wanted a front business — and, hey, the place was perfect as it was. If anyone came by wanting to make a purchase, he'd take a commission. This saved him having to amass stock of his own. Gonzalez couldn't have dreamed of a better tenant; he didn't relish the thought of moving a whole floor of antiques into storage through the Montreal snow, but he needed to lease that space. This way, he got to eat the pie and have it too. Cal liked to make people happy, and it wasn't difficult: you just found out what they most wanted and then gave it to them. Or promised to.

On the third floor was an office-apartment where the two parrots and Cal lived. The whole set-up admirably enhanced his image as a freelance entrepreneur, and more important, it gave those he was trying to impress an address, a place they could go to check that C. Calvin Broeker really existed. A place where they could observe his movements, see who visited him and check whom he visited. It would require so much paperwork, so many permissions, so much aggravation for a cop UC to acquire such elaborate cover that to do it on spec would be out of the question.

The first fish to swim into Cal's net was Tom Habib. A handsome Lebanese Christian in his early thirties, Habib was a peripheral figure with loose criminal connections to the Indians, the bikers, and the Italians. He was a criminal gadfly — a bit of this, a bit of that — and had a matching attention span. Cal first encountered him in Chateaugay, where he'd come looking for Ron Ong. Back then, he was keen to get in on the debenture racket, and word had it that Ong was the man to see. The inscrutable Ron Ong. No one seemed to know where Ong lived, but he'd made it known he could be found in Chateaugay. Habib found Cal instead. Cal cut him a lot of slack, just to see where the man might lead him. He even smuggled a tanker full of pirate gasoline across the border with Habib and then sold it to Elizabeth's gas station. It hadn't really been pirate gasoline, of course. It was normal gasoline, legitimately brought across the border with documentation from Brown's Customs Brokerage. Cal just made it look as if it had been smuggled so that Habib would think of him as someone who knew how to work the border.

Habib had begun calling the cellphone when Cal was still in protective custody in Vermont. He either had various deals or wanted various deals. You had to focus him or all you'd see was a blur of criminal wish-list. By the time he walked into the antiques store in Westmount, Habib had a load of hijacked cigarettes he wanted to get across the border. So Cal reeled him in. Carrying a wire built into a cellphone — the aptly named rat phone — or using a special briefcase fitted with a hidden mike and transmitter that were operated via the handle and catch, Cal was able to record these conversations for his handlers.

Tractor-trailers carrying a million dollars' worth of cigarettes are hijacked all the time. The truck is flagged down, someone points a shotgun at the driver, the load is stolen. That's it. However, it is usually done with some level of complicity from the driver. Complicity is needed, because these days the trailers are all tracked by satellite and rigged with silent radio alarms and other devices to make the small-time thief think twice. The driver has to identify and disarm these devices before the load can be driven away, so his co-operation is indispensable — and it's better to have him a willing accomplice than a reluctant one. That way, things go smoother and everyone is happy. Even so, the cigarettes are off-loaded from the trailer as soon as possible — or the trailer is buried somewhere — which means they have to be sold quickly. The Indians held all the cards in this game, though, because the autonomy of the reservations gave them some measure of security, as did their right to handle tax-free tobacco.

Tom Habib arrived at the antiques store with Jacky Ciotto, a bottom-feeder who had ties to the Italians, though he was far from being a made man. Heavy-set and short, Ciotto wore an open-necked black silk shirt, an outsized gold chain, and a rug that looked like a slice of frizzy-hair pizza. He looked like an extra from "The Sopranos," and he was so thick he could hardly breathe. Habib was positively elegant by comparison, his sultry Arab good looks nicely complemented by a cream designer sweater that had a monogram over the heart. The pair were energized about something, and they unknowingly babbled their complicity in numerous crimes into Cal's wires. The handlers were intrigued. It was clear that Habib and Ciotto were operating on spec for, among others, Larry Miller, trying to find buyers for a weekly diverted load of cigarettes. After much back and forth, Cal got the specifics out of them: DuMaurier filters, at $770 per master case of fifty cartons; a thousand cases, with duty seemingly paid, delivered anywhere in Montreal.

"Who're the players, Tom?" asked Cal.

The two parrots squawked at a private joke.

"People you know," replied Habib helpfully. Then he added, "We'd prefer to deliver them to the rez, though, at Akwesasne. Nice birds." He went over to the cage and strummed its bars.

Focus, focus . . .

"That's not the best place," Cal told him. "I can arrange a place, but I've got to meet the players, see their faces, know who I'm dealing with. . . . Don't do that: the birds don't like it." He also said he was worried about a rip.

Habib understood his concern, reassured him that he'd meet the people involved in good time, and told him to have the money ready to show them. He was about to change the topic when one of the parrots took a vicious bite at his finger.

Habib screamed, "It bit me! It fucking *bit* me!"

"What's your long-term goal here, Tom? Because I've got the companies, the know-how, the credibility to do this kind of thing, but I'm not going to do it for a one-off, fly-by-night operation."

"Flybanite!" the parrots repeated. "Flybanite!"

"Hey," said Jacky Ciotto, "dose fucking birds talk! Tommy, da parrots talk!"

"No, no, Cal," protested Habib. "These are serious people. You set up an operation that works, and we can do four containerloads a day of shit, from the U.S., Panama, South America, Vietnam, and the Middle East. All kinds of shit."

Habib told Cal how impressed he was by his efficiency. The set-up he had with Bulgaria was perfect. He added that his people were comfortable with Cal too, since he lived on the rez — and you had to be connected to do that or the Mohawks would kill you. His business ties had also been checked and were totally legit.

"Can we talk fees?" Habib asked. "How much are we going to make on this the way you'd set it up?"

Cal laughed. "You want me to set everything up and do all the work, and then you want fucking fees?" he said. "What are *you guys* going to do? What's your role? I tell you what, I'll take a commission of ten grand per container, flat fee. The rest is yours, but you collect from your investors, not me."

"Ten grand, ten grande, Tom-tom," said the parrots.

"Okay," said Habib tentatively.

"I'll facilitate everything. I'll set everything up," Cal added. "But you do the work. I'll simply oversee the whole operation, make sure it all works, provide all the documents, et cetera. But you gotta do the legwork. And I want to meet the top guys. I'm not dealing with minions, ware-housemen, runners. I go straight to the top or nothing. I won't give up my antiques business and risk my shipping operation on a bunch of flunkies."

"How soon can you be ready?" Habib wanted to know.

The parrots said, "Breddy-breddy-breddy!"

"Give me two months. I'll be ready by March 1. That's as quick as I can do it. And," Cal added, lowering his voice in a threatening manner, "no monkey business. No loads disappearing, that kinda shit. The Bulgarians don't play around — they just do business. We're tired of playing around, and it's gonna be painful if anyone tries. Understand?"

"You don't know who *we're* dealing with," Habib snapped, indignant at the thinly veiled threat, "but they're serious, dangerous people too. We're tired of shit from the Indians — rips and bullshit. We just want to do straight business, like you. And no monkeying around."

"We both understand that, we're fine," said Cal.

The parrots squawked rudely.

"Maybe Polly wants a cracker. Okay, Cal . . . er . . ." He appeared to have lost his train of thought. "Oh, right! Can you help us with a load next week?" This was something the Crown prosecutor would pick up on, since it was a clear indication that there was no entrapment here: Habib and his people were all set up and ready to go without Cal.

"You don't listen, do you?" Cal replied. "I said *I* will set up the opera-tion, *I* will provide the company, *I* will have end-user certificates from points all over Europe and Canada sent direct to your suppliers. Everything will be done properly because I will do it. Understand? And *that's* gonna take two months. Not a day less."

"Okay," said Habib, going on immediately to his next thought. "Listen, I've been having trouble with the Hell's here. They got a lot of heat around them, and I don't need that. I got containers of hash coming in from the Middle East. Can you deal with it for me?"

"Hashi-hashi," the parrots chorused.

"Maybe Polly wants a hash brownie 'stead of a cracker," Ciotto specu-lated. The birds watched him intently with beady eyes, then cackled, as if deciding he was the stupidest human they'd ever met.

"Don't feed 'em anything, Jacky, okay? They're sensitive," Cal told him. "Jesus, Tom! How many times do I gotta explain it to you? One step at a time. *One!* We're not kids in the schoolyard, are we? Let's do one thing at a time. And before we can do that one thing, I have to set up the company. Got it?"

"Er . . ."

"If not, which part of 'two months' do you not understand?"

The parrots laughed hysterically.

Habib was already onto another thought. Cal wondered how he managed to dress himself in the morning without putting his shoes on his head and brushing his teeth with the toast.

"You will be polite with these people when you meet them, won't you? How much money you gonna need up front?" These were Habib's new thoughts.

"I don't take nothing up front," Cal replied. "Besides, I don't know if I want to work with your people yet. We'll have to see."

"They wanna work with you. You've been okayed. Why do you think I'm here with this offer?" Habib was confused.

"You don't hear good, do you? I said that *I* — meaning me — I don't know whether I want to work with your people or not yet. I'll decide when I meet them."

"I know these guys will love this deal," Habib speculated, looking over at Ciotto. "They're not used to this kind of deal, but they want it, eh?"

"Dey want dis kind of deal," said Ciotto.

"I don't want no buddy-buddy stuff," Cal now told him. "I ain't looking to make new friends — if you know what I'm saying — just profitable business. We all make our own money and remain low profile, okay?"

"Profitable business, make money — it's perfect," echoed Ciotto.

"Mah-mah-mahni," said a parrot dubiously.

"If I can do business with you. *If.*"

This was the old push-me-pull-you routine. One step forward and two steps back. Lead 'em by the nose. There would be no getting out of introducing Cal to the principals, since he'd make it the deal-breaker. People like Habib were not used to dealing with someone who needed persuading. Bad guys tend to leap into the swamp at the first invitation — you don't become a criminal because you're choosy about who you deal with, after all. It served to make Cal all the more appealing, since everyone Habib knew would have stopped listening after hearing they'd make forty grand a day.

"I got a lot of stuff on the go," Habib then said, turning to Ciotto for confirmation.

"Oh, yeah," Ciotto agreed. "Lotta stuff on the go is right, Tommy."

The way Habib told it, you'd think he had several tractor-trailers full of contraband parked out in the street right now, their smokestacks a-puffing away. These boys were bouncing off the walls, they were so excited by all the crimes they were committing, all the hijacked or otherwise purloined stuff they had access to or were stuck with — depending on how you viewed their situation. There was hashish; there was cocaine; there was heroin; there was opium; there were arms and explosives; there was counterfeit; there was a big people-smuggling racket from the Orient; there was alcohol, tobacco, food, agricultural equipment, cars, fertilizer, clothes, bedding, furs, Persian carpets, pillaged antiquities, farm animals, blank passports, credit-card blanks, forged T-bills, a hundred thousand cans of Spam, a million spectacle frames, ten million doses of polio vaccine, and a container of human hair.

"Shit," said Cal, "maybe we should open a department store."

"Have to be a chain of 'em."

"Kwah-kwah," the parrots announced.

A meeting was set with Habib's people for the following Thursday.

Two months wouldn't usually be enough time to obtain the protocols and a go for a police sting. But the handlers had no doubt that this one would fly. And so Project Orienter was born.

### *Thursday, February 8, 1996 — Greene Avenue, Montreal*

Habib and Ciotto were accompanied this time by Jon Blake, a tall, well-built guy in his early thirties whose blond bangs, blue eyes, and sparse moustache gave him the appearance of a college linebacker. Cal locked the store door and led the three upstairs to his office-apartment, where Blake introduced himself as the lead man in the current enterprise. He said he'd worked six years with two different smuggling groups, both on the rez and off, in Canada and the U.S.

"I thought I made it clear," said Cal, wearily interrupting him, "that I wanted to meet the top people in the *new* operation, the one we are discussing, not some junior from an old operation."

The parrots laughed raucously, hopping around their cage.

"What do you mean?" asked Blake defensively. "Jeez! Don't those things ever shut up?"

"The way you dress, man, and your age — you look more like a college jock out for a good time than an international investor moving volume containers of contraband. You think you can play with the tough guys on the rez?"

"That's not fair, Cal," Habib protested. "Jon is well connected. He's got the go-ahead right from the top on this."

"That's my point exactly, Tom: 'the go-ahead from the top.' He's a fucking gofer, not a principal. And if he is a principal, I want proof from the top. Is that fucking clear now?"

The parrots screamed with mirth.

"You're right," Blake told Cal. "I'm gonna arrange it right for you next time."

"If there is a fucking next time."

"Tom and Jacky explained your position to me," Blake continued, "and I understand it. You'll get what you need. So let me explain our system, which is like this: we have moved around eighty plus containers to Akwesasne or Canada per year for the past five years. We got people on our payroll who work both U.S. and Canadian customs and pass the trucks through for us. In the past year alone, we moved around twenty trucks into Canada from the U.S. with this system."

"What about U.S. export control?" Cal wanted to know.

"All set up," Blake replied. "Our people . . . Understand this, Cal, my backers are worth about 30 million each. They're smart people. They know *of* you, but they haven't met you. Except one."

"Jaawwn!" yelled a parrot. "Jawn."

Blake looked over at the cage instinctively, then realized the birds weren't calling him.

"Oh, yeah?" said Cal. "So who are these $30-million men?"

"You know Damien Love," Habib said. "What about Larry Miller?"

"I met Love once, in his warehouse. And I've *heard of* Miller before — in my work with the Leroys and Transcorp."

Damien Love was king of the Indian smugglers, someone wanted badly on both sides of the border.

"Well," said Blake, "both Miller and Love want to start a new system, a better system, and they love the Bulgarian plan."

"Dey love it," Ciotto felt compelled to add. "Dey *love it,* Cal."

"Laaaarh-Cal, laaarhee," one parrot agreed.

"They need a more secure and less expensive method of transportation," Blake continued. "The Indians are always pulling rips. And the customs guys are getting greedy."

"What if one of these customs guys turns over or talks?" Cal asked.

"We'll blow away anyone who fucks with us," Blake stated. "I got the people to do it. Miller and Love got the money to protect themselves. I got the muscle to take care of all of us. You too, Cal."

"Skwaaah, Cal-cal," said one of the parrots.

Cal didn't miss the double entendre here — they'd take care of him or *take care* of him — and he threw in one of his own next. "I can take care of myself. Where do you dump the product in Canada?"

"Miller will explain all this when you see him."

"Who fucking said I want to go any further with this, Jon?" Cal glanced at Habib. "You keep fucking bringing in more people around me, don't you? And I'm alone, as always. Before long you're gonna have fifty guys at these meetings, and I'll still be alone. How many of your people are cops, eh, Jon?"

The parrots seemed excited by this, and repeated, "Kaaarhps, Jaawwnnn. Kaaarhps!"

"Don't worry 'bout that, Cal. These are all connected people with us — Italians, Orientals, Indians. Don't worry 'bout it. Listen, I'll show you how it works. We cross the stuff, right? It goes to a converted factory in Hamilton, Ontario, where a lotta truck traffic is located. The warehouse's got a million square feet, and Larry's installed movable walls so his shipments are hidden the moment they're in. You can't fucking see nothing. It's brilliant."

"How much does this warehouse hold?" Cal asked him.

"Waaaarh-ooo," one parrot announced.

"'Bout thirty full trucks. We drive 'em in, the wall closes, and any law shows up, you can't see nothing. It's brilliant! We use it for cars, drugs, everything. But we can have it only for this if you want, Cal."

"When can I see this building?"

"Any time you want," Blake replied. "Any time."

"I'm gonna want to meet with Miller and Love," Cal said, "and go over all the existing and the historical operations. If I gotta disclose my company's secrets, I wanna know yours, okay? This way I can arrange both existing and new operations in concert, see? You probably got systems and people as part of your old operation I can use in the new one, don't you?"

"I think we're ready to do that," Blake said. "When do you wanna start? Oh, and Larry wants to do some test runs with you before we go full bore. That okay?"

"Don't fucking push me, Jon," Cal told him. "I will develop the plan for you. It'll be like this: a Bulgarian company'll place the order from an existing Canadian registered company to a supplier in the States. It'll go in-bond to Canada, marked outbound to Bulgaria, and then it'll be received in Bulgaria empty, see? I will take care of all the internal arrangements, customs, et cetera. Understand?"

"Jaawwn-bum," suggested a parrot.

"I don't feel we been fair with you on the money offer," Blake said. "Seeing as you're the man on this deal, we wanna offer you twelve thousand U.S. on all containers for each shipment. Okay?" He paused, then said, "How much is a parrot like that?"

You didn't buy Cal Broeker like this.

"They're not for sale. Listen, Jon, I'll do my part," Cal said. "And | 145 we'll see what expenses develop as of the first load. We'll discuss the fee on volume and risk once the operation is totally packaged. Okay?"

"Yeah," Blake replied. "But we're gonna want you to set up an office in Toronto, as well as Montreal. Toronto's our biggest market to date. Also, can you help us find a safe warehouse in Montreal?"

"Who's gonna shoulder the expense of this set-up?"

"I tink," Ciotto said, "dat until you prove dis is really gonna work, and we all feel good wid one another, it'll have to be your problem. Right, Tommy?"

"Tommy-tommy-too," the parrots told each other.

"That goes for the offices only," Habib announced. "We're gonna pick up the warehouse, aren't we, Jon?"

"Yeah, agreed," said Blake. "We do the warehouse, you do the office and equipment. Okay? When you're ready to move to Toronto, Cal, you'll let me know, and I'll set the meetings and the tour. I didn't mean I wanted *those* parrots. How much do they cost in a pet store?"

"Can you be ready week after next?" Habib wanted to know.

"Don't push, Tommy," Blake told him. "We agreed to let things develop step by step, remember?"

"I gotta be in Bulgaria," Cal said, "for a period over the next two weeks. And I don't plan to be ready much before the end of March or the first of April. Those are rare parrots. You can't buy them here."

"Yeah?" Ciotto was trying to impress Blake. "We'll wait, den. 'Cause everyone wants dis done right. But we don't wanna wait too long, do we, Jon?"

Blake ignored him, saying to Cal, "In order to keep everyone moving in the right direction, get to me as soon as you can to look at the warehouse in Toronto. And find something safe for us here in Montreal in the next couple of weeks. Get your offices and equipment set up, your

Bulgarian people onside, and let's roll in April. Yeah?"

"Sounds good," Cal said. "But keep the date open. Listen, guys, I gotta run now."

"Fuk-kyu-fukkukoo," one of the parrots said in summation.

"You an' me both," Habib told him, standing. "But I'll see you tomorrow, okay?"

Cal took them down to the street. He knew where they'd parked, but he walked in the opposite direction. Habib, Ciotto, and Blake followed a few steps, then realized their car was the other way. Everyone turned and walked back to the car, where Cal said his goodbyes and took off.

Parked opposite the store on Greene Avenue was a plumber's van that held a couple of police photographers who now had pictures of the bad guys, head-on as well as both left and right profile.


CAL DIDN'T MEET HABIB the following day because he had ostensibly left for Bulgaria. The next time they spoke, it was by telephone.

When the familiar warbling ring sounded, Cal muted the TV, threw a beach towel over the parrots (who thought night had fallen and instantly went to sleep), grabbed the cellphone, and ran over to his fridge, hauling out a stack of TV dinners and plunging his head where they'd been in the freezer before he answered it.

"Hey, Tommy," he said. "Whassup-up, man-an?"

There was a great echo in that freezer.

"Jesus," said Habib. "Where the fuck are you? Up a mountain or something?"

Cal left a few moments for Habib to hear the freezer's motor throbbing before he answered. "I'm in-nin Sofia-ia, so reception-eption ain't so-wo great-ate. Can you hear okay-yay?" He was speaking into the frosted wall now, holding the phone down at the far end, where he leaned it against an ice tray.

Habib said the line was terrible, so he'd make it brief. Could Cal make a meeting on February 18?

"I'll do-oo my best-est, buddy-uddy."

He'd call if he couldn't make it.

After killing the phone, Cal shut the fridge door, shivering, and went back to the couch, turning up the TV and continuing to watch CNN. His curtains were drawn night and day, and the only light he had was on a timer that turned the store lights on and off too. The store was locked up, and a sign saying C. Calvin Broeker was out of town on business hung below the sign that said Closed. He was bored out of his mind watching the box all day and night, but he had few other options. One false move and he just might run into Blake, Ciotto, or Habib, or someone would see his shadow moving around the third-floor apartment. The only way he could be in Bulgaria without leaving Montreal was to barely stray from that couch, living on whatever he could prepare with his stale or dwindling food supplies (when, that is, there was enough daylight to cook by but not enough to betray his shadowy presence).

*February 18, 1996, 11:43 a.m. —*
*Moe's Deli & Bar, Fairview, Pointe Claire, Quebec*
Cal met with Tom Habib and Jacky Ciotto, who were so eager to know the results of the Bulgarian trip that they bobbed around holding their peckers until Cal told them it had been successful.

"But there's still a fair bit of work to be done setting up the infrastructure on this side. Organization like that's gonna require some thought and a chunk of money — if it's gonna support the kind of orders and volume we're talking about."

"What's needed if I want to go over with you next time?" asked Habib. "What do I have to get?"

Cal leaned over and grabbed his passport, which had been laying face up in case anyone wanted to check on his international mobility when he went to the john. He flicked through the pages until he found his Bulgarian visas and stamps. The dates on them were illegible.

"You gotta get a visa, Tom, like this." He showed the Bulgarian stamps to both men. "And you gotta be a straight shooter, because my people *are* the law over there. You make one mistake, fuck around just once, and — *zap!* — you're history, pal. My people are into this deal big time. Big commitments and big bucks. They don't want no mistakes; they don't want to be fucked around. So, Tom, I hope you're not bullshitting me about the other people involved with you."

"All da guys is ready to meet wid you," said Ciotto, "and get started on dis deal right away. Ain't I right, Tommy?"

"Jesus, not again!" sighed Cal. "I told you guys it was gonna take time. Well, I'm still not ready, and I won't be ready for at least three or four weeks. Can you just try to remember that for another month, eh?"

"Cal," Habib said quietly, looking sheepish, "Jacky an' me have a little problem. You see, we sold the deal so well to our people that Larry and Jon are now shoving our feet to the fire to get something going right away. So anything you need that we can set up, we'll do it, okay? Anything."

"Yeah," Ciotto added, "also I got some casino guys wanna talk wid you about machines and money, 'kay?"

"Shit," Cal told them, "if you really wanna fast-track this at such a speed, we're gonna have to use the old system and warehouse in Toronto as the launch vehicle while we're still developing the new Montreal system. Get me?"

"Dis is what we want!" Ciotto declared triumphantly. "When can you get down to Toronto and into the warehouse?"

"Relax, Jacky," said Cal. "Next week's the earliest I can do it. I have the antique business and other commitments to attend first."

"Oh, man!" Habib wailed. "Please! We're desperate to start. Come on! All the people we presented it to are in complete agreement that it's gonna work. Why can't you speed things up? Please!"

"For Christ's sake, Tom! As I've stated since the fucking beginning, it's gonna be slow but *professional*. Now here you are once again, pushing me to speed things up! You're driving me nuts! This is why I wanna meet the decision-makers — you guys just don't understand the process needed to make this work long term and secure. They do."

"We can do dose meetings when we go to Toronto, right, Tommy?" Ciotto said.

"I'll work this week on the Montreal office," said Cal, "and on the Bulgarian bridge. And we'll see if Toronto is in the cards for next week."

"You're right," Habib stated humbly. "We don't follow all the technical stuff you're giving us. But I'm worried the other guys will kick us out of the picture once they meet you, see? Can you protect us as part of your group?"

"No," replied Cal. "I work alone on this side. The only person you might meet, in the future, is a representative of Bulgarian interests. But he's gonna be around only at a later stage."

"Dat's fair," Ciotto decided, pursuing this theme of fairness. "We just wanna be secure for our money, is all."

"Why don't you make yourselves part of the ongoing operation in Toronto?" Cal suggested.

"We are. But I wanna be a part of this too. In Montreal."

"Let's see what you give me," said Cal, "and *then* we'll discuss it, okay? But I thought I made it clear in the meeting with Jon that I did not want any partners."

"Can you set up both the transportation and the resealing operation for the in-bond merchandise?" Habib wanted to know.

"I'm gonna work on it this week."

"We wanna do four trucks of milk to start," said Habib, meaning liquor. "As tests. They go okay, we move on to tobacco from Larry. We're in touch with other groups operating on the rez," he explained, "and we're gonna offer them this as soon as it's proven. Okay?"

"We got friends," said Ciotto, "dat wanna know 'bout money laundering. And dere's hash, too."

"No drugs," stated Cal grimly, wondering if Ciotto was catching the short-attention-span virus from his partner. "No drugs at all — at least, not right now."

"I got a powerful friend," Habib said, "down in Grenada. He wants to meet and discuss bringing rum to Canada. And arms. The guy's heavy into casinos too. And he's worked with a Canadian MP" — he frowned, as if thinking, then corrected himself — "or some high-ranking government official, on the potential sale of Canadian-made armoured rocket launchers."

"Yeah?" Cal tried not to seem interested. "You got a lotta friends, Tommy."

"Yeah. He said he needed help with contacts to sell these armoured rockets" — arms were clearly not Habib's forte — "as he's got a customer in Africa wants to buy."

"That right?"

"Just keep it in mind, okay?"

"Uh-huh."

"I wanna call you twice a day for updates, okay?"

"No way, José," Cal told him. "I don't need that kind of aggravation. If there's something you need to know, I'll tell you."

The meeting ended at 12:38.


A DAY LATER, Habib called. He was worried about being cut out and asked for protection again. Then he pushed for a meeting with Cal and Jon Blake, which Cal declined, saying he was too busy.

Habib called again the next day.

"Jon's excited," he said. "He wants an update on your trip, and he wants to set up meetings for Toronto. Can he meet with you on Wednesday, the twenty-first?"

"Listen, Tom," said Cal, "I'm extremely busy and I've got no time. Is that clear?"

"We'll come anyway and wait."

"Which part of 'no time' don't you understand, Tom?"

"Jon's gotta leave for a few days and he needs to talk."

"Shit. Okay, Tommy. Get back to me and confirm a specific time, all right?"


### February 23, 1996, 10:27 a.m. — 1350 Greene Avenue, Montreal

The Dynamic Duo showed up as Jon Blake's entourage and made it clear why anyone would want to edge them out of any deal: they drove you nuts. They drove you all the way to nuts and back. Blake looked tired of them already, and the day had only just begun. Dressed all in black, with a black-and-white-checked sweater, he had clearly just come from an appointment with his hairdresser — the blond bangs had bounce and definition — and he looked more like he was about to audition for a Monkee's bio-pic than break the law.

In between interruptions from Habib and Ciotto, he and Cal discussed the work that had been done to date on the project, and Blake didn't mind saying he was very happy with it.

"In fact, I'm ready to set up the Toronto visit," he announced.

"Pretty-pretty-preeaaaargh!" said the green parrots.

"You're gonna have all the principals lined up to meet me there, aren't you, Jon?" Cal asked.

"Larry and Damien," Blake said, pausing. "They don't go into Canada, but they'll meet you in New York . . . at Larry's house."

"They *don't go into Canada?* Why the fuck not, Jon? Why don't they go into Canada?"

"On one of his trips, Larry was asked to leave by Canada Customs. He's afraid of a set-up if he goes to Canada."

"Well," Cal told him, smiling coldly, "*I'm* afraid of a set-up if I go to the States. That's the problem."

"Don't be concerned, Cal. That's their turf. Larry would be informed of any investigation happening that side. Remember what I said the last time we met? Larry has people in the right places."

"What if *he's* setting me up, Jon?"

"I understand your concerns, Cal, but we deal straight."

"*You* might, that I believe, but what if *they* don't? How would you even know?"

"Listen," said Blake. "Larry started me out in business. I been with him since I was a kid. Now I'm tight with him, Cal. I'm part of the inner circle, which is just me, Larry, Damien Love, and Nick Miller, Larry's son. We're all tight. No one does anything without discussing it with the other three, understand?"

"I'll give you the benefit of the doubt, Jon. No more, though, understand?"

"I discussed the meeting you had four years ago with Damien Love," Blake said suddenly. "It was about money conversion."

"Yeah? So what?" Cal asked, masking the fear that had streamed through his veins the moment Love's name came up. Damien Love was about as well connected on the rez as any man not a full-blooded Mohawk could hope to be.

"They wanna talk about that again, as well as the new venture."

"Oh?"

"The reason being," said Blake, "that there was a falling-out between the Miller-Love group and Cookie Lamoure in regard to money lost on the racetrack in Malone."

"Doesn't surprise me," said Cal, recalling Cookie Lamoure, who gave the expression "two-faced, double-dealing con man" a whole new meaning.

"Rip-rip-ripper," said a green parrot.

"Damien was impressed with what you had to offer four years ago from what he recalls of the meeting. And he's ready to go with this new tobacco-alcohol deal. Listen," said Blake, lowering his voice and looking Cal straight in the eyes, "if you want, I can give you the total discounting and money-laundering operation for Love, Miller, the companies New York ATM and LBL, *and* the Russians Larry's working with."

"What Russians?"

"Raaa-raaasha!" a parrot decided.

"Larry's in the process of setting up a $22-million casino in Moscow" — Blake let this sink in before continuing — "with the Russian Mafiya. He's feeding this deal from the rez businesses. That's why he wants to increase his cash flow, see? To support the Russian deal and, long term, get out of the tobacco business altogether."

"Baaa-baakoh!" announced one of the parrots, then they both laughed.

"Why you telling me this now?" Cal wanted to know. He felt he was being suckered, and he wanted to make clear what he felt.

"Big-boy, big-big-boy," a parrot replied.

"Don't those birds ever shut up? . . . At our last meeting," said Blake frankly, "you were critical of my status. I just wanted to reassure you that I could, and *will*, place you in the centre of the money boys. That's all."

"What are the chances of meeting with them next week, Jon? February 28?"

"They're ready when you are, Cal. As long as Larry and Damien stay in the States."

Cal then gave Blake his proposed agenda, and they discussed various items on it.

"What I'd like to do," Blake next said, "is, after the meet with Larry and Dame on Wednesday, you and I take the Cornwall train to Toronto so we can discuss in depth what we're doing here — the whole operation. Can you do that, Cal?"

"Cal-calbro," a parrot stated.

If possible, Cal wanted to avoid situations where his handlers couldn't monitor his conversations. They would leave him open to suggestions of entrapment when the case went to court, and the cops didn't like him doing it. So he said, "I was planning to leave on my own terms, Jon. I got other business to attend, and I was going to take a suite of rooms in one of the Toronto hotels so we could hold all our meetings discreetly in one location."

"Hey," said Habib, who'd been visibly on edge ever since Cal and Blake had started talking more quietly, "why don't we all drive down together? You know, meet at some location and just all jump in a car together. And drive. Down. How 'bout that?"

"Yeah," Ciotto chimed in. "Good idea, Tommy. We's all drive down. Together. In a nice motor."

"Tommy-tom," one of the birds called out.

"No offence, boys," said Blake, "but I'd like to talk to Cal alone. Okay? Tell ya what: how about you two drive, so we have a car there? A *nice* car too. And if I can work it out with Cal, we'll do the train and meet you there."

It wasn't just raining on the boys' parade now — Jon Blake was *pissing* all over the thing. Both of them had faces like slapped asses.

"You don't realize how much money we're talking about," Blake continued, rubbing salt into the wounds, "with the laundering *alone*. Forget the cubes and liquid. I just need some time to explain it all to Cal, and the train would be perfect. Perfect!"

"Puffette-puffette," agreed the birds.

Blake then confided that he hadn't filed with the IRS in two years, and badly needed to rearrange his profile before he got caught. He had to get on the books to justify all the property he'd acquired recently — as well as all the property he was about to acquire.

"You wanna take care of that, Jon," Cal told him reproachfully. "That tax shit'll get you every time, man."

"Tasshit, tasssss-hit," agreed the birds.

"Yeah," Blake admitted, changing the topic. "Listen, I had time over the past two weeks to meet with all the people you suggested I align with, and I explained the project. I can't tell you, Cal — they were both so excited and optimistic about it."

"Good."

Cal noted that like most criminals, Blake occasionally remembered to talk in code, in case they were being taped. It might sound ludicrous, but in court a good defence lawyer would make much of such statements as evidence that Miller and Love were not the real principals.

"Lovey-dovey," cooed the parrots.

"Yeah," Blake continued, "they think the potential success of a legitimate cover for the diversion is fucking incredible. I mean, they been pumping hundreds of containers across over the years, and they always *wanted* to do it this way. They just never had an opportunity before. So they're real keen, Cal. Real keen." He looked down, thinking, then said, "Oh, yeah. Larry wanted to speak to you about Bulgaria, as he realizes you spent a year or so there, and when you came back you had a Bulgarian bank account, which for a grocery man is kinda funny."

"Funny?" Cal glared at him, wondering what this was about.

"I mean, not funny but a bit . . . odd," Blake explained. "Not odd to us, I mean, but odd from your business point of view."

"You don't know nothing about my fucking business, Jon."

"Don't take it wrong, Cal. Anyway, Larry wanted me to ask if your papers were still valid in Bulgaria?"

It was a trick question. Miller was trying to find out through Blake if Cal had really been in Bulgaria, and he clearly knew that a Bulgarian visa was good for a few years.

"Yeah," Cal told him, ice in his voice, "they're still valid, Jon. What I'd like to know is how the fuck did you guys get banking information on me?"

Habib confessed. "Hey," he said, "we just all like to know who is who in our group, Cal. And I stood for you."

"I don't need you to do anything for me, Tommy. Not *anything* — got it?"

"We'll also want to discuss the exchange-conversion idea," Blake said to defuse the tension. "Danny Surprise is in the process of opening a new office in Massena."

Surprise was another Indian smuggler working with Miller, but Blake meant that his people were opening the office.

"He needs advice," Blake continued, "and a strong connection in the Canadian banks."

"Cal is able to do that," said Habib. "Right, Cal?"

"Depending what is needed," Cal replied. "And as long as it's not illegal."

"We just want a big money machine to protect our new ventures and profits," Blake explained.

"How much could I guarantee my contacts in the banks?" asked Cal. "On a weekly basis."

"With Love, Miller, and everyone, about five hundred to one mill Canadian."

"Guaranteed?"

"I'll have to work on this," Blake said. "I just know that Cookie is running about five hundred per week without any competition. So if you have the best program, and you're part of the group . . . You get my figures?"

"No," Cal told him. "I need *absolute* guarantees. Understand this, Jon: we have gotta be absolutely correct and do class work. *Always*. On *everything* we do. Okay?"

"Dat's why we wanna get you in wid Larry," Ciotto announced, as if it was his first thought in ten minutes. "He needs someone to be *direct* wid his people in dis operation. Ain't dat right, Jon?"

"I think," Cal said, taking a piss on the parade himself, "that Larry didn't make millions being indirect with his people, did he? He's as direct as he needs to be. He certainly don't need me as far as direct is concerned — not in this operation or any other."

Ciotto looked beseechingly at Blake, who said, "Right on, Cal. But now we have the least options for him he's ever had, and he wants this to happen."

"What's the rest of the Toronto agenda gonna be?" Cal inquired.

The more he could get Blake to state for the record, the better the case would be. But Blake merely said, "It looks *great,*" adding that he'd work on the Miller meeting for Wednesday, and then the trip to Toronto.

"So," Cal asked him, "we look at the warehouse locations and meet the people on Thursday?"

"Yeah," Blake replied. Then he added, "Ya know, I *like* the hotel suite idea. Should impress the shit outta some of our people." He glanced over at Ciotto.

"Some of my contacts won't do da hotel ting," Ciotto announced to set the record straight. "Will you go to dem, Cal?"

"It depends," Cal replied. "But I don't think so. I just won't deal with them."

Ciotto protested: "Dey just don't like to be outta their areas."

"Poor things! I'm certainly way the hell outta *mine,* Jacky."

"I'll see what I can do to arrange a full two days," Blake said. "Would you consider living in Toronto, Cal, instead of Montreal? 'Cause I feel the major operations are gonna be based there. And Buffalo-Massena. For now, at least."

"Money," Cal replied, to make himself appear cautious, "car, and so on. I got rooms here, you know what I'm saying? But we'll talk, Jon."

"Yeah. Think about the train with me on Wednesday, Cal. Okay?"

Cal smiled at him. The meeting was over.

### Wednesday, February 28, 1996

Tom Habib and Jacky Ciotto met Cal at the Best Western motel in Cornwall, Ontario. They were driving a white Lincoln Continental, and Cal climbed into the back seat. It was 7 a.m. precisely.

"Nice car, Jacky," he said.

"I always get a nice set of wheels," said Ciotto, happily. "You *gotta* in dis business."

"Hey, Cal," Habib said hoarsely. "What did you do last night?"

"He means 'who' did you do?" Ciotto explained.

"We're ecology-minded," Habib announced, "so we shared a girl."

There followed the lengthy saga of how they lured a stripper back to their hotel room from the tits-and-ass bar, ostensibly to dance for them privately.

"Glad you had a good time," Cal said, privately rolling his eyes after the two had finished their tale, which they recited in excruciating detail. This pair made it easy for him to do his job. They belonged in the zoo, though, not the jail.

Next they discussed the weather, the meeting they were going to, and Larry Miller. Evidently, in the Moscow casino deal, Larry was in partner- ship with Chuck Norris — the actor and martial artist — as well as with the Russian Mafiya.

Ciotto was feeling expansive after his bestial night. "Da whole fucking world is a mafia," he said, "and we're all in it."

"So are your Italian pals in it?" Cal asked him.

"We're connected wid all different groups." He caught Cal's eye in the rear-view mirror, then, visibly bloating with optimism, said, "Ya know, Cal, dis company's gonna lead to big tings, real big tings. I *feel* it. Here." He smacked his chest.

"That's indigestion, Jacky," Cal said.

"Hey, Cal?" Habib asked, leaning back over the passenger seat. "You think I could introduce the Bulgarians to this friend of mine from Atlanta?"

"Sure, Tom. They'll fly over here from Sofia any fucking time just to meet a friend of Tom Habib's."

"No, I'm serious, Cal." Habib tried to make his face more serious, without much luck. "He sets up lap-dance bars and strip clubs, this friend of mine."

"I'm sure they'll be on the next fucking plane, Tommy."

"What I was thinking was I could do this over in Bulgaria. You know, a few classy joints."

"You ever see a classy joint where some chick is wobbling her knockers over the clientele's faces? It ain't classy by definition, is it?"

"You know what I mean, Cal, I—"

"What do you mean, Tommy?" Cal cut in. "You think they ain't got strip clubs in Bulgaria? That no one there is capable of dreaming up a place where overpriced liquor meets overpriced tits and ass? Don't be fucking naive!"

"No," Habib tried to defend himself, "I just thought that—"

"No, you didn't, Tommy. You didn't think at all. You're just hustling me again, and I told you to cut it out or I'll cut *you* out. Understand?"

"Boys, boys!" Ciotto said. "You's ruining the drive. We's all friends here. Let's keep it friendly, okay?"

They crossed the border into New York State uneventfully, and by 7:30 a.m., they were in Massena, where they pulled up at a truck stop, taking a table with six chairs at the back. Cal gave the waitress his order, then he went to the washroom, where he broke the seal on a liquid battery that powered the wire transmitter hidden in his coat. This was the first time Cal had worn a wire. He considered them too great a risk: they were bulky and easy to detect with a pat-down or a scanner. And the deniability factor with a wire was zilch. What were you going to explain it away as? "Somebody must have left it there. It isn't mine . . ." No, they found a wire on you, you were a dead man. On the rez, particularly; the handlers listening in would never make it in time to rescue him. But this wire was a state-of-the-art device developed by U.S. Customs, which wanted to try it out. It resembled a circuit board, not that this would have done much good if it were found. But Cal, endlessly inventive where his continued well-being was at stake, had come across a pamphlet from Microsoft on circuit boards, and he'd placed that alongside the new wire in an envelope addressed to Microsoft's customer-relations department. If the wire were discovered, he'd at least have a somewhat plausible explanation for its presence: his circuit board was malfunctioning, and he was supposed to mail it back for a refund.

The liquid battery had to be cracked open for the wire to begin operating, and such batteries were good for only forty-five minutes to an hour. Cal had to judge the timing just right. He didn't want to call attention to himself by going to the john at Larry Miller's place, and he also wanted to get Jon Blake on record regarding some specifics of their operation. He was cutting it fine, he knew, but his options were not that extensive.

Cal was back in his seat when Blake arrived at 7:42, looking very nervous. His tight buddies in the inner circle had clearly impressed upon him that much was riding on this meeting, and that any fuck-ups would be his fault.

"I'm real worried about the truck bonding," he told Cal, "and the legal procedure in regard to licences and the rest."

"Don't concern yourselves with small details, Jon," Cal told him. "Just KISS it, you know? Keep It Simple and Short. And allow me to do a test run with the op you already have."

"Larry's gonna want to know what you're bringing to the table, Cal."

"*Me.* I'm bringing me." Cal paused, then sprang the trap: "Jon, you think we could use the customs plan you outlined at our previous meeting?"

"Maybe."

"Just explain it again so I'm clear on all the details."

"Okay, but quick. We're late."

Thus, unaware he was even doing it, Jon Blake began transmitting via satellite to the U.S. Customs microwave receiver near Buffalo. His first transmission, appropriately, outlined the basic details of Larry Miller's smuggling operation.

"We buy alcohol and tobacco from various manufacturers, take it to a special border location, and then run it across during the midnight shift. We got *two* customs agents on that shift, guys we pay to turn a blind eye and make sure the trucks get through. Last time we used this system, in December of '95, we did between twenty-five and twenty-seven trucks per day."

"I want more information on this," Cal told him, "I can contact you for it later."

"You know," Blake confided, "this was always a short-term operation. I don't trust it. I also don't run it myself."

"Here." Cal pushed him a folder of Bulgarian shipping documents. "Take a look at these."

"We gotta go to Larry's now," Blake said, standing.

He had a brand-new four-wheel-drive Cherokee parked outside — loaded, British racing green, tan leather interior — and Cal climbed into it next to him.

"I'm still worried about the resealing of the trucks," Blake told him, making it clear that he did not understand much, if anything, about container shipments.

They turned off the main highway onto a rural sideroad, and after about a minute, they came to what looked like a farmhouse that had been converted to a mom-and-pop store or a restaurant. It was flanked by a big old barn on the wall of which, in faded green paint, you could just about make out the legend: Club 37. Blake turned into the driveway and parked around the back of the store. Over a side door hung a small sign saying Larry's Place.

"So, this must be Larry's place," said Cal, wondering if Blake could

see the humour in it.

He couldn't. "Yeah," he replied. "It's like a private club."

"Looks pretty public to me."

"Well, it ain't. You're invited, you come. You ain't, you stay the fuck away."

Inside, sitting in a rear bar area, drinking at 8 a.m., were four men and a woman. Indians, mostly, Cal decided at a glance. Tom Habib slithered out of nowhere and steered Cal up to the winner of the Mafioso Stereotype Pageant semi-finals. Appearing as more of an appendage to the bar than propping it up, the man was sixtyish, stocky, around five-eight, with a gut that a horse could have slept in. He was wearing a golf shirt unbuttoned, a gold chain as thick as his pinkie, a rug resembling a slab of fudge, and a cigar that could have been the last smouldering spar of that bridge back to decency he'd burned long ago.

"This is Dick Fanzetti," Habib announced. "He's got interests in the Vegas operations."

For a moment, Cal thought that Habib had got his name wrong, that he was being introduced to Larry Miller as a Dick Fanzetti. He was about to set the record straight when the man asked him: "You been to Vegas?"

"No." Clearly *this* was Dick Fanzetti. "That where you live?"

"I gotta place there," said Fanzetti in an after-hours growl. "I gotta place here too."

"Food's real cheap in Vegas, Cal," Habib announced, for no apparent reason. He was nervous around Fanzetti, Cal realized.

"I lose five hundred grand a week on fucking food," Fanzetti stated enigmatically.

"I . . . er, I meant in the restaurants, Dick."

"So did I. I own a few fucking restaurants there, dat's why I lose five hundred grand a week."

"Freebies to high rollers," Cal explained to Habib, rolling his eyes at Fanzetti.

He said, "Nah. High rollers, I get it back. It's fucking low rollers are the problem . . ."

"Low rollers! That's good, Dick!" Habib laughed for an unnecessarily long time.

"Shut the fuck up," Fanzetti ordered, chuckling to himself, then letting Cal in on the joke. "Don't Tommy here look like the lowest roller you ever saw?"

"Just wish he'd roll the other way sometimes," said Cal, winking at Fanzetti.

Then Nick Miller arrived. Tall, slim, in his late twenties, Nick had classic Indian dark good looks and bright, sparkling eyes. You wanted to ask him, "What's a nice boy like you doing in a dump like this?"

They all moved to a table at the opposite end of the room. Only too aware of his battery's brief lifespan, Cal knew he had to work fast without being too obvious about it.

"I just want to go over with you what I've been told by Jon," he said to Nick after introductions had been made. "So's we're all up to speed and talking the same language, okay?"

"Sure," Nick replied.

Cal went through the basic points of the operation as they had been outlined to him by Jon, and then he asked Nick if this was accurate.

"Yeah, I'm aware of all that. Uh-huh, I'm ready to supply the group with product from five different suppliers," he told Cal. "*As long as* you're ready to name me as the rep of your company in the U.S."

"I don't think that will be a problem," Cal replied, taken a little by surprise. "I'm gonna need a working proposal from you."

"'Kay," Nick agreed. "I'll draft one and fax it to you in Montreal. And," he said cannily, "I'll need one from you too. And I'd like a meeting with you on March 4."

"Too soon," Cal told him, to slow things down. "I'm not gonna be ready by then."

Prompted by Dick Fanzetti, with whom he seemed very close, tight, Nick Miller had Cal run through the major points of his proposed system, from point of pickup to point of diversion.

"Both of us is also concerned about our legal position," Fanzetti said when Cal had finished. "We wanna know, uh—"

"We want to be clear," Nick cut in, nodding at Dick, "where we stand legally on this."

"You gotta speak to your people about that," replied Cal, shaking his head. "I'm not your fucking lawyer, you know." He said it smiling, though. "That's gotta come from someone who knows precisely your exposure in every different area. See?"

"Fair enough," Nick decided. "Could you go over the Bulgarian side of the operation for us? Just so's we both know what the other knows."

"Yeah, go tru Bulgaria," Fanzetti agreed. "We don't want no secrets between friends, do we?"

Cal went through the details of the Bulgarian part of the operation, drawing on his experiences with Transcorp and Arroway to flesh out what would otherwise have been a series of international shipping and trade protocols. If he said so himself — and he did — it was more convincing than it even needed to be.

"Will the Bulgarian market handle legit products too?" Fanzetti asked. He'd warmed right up to Cal.

"Course it will, Dick."

"Then I got something for you!" He hauled himself up and — with surprising agility, considering the mare's nest of a gut he was carrying — darted into another room, returning to the table seconds later bearing a bale of blue denim. He peeled off the top pair of jeans and flung them into Cal's lap.

"Made in the USA," he said proudly. "One hundred thou of 'em at two bucks a pair. You can't go wrong."

Cal felt the fabric and inspected the style and stitching, then told Fanzetti: "I got cheaper pairs coming from Canada."

Fanzetti, like most older Americans, still imagined Europe as it was during the immediate post-war period of pro-American euphoria: jeanless, stocking-less, deprived of candy. Of the old Soviet Union, he had but a narrow, propagandized view: peasants straining under the yoke of tyranny, yearning for freedom in the form of Coca-Cola and rock music. Presumably, Fanzetti didn't get to accompany Larry on his business trips — didn't get to see that the world had moved on, that the peasants of Bulgaria, for instance, now strained under the yoke of a mafiocracy run out of Moscow. But Coca-Cola and American music were in plentiful supply. As were blue jeans, a fact that Cal tried explaining to Fanzetti, but he wasn't listening.

"I can let you have these samples with a pro forma," he said. "Then we see how it goes."

Nick Miller came to Cal's rescue — perhaps deliberately — by bringing up the subject of tracking beepers, or sensors, concealed in container loads. This had been raised a number of times already, and it seemed to concern them deeply.

"If you're being investigated," Cal told them, "I would worry. I can only speak for my own people, but we are *not* under investigation."

"Nor are we," snapped Nick. "If we were, we'd know about it."

"But I don't know *who* you are," Cal retorted angrily. "I came here to meet Larry Miller, is all I know, and I don't fucking see him, do you? How do I know you're not cops? I wanna know just who exactly you guys are."

"My father has cancer," Nick said in a tone that suggested Larry had a cold. "He just got out of hospital after the biopsy, so he's not feeling that good. And" — he looked Cal straight in the eyes — "we've got our concerns too. We've got concerns about *you*. Like, who the fuck are you?"

So much for Tom Habib's bullshit about how the Miller people had approved him already. Cal scowled at Habib, then delivered his standard bio — a grocer's story — and threw his wallet onto the table, saying, "Look through it if you want. Check everything out. Phone anyone. I've nothing to hide. Right now, I'm dedicated to my antiques store and work in general. I *like* work; I hate bullshit. But I've put my whole fucking life on hold to start this operation — and I'm serious about it. Are you?"

This speech seemed to do the trick. Criminals were unusually susceptible to accusations of ineptness or laziness — they were inherently inept and lazy, for the most part — and Cal had found that all he often had to do was turn their own fears back at them. Soon, they were discussing the procedure to be used for the proposed operation. They had even arrived at the division of responsibilities when Nick Miller suggested they save this for the next meeting.

"I'd like that to be in Canada," Cal suggested. "I don't want to meet in the U.S. I'm scared of RICO, you know — I could go to fucking jail for life just for talking to you guys about this."

"I gotcha. Meeting in Canada doesn't seem to be a problem," Nick replied.

The RICO (Racketeering Influenced and Corrupt Organizations) laws had everyone in the underworld worried. The new statutes had revolutionized the fight against organized crime in the U.S., and they meant, in effect, that anyone caught discussing a crime with known criminals was guilty of conspiracy to commit that crime. It enabled the police to apprehend bigger fish, the ones who were careful to keep a distance between themselves and the actual crimes they counselled others to commit. Along with what's known as proceeds — a law permitting police to seize money and assets that are known to be the proceeds of crime — the RICO statutes have forced organized crime to evolve upwards, seeking protection behind the veneer of respectability offered by "legitimate" big business. While it has a proceeds law, Canada has yet to develop the equivalent of RICO, which the civil-liberties people regard as a giant leap towards the police state. The absence of such legislation and the leniency of the Canadian courts are the chief reasons Canada has become a haven for organized crime.

"I wanted to touch on the subject of cash," said Dick Fanzetti. "Converting and laundering, know what I'm saying?"

"I have spoken about this briefly with Jon," Cal said. "As a long-term goal."

"If we like what you've got," Nick told him, "I can come up with five hundred grand a week."

"Yeah," Jon Blake said, "and I can round up Louis Richard, Damien Love, Danny Surprise, and others to come in."

These were all known Indian smugglers connected to Larry Miller, and between them, they had gambling, pirate gas, alcohol, firearms, and tobacco pretty much sewn up.

"One thing at a time," Cal said. "Let's focus on doing one deal, eh?"

"We'll build a phony company here," Nick offered, "if you'll take care of the organization and operation of the whole deal."

"Okay," said Cal.

"How long before we can start?" Nick asked.

"We'll have a better idea of the timing after our Toronto run," Cal replied. "And I need you to get me the documents on your proposal, Nick. I'll do the same for you by next week, okay?"

Fanzetti, who had left the room briefly, returned holding a sculpture of an eagle in quartz crystal.

"Cal," he said, "you know about antiques. What d'you reckon this is worth?"

Cal took the glass eagle and looked it over, well aware that Fanzetti was testing him, trying to find out if he was really an antiques dealer.

"This is Lalique," Cal announced appreciatively. "They made a number of these in the twenties and thirties — some of them as hood ornaments for cars, believe it or not." Cal felt he was starting to sound like "The Antiques Roadshow," a television program he now watched regularly with an avid professional interest. "I don't know what you paid for it, Dick" — or *if* you paid for it — "but in auction, this would fetch around twenty, twenty-five grand."

Cal hoped it wasn't a copy, though he somehow doubted that Fanzetti would go to such lengths. Fanzetti merely nodded in a non-committal way, then handed Cal a letter. It was from an antiques dealer in San Francisco, and it gave a value for the Lalique eagle of $25,000.

"Not bad," Fanzetti said. "Not bad. Think you can find a buyer for me?"

"I can try."


TOM HABIB AND JACKY CIOTTO gave Cal a lift to the train station, discussing the meeting with him. They were both now rather cocky, as if the proximity to criminal greatness had conferred some sort of validation on them.

"I don't know about Toronto," said Habib, referring to a location for the next meeting.

"My people don't like Toronto," added Ciotto.

"Your people sound like Agoraphobics Anonymous," Cal told him.

"I got some good people. You all should have people like my people."

"Cornwall's no good," Habib continued.

"My people don't like Cornwall," Ciotto announced.

"Maybe you should tell us the places your people *do* like," Cal said. "Be simpler."

"Cornwall is not a place to do business," Habib decided. "Cornwall is lousy."

"My people don't like Cornwall."

"Too political, too much growth . . ."

"Cornwall?" Cal wondered where Habib saw too much growth in small-town Cornwall.

"Cornwall's not convenient for my people," Ciotto said. "Dey won't go there."

"I hope Larry's health isn't going to be a problem," Cal said, climbing out in the station forecourt.

"Larry Miller," Habib told him smugly, "is a well-connected man with people gonna break you up with baseball bats you ever cross them — that's who Larry Miller is."

"Thanks for the tip," said Cal.

"Here, have a look at these." Habib handed him four sheets of itemized military hardware.

"What's this?"

"Mainly weapons," replied Habib. "See if you can find me some Indian buyers on the rez."

"You don't stop, do you?" said Cal, looking at the list. There were AK-47s, nine millimetres, mortars, rocket launchers, shells, bullets, and various kinds of explosives, like Semtex. "This a wish list, or you got the stuff?"

"I got it. I just need to get rid of it, is all."

When this little item was reported to the handlers, they just told Cal to forget it. It wasn't within the scope of the LOA, which targeted Miller only, and thus would be too complex to incorporate into the sting. The weapons were sold onto the rez, as it happens — though not through Cal. Where they went after that is anyone's guess, but known terrorist groups have often been observed shopping on the reservations. It is worth pointing out once again that the police don't choose to operate in this bureaucratic tangle, but rather that we have forced them to function in this way.

—

### *Thursday, February 29, 1996*

"If you was a chick, yous could ask me to marry you today," announced Jacky Ciotto, referring to the leap year.

"If I was a chick," Cal told him, "I wouldn't even *know* you."

"You're right . . . You'd be a fucking ugly chick."

Ciotto had come knocking on the door of Cal's suite in Toronto's Royal York Hotel to tell him that Tom Habib and Jon Blake were waiting downstairs in the coffee shop. He was wearing a bright red overcoat with a plaid shirt, and the hair on his vampire's wedge of toupee looked as if it had just been blow-dried with a flame-thrower.

"Little early for that coat, isn't it, Jacky?"

"Early?"

"I need welder's goggles, I'm gonna look at you."

"Pure cashmere, dis," Ciotto announced, smoothing the nap on his sleeves.

"Christmas present?"

"Nah," Ciotto replied innocently. "I got it made to measure."

"Same guy who does Santa Claus, right?"

"Fuck you. Yous don't know quality when you sees it."

"The trouble is I *do*," Cal said.

Over breakfast, Jon Blake continued his own education in the mysteries of shipping. He was not a good student, and Cal had to go over things like procedures for customs in-bond loads again and again — and even then, he knew Blake hadn't grasped it.

"I've got a company right here in Toronto that's done in-bond conversion," Cal told him. "We'll discuss the ins and outs with them, okay?"

Blake was pleased by the thought, and had to say how impressed he was with the progress Cal was making on everything. To make Blake happy, Cal realized, you had merely to take into account his learning disabilities, and promise that everything would be explained thirty times.

As they walked back to the suite, Cal heard a tinkling noise and wondered what it was. It ceased when they entered the elevator but started up again as they walked along the hotel corridor.

"You hear that, Jon?"

"What?" Blake stopped to listen, and the tinkling stopped.

Cal looked down and saw that Blake had silver spurs attached to his cowboy boots. "S'okay, Jon. Just the soundtrack to *Urban Cowboy* following us around."

"Oh, these." Blake seemed embarrassed slightly. "They came with the boots."

"If you say so."

Blake was also mightily impressed by the Royal York's lavish suite. There were fresh-cut flowers in the vases, and two bottles of Veuve-Cliquot in a silver ice bucket flanked by bowls of exotic fruit.

"Nice," he said. "Real nice. You live well, Cal."

"That's how I live, Jon."

Cal wondered what Blake would say if he told him that through the adjoining door was a room full of RCMP operatives who, with the aid of three spy cameras — one in a digital clock — and four hidden mikes, were recording every gesture and sound he made.


BY 9:30 A.M. THEY WERE on the road, heading down the Queen Elizabeth Way towards Hamilton, Ontario. They turned off at Centennial Parkway and went south on Highway 20. Taking the first light right, they went east on Barton, then turned at the second light onto Clavell. Just past Fred's Autoservice, at the bend, they came to the Fay Hoy Temple, a Korean joint. It was a vast complex, but in fact the temple itself comprised just a small adjoining room.

"This is the first warehouse," Blake announced, ordering Ciotto, who was driving, to pull over. "We lease the place from Koreans. They don't ask no questions. There's no heat or hassle. It's cool."

"We getting out?" Ciotto wanted to know.

"We're waiting for our contact," Blake told him.

"Any sign of him?" Ciotto asked a minute later.

Blake ignored him, then said, "I'm gonna phone." He got out and walked into a nearby store, whose many exhortations to business included one announcing its possession of a telephone for public calls. How quaint, Cal thought.

Blake was back in no time, looking pissed.

"Whassa matter?" asked Habib.

"Asshole," Blake muttered. "He was miffed we came to the site without his approval, wants us to do counter-surveillance."

Dutifully, Habib and Ciotto looked up and down the street, as if watching a tennis match.

"S'clear," declared Ciotto.

"James Bond got nothing on this baby," Blake said, then shook his head violently, perhaps trying to wake himself from this nightmare he was having. "We're to meet him at Piccadilly's in half," he added, gesturing for Ciotto to drive.

As they pulled up in front of Piccadilly's, in downtown Hamilton, Cal couldn't help noticing it was a strip club.

"For Christ's sake, Jon!" he said. "This is a fucking heat score, man. I don't wanna meet in places like this."

"It ain't even open," Habib observed.

"It's only 10:20, Jon," Ciotto pointed out. "Dey don't open till eleven."

"Guys, guys!" Jon yelled. "Jesus Christ! Don't it occur to you that maybe there's some influence here? It'll be open, don't worry." Then he turned to Cal and said, "The contact's upset. It's either here or we go back. He told us to go here."

"This one's on you, Jon," Cal said, getting out.

Blake shoved Ciotto out the door and slid over to the driver's seat, saying he was going to pick up the contact and would meet everyone back at the club.

Habib tried the door, expecting it to be closed. It wasn't, and he nearly fell over when it opened in front of him. Standing behind it in the shadows was Zorba the Greek, a great swarthy bear of man in a soiled T-shirt and dress pants. He had bulging eyeballs and a moustache like an old crow flying out of his nose.

"We're with Jon Blake," Habib explained.

The man looked up and down the street, then said, "Fucking funny. I don't see him anywhere. What you done with him?"

"Everybody's a fucking comedian," Ciotto said, brushing a hair from his crimson coat. "Ain't dey?"

"Naturally you're gonna think that, wearing that fucking coat," said the man. "Christmas was last month, Santa. Fuck off!"

Then, incongruously, Ciotto and the man hugged and kissed each other in between ejaculations of joy and the nature of time.

Inside, it was pitch dark except for a single spotlight on a small stage — more a podium, really — where a naked boy wearing only skimpy bathing shorts stood twitching like a marionette in the wind to a thumping techno beat.

"Yeah, great," shouted a man who turned out to be seated just in front of the stage. "Gotcha phone number, Misty. Gonna be calling you."

Misty slouched off the stage and trudged towards the exit. It wasn't a boy after all, Cal saw. Misty was a girl in no need of a bra.

"An' it's *Mystique,* not Misty," she yelled before vanishing.

"It'll make a big fucking difference, darlin'," said the man near the stage.

"What's going on?" Ciotto asked his long-lost buddy.

"Tryouts," the man replied. "You know: 'Ya wanna shake your tushy for a living, you come on down . . .' Whassa right word?"

"Auditions?" Habib suggested.

"Autrition, thassit! Yeah, they's autritioning. Only time we can fit it in." He yawned. "Some mornings, you just can't face the thought of another fucking pair of tits, know what I mean?"

"No," Habib said, then laughed.

They took a table to the side, about twenty feet back from the stage, and Ciotto's pal asked what everyone was drinking.

"You got any — whassit called? — Verve-Kleekwat?" Ciotto asked. "Dat champagne you had at da hotel, Cal? Da classy stuff?"

"Veuve-Cliquot," Cal told him.

"Lemme go look," the man said, disappearing into the shadows.

"Dream on, Jacky," Cal told Ciotto. "Be lucky to find Baby Duck in a toilet like this."

"Aw, Christ!" groaned Habib. "What's this? The fucking Miss Canadian Crack Whore Pageant?" He pointed to the stage.

"Whoa! Whoa! Nadine. Nadine, is it?" asked the man near the stage.

"*Nah*-dine, not *Nay*-dine," replied a plump black girl with pendulous breasts and a pair of pink candlewick shorts that looked as if another half millimetre of growth would make them explode.

"Okay, *Nah*-dine. Did you bring a tape?"

"No one say nothin' 'bout no tape."

"I'm sure they did, Nadine."

"Shee-it, you sure! Ain't no one mention no tape."

"Then what you gonna dance to, darlin'?"

"Don't you got no music here?" Nadine said indignantly.

"If her fucking tits are right," said Ciotto, "it's six-thirty already."

Jon Blake returned with the contact, a short, stocky guy in his forties wearing a brown leather coat, blue jeans, white socks, and loafers. He was introduced as Grant.

"Before we start, Jon," said Cal, "I want to say this: when we first met, I said I wanted to deal with only the top people. I didn't want too many others involved. All that's happened since then is — and no offence, Grant — I've met different people. On my side there's still just me, you'll notice. Who am I dealing with now?"

Zorba arrived with two bottles of Veuve-Cliquot he'd bought at the liquor store and five glasses.

"I didn't realize we were entertaining royalty," said Grant flatly.

"Well, you're not entertaining me," Cal told him, turning over his glass. Accepting such a drink was against the rules: technically, he would have been availing himself of the proceeds of crime.

"Cal, ease up, man," said Blake. It was clear he and Grant had "issues" between them.

"Fair enough," said Grant as the champagne was poured. "He has a right to know who he's dealing with. I gotta small operation here, Cal. I'm loyal to Larry and the Italian groups. And I been instructed to work with you, so that's what I'm doing. My operation moved twenty-seven trucks last December. It's a close-knit thing, you know — all *family*. We move about one truck a week normally, following a very strict procedure. Now" — he sat back and lit a cigarette, breathing in the smoke as if it was oxygen — "I'm expecting four trucks between tonight and tomorrow, and my problem is I don't know how to handle this amount all at once. It's gonna be complicated. Very complicated. So I'm not gonna be ready to handle you for at least two weeks."

He was expecting this to be a problem, that much was obvious, and was thus relieved to hear Cal say, "That's okay. I'm not ready either."

"So we're okay on this?" He seemed amazed. "Good. Then let me explain the warehouse situation to you. The Fay Hoy Temple, which you saw, is dead. Some people were pissed at us operating from that location. Anyway, the place was raided by the RCMP two years ago, but they missed the stock 'cause it was hidden behind a false wall."

This was clearly news to Blake, who looked embarrassed by it.

Grant continued, "I got two more locations I'm gonna show you. But I don't want you to point or even look too obviously as we pass by, in case there's RCMP surveillance. All right?"

They all piled into the car and drove out to the corner of Brampton and Parkdale, where they slowed down preposterously to make a turn past the 560 Carpet Warehouse.

Yeah, thought Cal, five big guys in a white Lincoln — subtle!

"This is my main operation," said Grant. "It's got eight bays. And across the street is a back-up location."

Everyone turned to look at another warehouse building called Neo.

They then headed back onto Parkdale and drove east, turning onto Rennie, where, near the corner of Woodward, they passed by the old Union Electric building.

"That's a *potential* new location," said Grant. "I'm in the process of negotiating for it, but I don't have it yet. . . . I take care of everything," he told Cal. "You know: lookouts and security for the loads."

They drove back to Piccadilly's, where their Veuve-Cliquot was still bubbling away in an ice bucket. The club was now open for the lunchtime trade, its tables occupied by the usual gaggles of chortling businessmen, eager students, and lonely old men.

"And now," announced Zorba's bored voice on the PA system, "all the way from Las Vegas, Nevada, please give a big hand — and you'd need big hands — to Miss Marie Van Mellonze and her bosom buddies!"

Onto the stage, dressed like a Christmas tree, strutted a statuesque platinum blond in a glittering bra big enough to house two bags of laundry.

"Holy shit!" said Habib. "Look at the knockers on that, J.C.!"

"Double dee-licious," Ciotto cackled.

They both scuttled off to the edge of the stage.

"I work with Larry and the Italians," stated Grant, "both for protection and for customers. It's a good relationship, mutually rewarding. But I don't like working with little boys, know what I mean?" he asked Cal.

"You or Jon can contact me any time, but I don't wanna deal with those two." He indicated Habib and Ciotto, who were busy stuffing cash into Marie Van Mellonze's capacious bra. "They're not business-minded. Right now they'd sell us all out for ten minutes inside her pants, understand what I'm saying?"

"Could you arrange the customs run if we need it?" asked Cal.

"If everyone approves," Grant replied.

He got up to leave, and Blake walked him to the door, where they talked alone for ten minutes.

Blake seemed excited and happy during the drive back to Toronto.

"Now we don't have egg on our face with Larry," he said. "Plus we got Grant totally impressed." He turned to Habib. "You guys heard anything about tomorrow yet?"

"I'll call when we get back to the hotel," Habib replied, thrilled to be included. "Way you're going, Jon, you're gonna be the next god-father, man!"

"I sure hope so," said Blake.

WHEN THEY GOT BACK to Cal's suite, Blake pursued his education in shipping arcana, asking endless questions related to bonded goods, some of which Cal couldn't answer off the top of his head. Habib and Ciotto had switched on the television, popped open a bottle of Veuve-Cliquot, and were surfing channels while discussing the many virtues of Miss Marie Van Mellonze, who had made an indelible impression on them.

"You got her phone number, right?" Ciotto asked.

"Nah," Habib told him. "But I gave her yours."

"Da fuck you did! Which one?"

"The home."

"My old lady's gonna take a message, is she? You fucking did dat, you's one sorry asshole, Tommy."

Habib laughed. "Kidding. I just gave her a fake one."

"Whassa fucking point of dat?"

"'Cause we don't have a number's any good to call us on."

"Yeah, we do." Ciotto thought about it. "We don't, do we? We should fucking do someting about dat, Tommy. She was hot for us too. Shit!"

Cal, meanwhile, called the Commerce Customs Brokers with Blake's inquiries.

"They've given me a contact," he told Blake. "A Mr. Thornbury. He's tied up right now, but I'll follow it up."

"Great," Blake said, looking unnaturally content. "I ever tell you about Larry's fishing trip?" he asked.

"Don't think so."

"What was dat?" Ciotto was saying. "Forty-four double D, I'd say."

"More like forty-eight," Habib replied, spreading his palm around an imaginary breast. "Monica was forty-six, and that bitch was bigger."

"Cost Larry three hundred grand," Blake said.

"I fucking hope he caught something," Cal told him. "Three hundred thousand bucks for a fishing trip? Where'd he go? Mars?"

"Was forty people, Cal. He took forty people with him for a week."

"What people?"

"Big shots," Blake replied, deeply satisfied by the thought of Larry's largesse. "Like a Las Vegas politician, an exclusive car dealer, Damien Love, and the rest were tobacco company execs and customers."

"Do the companies know who Larry is?" Cal inquired.

"Whadda you think?"

"So they're basically smuggling their own product, then?"

"It ain't that straightforward, but yeah, they are."


WHEN IT CAME DOWN to the figures, Cal realized that a tobacco company like R.J. Reynolds, for example, was doing around 60 percent of its total Canadian business in contraband. In other words, twelve out of every twenty Player's or DuMaurier cigarettes smoked in Canada were in fact smuggled into the country — most of them through the Akwesasne Reservation, a fact that could hardly escape the notice of RJR's senior executives. While they might — and did — argue that their responsibility ended at the point of purchase by a legitimate end-user, such an argument is specious because of the quantity of tobacco involved: five billion cigarettes a year. It is no different from trying to argue that the five kilos of cocaine in your trunk are for personal use. The cigarettes had to be going on into Canada, since there was nowhere else they reasonably *could* go — and that means complicity by the tobacco companies in defrauding the Canadian government of rightful tax revenues.

Of course, neither this argument nor the facts disclosed in this book were used when the case of the Canadian government versus RJR-Macdonald Inc., several related companies, and the Canadian Tobacco Manufacturers Council was heard in the U.S. district court in Syracuse, New York, in June 2000. The court dismissed Canada's case on June 30, citing the Revenue Rule, an eighteenth-century common-law rule that permits a court to decline to enforce another country's tax laws. Even the court, in its decision, admitted that if it was "writing on a clean slate . . . it would be inclined to find the Revenue Rule to be outdated." The district court simply felt bound by precedent set in higher courts. It did not, however, feel bound to address the factual merits of Canada's case, which had nothing to do with seeking to enforce Canadian tax laws through the U.S. courts. The government's allegation was that the defendants broke U.S. racketeering laws by their participation in the tobacco-smuggling scheme. Its beef with the Canadian Tobacco Manufacturers Council was that it was used to throw the government off the smuggling trail by blaming organized crime — which the council did in a report on smuggling it prepared for the government.

Canada's case is, however, at this writing, under appeal. The appeal will be heard in a higher court, which will be able to declare the invalidity of the Revenue Rule.

"DEY WEREN'T NATURAL, though," Ciotto was saying.

"Sure they were," Habib protested. "Originally they were natural."

"Hey, tit fans," Blake shouted. "Enough, eh? Tommy, what about tomorrow?"

"Oh, yeah," Habib replied. "Lemme make some calls." He grabbed the nearest phone and started punching keys.

"Grant wants the initial order to be quite specific," Blake told Cal. "Nine hundred cases of rye, three hundred rum, and four hundred vodka. This is the best mix for resale."

"I assume he knows his business," said Cal.

"I gotta line of information out of Ottawa," Ciotto announced, pouring the remains of the Veuve-Cliquot into his glass. "Yeah. My son works for Revenue Canada."

"The fuck he does," Blake told him.

"I ain't kidding yous," protested Ciotto. "But he's a good boy. Yeah!" He took a hefty swallow. "Dates a stripper, he does. Keeps his old man supplied with entertainment . . . when I need it."

"Fascinating," Blake muttered.

"We're all goin' out together tonight, right?" said Ciotto. "Tommy's brother's coming in."

"I wanted you to talk with him about his network," Habib told Cal, putting down the phone. "Everything's set up. We'll leave real early tomorrow morning, okay?"

"I can't be talking with no brother, Tommy," Cal said. Then, turning to Blake, he added, "And I don't want to waste another day driving around. I want to get back to work."

"Shit," Habib complained. "I want you to meet my people in Bowmanville."

He had some small-time scammer there moving containers of stolen potato chips and the like. It would do Habib a world of good to bring down the big guys, present them as pals: "See, I'm connected — right to the top!"

"Why, Tommy? So's you can show off?"

"No, Cal. C'mon, man. It'll be good for business."

"Monkey business."

"I gotta few things to do," said Blake, "so let's take a break now and leave the decisions for later, okay?"

———

**Schwartz Adler Co.**
**Memo**

**Schwartz Adler Co. is prepared to represent the company Omnigroup of Bulgaria, to establish a Canadian-based North American office. S.A. Co., on behalf of Omnigroup Bulgaria, is prepared to offer a North American agency agreement to N.D.M. Co. of Massena, N.Y., to represent the company in the U.S.A.**

S.A. Co. will reform and transfer proforma offers from Omni-group Bulgaria to our U.S. agent, N.D.M Co. N.D.M. Co. will then place said proforma orders with the select suppliers and providers of its choice.

N.D.M. Co. will set up all shipping and transfer logistics for an in-bond transfer of all goods, where applicable, to a pre-selected bonded yard, located in Canada, for in-bond transfer to Port Canada for shipment to Bulgaria.

S.A. Co. will organize and supervise the release from bonded yard and transfer to port. S.A. Co. will also assist N.D.M. Co. on each and every order from point of supply to destination.

S.A. Co. will hold its cash in accounts established in Montreal, Quebec, for deposit and wire transfer of funds for orders initiated by S.A. Co.

I hereby authorize the use of these names on my business cards for the company S.A. Co.:

Jon K. Blake
Tom Habib
Jacky Ciotto

C. Calvin Broeker

The fact that they had actually signed their names to this document would go a long way towards keeping Cal Broeker out of court when the time came.

### Wednesday, March 20, 1996

Habib and Ciotto showed up at the Greene Avenue store grumbling.

"Your fucking truckers, man," said Habib, "they want too much money. We're not gonna make the kind of money we thought we would, and what with the seal problem, we're getting concerned."

The "seal problem" was a reference to the customs seals, which would have to be broken and then resealed, a process Habib was beginning to think of as phenomenally expensive, if not impossible.

"There's no problem," Cal told him. "Except the problem that I was instructed to provide a service that had associated costs I was not aware of at the time. Understand?"

"Let's go over how this started," Habib said, counting off fingers. "Myself, J.C., Jon, Larry, Dick, Nick, and associates — we were discussing ways to increase the volume and safety of our fucking smuggling operation. So we discussed diverting bonded loads, and that was when I thought of you with your grocery connections."

"I never realized you were part of Larry's inner circle, Tommy," Cal said.

"You know what yous need to know," Ciotto announced, looking pleased with himself.

"I came to you," Habib continued, "to see if you could assist in providing a bonded carrier that would divert loads."

"I know," Cal told him. "I was fucking there too, wasn't I? What's all this leading to, Tom?"

Habib, having delivered his speech, returned to normal and said, "Listen, I know it's not your fault, but can you see what you can do to reduce costs?" He looked around the room, puzzled. "Hey, what happened to the parrots?"

Cal had given them back to Mr. Gonzalez, who'd relocated his office next door and missed the birds.

"They escaped."

"No shit? I liked those birds."

"Dey were pretty birds," Ciotto commiserated. "Dat's a real shame."

"So try to get the costs down, Cal, eh?" Habib said.

Obviously, Blake or someone in the Miller group was pressuring him to get a price break. It was just like real business.

"Yeah," Ciotto chimed in, "and you gotta speed things up. Why's it going so slow?"

"You guys know how many trucks a week you wanna do yet?"

"Yeah," Ciotto replied. "Course we do. Two, maybe four. As many as we can."

"Right," said Cal. "Two, four, or sixty. I'm gonna call the truckers, set up a meeting, nail this down, okay?"

—

IT WAS AROUND NOW that Cal was instructed by his handlers to bring an RCMP operative into the operation, for back-up and to help with arrests. As he was not a Canadian, let alone in the police force, Cal could not arrest anyone or even apprehend them. He was merely a conduit for information — information that would not, however, have existed without him.

He could not have asked for a better partner than Bill Gordon, a twenty-three-year veteran of the force with expertise in organized crime, smuggling, money laundering, and the Chinese Triads (subjects on which he had published in both national and international police journals, as well as given expert witness testimony). Bill Gordon was thenceforth to be known as Bobby Paulson, trucker, owner of a bonded licence and a trucking outfit shipping between Canada and the U.S. It was a good front: the company had been in business for fourteen years and was easily checked out as legit. Cal simply had to find a way of introducing Bobby without anything appearing out of the ordinary.

### Friday March 22, 1996

Habib and Blake arrived at Greene Avenue dressed in nearly identical cowboy outfits — boots, jeans, denim jackets — with Ciotto looking like a portly vampire bank clerk.

"Yeah," said Blake as Cal greeted them, "it's the good, the bad, and the fucking hideous."

"You two call each other before dressing *every* day? How sweet!"

"It was a coincidence," Habib said, as embarrassed as Blake clearly was.

"Tom's gonna take care of the seal," Blake said when they were sitting in the upstairs office. "Personally. He's gonna cut the original seal, then either resolder it or glue it back together."

"Glad to see you've found honest work, Tom," said Cal. "What's J.C. here gonna do? Observe?"

Blake told Cal they were going to bring the first load to a bonded yard at the Detroit border.

"We'll get you cash by next Wednesday," Blake added. "Canadian funds. You'll wire it to Nick, and he'll start the order. It's a distillery in Minneapolis. We're gonna be off-loading to customers in Hamilton and

Bowmanville. Then we got another location to reload the truck with sand and do the seals. Can you cover it, Cal?"

"Sure. I'll make certain you're not followed," Cal told him. "Now, the truckers have agreed to reduce the price to eighteen grand USD per load, okay? They're gonna take ten and I'll take eight."

"That's fine," Blake said.

"It's gotta be fine," Cal added. "That's their final decision."

"What about final shipping dates?" Blake asked.

"Again, that's up to the truckers. They've set up a parallel company to handle this, Jon. These are good people, serious people. And listen" — Cal sat back and sighed — "if any of your people should happen to meet these guys, let's not get into any personal talk or death threats, okay? These guys don't respect that kinda talk. Are we clear on this?"

Blake nodded circumspectly, then said, "I need a firm shipping date."

"Let's call Bobby Paulson now," Cal said. "He's the trucker. Okay?"

"Sure," Blake replied. "Tommy, you talk to him."

"He'll be on the road," Cal told them, "but he answers his pager."

———

*From the notes of Inspector Bill Gordon, officer in charge of the Proceeds of Crime Section in "A" Division, Ottawa, Royal Canadian Mounted Police. From the court brief of Project Orienter, Cornwall Regional Task Force Investigative Unit.*

*15:45 hrs:* receive page to call 514-935-XXXX

*16:00 hrs*: the number and spoke Cal. The same the person as introduced by Sgt. D. Cal stated Tom was on the line with him and he wished to speak with me.

Tom gave his name and I gave name as Bob. Tom requested a meeting this weekend in order to get things off the ground. I had advised it is impossible as I had another thing happening which would be taking me south. Tom asked for a meeting by Wednesday at latest to get things going. I advised I would not be back until late Wednesday. Tom expressed disappointment as he hoped to meet and move within 10 days. I explained my speech therapist (lawyer) was busy setting things up as I wanted to ensure we had a long-term commitment and that it was taking longer. I advised that I had only been brought in at the last minute and therefore was having to put things together. Tom asked where I lived as he would like only a one-hour meeting. I stated between Ottawa and Toronto, and . . . that I wanted to meet at which time I would give them some contact numbers. Stated he had a lot of customers and he didn't want to disappoint them. Talked to Cal, explained the lack of availability. Cal told him I hadn't spoke to our friends and therefore wasn't aware of direction. Cal expressed hope we could meet for at least one hour over weekend and that he would still get carpet. Call concluded.

*Telephone conversation*
*Conference call, Cal Broeker, Jon Blake, and self*
*96-03-28*

*16:50 hrs* page received. Called and spoke to Sgt D, who gave me telephone number of 514-935-7054. This number for Cal, and Cal to arrange conference call with Jon Blake for the purpose of stalling any business activity in light of operation approval still being sought.

*17:15 hrs* call number and speak to Cal. General discussion about using disguise — there is heat in light of arrests in Ontario and especially seeing Tom wanted delivery in Bowmanville reason to postpone. Cal advised he wanted to conference call with Jon — Cal agreed to set up with operator — put on hold — after a few seconds Cal heard talking to a male. Cal explained he was getting a lot of heat from Tom, and that Bob and Gary staying outside during due to our acquaintance. I then explained I was concerned about all the heat from the takedown and that I didn't want to drive 110 K machine into a loss. Jon stated the heat was an undercover operation by OPP involving a ring of people who dealt through a farm and that he was keeping an eye on things. I stated I have to wait a couple of weeks as RevCan hadn't issued bond and that my lawyer was working on it but they wanted to talk to me. According to my lawyer this would take a couple weeks — two weeks would allow time to assess the heat. Jon agreed and Cal asked why we were getting so much heat from Tom — Jon stated they had customers but all he needed was a date and that we would only have to do one stop from Detroit bonded yard (free-trade zone) and stop west of Toronto. I stated that before proceeds I would like to meet. Jon and Cal agreed. Suggested I wouldn't meet until my end was together — approximately two weeks. Jon advised he needed seven days advance notice to get order. I advised this time frame would be good and that I'd appreciate he (Jon) keep Cal abreast of any heat. All agreed. Stated I looked forward to meeting in person. Call ended.

*Meeting with Cal Broeker*
*Montreal, 96-04-22*

*21:00 hrs* met with agent Cal Broeker at Les Nouvelles Hotel in Montreal. General discussion on background — living in Asia, antiques, previously doing business in carpets — will be asking for 35-50 K for costs are attributed to setting up our end. Our objective would be to get 25 K — meeting to be arranged at Holiday Inn, Chinatown, Thursday, 14:00 hrs and to meet agent at 10:00 hrs.

*Saturday, April 6, 1996 — 1350 Greene Avenue, Montreal*
Possibly Habib had been instructed not to wear an item of cowboy attire, or perhaps he had merely decided to be prudent, but whatever the reasons for it, he never again appeared wearing so much as a silver-and-turquoise belt buckle. Jon Blake, on the other hand, looked like he'd stepped from the cover of a John Denver album at nearly every meeting from then on. And Ciotto had his own unique style. These boys were

as vain as runway models, and touchy when it came to humour at their expense.

"I look at you, Jon," Cal said, "and I can smell that Rocky Mountain air."

"Yeah, okay, enough," Blake growled. "Listen, Cal," he said in a low, urgent tone, "the rez has fucking dried up, man, and everyone's hot to trot to start this deal ASAP, get me? Danny Surprise's ready to start moving money across at a hundred grand per trip. And Headlight's the only guy there still in full operation as far as smuggling goes, and he's said he'll work with us as partners on anything we like."

"I don't want no Indian partners," Cal stated, remembering vividly his experience with Headlight. "I'm not interested in starting anything new, anything other than what we got going now."

"Larry's due back from Russia next Tuesday," Blake told him. "And I think that he and Damien Love might be up to having a meeting here in Montreal as soon as I can arrange it. Cal, you gotta classy place we can meet here? You know, like what you put together in Toronto?"

"I got pretty solid relations with the Holiday Inn group, got a corporate rate position with them. Yeah, I can get us a nice suite there."

"Okay, then I'm going to work on a meeting for May. Sound good?"

"Fine by me," Cal replied. "Oh, by the way, guys, I need you to put $550 towards the cost of the new business cards and the letterhead with your names on them. Okay?"

"Sure." Blake dug into his jeans and counted out $130, which seemed to be all he had on him.

Cal looked over at Habib and Ciotto.

"I'll give you mine when I get the cards from you," Habib said.

"Yeah. Me too," added Ciotto.

"I wanna stress," said Blake, "how happy I am with the program, Cal. I can't wait to do this first deal, man. I'm gonna be coming up again next week with Dick, if possible, since Dick has now got to all his people with what we're doing and they're very excited. They're over the fucking moon, Cal."

"They're not gonna be disappointed, Jon."

"I hope not. The rez was hit pretty hard by the recent busts. They're suffering there. Nobody trusts anybody any more, you know how it is. And the clients are going dry. It's got everyone mad. The Kahnawake people have told us they're gonna get nasty. They're gonna start hijackings and outright heists of product here in Canada. The market's totally fucking dry, so's you can't blame 'em."

"Whadda fuck dey s'posed to do?" Ciotto chimed in. "It's *dry* out there."

You'd think that Prohibition had returned to hear these guys speak, thought Cal.

### Thursday, April 11, 1996 — 1350 Greene Ave, Montreal

Dick Fanzetti arrived with Jon Blake, who wore the kind of cowboy boots you normally see only in the window of some showbiz cowpoke outfitters like Nudie's in the San Fernando Valley: a mix of hornback toad, snakeskin, and ostrich in various hues, they had Indian bone bracelets dangling around the calves.

Cal looked down at them and then up at Blake, who said, "Don't even *think* of calling Dick 'Tonto,' Cal."

"Whassat?" asked Fanzetti. "Tonto?"

"It's our joke, Dick," Cal explained. "Every time he shows up here, I wonder where he's left the horse."

"What horse?" Fanzetti was no fun.

"What updates you got for us?" Blake asked.

"I ain't heard nothing yet from Bobby so far."

"Well," Blake said, sighing, "as you know, these busts on the rez have left the customers screaming for product. We gotta do *something*."

"When we're ready, we'll move. Not a moment before."

Like all criminals, they were used to making quick money. But as Cal had tried explaining to them, money isn't made that quickly. Money needs time, it needs patience, and it needs a lot of documentation to coax it out of hiding. The problem was that people like the rez smugglers were used to the quick fix. Cal recalled Thomas Michaels once paying $60,000 cash for a load, which he then drove about half a mile and sold to someone else for $80,000. Twenty grand profit for about half an hour's work — not bad. And that's how they viewed all business. Which in turn made them fish in a barrel when it came to round-up time. And the information that Orienter was bringing in had already resulted in a series of RCMP lightning raids to weed out the little guys, the small operators. They didn't want the waters muddied by small fry when they went after the bigger catch.

"Everyone's real impressed with the op to date," Fanzetti told Cal. "You done everything we asked, and we appreciate that. But . . ." He pinched the bridge of his nose and looked pained, exhaling with a hiss through his teeth. "What I gotta discuss with you now is very sensitive, so I hope to fuck that you ain't wired." He leaned over and started to pat Cal down, carefully feeling his back and the lining of his jacket.

"Why'd you remove the birds, Cal?" Blake asked gravely, gesturing to where the parrots' cage had been.

What did this prick think? Cal wondered. The birds had been removed to make taping easier? What a crock.

"They weren't mine, Jon. They belonged to Mr. Gonzalez, and he took them next door. . . . Fuck this shit!" Cal, his heart pounding, started patting down Blake. "Maybe *you're* wired, eh?" Then he moved on to pat down Fanzetti. "Or you? 'Cause if you're gonna play fucking pissy little games like this at *this* stage of things, I'm just gonna send you a bill for thirty-three grand USD — my services to date — and you can forget the fucking deal. Okay?"

"Hold on, Cal, I—"

"Hold on, *bullshit!* It's me that's fucking concerned about cops, not you."

"What you mean?" Fanzetti asked.

They were both glancing anxiously at each other, and Cal knew he had the upper hand. He hadn't been wired, of course, because the wire was in the rat phone on the table in front of them, recording every word.

"I'm concerned about Tom and J.C. being cops, is what I mean."

*When an enemy employs an unexpected strategy, simply use the same strategy on him to regain the upper hand.*

"Why would you say that?" Blake asked, now ashen-faced.

"Ever since I fucking known Tommy," Cal replied, "he's always promised — promise, promise after fucking promise — but he's never delivered. Going back years now, this is. Then he wants to introduce me to his people in Bowmanville — when we were in Toronto, Jon, remember? — and now these people are suddenly in fucking jail."

"Yeah?"

"The problem with this is that if they're *his* fucking people, how come *he* ain't in jail too? And when I bring up the busts in Ontario, he tells me not to worry. I say, 'Tommy, all my people are worried.' Isn't it strange that *we* are and *he* isn't? Ain't that a bit too fucking odd?" Cal stared from Blake to Fanzetti and back again, putting as much dark anger in the stare as he could summon up. "Jon, Dick," he continued, "maybe you guys should check your own fucking house before bringing this shit to me! What if I would have gone to Bowmanville, eh? What then? Well, I'll tell you what. Maybe we'd all be fucked by now, and little Tommy and J.C. would be telling some other poor bastard not to worry, eh? Whatta 'bout that! Shit! Those fucking low-rent assholes — they can't even pay me $150 for their fucking business cards, and these are the kinda people you deal with! I'm fucking mad. I'm so pissed, I wanna end this right now!"

"I really don't think you gotta worry," said Fanzetti meekly.

"Why do you guys try to placate me with that 'no worry' shit?" Cal saw that he had them on the run. "I'm always gonna worry — *always!* — and hopefully I'm always gonna stay outta jail too." He turned to Fanzetti. "Dick, for Christ's sake just *think* about this last bit of information. Think! Why were Tom and J.C. pushing me so hard right up to the bust, but now — *now* — I don't hear a fucking peep from them? Why's that, eh? Maybe because they couldn't get me into the Bowmanville bust. Maybe they wanted to do a quickie run and make ol' Cal trip up. Just fucking think about *that* for a moment. And," Cal continued, knowing he was home and dry, "the changes that Tom mentioned in the load sealing — that bothers me as well. Now he *doesn't* wanna do it? Why's that, eh? So some other sucker takes the fall! That's fucking why."

"You gotta good point there," Blake said. "But I think they're desperate. That's why we're here today. They owe me thirty grand USD, and they haven't paid me back. I've done several runs over the past few weeks just to make some cash. And I gotta front the first load myself before any of the boys get involved — they won't risk it, see?"

"I got Mafia will burn any fuckers," Fanzetti snarled, teeth gritted. "And Larry's got the Russians over here now. Tom and J.C. were told the same as you, Cal: we gotta protect our ass, and we will. These people will fucking maim and kill you *and* your dog and cat if you fuck with 'em. I personally don't think Tommy's *that* stupid — he's just dumb." Fanzetti relaxed a little, sighing. "Which brings me to the real reason we're here, Calvin. I represent the Genovese interests in tobacco and other products, understand? And I got an offer to make to you."

"Who are these Genovese people?" Cal asked innocently.

Fanzetti was incredulous. "You don't know the *Godfather* movies? Where you been? *The New York Genoveses?*"

"I don't pay much attention to things don't interest me," Cal told him icily. "And that doesn't. As a matter of fact, why the fuck would I want to deal with people who are always threatening to whack me one way or another and talking shit? Hmmm? Why? Because, Dick, I don't scare, and I don't care — *and no one fucking owns me.*"

"Hey, Cal," said Blake, palliating. "Just listen to Dick, man. Everyone trusts you, and I will take Tommy and J.C. off your back. Okay?"

"The Genoveses need a legit front company," Fanzetti continued. "Just like your truckers. They wanna run tobacco deals. Their two companies are in Vegas, and I'll make the arrangements to supply Marlboro cubes, okay?"

"I don't have much faith in any Marlboro deals," Cal told him, "as Philip Morris controls all their quotas and production."

"Don't you realize," Fanzetti said, "that Larry and all these people have made their fucking millions in tobacco? *Tobacco!* They're all connected people, Cal."

"I'm really stupid, Dick, so you better explain the whole program so I can fucking understand who is fucking who. And if you're gonna run this, I need pro forma and product contract verbiage and terms and conditions in order to tender this offer."

"Like what?"

"CNF, FOB, CIF, location, terms of LC payment, dating, and so on. If you don't know this, Dick, then I have to talk to these guys — because I'm not going to fucking train you as well as do the job."

The acronyms were all real items related to shipping, but Cal knew Fanzetti didn't have a clue what he was talking about.

"If I give you this," Fanzetti said quietly, looking Cal straight in the eyes, "and you fuck with these people, you're dead fucking meat, pal."

"Cut that shit out, Dick," Blake said. "We don't have to hear it again."

"It's my ass too, Jon," Fanzetti told him defensively. "And my people don't play."

"Dick?" asked Cal. "With all of this Mafia talk, supposing I asked you to arrange a hit, or for someone to be beat up — you could arrange this?"

"No problem. Who is it?"

Cal smiled ruefully, saying, "I don't know whether I wanna get involved with organizations like this, Dick. You know, the littlest screw-up and it's bye-bye."

*Get the enemy to come to you, never go to them. Be like a reluctant virgin.*

"Okay," said Fanzetti, as if teaching it to a child. "Here's the set-up. I am a representative of Genovese, New York. They have a contact in Philip Morris, Virginia. This contact will give me an allocation of ten containers for a twelve-month period at $268 per master case, packed 900 MC per container, each MC packed fifty cartons. Got it?"

"Okay."

Cigarettes are sold in quantity by allocation. An entire year's production is allocated in advance. To get an allocation, you have to either be a licensed distributor or have a licensed distributor to whom to sell your allocation. You need a legitimate end-user. And you must not be encroaching on anyone else's existing territory. To ship offshore, you need even more documentation. Or you need inside contacts, someone to allocate you ten containers a year for a little kickback under the table. To understand the sort of profits involved, consider that with a wholesale price of $268 — a mere two dollars or so per carton — a master case would have a retail price in Canada, depending on the province, of somewhere between $2,000 and $4,000. Even with a 100 percent profit for the retailer — and it's usually far less — there would still be a profit of nearly 300 to 600 percent on the wholesale price, or between $500,000 and $1 million per container *after costs*. That's how Larry Miller made his millions.

But of course, it works only if the tax isn't paid — because some 75 percent of the cost of a packet of cigarettes is tax (and it can be argued that governments have made far more money from cigarettes than tobacco companies or smugglers ever did). Miller was a middleman. His end-user, for a long time, was Damien Love on the rez. But Miller could not have smuggled the quantity of cigarettes he did without the co-operation of Northern Brands International, a distributorship and subsidiary of RJR in Buffalo. Northern Brands was set up in 1993 by Les Thompson, who was also director of sales for RJR in Canada. This was, by coincidence, also the year that Ontario's NDP government raised taxes on cigarettes to unconscionable levels. Two years earlier, the federal government had already nearly doubled the price of a pack with increased taxes. Les Thompson has stated that during its very first year of business, Northern Brands averaged $1.3 million (U.S.) *per week* in profits, and that the firm was considered the single most profitable business unit in the RJR Nabisco family of companies. It could be argued that Les Thompson, in allocating to his own company and moving product to Larry Miller, was doing legit-imate business. He claims he was told by RJR lawyers that he was working in a legal loophole. It could be *argued* — but can it be *believed?*

RJR blames Thompson for its legal troubles, labelling him a rogue executive on the take. However, the industry teems with Thompsons — many of them once entertained at fishing lodges and in Las Vegas by Larry Miller and his associates in organized crime. On January 18, 2000, Les Thompson was sentenced to a six-year prison term and a $100,000 fine for laundering $72 million in profits from contraband cigarettes. He claims not to have any of the money, and he had to cash in his pension to pay the court's fine.

Thompson is anything but the patsy in this conspiracy — he knew damn well that the cigarettes were being smuggled — but he is a scape-goat. The real question, however, is whether the entire tobacco industry is being made a scapegoat for governments whose profits from cigarette taxation far exceed those of the tobacco manufacturers themselves, and whose so-called sin taxes reveal complicity in the deception they claim big tobacco has been perpetrating on the public, since they prove prior knowledge of smoking's dangers.

"Because I don't have a licence to distribute this product," Fanzetti continued, "I had to do a deal like yours, find a legit supplier that has faith in me and my connections. Okay?" And here Fanzetti revealed a lot more than he should have done. "So these suppliers are David Raven-scroft of Las Vegas, who's worked for Philip Morris for fifteen years. He owns Dawn Horse Distributing." Fanzetti rattled off the phone number from memory. "702-367-XXXX. Got that down?"

"Yeah." Cal was busily taking notes, as he often did.

"Ravenscroft's partner is D.C. 'Nobby' Neeson, of NDN International — 702-871-XXXX or 702-367-XXXX. My fax there," Fanzetti added, "is 702-655-XXXX. Now, these guys will work with you on a legit sale of Marlboro. You find the buyers and add on your commission, and I am taken care of by the family. If you pull this deal off successfully, Cal, we can offer a shitload of products for your Canadian operation. These guys are heavy into money laundering too, and they have taken care of all the people you know from the Massena group at one time or another. I told them about your amounts and your Royal Bank account, and they said they could put that anywhere you want at any time you want, without any tracing. Cal . . . *Cal*," he said theatrically, "we can do a lot of business with these people, and this is no Mickey Mouse shit."

"If I do start anything with these groups, Dick, I will take my time. Okay?"

"Don't make any promises you can't keep," Fanzetti advised. "Keep your mouth shut, pay your debts, and we'll do great. We need a guy like you, Cal. Jon's gonna take care of the Tom and J.C. thing. . . . Don't worry 'bout it."

Cal then got Fanzetti to call David Ravenscroft in Las Vegas — using Cal's calling card, so there would be a record. Cal spoke with Ravenscroft for a while, each testing out the other's skills and knowledge. As usual, Cal managed to establish a quick rapport, and Ravenscroft told Fanzetti before hanging up that he was satisfied a deal could be done.

"Be aware, Dick," Cal said, "that I'm gonna ask you to repeat all this to the trucker, because he's one of us and he should hear it. I want him totally aware of all the implications."

"Okay."

The meeting was over and Cal walked the two of them down to the street, where Fanzetti asked if they could speak alone for a moment. They went back upstairs, leaving Blake on the sidewalk.

"Listen," Fanzetti said, "I apologize for any bullshit back there, but you know how it can get."

"It's okay."

"I'm gonna give a great report on this meeting when I get back — don't worry 'bout a thing. A fucking great report."

"Good. I've been straight with you guys. I just expect the same."

"And you'll get it." Fanzetti started to leave but turned back. "Er, Cal," he said, "did you get any interest in that glass eagle of mine?"

"Not yet."

"Just wondered, is all."

"I'll keep trying."

"So where are the birds, next door?" Blake wanted to know when they returned.

"Jeezzzz!" yodelled Cal. "He still don't believe me!"

"Forget it, Jon," Fanzetti said.

"Forget shit, Dick," Cal told them. "Follow me, guys — or do I gotta drag you?"

They marched next door and were buzzed in, then walked upstairs to the office of Mr. Gonzalez.

"Sorry to bug you," Cal told the old man, "but my friend here got pretty fond of your parrots while they were up in my place. Could he possibly see them for a minute?"

"Of course, Calvin, of course he can. Welcome, welcome." Gonzalez ushered everyone into the adjacent rooms, where the parrots were as noisy as they ever were.

"I give you a spoon?" Fanzetti asked Blake. "Or you gonna lick the egg off your face?"


ALTHOUGH THEY HAD THE INFORMATION, it is not known whether U.S. authorities followed up on the potential of connections among Fanzetti, the Genovese crime family, and some senior tobacco company executives. Or whether such connections still exist.


### Thursday, April 25, 1996 — 1350 Greene Ave., Montreal

BOBBY PAULSON, the former Insp. Bill Gordon, RCMP, arrived at the Greene Avenue antiques store just after 12:30 p.m. He'd spoken to Cal by phone before, but this was the first time they'd met. It was also the first time the knight errant had worked with a partner, and he wasn't sure he'd like it, or even that it would pan out. He pictured his handlers trying to play bad guy, using terms like "swag," "piece," and "hood," wearing the windbreakers and cheap loafers they favoured off duty, with their five-dollar barbershop haircuts and Sergeant Pepper moustaches, smelling of Brut.

It gave him the chills just thinking of it. You might be able to get by Tommy and J.C. with that, but someone like Dick Fanzetti would smell a sewer full of rats before he even got through the door.

"Jeez! Mr. Liberace, do come in," said Cal, opening the door to Bobby. "I'm assuming you're in disguise," he added. "If you're not, I'm real sorry . . . for you."

They shook hands and went up to the office-apartment.

The cop looked a good deal younger than his forty-eight years. Darkly handsome, he'd grown a goatee and had his hair layered short and spiky. The clothes were right too: flashy but expensive. It all said taste and money, and a taste for money was what criminals had in common.

"What do you think?" Bobby asked, referring to his getup.

"Looks rich," Cal told him. "Looks bad. Looks a bit gay too."

"Gay!"

"In a good way. You know: perverse and dangerous."

Bobby looked down at himself quizzically, as if he'd betrayed himself. "Yes, well," he said, "I was going for a bit of danger. . . . It's not too faggy, is it?"

"Listen, I got nothing against faggots," Cal assured him.

"I'm not," protested Bobby.

"Relax. It's good. Like some coffee?"

They sat drinking coffee and discussing antiques, a passion they both shared.

"Of course," Bobby confessed, "on a cop's salary, I can't indulge that often."

Cal wondered whether Bobby was one of those cops who thought people like him were overpaid scum, and he felt obliged to point out that he would get paid only when or if there was a successful conclusion.

"There will be," Bobby assured him. "The work you've done so far is really first-rate. We'll get these bastards, all right."

Cal relaxed. These guys didn't hand out compliments very often.

"I forget what it's like to have a regular paycheck," he said. "I miss that security."

"By the time the government's finished taking its cut, you don't feel so secure," Bobby said.

"The silent partner."

"Partner! Wish he'd do some of the work. I don't mind silent — it's the silent parasite I can't stand."

They both chuckled about bloated government and excessive taxation, and then they got onto the subject of living in the East. Bobby had been stationed in Hong Kong, working on the Triads, credit-card counterfeiting, and money laundering. Cal recalled his days in Thailand, and both admitted to missing the colour, the mystery, and the relative simplicity of life there. Before long, Cal knew he liked this man and could work with him. He was blessed to have been sent so capable and distinguished an officer — after all, how many like this did the RCMP have on call? He hoped Bobby felt the same way, and most of all he hoped the job would just go smoothly for both of them. He didn't often let himself think of worst-case scenarios, but with Bobby here he suddenly felt protective. This was a nice man, a good man — he shouldn't end up with his brains smeared across the sidewalk.

Before long, footsteps coming up the stairs signalled the arrival of Jon Blake and Dick Fanzetti.

"Show time!" Cal whispered.

Bobby winked at him.

"Gentlemen!" Cal said as the bad guys appeared. "This is my main man, Bobby." He introduced everyone and ushered them to chairs.

Referring to Fanzetti and Blake occasionally, Cal presented an overview of the project for Bobby. It was partly so Bobby wouldn't appear too knowledgeable for someone just brought in and partly for the rat phone. Every time Fanzetti or Blake said "Yeah" or "That's right" to a summation, it would be taken as a statement of intent to commit a crime: conspiracy to defraud a government.

They next discussed the $50,000 bond that needed to be posted, and Cal asked Fanzetti and Blake if they could help with the costs.

"I'll tell you what," he boomed in the voice he reserved for gestures of largesse, "I'll put up twenty-five grand. Howzat? Half!"

He might as well have said twenty-five cents for all the impact it had.

"We'll deal with it," Bobby said. "If it's okay, first off, I want to air a beef I got."

"Go ahead," said Fanzetti, narrowing his eyes.

"I'm not impressed with this Tom guy you got working with you."

"He's not an impressive guy," said Fanzetti, laughing.

"We're not impressed either," Blake added.

"He's a fuckwit," Bobby said. "He knows shit. He's a fucking liability."

Steady on, Bob, thought Cal.

"Weren't you looking into that, Jon?" Cal asked.

"Yeah," replied Blake.

"He's not professional," Bobby complained. "We wanna establish a viable entity here, something that's gonna survive the long term. No?"

"They've gotta come out of the equation," Blake announced. "Tom and J.C. Are we agreed on that?"

Everyone agreed. Habib and Ciotto were history. Supposedly.

Next, each person present reviewed his expenses to date, and then Bobby made a superb presentation of his company's activities and his personal aspirations. Just as he was wrapping it up, his cellphone warbled. Why hadn't he turned the fucking thing off? Cal wondered.

"Yep?" Bobby snapped. Then, covering the mouthpiece, he said to everyone, "'Scuse me a second, I gotta take this." He walked over to the door between the sitting area and the main floor.

Cal tried to get Fanzetti and Blake talking about the project, but he just got shrugs or nods in reply. It was clear they wanted to eavesdrop on Bobby's call.

"Don't fuck with me," Bobby was saying. "I already got my people in Vancouver. . . . Yeah. . . . No fucking way! It's still eight points. . . . Right, right. . . . There's fucking nothing to talk about. . . . That's right. . . . Nope, don't wanna discuss it further. . . . Eight or nothing. . . . Fucking right!" With that, he hung up abruptly, walking back over to the others. "Sorry 'bout that," he said.

"Don't worry 'bout it," Fanzetti told him.

"I got this thing happening," Bobby explained. "I fucking hate people who reopen negotiations after an agreement's reached."

"Know what you mean," Fanzetti said.

"It's the fucking Colombians," Bobby continued.

Cal was praying he'd shut up, can it, but he didn't.

"They got these boxes of cash need cleaning," he said. "I told 'em I need eight points plus expenses. It's *reasonable!*" He looked around, daring anyone to dispute this. "Assholes think I'm gonna go down, they can fucking find someone else. Am I wrong?"

Fanzetti chuckled, saying, "You gotta Jew attitude. *Fuck you!*" He chuckled again. "I like this guy!"

Cal started breathing again.

It was clear that Fanzetti and Blake were won over: a level of comfort had been achieved between them that prompted Blake to spill a few beans of his own.

"You probably wanna know what we do?" he said. "Well, I been doing this work for five years now, moving containers. The profit's around $180,000 per load, including $10,000 to the driver. I'm in at every level, any product, and I'm moving loads right now without any help."

"He works with Larry Miller." Fanzetti felt the need to interject. "Larry made him a rich man."

"I work with the Miller group and alone," Blake said, giving Fanzetti a frown. "Like you, Dick."

"What we need," Fanzetti said, "is a new route and some *regular* business, something we can rely on."

"We wanna do ten loads a week," Blake stated flatly.

"Jon," Fanzetti asked, a tinge of irritation in his voice, "what's gonna happen if your buyer can't handle all the product, eh?"

"I got one person, *one* — who you know, Dick, he's Mafia — who wants 2,500 cases of liquor a week. A fucking *week!*" Blake looked around at everyone, then felt he needed to elaborate. "One truck," he continued, "is only 1,600 cases, so I *know* I can easily move three loads a week."

"You were saying ten just now," Fanzetti pointed out. "Which is it?"

"Building to ten," Blake told him irritably. "*Building* to ten."

"I don't wanna get greedy," Bobby said, helping Jon out. "I wanna take it slow."

"Right," Blake agreed.

"After moving one, I wanna regroup with you guys and discuss the problems, okay?"

"Perfect," Fanzetti said.

They moved on to discuss the responsibility of NDM, the Miller group's company, and how the shipment would move. The plan, as Cal noted it down, was this:

Jon Blake brings the money by boat to Canada and gives it to Bobby in Cornwall.

NDM faxes a pro forma and an understanding of responsibility.

Cal and Bobby's group faxes back an order and wire-transfers the funds to NDM.

"Wait a minute," Fanzetti said at this point. "I don't wanna get into a tax situation here. I never pay any taxes."

"I'll make sure it's only the cost that's wired," Blake told him. "The rest you'll get under the table, okay?"

"Don't fuck it up," Fanzetti cautioned. "You know what the fucking IRS is like."

NDM then places an order with the supplier.

The supplier then loads a van, since they will not fill containers.

NDM next delivers the van to a bonded yard, using D & N Transport, Minnesota.

NDM unloads the van and reloads the product into a shipping container, where the load is wrapped. The container is then sealed.

NDM then coordinates with Cal and Bobby's group, RGP Inc., to connect the loads.

RGP picks up the load in the bonded yard and drives it across the border.

The load is delivered to a warehouse in Hamilton for unloading.

At the warehouse, Jon Blake breaks the container's seal, unloads the product, reloads the container with the same weight in sand, and then reattaches the seal.

RGP's driver then pulls out of the warehouse and drives to Montreal, where the container of sand is shipped to Bulgaria.

The idea, of course, was not to sell the Bulgarians sand instead of, say, tobacco or alcohol, but rather to give them a share of the profits from the illegal sale of duty-free liquor or cigarettes in Canada. Those who received the shipment in Bulgaria would never complain that it was only sand, so no one would be the wiser. It was a near-perfect crime, and its only victim was the government. Who could get that upset over this in a country as overtaxed as Canada?

The trouble was, however, that the products shipped in this fashion were not limited to alcohol and tobacco. They could just as easily be arms and explosives, which instead of going to a distant country would be sold to the highest bidder within Canada — and that bidder was more than likely not a collector of weapons or an unsporting hunter. He was a terrorist of one stripe or another, or some kind of fairly dangerous criminal whose targets were all of us. Blake and Fanzetti wouldn't care who bought their product, and they most probably wouldn't even know. They were just concerned about making their cut and then shipping another load. The way it was set up, this was easy work for big profits. All it required was a total lack of conscience.

The money was scheduled for transfer on April 30 in Cornwall, Ontario. The first order was going to be placed on May 6, for delivery in Canada on May 9, 1996. The four men shook hands and patted each other on the back. It was a good day's work that, if everything went as planned, would make them all very rich in a very short time indeed.

# 7

## Miller time

*Lawyers spend a great deal of their time shovelling smoke.*

— OLIVER WENDELL HOLMES, JR.

### April 29, 1996

Cal Broeker telephoned Nick Miller at the offices of NDM Inc.

"I need your company registration documents for our files, Nick," he said.

"I'm not giving you anything, Cal," Nick replied, "until *you* give *me* a purchase order based on the draft you sent us back in early March."

He was a shrewd customer and wasn't making the mistakes his father had made at the start of his career.

"Then send me some more banking coordinates for NDM," Cal pursued.

"No more paper! Until I get something from you, we have nothing."

"I'm gonna contact Bulgaria and have your file for tomorrow."

"That's good, Cal."

Did he suspect something? Cal wondered. He contacted the Cornwall Regional Task Force and requested permission to fabricate a file with agreements and an irrevocable confirmed purchase order (ICPO) from Bulgaria. It was granted.

Cal sat down at his computer — the forger's friend — and, from blank sheets of paper, created a twenty-three-page file of documents, complete with letterheads, seals, and signatures, including:

202 |

- *Bulgarian company registration for C. Broeker Ltd.;*
- *the same for Omnigroup;*
- *agency appointments for both companies to NDM Inc.;*
- *general information pamphlets on Bulgarian trade;*
- *information on the Vitosha Hotel; and*
- *the ICPO document.*

He faxed all this off to Nick Miller two days later. The same day, he received back the NDM banking information.

### April 30, 1996 — Wal-Mart, Cornwall, Ontario

Driving a brand-new white Lincoln Continental, Bobby Paulson pulled into the Wal-Mart parking lot looking for the Quacker. He wore a black-and-white-checked double-breasted suit with a black silk shirt, no tie. The Quacker was a green Chevy 4 x 4 with a white canopy; inside it was an RCMP operative with sound-recording equipment that would pick up every word said in Bobby's car. Bobby saw the Quacker down near the Norcan money exchange and parked in the spot opposite it. It was 10:45 a.m.

Ten minutes later, a black Chevy bearing a New York licence plate pulled in right next to the Quacker. Jon Blake got out of it, wearing pale blue pants, a pale blue T-shirt, and a red-and-white windbreaker. He walked straight over to the Lincoln, opened the passenger door, and got in.

"Everything's cool," he said.

"Good," replied Bobby. "I've set up the business and have now received the bonds. It's set me back eighteen grand in legal fees, Jon."

"Yeah, well, things are tough all over, Bobby. I'm shelling out $3,500 a month for the fucking warehouse, man."

"Cal told me you got some problems with heat your end?"

"Nah, not really. It's with our contact in Hamilton, and it ain't a serious problem." Blake looked out of the window, thinking, then added, "Cal's met the Hamilton end. If you want, you're welcome to go meet him yourself, you know. See there's no cause for concern."

"S'okay, Jon. I trust you. But you can't be too careful, right?"

"Oh, yeah. Careful's gotta be our middle name."

"Jon, I gotta say that I'm not too impressed with Dick — he doesn't seem to understand the business."

"He's new to the business, Bobby, but he's a very bright guy. *Very* bright. He's vice-president of Arizona Charlie's casino in Vegas, for fuckssakes." Blake paused, looking quizzically at Bobby. "You know the business is Larry's, don't you? Cal musta told you 'bout Larry, didn't he?"

"Some."

"Well, Dick's handling everything for Larry right now, 'cause Larry's tied up on this Russian casino deal. But in this business, Bobby, Larry's the fucking king. He's made *millions*, millions and millions."

Blake then reached into his coat pockets — there were four of them — and pulled out four bundles of Canadian hundred-dollar bills, glancing around to make sure no one outside was able to see. "There's thirty-eight grand Canadian here," he told Bobby. "You're gonna wire twenty-seven grand U.S. to the account that was faxed to Cal. I'm gonna be paying the additional monies to Dick myself, directly, under the table." He then peeled two bills from one of the bundles, saying, "Using the 140 figure we discussed, the total amount should only be $37,800. Unless you prefer I leave the two in?"

"Yeah, I would, Jon." Bobby took the bundles of cash from Blake and leaned over to place them behind the centre armrest on the back seat, adding, "Never know what you'll find in a leased vehicle, do you?" He then looked Blake in the eyes and said, "Should I be concerned about the money?"

"Concerned?"

"You know, Jon. Cops have a way of marking it. I can run it through a casino and then go to a friendly banker if you think it might be necessary?"

"There shouldn't be a problem." Blake paused. "But the cash did come from the business — 'bout a year ago."

"So it's dirty?"

"Yeah."

"I ain't taking any chances, Jon. I'm gonna run it through a casino, clean it. Sorry, but it's not I don't trust you. I just learnt to be careful — the hard way. Few years back in the drug racket, you know?"

"I'm happy to learn from other people's experiences."

"Better than your own, eh?" Bobby laughed.

"Dick wanted to move to three loads a week, Bobby. But . . . well, I realize we gotta take it slow and easy. You know: to get comfortable." Blake examined his fingernails for a few seconds before continuing. "I thought your suggestion we meet after the first load, discuss problems . . . I thought that was a great idea. It'll make sure we keep professional on this."

"That's why I wasn't comfortable with Dick's lack of experience."

"I'm gonna arrange for you to meet Larry and discuss it all with him — you know, before we get any bigger."

"Great, Jon."

"When you gonna send the money?"

"Tomorrow. When do I get my $18,000?"

"The moment the load arrives at the warehouse. I'm gonna be there, so don't worry. You wanna come to Hamilton with me, check it out?"

"Nah, it's okay, Jon. I got some other business to look after." Bobby lowered his voice. "Yeah. They just passed some new laundering laws down in the DR, and I got over six mill to move as a result."

"The DR?"

"Dominican Republic."

"That's a lotta cash."

"Right, so I'm not gonna be available till next week."

"Shit, Bobby, that's gonna make it too tight if we gotta do a load."

"I'm happy to leave it in your hands, Jon. I gotta good feeling 'bout you."

"Larry does wanna meet with you anyway," he said. "He's got other business to discuss as well — possibly in the West."

"At the right time, Jon, I can put together a meeting with my Asian contacts. That could do all of us a lotta good."

"With Larry we can all make some very good money, Bobby. *Very good money!*"

They shook hands and Blake climbed out of the Lincoln, walking back to his own car, next to the Quacker. Bobby pulled out immediately, circling the area on the lookout for tails. It was 11:10 a.m. Satisfied he wasn't being followed, he took off, heading for Ottawa with the cover team in tow.

### May 15, 1996

It was going to be a long, busy day. Bobby Paulson left for Windsor, Ontario, first thing in the morning, driving a new red Lincoln Continental and wearing a suit of shimmering green mohair with a black silk shirt. He was followed by Staff Sergeant Phano, a member of the task force. At 9:20 a.m., Bobby telephoned Sgt. Yves LaPorte, who, although he held a lower rank than Bobby, was in charge of Project Orienter. LaPorte told him that Clyde — the driver for Bobby's RGP trucking company front — was now on the U.S. side of the border and at the warehouse.

There had been numerous foul-ups over the preceding two weeks — papers weren't in order, containers weren't available, Jon Blake couldn't find any sand — but finally everything and everyone was ready to do the first load.

At 9:55, Bobby parked in a lot by a McDonald's, just below the bridge leading to the U.S. He had some breakfast and, exhausted from the long drive, lowered the seat and dozed for an hour. At 11:05, he telephoned Clyde, who said he was still loading the truck and would be another half-hour.

"Oh, Bobby," Clyde added, "they're gonna be putting a red U.S. Customs seal on the trailer. Okay?"

"Fine."

Bobby waited again. An hour later, Jon Blake called.

"I just spoke to my driver," Bobby told him. "He was still loading. Once we're on our way, we'll be about four hours, okay?"

"When you get to the intersection we discussed," Blake told him, "turn left. Got it?"

"I'll call when we're within twenty minutes."

Ten minutes later, Bobby called Clyde, who said he was now loaded but waiting for one of Joe Lutheran's people to bring him papers from U.S. Customs. Because they were reputable companies that the border authorities knew, Lutheran and Fritz and Co. were the agencies Cal Broeker had enlisted for NDM, the Miller group, to use in its shipping of the loads.

At 12:33, Yves LaPorte called. Apparently, there were more problems with the paperwork.

"We may need Cal Broeker to do a power of attorney," LaPorte told him. "Wait to see what Clyde says."

Clyde called at 12:55, seeking an update himself. There were problems with the paperwork, he confirmed. They didn't have a bill of lading, for example. For professional smugglers, thought Bobby, the Miller people were a joke. He phoned Joe Lutheran.

"I'm getting it in order," Lutheran said in a bored voice. "No bill of lading was supplied, so I'm making one out. Also, you got the wrong bond number on the invoice. I corrected it."

"I wanna get everything right, Joe, so the process is smoother on future orders."

"Marty tells me you got another load scheduled for Monday?"

Marty Block was with Fritz and Co.

"That's news to me, Joe. I'll look into it."

"I 'preciate you stayin' on top o' this, Bobby."

"I'm in business, Joe. I'm not fucking playin' . . . like some."

"Yeah."

"I'll call you end of the week or the first of next, okay?"

Bobby hung up and called Blake. He wasn't available. He called again two minutes later. Blake still wasn't available. Then he called Nick Miller.

"Hi, Nick, it's Bob. The paperwork's all fucked up. You aware of that?"

"Refresh my memory," said Nick. He clearly had no idea who was calling.

"It's Bob Paulson of RGP Transport."

"Oh, yeah. Okay, what's the problem?"

"The paperwork's screwed up."

"Is the truck loaded?"

"Yeah, but it can't leave."

"Is it still in the yard?"

"Yeah."

"Is there anything I can do?"

"I'm dealing with Joe Lutheran. Hopefully we can work it out. But I been trying to contact Jon to tell him we're delayed."

"I'll pass the message along," Nick said.

At 13:20, Yves LaPorte called and told Bobby to meet him at three o'clock in the local Becker's variety store. Five minutes later, Clyde called to say there was now a problem with the U.S. broker's paperwork. Bobby told him Joe Lutheran should be able to straighten this out. LaPorte called back at 13:58 to say that a power of attorney was definitely needed from Cal. He wasn't certain how such a document should be worded, so Bobby dictated it. LaPorte said he'd get hold of Cal. Ten minutes later, he called again to say that it was Nick Miller who'd called Cal requesting the power of attorney.

"Can you check this out with Joe Lutheran?" LaPorte asked Bobby.

Bobby called Lutheran. He was tied up on the phone with U.S. Customs trying to get the load processed, according to the woman who answered.

"The 7512 is filled out wrong," she said. "So now Schwartz Adler is required to give power of attorney."

"I'll try to expedite this," Bobby assured her.

At 14:15, LaPorte called back to say that Cal had been told to send the power of attorney. Just before 14:30, Jon Blake called.

"Finally!" Bobby said. "The paperwork's all fucked up, Jon. Fritz and Co. screwed up here. We're still trying to straighten it all out, so it's gonna be a while."

"Hang in there, buddy," Blake told him.

Clyde called two minutes later.

"I been sitting in a fucking room twiddling my thumbs," he complained. "No one's told me anything."

Bobby brought him up to date, then told him to get a copy of the power of attorney from Joe Lutheran.

"It's being sent by Schwartz Adler, tell him — the consignee."

LaPorte called a minute later.

"Can you meet me at Becker's in a half?" he asked.

"I already told you I would, Yves."

"Okay. See you there."

Just before three, Bobby stood inspecting cans of baked beans in Becker's with LaPorte and Staff Sergeant Phano. They discussed a stall tactic for the next load, eventually agreeing on complications relating to a shortage of containers. Bobby was going to say that unless the load was in a container, it might well be checked at the port in Montreal. They'd have to hold off until the following Thursday to do the second load.

At 15:20, Clyde called.

"All the paperwork's . . . *spaggen brrr-att taddi* . . . *opppti* . . . *aaackle* . . ."

Bobby held his phone at arm's length, then shouted into the mouthpiece, "CLYDE, I CAN'T HEAR A FUCKING WORD. GONNA CALL YOU BACK."

Back in his car, Bobby called Clyde.

"All the paperwork's together," the driver told him. "Now it's been taken for certification at U.S. Customs."

"Then you're off?" Bobby asked.

"Then I get given a copy," Clyde said, exasperated by bureaucracy, "which I'll have to get restamped. But at least we've got a red ball seal from U.S. Customs, so I don't think there'll be a problem on the Canadian side."

He said he'd call again when he was mobile.

Ten minutes later, he called back to say he was on his way and would call again only if there was a problem at Canada Customs.

At 16:25, Clyde called.

"I need a fucking letter of authority from you to drive a rental truck on your behalf."

"Jesus!"

Bobby drove over to the Canada Customs bond yard to meet Clyde, wondering all the while why the RCMP and Canada Customs couldn't co-operate a little on a venture like this, if only to avoid such time-wasting situations as the one that had come up. Clyde, a gaunt, sallow man in his late thirties, with a tangled mop of sandy hair, bad teeth, and an expression of perpetual sorrow, really looked like a trucker. He really looked like a trucker having a bad day too.

"Are you a representative of RGP Transport?" asked a poker-faced female customs officer whose mouth was barely wide enough for a teaspoon.

"Yes, I am, ma'am," said Bobby.

"Can I see some identification?"

Her eyes were the colour of tobacco smoke, and her hair had been pulled back so tightly into a ponytail that it looked painful. Bobby noticed that her lipstick was designed to make her lips, which were fuller than they actually seemed to be, the same parchment colour as her skin. He wondered if the job required this, or if she merely thought she needed to acquire more severity in her appearance. Dealing with truckers was no cake walk, after all. He handed her his driving licence.

"This is a driving licence," she observed.

"Right."

"I need identification that shows you are a representative of RGP Transport," she told him in a dead monotone. "Not identification permitting you to drive a motor vehicle."

"It's my company," Bobby said. "RGP . . . my initials."

"Your driving licence says William Robert Gordon."

*Shit.* Bobby made a mental note to bring the right driving licence with him in future. Next time it might not be a customs officer who noticed the disparity.

"Yeah. RGP — Robert Gordon and Partners, see?"

"No, all I see is B.S. I'm going to require proper identification."

"Is there a problem?" Bobby inquired.

"I am concerned about the lease arrangement you have with this truck."

"Everything's in order, I promise you."

"I don't need your promise, I need your identification."

"Why don't you call the leasing company?"

She looked at him without blinking, perhaps seeking the tell-tale signs of a liar. Bobby wondered what was going through her mind. If the eyes are the windows of the soul, he thought, then someone's closed the drapes. Whatever was in there was veiled by a pale smoky screen.

"What's the number?" she said at length.

"Um . . ."

Bobby looked anxiously at Clyde, who started rummaging through his coverall pockets. The customs officer looked back and forth from Clyde to Bobby.

"Any other ideas?" she asked after some minutes.

"Here it is!" Clyde yodelled, joyfully waving a crumpled carbon copy.

"Wait here," the officer told them, walking back to her desk to make

the call.

At 17:50, Jon Blake telephoned.

"We're tied up right now at Canada Customs," Bobby told him. "With some officers."

"Heat?"

"Nah."

"Trouble?"

"Not really. We should be done in an hour, hour and a half. I'll call you then."

Bobby hung up and called Staff Sergeant Phano to brief him on the situation and the concern about lease arrangements for the truck.

At 18:10, Cal called. Bobby told him about all the paperwork snafus. "When you're speaking to Nick," he added, "do mention our total fucking dissatisfaction with the way this thing is unfolding. And make sure he understands he's gotta cover another five grand in costs. Also, can you arrange a meet next week to discuss the future?"

"Imagine what working with amateurs would be like," Cal told him, his laughter rattling the earpiece of the phone.

Finally, the customs officer returned.

"I need to see the leasing documents," she announced.

Bobby looked at Clyde, whose features recomposed themselves, upgrading from an expression of sorrow to one of abject despair. In his orange coveralls, he looked like gift-wrapped cancer. It's enough to make a cat laugh, thought Bobby, whose mohair suit now seemed luminous in the low sunlight of the spring evening. His many bracelets and rings rattled in contradiction to everything he said. If he told this woman they were cops, she'd pop a vein. He didn't even *feel* like a cop. He felt like Lenny the Lounge Lizard.

"The leasing documents," Bobby repeated.

"Yes, they would be the ones." The customs officer tapped her ballpoint very, very slowly against her mannish fingernails.

"In the truck?" Clyde asked himself.

"No, I'd like to see them here," said the officer with the patience of Job.

"She'd like to see them," Bobby told Clyde.

"Here," added the officer, tapping.

Clyde walked over to the truck.

"Sorry for all this trouble," Bobby offered, feeling he'd told her to go fuck herself.

"It's what I'm paid for," the woman replied with stupendous sarcasm.

"You find the guys just love a gal in uniform?" Bobby regretted saying this as soon as the words were out of his mouth.

The customs officer merely looked at him, as if she was deciding whether he'd be better flayed or hung, drawn, and quartered.

Clyde seemed to be having some trouble with the truck door. He was hanging off the handle with both feet clamped on either side. Then he sprang back to the ground and started hammering with his fists on the panelling.

"Whassa problem?" Bobby yelled.

Clyde had dived beneath the truck and was on his back in the greasy gravel, reaching into the chassis. "A blotted duckling skis in!" he appeared to shriek back.

"Eh?"

Clyde wriggled out, covered in patches of damp, oil, and shit. "I've locked the fucking keys in it," he enunciated.

Bobby heard the customs officer exhale.

"Never rains but it pours," Bobby told her.

"I carry an umbrella," she said, "and listen to the forecast."

Bobby went over to help Clyde.

"There's an emergency door release," he whispered. "Somewhere."

"What you think I'm looking for?" Clyde said. "Easter eggs?"

It took them nearly twenty minutes to locate the door release, during which time the customs officer stood tapping out a requiem mass on her fingernails. Fortunately, the leasing documents were in the huge glove compartment.

"I need copies, not originals," the woman said as Bobby handed over the papers.

"Can we use your Xerox?" he asked her.

"No. You are required to provide copies, but we are not required to provide you with a photocopier."

"Then how do you suggest I make copies?"

"I don't suggest it — I'm telling you it's a requirement."

Bobby looked her in the eyes, thinking how perfect she'd be as the poster girl for *Ilsa, She-Wolf of the Nazis*. "Oh, come on, please," he said. "Give us a break. . . . It's been a really long day."

"And it's not over yet," she told him.

Then she took the leasing documents and went back into the customs building.

"No wonder crime pays so well," Bobby said. "We're all that stops it, and we can't even get from A to B without crashing into Z."

"Huh?" said Clyde.

The customs officer returned after ten minutes, holding copies of the leasing papers. She gave back the originals and said, "In future, make sure you have copies of these documents with you."

"Yes, ma'am."

"Now I need a letter from you," she told Bobby, "authorizing the use of this lease and confirming that this gentleman is your employee."

"I—" Bobby began to say, but she cut him off.

"You may use my typewriter."

"I have some letterhead in my car," Bobby announced.

"I'm sure you do," the woman said, looking him up and down. Then she said, "Bobby and Clyde, eh?" and the faintest wrinkle of a smile barely creased her cheek. "How sweet."

Finally, after two hours, the truck was released and sealed by Canada Customs.

"What a fucking bitch," Bobby muttered.

"I thought she was kinda cute," said Clyde.

Bobby looked at him. Maybe Clyde should get some R and R?


"WE'RE AIRBORNE," Bobby told Jon Blake at 18:39.

"You are?"

"I'm following the truck. We should be there around eleven-thirty. I'll call when we're twenty minutes away."

Blake called at 20:18.

"How's it g— *ggrrrk crippittorrrrrrk-mmkkkrlllnrrrr?*"

"Eh? Can't hear you, Jon."

"*Sssmmorrrkk . . . -attery . . . -eeds . . . kkkkrrk-arging.*"

"Or something."

The line went dead. Bobby saw the truck ahead of him pull into the | 213
Husky Service Centre, and he pulled in behind it, parking in the lot. He and Clyde went into the restaurant for some dinner. By 21:08, they were back in their vehicles, with another hour and a half at least to drive before they reached Hamilton.

At 22:18, Clyde called Bobby to say they were about twenty minutes from their destination. Bobby called Jon Blake repeatedly but got through only after ten minutes of trying.

"We're around ten minutes away," Bobby told him.

"Can you make it fifteen?" Blake asked.

"I suppose so. I know where it is, so we'll see you there."

"Great."

Bobby called Clyde to let him know contact with Jon had been made.

At 22:45, the truck pulled off Brampton Street, at the corner of Parkdale, and, following Bobby's Lincoln, drove to one of the side bays of the carpet warehouse. The moment it stopped, Jon Blake appeared.

"We gotta wait a coupla minutes," he explained to Clyde and Bobby. "Grant's on his way with the keys."

"What a fucking cock-up, Jon," Bobby said angrily after introducing Clyde. "The fucking paperwork nearly got the load seized. I can't believe how sloppy it all was!"

"I'm so fucking pissed with you, Bobby," Clyde hissed. "Getting me involved with a Mickey Mouse deal like this. It's a fucking miracle we didn't go down. They took away my licence, man, you'd have fucking hell to pay."

Clyde was only pretending, but he was real good at it.

"I'm so sorry, guys," said Blake sincerely, looking down like an errant schoolboy in the principal's office. "I really am. Let's go through the day and try to find where the breakdown was. All we can do is make sure it don't happen again."

"I'd say it was Marty Block," Clyde told him.

"Me too," Bobby agreed. "Fritz and Co. really fritzed it up."

"Yeah. Maybe we're gonna have to find a new broker."

"What's wrong with Cal Broeker?" Bobby joked.

"Cal?" Blake didn't get it at first. "Oh, Cal *broker*, right." He smiled, as if the assonance had never before occurred to him. "Cal *Broeker*. That's a good one!"

"Broke her? I'm not surprised, guy that size." Bobby wondered how Blake was with puns. "He must be hung like a horse."

Blake merely looked puzzled. Bobby told himself to shut up — the fatigue must be getting to him.

A car pulled in off the road and Grant got out, looking as if he'd been woken from a deep sleep.

"C'mon, open up," Blake told him.

Grant opened the massive doors and told Clyde to drive the truck inside. As it began to move in, two men appeared from the shadows. Blake introduced Bobby to Tom Habib and someone named Scott — a big, dangerous-looking guy with short black hair and wire-rimmed spectacles. He'd pumped a lot of iron in his time.

"Don't get into any conversation with these guys," Blake told Bobby out of earshot. "They're just here to help, and they don't need to know all the details of our business, okay?"

"Gotcha. Here." Bobby handed Blake one of his new business cards. "You gotta come see our new office. We'll have the meeting there next week."

"Sure."

"We spoke by phone, right?" Bobby asked Habib, approaching him.

"Yeah," Habib replied. "I'm a good friend of Cal's. We go way back. You gotta great partner there, Bobby. Cal's gonna make you lotsa money."

"Cal Broeker the broker," Blake said, and laughed.

"What's so funny, Jon?" asked Habib.

"Nothing," Bobby told him. "Habib? What is that — Pakistani?"

"Lebanese," Habib replied, looking worried that a dose of racism was about to be dished out.

"Where's Lebania, then?" asked Bobby, just to keep up his dumb-buddy front.

"Lebanon," Habib corrected him. "Middle East."

"Oh. I was thinking near China. . . . You know, Chinese — China; Lebanese — Lebania."

Once the truck was inside, Grant closed the warehouse doors. As Clyde got out, Bobby told him not to forget the papers he'd left inside. Tom Habib went to the rear and started to cut the seal. Clyde unlocked the doors and climbed into the truck, taking the quire of papers attached to the first pallet. Jon Blake dragged off the tarpaulin concealing a pile of cement breeze blocks, while Grant and Scott jumped into two Toyota forklifts and began unloading the pallets. Habib then left the warehouse holding the pieces of the seal he'd cut.

At 22:58, Bobby called Sergeant LaPorte to say that everything was going smoothly, and that he and Clyde would be about half an hour more. They waited by the breeze blocks while Grant, Scott, and Jon continued unloading pallets from the truck.

At 23:03, Staff Sergeant Phano called.

"Everything's fine here," Bobby told him, using a prearranged code. "Is the weather any warmer where you are? . . . Okay. . . . *Good!*"

Jon was standing nearby, so Bobby told him there didn't appear to be any heat. Then he added, "I shoulda stuck to moving fucking money — it's safer. You know, Jon, the only reason I got involved in this is Cal told me you guys had done it plenty of times and were professional. What I seen, I don't believe him."

"I don't understand what went wrong," Blake said, shaking his head. "Through NDM, we done this maybe six, seven hundred times over the past few years. Seven, eight loads a week to the rez. It's a fucking puzzle, is what."

"And the fucking container, Jon. You guys were gonna supply that, now we're left scrambling. What's that about?"

Blake was called over to the truck. The pallets were deeper in now, and Scott was hooking a chain onto one of them. Blake attached the other end of the chain to Grant's forklift and fed it out as Grant dragged the pallets to the edge, then drove back to scoop them out. It was a pretty fancy manoeuvre.

"You've done this before," Bobby joked to Grant, who laughed like a drain.

"A few times," he said. "A few. Hey," he added, "nice work with the pallets, Clyde. One load a few weeks back had 'em in sideways, and when we fucking tried dragging them, they broke. You done a good job, man."

Clyde acknowledged the professional compliment, then in a low voice asked Bobby if he thought the cement blocks were necessary.

"The scales aren't gonna be open," he said. "We can just guise it and run straight through."

"Yeah." Bobby thought about it, noting down the licence plates of two rental trucks that were also in the warehouse, one of them from Quebec.

Jon Blake, still uncomfortably embarrassed around Bobby, announced that he wanted to settle up for the hauling and pay him for the next load too.

"I gotta keep Clyde happy too," Bobby told him. "He lost a long haul to California because of this, and he's out five grand."

"Canadian load?" Blake asked.

"Yeah."

"I'll cover half of the five with you."

"'Preciate it, Jon."

Two other men arrived — real low-lifers, with sallow, jailhouse complexions — and started to help with the unloading. One of them, his teeth missing, had to be in his seventies. In running shoes, jeans, and a T-shirt, he looked, incongruously, like a prematurely aged adolescent.

"This is Paul," Blake announced, introducing Bobby to the old-timer. "He's Grant's dad. C'mon," he added in a lower voice, "let's get the money while the truck's unloading."

He led Bobby out through a side door and onto Parkdale. They walked across the street towards a doughnut shop, then Blake announced he'd forgotten his keys and told Bobby to wait while he went back to get them. Bobby felt a little uneasy. Farther down the road, he noticed two men sitting in a brown Chevy pickup with a canopy. It had an Ontario licence plate reading PORKY. Blake returned quickly, rattling his keys. Bobby noticed Grant's dad, Paul, come out of the warehouse too and head over to the pickup. Bobby walked with Blake to a black 4 x 4 and got in the passenger side.

"Wait here," Blake said. "I'm gonna get the money."

In the side mirror, Bobby saw Paul open the back gate of a Chevy station wagon and pull out two cylindrical objects. Blake left the 4 x 4 and walked over to where Paul was, taking one of the objects from him. When he returned, Bobby saw he was holding a large Thermos. Blake had just closed the door behind him when a white Dodge K Car drove up the street towards them. There were two men in the car, and as they passed by, the driver waved.

"You know that guy?" Blake asked.

"No," said Bobby. "I fucking hope you do."

The car stopped, did a U-turn, and then pulled in behind the 4 x 4. Bobby saw Paul walk towards it.

"If I don't," Blake said, "I'm gonna fucking whack him."

He got out. As he walked towards the white car, Bobby saw the pickup start and back up into the doughnut shop's laneway, facing him. The two men inside appeared to be watching what was going on.

"It was Paul's son," Blake announced as he got back in. "I'm glad I knew him or the fucker'd be laid out."

"Grant's brother?" asked Bobby.

"What?"

Blake opened the Thermos he was still holding and pulled out four bundles of bills — hundreds and twenties. He dumped them in Bobby's lap, saying, "Fifty grand."

"You're short," Bobby told him immediately.

Blake laughed. "There's another one," he said.

"It should be twenty-five Canadian for hauling," Bobby said, "thirty-seven for the next load, and twenty-five-hundred for Clyde."

"Hang on," Blake told him, getting out again.

He was back in a few seconds with the other Thermos, from which he counted out another $14,500.

"There's another thirty left," he said, more to himself than to Bobby. "I gotta pay some other people."

"How're we gonna handle the paperwork problems?" Bobby asked.

"This has gotta be professional, Bob. I swear to you these fuck-ups won't happen again."

"Well, maybe I was just unlucky," Bobby said to make Blake feel better. He knew he was supposed to be more relaxed now that the payoff had happened.

"You know," said Blake, now in a meditative mood. "I may not be that old, but I've learned a lot over the past seven, eight years. And one thing I've realized is . . . is that it's really, really important to be on time."

Slow learner, thought Bobby, saying, "Yeah, absolutely. When I was moving powder, someone's even five minutes late — I ain't there."

"Right." Blake nodded, then, wrestling himself from some reverie, he said, "Can you wire the twenty-seven U.S. either tomorrow or early Friday, so the order can be placed Friday aft?"

"Sure, but the load can't happen before Thursday."

"Agreed."

"Can we meet, say, Tuesday?"

"Not a prob," Blake replied.

"Ottawa would be really good for me."

"Ottawa it is, then."

"I feel like saying it was a pleasure to do business with you," Bobby said.

"But it wasn't?"

"It will be next time."

"Better fucking be. You wanna lift back to your car?" Blake asked.

He took Bobby back to where the red Lincoln was parked. Bobby took the money, placed it in the trunk of his car, and returned to Blake's vehicle.

"Never know what you're gonna find in a leased car," Blake said.

They both laughed.

"Much better to have leased wheels if there's a bust," Blake told him.

"You're preaching to the converted, Jon." Bobby pointed to where Clyde's truck was now parked outside the warehouse. "It's leased," he added, since Blake didn't seem to be getting the point.

The truck was alongside the white K Car, and Paul was now speaking to the driver, who resembled a much younger version of himself. Seeing Bobby and Blake looking his way, the driver leaned out and shouted, "Hey, Jon, when're you getting your boat out?"

"I haven't had time," Blake shouted back, getting out.

Bobby joined him and they walked over to the truck, where Habib was now replacing the seal.

"Don't you want the blocks?" asked Blake.

"Nah. The scales'll be closed. We're just gonna run them," Bobby replied. "Hang on to them, though — in case we do an earlier load."

"He's been practising this all week," Blake said, indicating Tom Habib and the seal. "Got it down to a fine art. But just in case he hasn't, you might need this." He pulled a similar seal from his pocket and handed it to Bobby.

"Number won't be the same," grumbled Clyde, who'd just appeared from the warehouse. "Still, better than fucking nothing."

At 23:55, Bobby called LaPorte and told him they'd be leaving shortly. When he hung up, Scott walked over and stood with them, watching Habib work on the seal.

"Moving fucking cash is easier than this shit-ass hassle," Bobby muttered.

"I been working with Jon three, four years," Scott told him. "Usually everything goes smooth."

"Usually."

Habib eventually declared he was done, so Bobby and Clyde walked over to examine his work.

"Looks good," said Clyde.

"Yeah, it does," Bobby agreed.

"I must've gone through a hundred seals getting it right," Habib told them, flushed with pride. "I tried all kinds of tools to get the cut right. See?" He plucked two pairs of pliers from his pocket, a cutter and a needlenose. "These are the only ones'll do the job. You gotta get in there, see, and grip the wire from the inside. This is the only tool you can do that with." He brandished the needlenose pliers. "Wanna know how I worked this out?"

He went on and on about his feat of fakery while Clyde backed the truck out onto Brampton Street.

"I gotta friendly agent in Montreal's helping me out with the container," Bobby told him to terminate the saga of seals and tools, of how he discovered this and how he realized that. "For fifteen hundred."

"Fifteen hundred ain't bad," Habib said, weighing the sum. "Well, as they say, a bull and a cow to feed, and a sow to market."

"Who says that, Tommy?" Bobby inquired.

"My mother used to."

"What the fuck does it mean?"

"You know . . . if no one gets greedy, everyone can make some money."

"A bull and a cow . . . I don't see how it means that, Tom."

"And a sow to market," Habib reminded him.

220 | "So? You sell the fucking pig, what's it got to do with the bull and the cow?"

"You have to feed them."

"I'd sell the whole fucking farm if I was you, Tommy," Blake called out, walking over to where they stood. "You ain't no farmer, pal."

"It's an old saying," Habib protested, a little hurt that his mother's proverbs were being trashed.

"Sounds like one," Blake told him. "You should be able to afford some new ones now, eh?"

"Thanks for your help, Tom," Bobby said, shaking his hand. "And I think your mother was right . . . about the greedy part." He winked.

"She was right about a lotta things," Habib said somewhat sadly.

"Be sure to send the cash early Friday," Blake told Bobby.

"Yeah. I'll see you Tuesday, Jon," Bobby replied, walking to his car.

"Bobby and Clyde, eh?" Blake called after him. "Faye Dunaway's a lot better looking."

Should never have introduced him to the mysteries of language, thought Bobby. He followed the truck — and Clyde — left on Brampton, turning around at the first corner, then heading along Parkdale to Highway 403. It was 4:00 a.m. when he'd completed his notes and placed his head upon a pillow — which was lumpy because there was $64,500 in a bag beneath it.


*May 25, 1996*

The second load, shipped on May 21, proceeded a good deal more smoothly. Everyone was happy — so much so that Larry Miller wanted to meet Cal and Bobby. Finally. When Cal, Bobby, and the other cops had discussed how things should be arranged so that Bobby could effectively supplant Cal as the Miller group's main contact, it had been decided that RGP Transport would buy out Schwartz Adler Ltd., Cal's company.

What was needed now was concrete proof of Miller's involvement in smuggling. The instructions were to get him on tape discussing his operations and actually using the term "smuggling."

Cal and Bobby met with Yves LaPorte and Staff Sgt. Ted Phano — who was heading up the operation on behalf of the OPP — in a motel near the border. Phano wanted Cal to wear a wire. Cal refused.

"It's too risky," he said. "They can pick up the signal too easily."

A device anyone could buy at Radio Shack would identify the transmitter's signal.

"You don't have any say in this!" snapped Phano. "You're nothing! You'll do as you're told."

"I don't have any say in my own safety?" Cal said, incredulous.

"Let's get the rat phone down here," Bobby said. "If Cal doesn't feel safe with a wire, he's not gonna wear it."

"Keep out of this, Gordon," Phano told Bobby. "I'm in charge of this part of the operation."

It was a problem having a senior inspector taking orders from a constable and a sergeant, but that was how Orienter had been set up.

"The fuck you are!" shouted Bobby. "You're not risking my agent just to save fucking face."

The two of them went at it hammer and tongs, with LaPorte trying to calm everyone down. In the end, Phano was out-voted, but he wasn't about to forget the incident.

Cal took the rat phone with him.


LARRY MILLER WAS A small, thin man in his sixties, with close-cropped grey hair and a rasping, guttural, street-smart voice. You couldn't see much Indian in him, except for the dark, suspicious eyes that squinted from hooded lids. In his blue work shirt and jeans, he looked like any other farmer from the Massena area, or indeed anywhere else in rural America. Cal and Bobby met him in the bar of his "club," with Jon Blake, Dick Fanzetti, and Nick Miller.

"I hear you work for Bobby now," Fanzetti said, referring to the buyout.

"Yeah, I should get a percentage of that, shouldn't I?" Blake joked.

"You know Cal," Bobby told them. "He lives so high on the hog, he was costing me too much in expenses as a partner. But he's not much better as an employee."

"More expensive than me," Cal said, to turn the conversation to business, "is the lack of professionalism we've seen from NDM with that first load, and the lack of communication between us."

"I gotta admit I was surprised by the lack of professionalism," Bobby added. "Especially considering Larry's had so much experience in this kind of operation."

It was a little heavy-handed, Cal thought. But Larry didn't seem to be bothered.

"We'll clean it up," he said simply.

Bobby then emphasized his vast experience with shipping and transportation; how he'd worked in Vancouver and the Far East, with the Colombians and the Chinese; and how he'd once worked in drug trafficking but got out.

"I had a partner," he said, "who's pushing up daisies now. That's why I got out."

Bobby was as bad as Dick Fanzetti when it came to hinting at violence. Cal felt that they should keep this on a business level — that this was the way to pull in the really big fish, those who ordered executions but were never anywhere near them.

"Where you living now?" Nick Miller asked Bobby.

"All over," Bobby replied, quickly changing the subject. "Another concern of mine is all the new faces that appeared when we were working in Hamilton. That kinda thing disturbs me. I shouldn't have to be exposed to all those people."

"I understand," said Larry.

"Then, perhaps, Larry," Cal cut in, "you could identify who's who here. You know, in terms of our working relationship."

"We're all in this together," replied Larry, "as far as I'm concerned."

"Good. That's my understanding," Cal told him. "I don't wanna work with kids. I'm doing this because you're involved, Larry. That's why I'm willing to share the Bulgarian side, and that's the reason for this meeting."

"Cal deals with the Bulgarians," Bobby said. "I won't do it. I don't understand your deals with the fucking Russians either, Larry. They're worse than the fucking Colombians."

"Much worse," agreed Fanzetti.

"What's this other deal Nick mentioned?" Bobby inquired.

"It's Nick's deal," replied Larry.

"I don't know nothing about any other deal," Blake complained. | 223 "I don't want it affecting what we already got going here."

"Is it cigarettes?" Bobby asked.

"Yeah, but it's Nick's deal," Larry repeated. "It's for him. It's a good, safe deal."

While Bobby, Nick, and Jon Blake discussed this other venture, Larry talked with Cal. The rat phone was on the table between them, the way Cal normally had his cellphone.

"Tell me about Bulgaria," Larry said. "How long were you there?"

"About eight months total."

"How many strong contacts you got there?" Larry narrowed his eyes to slits. It was a sign that he was intensely interested in a topic.

"Government," Cal replied. "Customs. Economic groups."

"I got strong Russian connections."

Cal wasn't sure whether this was a threat or a boast. Larry didn't give away much.

"Mafiya? Government? Who you got?" he asked.

"The top. The *most* powerful."

"Then what do you need me for?"

"I need a trusted person to set up an operation smuggling items into Russia from different places. Can you do it?"

"Depends on what and where."

"An example," Larry continued, leaning closer to Cal, who could smell something rancid and cancerous in his breath. "I gotta supply two chemicals into the States that are controlled items. One is potassium perchlorate."

"Hold on, Larry," Cal told him, asking Bobby for some paper to write this down.

Bobby took some RGP letterhead from his briefcase. Cal told Larry to carry on.

"Potassium perchlorate," Larry repeated. "And the second is aluminum powder. It's for fireworks and explosives. It's called German black and comes from Deutschland." He pronounced it "Doochlund," and Cal wondered why the concession to language. "It's a very sensitive product," Larry went on. "I'll take care of the cross-border problem myself."

Presumably he was going to bring it through the rez.

"You got customs lined up, or you gonna find them once you got a stockpile?"

"We got all we can sell pre-sold," Larry confided.

"We got some history in moving Canada–U.S.A.," Cal let him know. "You need us to haul it?"

"If your way is better and cheaper, and we can trust your people, then yes, I will use you. But you gotta remember, this is fucking sensitive material. We gotta be very careful."

From subsequent hints, it seemed likely that his customers for these key bomb-making ingredients were Russians living in the U.S. But it is not known whether this lead, like so many other tantalizing leads Cal offered to the authorities both before and after, was ever followed.

"So," Cal asked, "specifically, what you want me to do?"

"Work for us setting up Canada to receive the chemicals, and give me a plan on transportation I can look at. Also, set up the Bulgarian side for us and my Russian partners." He leaned even closer, his voice lowered to a scraping hiss. "You'll make more money than on these little fucking deals."

"How much?"

"Millions. I trust my Russian partners."

"Well, I don't," Cal told him. "I don't even trust my Bulgarian partners — only as far as the money goes."

"I'd like to see your Bulgarian papers," Larry said. "Can you show them to me?"

"They're in Ottawa."

"Your people still good over there?"

"You tell me. Did you make money on the last two loads in Hamilton?"

"Yeah. Your people," Larry pursued, "can they handle Bulgarian customs? Are they doing business into Russia now?" Larry paused, then asked, "What's the tariff on booze, d'you know?"

"Yes to the first two," Cal replied. "As for the tariff, I can't be sure. I pay the Bulgarians to take care of their end. I think it's 12 percent of the total invoice amount and the duty. . . . I don't know for sure."

"Will you go over there for me and do a work-up? So we know for sure?"

Cal turned to ask Bobby if he could spare him to go to Bulgaria on Larry's behalf.

"No fucking way!" Bobby replied. "I need you here for the next coupla months to get a comfort level going on this project."

"If I *do* go," Cal told Larry, "someone pays expenses or it don't happen. I gotta program, Larry, that fucking speaks for itself. That's why Bobby's paying me till it hurts him. I *produce*, and I will produce."

"Okay," agreed Larry. "We'll discuss your terms when you see if we can do it. I also wanna send cigarettes and alcohol into Russia through somewhere to avoid taxes and duty. We can do cars too, and other things." He looked at Cal directly, eyes mere slits now. "I want you to work with me," he said.

"What can we do right *now* to fill the war chest?" Cal asked him.

"I got 141 containers of vodka in Kotka, Finland," Larry announced. "My people wanna smuggle it into Russia. Give us a quote for delivery from Finland to Bulgaria to Russia. Check it out with your friends, and we'll split two bucks a case — depending on how much your friends charge."

"What exactly is my position, Larry? You gotta spell out precisely what you want, you know, so I don't have to make a thousand fucking phone calls."

"Gimme a quote for delivery of 141 containers — that's packing sixteen hundred cases per — to Russia, anywhere in Russia, and we split two bucks."

"It's gonna be a problem," said Cal, "'cause we're gonna have to take it from rail to a Black Sea port or overland."

This was when Bobby made a big mistake. He cut into the conversation, saying, "No, we'll just take it directly by rail, straight to Moscow from Kotka."

The problem is that you can't do this. Because of NATO regulations designed to limit the old Soviet Union's capabilities of incursion into

Europe, or NATO's into Russia, the rail gauge changes at the border. Only specially designed trains can cross over, shifting their wheels to accommodate the different gauge. They had to be booked up to a year in advance. It was clear that Larry knew this and was disturbed by the fact that Bobby did not. Cal, who was aware of the rail-gauge problem, tried to salvage the situation.

"C'mon, Bobby," he said. "You've never done this before. I *have.* And there's things I didn't tell you." He explained the problem. "I gotta have a few secrets, don't I?" He laughed.

So did Larry. Fortunately. Cal went on to suggest that the loads could be piggybacked, or that they could be off-loaded onto different trains — if, that is, they couldn't arrange a train with drop-wheels.

"You only want the smuggled price, right?" he asked Larry. "Not the regular delivery."

"Fucking right! The taxes kill us, and this stuff is priced right — "

At that point, Bobby's phone rang. It was, presumably, another one of his arranged calls from Phano, but all the room heard was: "Yeah? . . . Where they want it picked up? . . . Uh-huh. . . . No way. Gotta be a fucking point more. . . . Right! Okay. That's a deal? . . . Good." Bobby hung up and apologized for the interruption, adding, "I just made twenty-five grand on that."

There was general joy — the joy of scammers — and people shook his hand.

"Split three ways, right?" joked Jon Blake.

Blake had picked up the rat phone and was idly looking it over. Unlike most cellphones, it did not have a read-out screen, which must have piqued Blake's curiosity. Normally this would have been okay, but when the phone was transmitting, you couldn't make calls with it. If Blake wanted to try it out, there was going to be trouble.

"Did I say 'grand'?" Bobby played along. "I meant twenty-five *hundred!*"

Fortunately, Blake soon lost interest in the rat phone and replaced it on the table. It had been a close call.

Cal returned to Larry Miller, saying, "Please try to come to the offices in Ottawa. I just don't feel comfortable speaking in restaurants and bars, you know?"

"Gimme a reason," Larry replied, "and I'll see what I can do. You work out something on the Bulgarian stuff — the vodka or the chemicals — and I'll come up there. I wanna see *results* first."

The talk about him not being able to get into Canada had been bullshit. Anyone with his connections on the rez could move across the border at will without ever seeing a Canadian immigration official. It was one of the many services offered by the Indians — for a price.

"You got results on the Hamilton products, didn't you?" Cal said.

"Oh, yeah. Your people did a great job." Larry narrowed his eyes again. "And you're well paid for it, I imagine?"

"Not enough."

"Well." Larry shrugged, staring at the ceiling. "We can do a load of tobacco from Seattle, Washington, to Vancouver right away. That's big money. Just like this Miami to New Jersey is big money."

"That Nick's deal?"

"I done it before. He's doing it now. It's safe. I got all I can handle right now taking care of Russia — and it's costing me plenty."

"How much is there in the Vancouver deal?"

"A lot. Talk to Nick." He leaned closer again. "Listen, Cal. Get me the info we discussed, and you an' me can go to Bulgaria — or wherever — and make some fast money. You work out the details. I'll be outside."

"Hey, Bobby," Cal said. "You working Monday?"

"Yeah. Why?"

"Is the Vancouver scene doable right away?"

"We got too much on our plates right now," Bobby replied. "Let's discuss it Monday. I'll contact Wong."

Wong was a fictional West Coast contact.

"I gotta go now," Larry announced, rising to leave.

Farewells were said, then Nick asked if anyone wanted a drink. Bobby and Cal politely refused.

"You guys ready to do a load to Ottawa?" Dick Fanzetti asked them. "We gotta great fucking warehouse there now. Very secure."

"That's a bit too close to our back door, isn't it, Bobby?" Cal said.

"Depends," replied Bobby.

"Who?" Cal asked Fanzetti. "Or is it your people?"

"It's Larry's customers, but we don't know the set-up. We're gonna head up there on Tuesday to check it out. You gonna be there?"

"It's up to Bobby," Cal replied.

"If it's an old customer of Larry's," Bobby said, "I wouldn't worry. D'you wanna use the office, Dick?"

"No, but thanks."

Nick then mentioned a scheme that involved using a replica of an old-fashioned riverboat as a floating casino.

"It's sweet," he said. "You pick up the passengers in Buffalo or wherever, and then float 'em down to Akwesasne, where they can gamble. Dick lined up the boat for Damien Love."

"Yeah," said Dick Fanzetti. "I gotta contact built this fucking boat for gambling and it's never been used. He was originally asking twelve mill for it, but the price has dropped to six."

"Love's only aware of 9.5 million, though," Nick added. "'Cept he won't give back the proposal."

"I should fucking run down to Damien and offer it for seven," Blake threw in.

"Yeah," said Fanzetti, "you do that, you're gonna be pushin' up daisies like Bobby's fucking partner."

Cal and Bobby got up to leave. Jon Blake said that he'd see them out, that he wanted a word alone. While Bobby went to the washroom, Cal and Blake walked to the parking lot.

"You know," Blake said, "I can give you guys all the inside stuff you need on the Millers."

Cal was suspicious. "What do you mean?" he asked.

"Whatever you need to know," Blake replied. "Like for this tobacco deal."

"Yeah?"

"I mean, you don't need to go through Tom and J.C." Blake seemed to be backing away from his original suggestion. "They don't need to know anything."

Bobby joined them, saying, "On the last deal, there was a guy sitting in the car with Tom, had a fucking rug like the toe of a hairy cowboy boot."

"Oh," Blake told him, "that was J.C."

"Right," confirmed Cal. "Unmistakable."

"I fucking looked like that," said Bobby, "I'd shoot myself."

They all laughed.

"I'm a bit pissed that Nick contacted you direct on this last deal," said Blake. "Without filling me in."

"They only offered ten grand," Bobby grumbled. "I don't think I can do it for that. It's chicken feed."

"Don't worry," Blake told him, "you guys are in now. I'll speak to Nick, get you thirty-five or forty. Listen," he added, lowering his voice, "the Millers are tight-asses when it comes to money, but I know how to work 'em. They'll make a hundred grand, you know, and pay the guy who takes all the risks a grand — if they can get away with it."

"Everyone should get a fair shake," Bobby said.

"Right," Blake agreed. Then, looking at Cal's Tag Heuer wristwatch, he asked, "What kinda watch is that?"

"It's a *man's* watch, Jon," Cal replied. Then, lisping, he added, "Unlike Bobby's, which is only for *therrtain* guys."

Laughing with them, Blake said, "You wanna Rolex, Cal? It's new. It's not original, you know, but it's, like, a good fake. Know what I mean?"

"I don't think so, Jon. "

IN THE CAR DRIVING BACK across the border, Bobby said, "That call I received, Cal—"

"Fucking brilliant, Bobby. Twenty-five grand!" Cal laughed.

"It was LaPorte telling me we're shut down."

"What? That asshole Phano?"

"No. The Crown told him we're breaking the law helping these guys ship liquor into Canada. We'll be arrested if we continue."

"Ah, Jeeeesus," Cal sighed, burying his head in his hands. "After all this work."

"Yves's gonna fight it for us, try to work something out. But we gotta slow it down until we're clear."

"Whose side's this Crown on, Bobby?"

"This is policework. This is what we're up against every day. But we gotta stay within the law or we're fucked in court, you know?"

"Yeah." Cal bit his tongue, wanting to vent more spleen. But Bobby didn't need to hear it. "I got a lot invested in this, Bob," he finally said.

"I know you have. So does Yves. He's gonna fight for us," Bobby said. "He's got a lot riding on it too. We all have."

AT THE MOTEL, they were further briefed by LaPorte on what had transpired and the problems that the Crown prosecutor had with the way the operation was going.

"I understand his side," said LaPorte, "and I think he understands mine. We just gotta work out a compromise. I'm not gonna let this go down. I'm gonna fight, don't you worry about that. Just hang tight in the interim, okay? We got some great stuff today. And, Cal, you did a great job out there."

This was said so that Ted Phano could hear it. He was still smarting over the morning's humiliation, and he wasn't a happy unit. As luck would have it, Cal was obliged to ride back to Ottawa with Phano in the car containing the equipment that was used to monitor the rat phone's transmissions. You could have cut the air between them with a knife.

After half an hour or so on the highway, Cal noticed ahead of them a beat-up old four-door saloon careering from lane to lane and even off onto the shoulder. The driver was a grizzled oldster in overalls and a greasy baseball hat, but in the back seat Cal could see two little heads.

"It's not for me to tell you your job," Cal said to Phano as diplomatically as he could, "but that asshole's gonna kill those kids the way he's driving. He must be drunk or on some medication. Shouldn't you pull him over?"

"Don't you fucking talk, okay?" barked Phano. "You don't tell me what to do. Just keep your mouth shut." Then, clearly realizing he was sounding unreasonable, he added, "This is an undercover operation. No one must see you, understand?"

"I'm not telling you your job," Cal persisted. "But isn't there something you can do? Radio ahead, give the licence plates, get a car here? I mean, shit, look at him — he's doing 120 and weaving all over the place. I just don't think it's fair on those kids."

Ted Phano was seething, but he could hardly argue with Cal over the safety of the two little passengers ahead of them. So he radioed the local OPP, only to be told they didn't have any cars in the area. The operator instructed Phano to pull the vehicle over himself and wait with it for back-up to arrive. Now he was really pissed.

"You just shut your mouth," he told Cal. "Don't talk about this again, got it? I'm violating all my protocols with this fucking shit."

"For saving the lives of two kids?" Cal couldn't believe this guy. "There isn't a judge in the world who'd say you did the wrong thing here, Ted."

"Just fucking shut up and stay in the car."

Phano had no option now that the call had been made. He got the car to pull over and went up to the driver holding out his badge. The old man got out of the vehicle, as he was instructed, but was so shit-faced drunk he could hardly stand. Real rural white trash. Probably his grandchildren, Cal decided, looking at the sweet-faced boy and girl on the rear seat. He wondered if they would make a better life for themselves, thinking of the hardships of his own childhood and the struggle to rise up and out of the narrowness and pettiness of a small town — a struggle that was still not over. Perhaps it would never be over? All he'd ever wanted was a family and a business of his own — and he still wanted these things deep down.

The warriors of old had no such baggage, not even a childhood. They were trained as soon as they could walk for one task only, and when they were performing that task, they didn't have to worry about legal red tape. They didn't have back-biting brothers-in-arms either, knights who were committed only nine to five, who said, "Oh, sorry, can't fight tonight. I gotta take my boy to little league." But perhaps, Cal considered, it was partly envy that made this bother him. He had no one to go home to, not really. And he wanted someone. He was getting weary of fighting a world that wouldn't or couldn't change. Bust one group of bad guys and there were always more to take their place — and always would be, the way things were set up. You couldn't use the Queensberry Rules to fight a guy with a MAC-10 and a chainsaw. Along with Bobby and LaPorte, Phano had done a phenomenal job with Orienter so far. Everyone wanted recognition, and Cal just wasn't a member of the club when it came down to it. He never would be — that's just the way it was. It would always be an uphill battle. Always. Suddenly, he wasn't sure how long he could go on fighting under these conditions. Even his idealism bothered the cops. Maybe it reminded them of the ideals they'd once had themselves; maybe it just scared them. He was a loose cannon, that's what they probably thought of him. He didn't fit in.

Phano had to radio back to say he was arresting the guy, he was so drunk. While he was doing it, the old man got back in his car and attempted to drive off. Phano had to rush over and tear out the keys. Then they had to sit and wait for most of an hour before some local officers arrived to take over the problem. Ted Phano would now have another page or so to write out in his notes for the day. With the operation now in jeopardy because of the Crown's apprehensions, Cal knew he didn't need that.

### *June 4, 1996 — Offices of RGP, Ottawa, Ontario*

Whether through the agency of Sgt. Ted Phano's dislike for him or not — he would never know for sure — Cal Broeker was suddenly taken off Project Orienter. At least, he was informed he'd no longer be needed in the field. But as Bobby argued, he was still indispensable in the RGP offices. Larry Miller and the others would be suspicious if they could no longer reach him, and besides, no one else could continue to keep up the (heavily documented) pretence that the Bulgarian project was still under way. Nonetheless, it was, for Cal, a slight — unnecessary, vindictive, unprofessional. Although they weren't about to question the chain of command, let alone bad-mouth colleagues, Cal's close associates on the case let him know that they didn't feel he'd received fair treatment. After all, the project would not have existed without him.

Yves LaPorte had fought heroically with the Crown to keep Orienter alive too. They'd reached a compromise: the RCMP would be allowed to pick off selected loads after they left Grant's warehouse in Hamilton. This way, the Miller group would not be affected — they'd have already made their money and wouldn't care — but it would send ripples through the buyers and back to Grant. The first bust seized one hundred cases of booze from a van in the Toronto area on June 3.

It was much on everyone's mind when Cal and Bobby met Jon Blake, Tom Habib, and Jacky Ciotto at the RGP offices. RGP's headquarters had been carefully organized to appear totally authentic, with maps, monthly shipping schedules, trucking documents all over the place, and a secretary on the phones dealing with orders.

Predictably, Jon Blake was not too concerned about the seizure of the one hundred cases.

"Grant cleared the load last night as okay," Blake said. "The van that got busted was loaded from a smaller truck away from the warehouse. It was taken outside of Kitchener — that's around thirty miles from the warehouse. Listen, it happens all the time. As far as we're concerned, the deal's still on."

"I don't like it," Cal told him. "I've shut down the load" — he meant further transportation of the empty truck — "and I'll reopen it only on your instructions and even then only with Bobby's approval. Take a look at this, Jon." He handed him a flow chart he'd drawn up that established a risk factor of 20 to 70 percent. "Bobby and me feel this kind of risk is too high to continue."

"Grant cut the numbers off the boxes too," said Tom Habib.

"And you don't have to worry about Grant rolling over if he's burned," Blake added. "He's a stand-up guy."

"I don't know these people," Bobby said. "I don't know the status of the guy that was busted. We need to feel comfortable about everyone in this deal."

"Grant's insulated from this guy even if he puked," said Habib.

"I've had a lot of trouble getting hold of Larry," Cal said. "I need certain information for the Bulgarian file. It's gonna cost, and I'm not gonna be able to get the fucking quotes without it."

"Larry left for Egypt last night," explained Blake.

"Shit. Well, why couldn't he contact me before he left? This is really fucking unprofessional."

"Larry knows you need some expense money," Blake said. "But there's a problem. He was tipped off that he's under investigation for tobacco deals he worked on between '92 and '94. He didn't want to expose you or Bobby until he's sure this thing's been cleared up."

"Who the fuck's investigating him?" Bobby asked in a worried tone.

"It's the IRS," replied Blake. "But he paid out eight million in taxes last year, so he's not too worried about it."

"Yeah, well I am," Bobby told him. "Are they gonna look into NDM?

And we transferred funds direct into Larry's account on the first three deals — what's that gonna do?"

"Don't worry," Blake urged. "NDM's not connected to Larry, and anyway, the investigation's not going past '93–'94. Larry's on top of it, and he ain't concerned."

"Is it worth five grand to make sure what kind of investigation's going down?" asked Bobby. "I got contacts through the mob out West can check out this kinda thing."

"Yeah, it's good, Jon," Cal said. "Comes back in writing on official letterhead, totally accurate."

"Larry probably would be interested," Blake decided. "I'll mention it to him."

"Any risk to me, I'm gonna talk through with my lawyer," Bobby said.

"You know what agencies are involved, Jon?" asked Cal.

"I'm not sure, Cal. But they're all U.S. There's no Canadian. You don't have to worry, guys, honest. You're not involved."

"I fucking hope you're right," Bobby told him. "And about our busted load . . ."

"I've lost loads before," Blake told him. "Most of the time, the Mounties just seize the stuff. I was even let go once without a fucking licence check. Trust me, this'll be forgotten. It was a weekend bust — the cops won't wanna do the paperwork."

"Da load's okay," announced Ciotto, resplendent in a Hawaiian shirt, canary yellow pants, and white patent-leather loafers with gold chains. "We gotta run it because next week's a down week. We doan wanna lose our money."

"We don't wanna lose our company," Cal told him. "Let me do some risk equations on the computer."

To buy more time and slow things down, Bobby had declared the following week down time, saying he'd bought one of his customs people a vacation and the man could only take it then.

"I run a probability vector along the X parallel," Cal explained, generating a riot of algebra on the monitor. "Then I divide the AB repeatability harmonic by the Y factor — that's you and Tommy," he told Ciotto. "Giving me 2 xy2 x pn3, which is ratified by the logarithm RC, then added on a Q vector."

Ciotto was deeply impressed. It was complete bullshit, of course — Cal just wanted to see how stupid they really were. His opinion of criminals, never high, had been steadily sinking. Most of them were flat broke half the time, and they lived in cheap rental accommodation with broads who were usually strippers or ex-hookers. True, when they went out, they had the $800 shoes, the $400 shirt, the leased Lincoln. The market in dia- | 235 mond pinkie rings would collapse without them. But it was mostly sordid little stuff of which their lives were made. And then there was prison.

Prisons, Cal had come to see, existed not to deter criminals from crime, but to deter the rest of us from crime. No one is rehabilitated — this is merely the myth that justifies their existence and our lack of any other solution to crime — and many quite enjoy their stay. Prisons are an honest man's solution to crime; if you want a real solution, ask criminals how they would solve the problem. Organized crime tends to be a lot tougher on infractions of its rules than disorganized society — and you don't hear a peep from the civil-liberties people about it. Buddy knows the penalty for theft if the victim is also one of the buddies. He's just not clear on what it is as far as we're concerned — and nor are we.

"My son's a computer whiz," Ciotto announced. "Yeah, he works in dat area for RevCan."

"Fucking support we're paying *that* company," said Bobby, "they should loan us his services."

Bobby then received a phone call. It was from Sgt. Bob Osler, who headed up Proceeds in Toronto.

"Your plate has been queried by Metro Toronto 21 Division," he said. "I'd like to discuss this with you."

"I'm in a meeting right now," Bobby told him. "Gonna have to get back to you on that order." He hung up. "Jeez," he told everyone, "business is booming!"

"What about the Vancouver thing?" asked Blake. "Nick's thing?"

"Doable," replied Bobby. "I can do it, but Cal's gonna be too busy."

"Okay," said Blake. "Great! Just don't fuck with those guys out there, is all, or there'll be bodies all over the place."

"Fuck you, Jon," yelled Cal. "Quit it with the threats."

"I wasn't threatening," Blake protested. "I was just pointing out that they were dangerous and you shouldn't fuck with them."

"You mean like we fuck with everyone else?" Cal said, pointing his finger at Jon Blake. "I'm getting fucking sick of having to prove myself to you people. I just wanna do business. I think I've proved enough."

"I'm not even talking to you," Blake told him in a "na na-na na na" tone. "Bobby's gonna be doing the deal, not you."

Blake was already seeing where his bread was buttered. So much for honour among thieves. *Fuck you, Jon.* Cal knew he'd be having the last laugh, so what did he care? It was odd, playing a game when you knew how it would all turn out. You knew the ending — you just had to get there. Unlike real life.

Cal tapped a few more fictional figures into the computer, saying, "And now, gentlemen, I present for your approval, the new and totally-revised-in-the-light-of-new-information *risk factor.*" (Actually, he'd just typed $19 \times 2 + 100 - 70 + 22 - 52 = ?$) "And I'm predicting under 40 percent. What will it be? Place your bets."

He hit Enter. A big 38 percent appeared on the screen.

"Wow!" exclaimed Habib. "I'm impressed."

"You're gonna have to show me how to do that one day, Cal," Blake said. He wasn't joking either.

"That's more acceptable, isn't it, Bobby?" Cal asked, referring to the new risk factor.

"Definitely a fucking improvement on the last one," Bobby replied. He paused before adding, "I think we can proceed with those odds."

There was general jubilation, especially from Tom Habib and J.C.

"Can I speak with you alone a minute, Jon?" Bobby asked.

They both went into the private office, but they left the door open.

"I've looked into that other matter on the money for you," Bobby told Blake. "I've gotta company on the shelf I could fix up for you. It'd cost eight hundred Canadian. And for money cleaning, I could do it for one-three-six. After three months, you could be earning dividends, Jon, and the money will be protected like Mother Teresa's virginity through a lawyer I've used for years. But the minimum amount's gotta be five hundred grand."

"I like it," Blake decided. "I like it a lot. I'll definitely do something soon, okay?"

"Great. But, Jon, don't let Larry or Nick know about it, okay? I'm doing it solely as a favour for you, all right?"

"No prob. I appreciate it, Bobby."

They returned to the main office, where everyone said their goodbyes.

"We should have a meeting like this every coupla weeks," Blake enthused.

"Yeah," J.C. agreed. "Dis was a fucking good meeting, wasn't it, Tommy?"

"Oh, yeah! One of the best meetings I ever had."

"I'll get back to you soon, Bobby," Blake said. "I don't wanna carry these papers over the border. Not a good idea."

He waved the sheaf of documents relating to the next load.

"You're right," Bobby told him. "Cal, can you make sure you fax Nick and Jon the docs?"

"Sure thing."

Bobby's phone rang again. Sgt. Bob Osler was on the line.

"Hold on," Bobby told him, ushering everyone out.

"Hey, Bobby," said J.C.

"What?"

"You gonna be having da cars shadowing da truck again like you did before?"

"Is the pope a Catholic?"

"Course he fucking is. Isn't he?"

"I must say, J.C.," Bobby told him, deadly serious, "you look fucking brill today, you really do. Where'd you get those white loafers, man?"

"Vegas." J.C. affected an aw-shucks expression, picking at his sartorial nightmare. "You like da get-up, eh?"

"You are just one helluva natty dresser, ain't he, Cal?"

"The reincarnation of Beau Brummel himself," Cal agreed. "I'm only surprised women don't jump you in the street."

"Yeah? Well," J.C. chuckled, "mebbe dey do."

Cal led everyone out, and Bobby returned to his call.

"Sorry to keep you waiting, Bob."

"I thought it was trucking, not male modelling," Bob Osler said.

"Diversify, diversify — you're behind the times, Bob."

"And glad of it. So what are we gonna do about your vehicle being run?"

"You think it warrants any action?"

As they discussed this latest development in inter-police non-communication, Bobby watched through the window as Cal herded everyone into Habib's grey Cadillac.

238 |                                        —

June 23, 1997
News Release from United States Attorney
Northern District of New York

United States Attorney Thomas J. Maroney today announced that the following individuals have been charged with conspiring to conduct financial transactions which promoted a massive scheme to defraud the United States and Canadian governments of tax revenues due in connection with tobacco and liquor products which were smuggled into Canada.

John W. "Cookie" Lamoure, age 56, of Malone, New York
Damien M. Love, age 38, of Bombay, New York
Daniel L. Surprise, age 49, of Hogansburg, New York
Larry V. Miller, age 52, of Massena, New York
Nick L. Miller, age 31, of Massena, New York

[twelve others were also mentioned]

The money-laundering charges were included in a sealed seven-count indictment returned by a Federal Grand Jury in Syracuse last Friday. The indictment, which was unsealed by Chief U.S. District Judge Thomas J. McAvoy in Watertown today, also charged the following defendants with conspiring to (a) defraud agencies of the United States Treasury Department, and (b) aid and abet individuals engaged in smuggling tobacco and liquor products from the United States into Canada:

Richard A. Fanzetti, age 61, of Las Vegas, Nevada
Larry Miller
John Lamoure
Damien Love
Nick Miller

Upon conviction, each defendant charged with participating in a money-laundering conspiracy faces up to twenty years in prison and a fine of $500,000 or twice the value of the under-lying transaction. The indictment also seeks forfeiture of $478,061,239, as well as substitute assets which the defendants have acquired throughout the United States.

Each defendant charged with participating in a conspiracy to defraud the agencies of the United States faces an additional term of incarceration of up to five years in jail and a $250,000 fine.

The final count of the indictment also charges former Akwesasne [St. Regis] Mohawk Tribal Chief L. David Jacobs and Danny Surprise with conducting the affairs of the Akwesasne–St. Regis Mohawk tribe through a pattern of racketeering consisting of bribery and extortion which deprived the people of Akwesasne of the rights to the faithful and loyal service of their elected representative. L. David Jacobs and Danny Surprise face up to twenty years in prison, a $250,000 fine, and forfeiture of $185,000 in cash or substitute assets.

Evidence of the underlying criminal activity was developed through the cooperative investigative efforts of the Internal Revenue Service, the New York State Police, the United States Customs Service, the Bureau of Alcohol, Tobacco and Firearms, the United States Border Patrol, the Federal Bureau of Investigation and the Royal Canadian Mounted Police. The contribution made by dedicated agents and investigators from each of these law enforcement agencies has been essential to the success of this undertaking.

LARRY MILLER WAS IN Russia when the indictment came down. He was persuaded to return for his trial only upon hearing that if he did not, Nick Miller would be tried for the sins of his father, as well as for his own. Both were found guilty as charged.

# Cold Shots:
# Coming in Heavy

*In ceremonies of the horsemen, even the pawns must hold a grudge.*
— BOB DYLAN

The criminal underworld is a place of rumours and smoke, a constantly shifting verbal subculture where hard facts are a scarce commodity. There is no *Wall Street Journal*, no *Report on Business*, no *Barron's*, no *Who's Who*, no Standard and Poor's. It is a vague, fugitive world, tantalizingly imprecise. To make things even more difficult for the working hoodlum, the global trend that had been transforming legitimate business in the 1990s was having its own effect on the parallel world of contraband. Things were changing fast in the realm of crime. There were many disparate groups of buddies doing business on the international black markets, but their connections were tenuous, often existing solely on a deal-by-deal basis. Business recommendations came in the form of personal referrals — "He's a good fella," was the classic form of introduction in the old style — but geographical distance and inter-ethnic considerations meant that such hearty connections could not always be made in person. Deals could fall apart at any time, and the rip was always there, waiting to happen. The disorganized nature of organized crime was custom-made for undercover agents to exploit. In a world where it was bad form to ask for even a last name, they could manoeuvre, prevaricate, sail along on sheer bluff.

For instance: in the spring of 1996, when Cal Broeker returned to Montreal from protective custody with the Secret Service in Vermont after the arrest of Réal Dupont, Pierre Maille's people came and found him at the antique shop on Greene Avenue in Westmount and demanded an explanation. Justinian Sabot and an Iranian buddy named Reza Kashani turned up at Cal's borrowed store under the pretext that the latter was looking to sell an antique scimitar with a mother-of-pearl inlay on the handle. He maintained it had been in his family back home in Teheran for generations. Big Cal, connoisseur of military artefacts that he was, wasn't impressed with the weapon; they were a dime a dozen in the Near East. This one looked like it had been purchased at an airport souvenir stand. But the scimitar wasn't really what Sabot and Kashani were there to talk about.

"Maille wants to see you," Sabot said.

Broeker had been expecting this visit ever since the Dupont takedown. He didn't blink. He was ready as Teddy.

"Fine," he said, "Set up a dinner."

PIERRE MAILLE, WITH HIS Kestrel Investments, had been the money man behind Réal Dupont. He was planning to take the $16 million the jolly Dupont was going to make from the counterfeit deal and move it offshore for him, facilitate that Caribbean fantasy. He allegedly performed similar services for the Mohawk runners. Maille's set-up was — what else? — shady import-export. Kestrel was similar to the Leroys' Arroway Ltd., but Maille made even less of a pretence of carrying on legitimate business. Kestrel was a flat-out front. Maille had fishing boats in Nova Scotia that took loads of potatoes down to South America and returned with doubtful cargoes. Kashani was his "consultant" for Middle Eastern activities; he was to Iran as Vulko Markov had been to Bulgaria. And Maille had strong connections to the multitudinous gangs that did business in Montreal.

The authorities were aware of Maille's activities, but they had never been able to make a case against him. He was thin and dark, in his mid-thirties. He wore his hair in a carefully maintained lounge lizard quiff and wore expensive casual clothes. He had several Porsches in his collection of fine automobiles. He owned a restaurant called Chief Joe's, a steakhouse in downtown Montreal, on Peel Street, and it was there that | 245 he and Sabot sat down with Cal Broeker.

The decor at Chief Joe's was standard-issue southwestern, with the usual Navaho blankets, mounted buffalo heads, and Apache head-dresses. Cal wondered what the Mohawks made of it. He saw that Maille and Sabot were looking sideways at him under lowered lids. Maille reminded him of Robert Goulet. Their suspicion was palpable; it hung heavy in the air. But after a few pleasantries, Maille was direct. He wasn't a killer himself, but Cal knew all the guy had to do was pick up the phone. Somebody like Little John, a member of the notorious Rizzuto crime family, would see to the rest. C. Calvin Broeker would be turned into a grease spot somewhere, then just a memory. All the same, Maille and Sabot proceeded with caution.

"What are you?" Maille asked. "A cop?"

Okaay.

Cal took a deep breath. He remembered that rumour was the greatest power in the world. During Cal's basic training in the air force, an instructor had gone to the first man in a room of fifty trainees and whispered in his ear, "The Russians are Communists." He had this man turn and whisper the exact same sentence to the man behind and so on, until it reached the last airman in the room. When this guy repeated the sentence back to the instructor it had become "We have to rush faster at our meals or receive punishment."

"Look," Cal said evenly, "Dupont got greedy. He tried to do a last-minute deal; he tried to fuck me, so I fucked him. If you're gonna rip me, you're gonna go to jail, I'm not. You interested in history, or you want to go forward with the deal I'm working on now?"

"You're a fucking cop," Maille insisted.

"Oh, yeah? How come I've got a casino with the Mohawks?" said Cal. It was sheer bluff.

"You crazy?" said Sabot. "They're gonna slit your throat, you go back there."

"Been living there the past year and a half," Cal announced with enormous satisfaction.

He hadn't, of course — hadn't been on the rez at all. And there was no casino. But if you're going to tell lies, why bother with little ones?

"Look," said Cal with enormous patience, "everybody lost face with Dupont. I lost money. I got hung up with the RCMP, the Secret Service. Nothing happened to you. You didn't lose any money. So don't fuck with me, or you'll end up like Dupont."

That tough kind of talk sold them. When Cal got down with his brutal-gangster jive and made with the threats, he was damn intimidating. Cops didn't talk like that. Maille and Sabot didn't know what really happened with Dupont; they were so scared of the guy, they hadn't even talked to him after the bust — nor did they go to his trial. Like everybody else, they were relieved he was off the streets. They too had been on the receiving end of his threats of terrible mayhem.

"How come you're back in Montreal?" asked Maille, somewhat mollified.

"I was arrested by the Feds in the States," said Cal. "But I'm not going back."

It took a few more meetings and phone calls to satisfy Maille and Sabot. Cal talked and talked. Once he got started, he was impossible to stop, a mellifluous stream that meandered in all directions through the underbrush. A couple of hours with Cal could make the head spin. It all sounded impressive, but you just couldn't put your finger on any of the details. It was clear who he was: he was undeniably C. Calvin Broeker. What he was — that was something else. He wasn't Constable Jones posing as Bad, Bad Leroy Brown. He wasn't Ratso Rizzo looking to snitch off a buddy to cop to a lesser jail term. What the fuck was he?

If Cal was indeed police, Maille had to think twice about where ordering him killed might lead. If he was connected to the Mohawks, that might not be so good either. Killing him might lead to retribution from that direction. Then there were the Russians. They tortured folks — there was amateur dentistry, electric prods, amputations. You ended up toothless and blind, with your scrotum stuffed in your mouth. It was safer just to leave him alone. For the moment. In the end, Maille offered Cal a place at Kestrel and his name on the desk. No longer threatened by him, Maille and Justinian Sabot went back to sleep.

WHEN ORIENTER CAME TO a conclusion in 1997, Cal went once again to Montreal and set up in the Manoir de Belmont on Sherbrooke Street. Agent O.4649 was on a roll. Both Orienter and the Dupont bust had been hugely successful; the former had paid $20,000 and the latter $100,000 (if over three years). Plus expenses. When an LOA was in force, he got a weekly salary, plus a bonus in increments. He had decided to devote his life to undercover work. It was fighting the good fight, and the pay wasn't that bad. It had the makings of a life. And Cal was making himself a new life in Montreal, one that could blend seamlessly into UC projects when it needed to, one that erased the betrayal and humiliation of the past and erected a new C. Calvin Broeker on the foundations of the old. He'd shriven and purified himself as a lone warrior long enough. Now he wanted to build again, throw down roots, stay awhile. He wasn't certain anyone could incorporate this sort of work with a normal life, but he was sure going to try.

But he also tried to visit his two sons down in New York State whenever he could. And he was still looking for Ron Ong. He had discovered that everything in Ong's life was rented or leased: the houses, the cars, the whole deal. Anywhere he perched, he was able to disappear overnight. The man had talent.

Cal was cultivating a certain big-city polish too. He grew an urbane beard, which he wore close-trimmed. The apple-cheeked country boy from upstate was developing a distinct resemblance to the bearish rockabilly shouter Ronnie Hawkins in his early sixties prime. Now Cal had an elegant apartment, a vintage black Mercedes, and a closet full of stylish suits.

Who said crime doesn't pay?

Elizabeth wanted to get back together, but there was no way now that he could live on the rez. Besides, he was seeing another woman, a glamorous one for sure. Simone Vega was a well-known actress and singer in Quebec; she had more than a dozen CDs and a score of movies to her credit. She had come up from a rough-and-tumble childhood, through singing in strip bars and vaudeville houses as a teenager, to a solid, respectable career in the self-contained entertainment world of francophone Quebec.

Dark, beautiful, cultivated, Simone spoke five languages. She owned a house in fashionable Outremont. She had hair the colour of the gold in old paintings. In Montreal, she was definitely a celebrity, a star, an estimable beauty. Simone had been through a marriage to a European aristocrat that had resulted in two teenage sons. There had been a lengthy relationship with a jet-setting financier. There were plenty of women in this time of savage money-hunger who fervently believed life with a wealthy man spelt unalloyed happiness, but Simone Vega could tell them a horror story or three about the world of yachts and private helicopters.

Cal met Simone just as Orienter was getting under way. They met at a party at the antique store on Greene Avenue, a reception for a concert pianist. The building was one of those former mansions built in greystone by the Anglo-Scottish bankers of Victorian Montreal. Cal was preparing the hors d'oeuvres and serving them, wearing his apron and tie, making polite conversation. No matter how far he got from the grocery store in Chateaugay, Cal maintained a continuing interest in food. Besides, it didn't matter whether it was villains or violas, there was no milieu extant into which C. Calvin Broeker couldn't insinuate himself. He took pride in the growing stock of roles he knew he could play if he had to — and in this work, you never knew when the opportunity would arise.

Simone had been invited to meet *un antiquaire*. When she first laid eyes on Cal, he was so big and tall that she thought he had to be standing on a box. When he stepped out from behind the table, he noticed that she was staring at one of his size-fourteen-plus brogans.

"Is something wrong with my shoe?" Cal enquired.

After some further conversation, he asked her if she would like to see his collection of Celtic runes. It wasn't the most original come-on she had ever heard, and a woman as attractive as Simone had heard plenty in her time. Still, it was kind of amusing. She had never met anyone like this American with the outsized personality. He appealed to her. She forgot all about *l'antiquaire*. They had a laugh when she later discovered that Cal himself was the man she had been invited to meet.

Soon, they were seeing a lot of each other. Eventually, feeling he could trust her — since, after all, there was no question that she was who she purported to be: a novelty in itself — Cal told her what he was doing with his life. It didn't faze at her all; in fact, she was fairly intrigued. Ladies love outlaws, they say. If Cal wasn't a really bad boy, he wasn't your average straight citizen either. In the showbiz world in which she moved, he was certainly an exotic. Simone found his mission against the world's monsters heroic, noble too. She'd seen her share of villains — in showbiz who hadn't? — and she'd always felt that they shouldn't be allowed to get away with it forever, that retribution should come. Cal the Sword of the Lord seemed to be bringing a little much-needed balance into the world, and without being too preachy about it. She liked that, liked it a lot. The men she had known were all singular personalities, exceptional individuals. And there weren't two Cal Broekers around either.

For his part, Cal was knocked out and a little astonished that a woman as beautiful and celebrated as Simone would even give him the time of day. Like they say, you can take the boy out of the country, but you can't take the country out of the boy. There was a problem, however.

Simone was often recognized on the streets, and she was afraid that this would cause trouble for Cal, who definitely did not want to be noticed, especially by any associates of Larry Miller, Dick Fanzetti, Jon Blake, Réal Dupont, the Mohawk smugglers, the Genoveses, the bikers, or the Russians. But apart from that, it was the love affair of Cal's life. Simone was doggedly loyal in terrifically difficult circumstances. After the betrayals he had suffered at the hands of his brother and his ex-wife, Cal profoundly respected loyalty. Together, he and Simone made a formidable couple.

AS SUMMER TURNED into fall, he started loading LOAs as fast as the RCMP would let him. Cal was developing law enforcement into a freelance entrepreneurial activity, another form of gonzo capitalism. He was a new kind of bounty hunter. Soon he was hacking his way through a dense thicket of undercover operations.

As well as looking into Maille's activities, he was asked to work on Project KGB, a Mountie investigation into Montreal's Russian and East European gangs. The Vic MacLoden arms probe was going on, and then one of his Mohawk contacts, a guy named Joey, told him about an upstate New York produce company that was smuggling tobacco at the same time as it was bringing fruit and vegetables to market in Montreal.

Joey said the Americans were unloading the trucks at two different isolated spots in the rez. Cal had been told by his RCMP handlers that if he went on the rez, it would be the last time he worked. They just couldn't take the chance. But Agent O.4649 was the stubborn type.

He met Joey at Matisse's. The Mohawk wanted him to either buy product from these loads or else ship something back in the empty trucks — or just front some money to the runners on behalf of his legendary East European connections. Russians, Bulgarians — they were all one to the Indians; they didn't make much of a distinction. But then, Larry Miller himself somehow thought that Cal was a Russian. Once Andrei Lukanov had been gunned down at his front doorstep, Cal's contacts in Bulgaria weren't worth a dime, but none of the bad boys in Montreal exactly kept current with events in Sofia — and Cal wasn't about to help them out.

Joey said, "If you want to meet some of the guys, show up at Reboska's." It was a little diner downtown on the rez. He decided to take the chance.

NOW IT WAS WELL into autumn; the night was dark and rainy on Akwesasne. He pulled on a set of camouflage fatigues that dated back to his air force days. He had a car drop him off on the autoroute near the rez. He climbed the fence and went through the woods, armed with his cellphone and a pair of binoculars. He set himself down in the woods and peered through the binocs.

He could see the smuggler's trucks unloading in the moonlight. He got the numbers on the plates; he got the company names on the side of the trucks. And he phoned the information to his handlers. Then he got up and trudged back through the wet woods to the autoroute, where his ride picked him up. He made some notes, then called Staff Sgt. Brian Byrne at the RCMP's customs-and-excise branch. He told Byrne he had just seen the trucks. Byrne told him they just wanted to do a quick in-and-out kind of deal. When he heard about the next load, he was to tell them and C & E would pick them off as they exited the reservation.

In a semi, there was a ledge for a reefer, "the shelf," they called it. The

New York truckers had built up a bulkhead that could hold ten master cases of cigarettes. Then they welded the bulkhead shut for the run up to Canada. The trucks, crammed with produce, were crossing the border and emptying their load. On their way back empty to the States, they would stop at the rez, fill the bulkhead with product, and re-weld it, or if rolling empty, just keep the welded plates on the floor of the trailer.

It was sweet, real sweet.

The next time a big load was coming up to the rez, Big Cal went into his swamp-crawling routine again. Wearing those camouflage fatigues and toting the cell and the binoculars, he watched two trucks unload. This time, two C & E undercover cars carrying Byrne and Cal's coverman, Charles du Lac, followed the smugglers on the autoroute back to the border. When the smugglers came back north, the authorities were waiting. The C & E dudes stopped the trucks at the border and ripped them right apart. They seized both trucks and all the contraband. Big Cal wasn't looking for a payment this time. He was a generous fella, and he was throwing C & E a freebie, just a little taste — doing his pals a favour on a slow evening.

AT THE SAME TIME, Cal had started work on the KGB file. He agreed to a cold approach with the RCMP, an operation targeting a Bulgarian gang in Montreal that was counterfeiting the tax stamps on imported vodka. The cold approach meant that Cal would make contact with a suspect with no introduction, no knowledge of his organization or his routine, and only a basic briefing.

Irina ran a restaurant on rue St-Denis. The Mounties suspected her husband and his friends of moving large amounts of weapons from Russia to Canada and over the border into the U.S. They were a rough bunch. A young, inexperienced undercover agent had proceeded Cal in trying to infiltrate the Bulgarians who hung at Irina's. They had sniffed out something wrong about him. They didn't look on outsiders prying into their business with any degree of benevolence whatsoever. They took the kid down to the basement in the restaurant and carved his face with knives. The rookie agent lost an ear. There was a lot of blood. Undercover police-work was no game for beginners.

Cal was given a photo of the couple, the address, and all the best wishes for success. Go to work, bub. But do not break any laws, or entrap, or threaten or coerce, or promise or accept money or gifts, or take drugs, or, or . . . If everything went right, Cal would not have to appear in court, as the alleged criminal would, of his own free will, provide the necessary acts, crimes, and violations to completely screw himself and most of his operation. All Cal had to do was put his life on the line. If anything went wrong, he could end up in jail or dead.

Cal decided to develop a relationship with Irina and her husband. When he walked into the restaurant, all he encountered was hostility. The Bulgarians just bridled at the stranger in their midst, turned their broad backs. The first thing he did was to cultivate the bartender. Right away. The man or woman behind the bar is a critical factor in any nightspot. He can make or break the business, strip the place bare or make it a howling success. You didn't want to come in too quick, make too big a splash, or they'd think you were a fool. You just wanted the barkeep to wake up a little. Heyyy, buddy. . . . First rule of the cold approach: money talks, bullshit walks. So Cal would tip the guy twenty dollars on a hundred-dollar tab.

"Man," he'd say, "this place is great."

Then Big Cal would buy a round for the whole bar. Next, he'd let drop that he'd been in Bulgaria, just came back. Loved the fuckin' country. He laid on the flattery with a trowel. But Cal had a deft touch. The crowd at Irina's were like anybody else: they enjoyed being stroked. In their world, it didn't happen all that often. Besides, when Cal Broeker chose to flatter you, it was if some huge force had taken you in and decided powerfully, enthusiastically, and unconditionally in your favour.

It felt gooood.

"Say, I'm lookin' for a recipe for *schema chorba*," he said. "Tripe soup. Know where I can find it?"

Well, what do you know? *Schema chorba* is the house specialty.

Soon he was going into Irina's two or three times a week. He loved that goddamn tripe soup. Got to know all the regulars. He would warm up with a few drinks in a bar nearby and get into character. Simone Vega, back at the Manoir de Belmont, could see the change come over him as

Cal got ready for work. His eyes would narrow and go cold; it was like he was transforming into the Warrior.

Next, he brought a topographical map of Bulgaria to the restaurant as a gift. The barkeep couldn't wait to introduce him to the owners. They framed the map and put it over the bar. Then everybody in Irina's was hearing Cal's war stories. Hell, I lived on the rez. Man, you shoulda seen some of the shit I saw go down in Bulgaria. Yeah, I even met your goddamn president. And all the time he was flipping money on the bar. He was loud; he had a wad. The vintage black Mercedes was parked nearby. With its oversized grille and searchlight-style headlamps, it got Cal noticed too. Not that getting noticed was any problem for him.

"Hey, Cal, why you all dressed up?"

"Hell, I got a date. Yeahh. I mean with two or three women."

That was a tall tale too. But pretty soon, Bartender is pouring free drinks.

Next, he meets the owners. Jeez, you gotta meet this guy. So Cal's talking to the criminal owner and saying the kind of things that mark him as a soulmate to rounders everywhere.

"Man, you gotta go to Amsterdam. I think my dick has left me for Amsterdam." In the new world of the buddies, Amsterdam, with all its legal dope and pussy, has replaced Las Vegas as their idea of Valhalla.

Now they can't help popping the question.

"So, Calveen, what do you do?"

"Ah'm pretty much retired," he'd tell them. "I've made just enough money to lie back and enjoy my life."

What with the Mercedes, the plush apartment, his easy spending ways, he seemed to be a wealthy American businessman. If there were any doubts on that score, he just showed them the bank statement for the $16 million the RCMP had deposited in his account during the Dupont sting.

He'd tell them about his experience in shipping and banking, then add, "Just looking to do a few deals here and there, don't you know."

He let it be known that he had good connections in both the legit and the criminal arenas of business. Soon enough, they were hooked.

With the Bulgarians, Cal reversed the smokescreen. In Orienter, he drew Miller and company into a deal with fictional Bulgarians who turned out to be RCMP. This time, he drew the Bulgarians into a deal with fictional Indians. The key to undercover work, as Cal saw it, was to figure out what the targets most wanted and then become the man who could provide it — big time, big volume. As soon as they heard he had a fool-proof way to get contraband into the U.S., they wanted to hear more.

The Bulgarians at Irina's didn't know Mohawks from mohair, but they knew the Indians controlled the rez and the river and had the smuggling down pat. And on the other side, Cal's Mohawk contacts wanted to connect with the "Russians," as they called them. They had connections to Europe; they were tough and they were rugged.

It was easy for Cal to play one off against the other because there were few real connections between the two worlds. Each thought the other ran a lucrative enterprise; each thought the other a dangerous bunch. Damien Love wanted him to smuggle Marlboros to Bulgaria. The boys at Irina's were always looking for a safe route into the market across the border. Both sides were burning with the fires of greed, and Cal just fed the monster.

Soon he had a pair of RCMP covermen, Sgt. Serge Colombe and Const. Yves LaPorte, sitting outside Irina's in plainclothes and an unmarked car. As far as Cal was concerned, it was a kind of half-assed arrangement. He didn't even have a panic pager to hit if things went wrong and the Bulgarians started to carve on his ass. If the shit hit the fan, the best he could do was somehow get to the restaurant's window and wave feebly for their attention as they sat there drinking coffee. Just to make sure nothing close to that would happen, he started packing two razor-sharp knives himself, tucked away in leather sheaths on the back of his hip. One was a big Bowie doorstopper, and the other was a little surgical slicer with which he planned to open up a few Bulgarian veins, if the situation called for it. He practised with both of them. If he couldn't get to his blades, there was no better weapon at close quarters than an ordinary glass ketchup bottle, or he could try stomping the leg off a wooden chair and using the splintered end as a spike and the chair as a shield. He had seen what those homely bludgeons could do back in Thailand. Cal Broeker planned on keeping both ears.

One night, he walked down to the basement of Irina's on a scout, just to see what was down there. There were a lot of little rooms with closed doors. He wiggled the door handles and walked around. If somebody catches me, he thought, I'll just tell 'em I'm looking for the bathroom. He then went through a steel door at the back and crossed a small alleyway into another basement. There he found a stairwell going up to more rooms. It was like a dream.

Next to a bathroom he found a door with massive bolts, plate steel | 255 like it came off a battleship. He pulled the door and it opened to a group of large Bulgarians having a meeting. They reacted to the sight of Cal Broeker with a roar of outrage. They pushed and shoved. In a flash, one of them was right on top of him. He had had his ear chopped off too. In the world of the Bulgarian underworld, ear-loss was the penalty for stealing. The dream was suddenly turning into a nightmare. Cal was forbidden by the terms of his LOA to physically harm anybody he was investigating. But now was not the time for legal niceties. Cal pulled his huge Bowie knife from behind the small of his back, grabbed the thug, and held the knife to his neck.

"Back off or I'll cut your fucking throat!"

The Bulgarian backed down. Cal made it back to the restaurant proper without further incident.

In Irina's, this type of savagery was routine. One night, Cal was sitting there when Irina and her husband suddenly appeared, talking a fast Bulgarian. Then the man grabbed her by the hair and just hauled off and slapped Irina so hard that she flew in a complete circle before crashing to the floor.

Cal couldn't risk his mission by interfering, although he had wanted to. Wife abuse, no surprise, was common among the buddies. Cal was of two minds about it. On the one hand, he was sorry for the women, who just had to take it and keep quiet. On the other, he thought that they knew what kind of animals they had hooked up with. They could get out or accept the consequences. On the rez, however, things were different. Domestic violence was rare and was dealt with by the tribal council, which, whatever it did, did it very effectively.

AS WINTER TURNED into spring in 1997, Cal was approached by the Falcon Task Force, led by Insp. Luc Demaine. They wanted him to infiltrate a gang of old-school French-Canadian Mafia working out of Laval. These guys specialized in counterfeit and were working with the Colombians, with some Arab connections thrown in for good measure. They also trafficked in stolen cars, drugs, and other assorted contraband. The Mounties wanted him to do another cold approach. Was he up to it?

256 |  Agent O.4649 didn't have to be asked twice. He always wanted another file, another project. His appetite for UC work, despite the risks, was bottomless.

So Demaine set up a meeting downtown in the boardroom at the Sheraton with Cal and Gilles Chambertin, his partner. Inspector Demaine was heavy-set. He had a big handlebar moustache that made him look like an RAF pilot during the Battle of Britain. The targets in question were an old lag named Philippe Beaudoin and his partner, Roger "Roddy" Zeppo. The Falcon Task Force had a wiretap on their warehouse in suburban Laval, where they dealt in stolen blue jeans and coffee. They had discovered that Beaudoin and Zeppo planned to bring a shipload of cocaine up from Colombia — 40,000 metric tons of marching powder concealed in tunafish tins. Forty thousand metric tons! The huge amount spoke volumes about the demand in North America. It was a whole freaking mountain of blow! It was enough to keep the entire east coast of the continent on a hair-trigger all winter! There was definitely something Paul Bunyan-esque about Cal Broeker. Like America itself, everything he touched was super-colossal.

The big nose-candy mountain was going to be sent up to Canada within six months. Cal's job was to get the name of the ship, the departure date, and the ship's manifest. It was quite an undertaking, considering that both the bad boys and the Mounties were francophones, and he had just two words of French.

At a meeting with Demaine, Cal signed the LOA. Demaine slipped it in a red-tagged pouch. The sealed envelope was then put in a safety-deposit box. It's one document you don't want the bad boys to get their hands on.

Demaine and Chambertin had intercepted a phone call that Philippe had made to a chief on the rez looking for "the shipping guy." Student of military history that he was, Cal decided on a quick, Patton-like thrust of armour. A bold move. Whoever the Mohawk shipping guy was, he would impersonate him and hope like hell the real thing didn't walk through the door.

Balls of brass, man. Big balls of brass.

He hopped in a taxi and drove up to the warehouse in Laval. He just walked in cold and asked for Philippe. The Colombian receptionist called her boss out to the front. Philippe was short, heavy, stocky, in his late fifties, a casual dresser. He talked a rough *joual*. His complexion was grey, he chain-smoked, and he had a bad cough. Cal had decided to come in heavy, a veritable steamroller of intimidation.

"Somebody on Kahnawake told me you were looking for me," he said.

"I don't know who the fuck you are," replied the old lag.

"Don't play fuckin' stupid — you made a call to the chief on the rez to get the European guy with the shipping. I got a call to come here, I'm here."

Philippe looked him over. Cal loomed over the man. He looked like a 300-pound NFL linebacker next to a prematurely aged and somewhat sinister schoolboy.

"Come in my office," Beaudoin whispered out of the side of his mouth, as if Cal was in the next cell during one Philippe's frequent removals to the pen. The guy had done plenty of jail time already.

"Hey," said Cal, "I'm talkin'. I'm not whisperin'."

They went to Philippe's office. Cal saw that the guy had a lot of Colombians and Cubans working for him.

"Tell me why you're here," he said.

"I was told to come here," said Cal, "because I got a call that you were looking for the guy that does shipping for the rez. From Europe. I'm outta Bulgaria. I've got my documents with me if you want to see my company. What are you lookin' for and what can I do for ya? If you're lookin' for me, I'm here. If you're not, I'm outta here."

"Why did you pull up in a cab?"

"You think I'm gonna let you plate me? If somebody's photographin' you out front and I pull up in my ride, I don't even know who you are. We haven't even made introductions yet."

Philippe calmed down and called in his partner, Zeppo. Another stocky little Quebecker in his fifties. He was more dude than partner; Zeppo favoured suits and ties. Together, they looked like a pair of retired furniture movers. Cal went through the drill with Zeppo too.

He said, "If you want to continue with this, I suggest we meet in a restaurant. Pick a place."

So they picked the Crystal Palace, a busy Chinese restaurant in Laval across from a mall. At lunch, they served a buffet. Cal met Philippe and Zeppo there the following Friday. Luc Demaine positioned a couple of plainclothes Mounties at a table not far away, keeping an eye on things. Philippe told Cal they had made another call to their contact on the rez, just to make sure he was the right guy. Cal had to put a stop to these calls quick.

"Let me tell ya somethin' right now," he said. "If you keep phonin' those guys, they're gonna want a piece of your deal. You can pay commission if you like or get ripped, but I don't do business like that. So if you're comfortable, we go on — and we don't have any more calls."

Philippe and Zeppo backed down. Then they told him what they wanted. They wanted to bring the blow mountain up in a ship, offload it in the port of Montreal, bring it onto the rez, and store it there so it wouldn't get hit by gangs and cops. Hide it there until the heat died off so they could deal it out of Laval. They said they had done business like this before.

At first, Philippe and Zeppo were talking in vague circles, saying, "There's products we want to bring up from South America, but it's very sensitive." So it was Cal's task to get them to identify what it really was they were talking about. Was it coke? Was it hash? Was it a cure for cancer? If he couldn't get them to be specific, the sting could stop right there.

This was the tough part. Now it was either talk or walk. This was where an undercover operation was made or broken. Cal told them the deal had to be quick. Had to happen within two or three months. He pitched them on what he could do as a legitimate shipper.

"I can get you through customs, pre-cleared," he said. "It goes onto trucks, they'll pull it wherever you want to."

Philippe and Zeppo had to worry not only about the authorities, but also about being ripped by other gangs, especially the Italian Mafia, which was still all through the Montreal docks, one of the few sacrosanct territories they had left since the Russians moved in and showed crime what terror really looked like. Cal offered the duo a window into the world of big-time freight, with its waybills, powers of attorney, bills of lading. He could furnish a phony paper trail that would make it look as if the freighter had come from London or Cyprus rather than tell-tale Latin America. Any boat from south of the equator was automatically suspect.

What he told them was all bullshit, except for one thing: with his RCMP contacts, Cal *could* get any load through customs without a check. It was just that a SWAT team would be waiting at the other end when Philippe and Zeppo came to claim it.

Whoever the real Mohawk shipper was, he never showed up. Philippe and Zeppo were sold. They bought the notion that Cal Broker was in tight with the Indians and had strong Russian connections. Cal was in business.

NOW HE WAS WORKING the Bulgarians and Philippe and Zeppo at the same time as he was probing Pierre Maille. He worked the three projects into a daily routine. In the mornings, he would go out to the warehouse in Laval. Afternoons, he checked in with Kestrel, and then it was time for *schema chorba* on rue St-Denis.

A Bulgarian "immigration specialist" named Georgi Zhikov offered him stolen credit cards, bank cards, steroids, a whole garbage bag full of blank Canadian passports. He said he could get Cal married ten times a year, just to get women into the country. Fun *and* profit — you might even find one you like. . . . Cal had to walk away from all of these deals because they weren't within his mandate, as specified in the LOA. Snowed by fine print. So everything went on the street, all the contraband. It frustrated Cal because the Bulgarians could have been a huge project. There was prostitution involved, and drugs as well. You name it, it was probably in there somewhere.

He brought a couple of the Mohawks into Irina's, hulking, big-faced, moody guys. The regulars were pretty impressed when they walked in, and Irina was all over him.

"Calveen, my Calveen, come here and sit down."

He would introduce the Mohawks around. Or he would take a couple of the beetle-browed Bulgarians over to Reboska's on the rez, and the large Native woman there would come out from behind the counter and give him a big hug. He never initiated a discussion about possible deals. He always waited till they made the first move; he was seldom disappointed. He'd made this a science.

With Philippe and Zeppo, he was having trouble making the deal jell, however. Its ends kept flapping up in the breeze. They told him he had to go meet the Colombians, had to fly down there. He couldn't do it. He'd have liked to, but no dice.

"I'm not goin' anywhere. You tell those Colombian motherfuckers to come up here and sit in the chair and we'll talk."

Philippe and Zeppo. It sounded like a circus act. Old clowns in silly clothes.

"I'll clear it," he told them, "do the brokerage, get the power of attorney. All you have to do is get it on the boat. I don't care how you do it — whether you ship it in cans of tuna or pillars of cement."

Now they wanted him to go down and supervise the loading. There was nothing Cal Broeker would have liked better than to go down and start messing with the Colombians, but the Crown attorneys working with Falcon wouldn't allow it. No way. He couldn't help the deal down south at the other end; it would edge well over into the legal definition of entrapment. It'd be out the other side.

"You're exposing me to people's faces I don't want to see," he told Pierre. "People I don't want to know."

First they said the cocaine was to be concealed in tunafish cans. Then it was to be in the floor of a ship, with raw fish piled on top. Then they were going to fill potatoes with it. *Pommes de blow.* They talked about paying him in product one moment. The next, it was to be pesos out of Panama. Then Brazilian automatic rifles and ammo — weapons for sweat equity. Indecision was the order of the day. It ruled.

Philippe and Zeppo would disappear for two weeks down to Colombia, down to Cuba. Somewhere hot. They brought back a box of cigars that they sold to Cal for $600. The stogies turned out to be counterfeit. Pity — Cal enjoyed a good burn. But he kept buying them dinner all the same.

Then Philippe set a trap for him. One day out at Bosco Distributing, their company in Laval, they left him alone in the office and set out all kinds of bait, just left agendas open, phone numbers and file folders lying around. Philippe and Zeppo went out and shut the doors. Cal just sat there. He assumed they had some kind of surveillance camera on him. He didn't need to see their secret papers anyhow; they weren't part of his objective. And what the fuck could they possibly be keeping from him anyway? All he cared about was the shipload of blow specified in the LOA.

Philippe and Zeppo came back into the room. They were real happy. Philippe took him out front and showed him the monitors where they had been watching him. Next, they took him back into the warehouse and revealed their latest adventure in contraband: computers that had fallen off some truck. Hundreds of them. They were going to ship them to Saudi and make 20 percent. Cal wasn't impressed. He was going to make $100,000 busting them.

After four or five visits to Bosco, he began wearing a wire, a terrible girdle-like contraption with a battery pack that stretched so tight you could see the seam through his shirt. His coverman was across the street in a telephone-repair van. Cal would open the window blind so the Mountie could take photos. Front and profile, just like he'd done with Tom Habib, J.C., and Jon Blake. And just as he did with the Bulgarians, he made meticulous notes after every single encounter with the pair.

Photos, notes, tapes . . . the world of the justice system was the mirror opposite of Planet Buddy, with its boiling atmosphere of vague rumour, wild speculation, paranoia, and wicked gossip. In court, the Crown would present an array of microscopically precise facts. Smoke and ambiguity would not exist. Never did. Even before the bust happened, buddy would be trapped, dead to rights. In court, he would be ground into a fine dust. All he could do was arrange a plea bargain. The tribe had spoken.

Philippe and Zeppo were a luckless pair. You felt kind of sorry for them. Once, supposedly just back from Europe, Cal called them up. As usual, he'd represented himself as constantly travelling, available only by cell-phone. But Philippe, sounding older and frailer, didn't seem to recognize his voice this time. He coughed a couple times. He sounded bad. Finally, he seemed to recall who Cal was. Yet Broeker was unfazed.

"How ya doin', pal?" he said.

"Not so good," allowed Philippe.

"What's the matter?" Cal asked, all concern.

Well, he had had chest pains the previous morning, went to emergency, had to go through a lot of tests. The valves. It was bypass time. Cal had nothing but sympathy. His father had had similar problems. And life was tough enough without these things, wasn't it? Then, relentless, he moved Philippe back on track. Forget the heart attack. Let's go for blow.

How about our deal?

Philippe coughed a couple more times, then hung up. He was in no condition to talk about 40,000 metric tons of cocaine. Just the thought of it raised your blood pressure.

It got even better.

Philippe took him to meet a Lebanese buddy, George. It was at a restaurant in Laval, a restaurant of a very special type: it never, ever opened. The place was a total front. Even though there were no customers, there was this huge motherfucker at the door standing guard. Made you want to go in, see what was happening that needed such security.

Cal went in with Philippe, met the guy. George asked Cal whether he could move stolen cars, drugs, guns. Basically, what do you need, where do you need it, what you got going? Cal's strategy, natch, was always to show vast reluctance. Woo me . . .

"I don't know you," he said. "I don't know what you're into. And I definitely don't wanna go down for a stolen car. How much we gonna make? $1,500?"

More, as it turned out. Much more.

But it was no thanks all the same. Cal wanted to keep the focus on Marching Powder Mountain, so he nixed George and got the hell out. Five minutes after he'd left the restaurant, George was busted by the Sûreté du Québec for stolen cars. Philippe and Zeppo were having a shit-fit about that little coincidence when, the following week, two hours after Cal walked out of the Bosco warehouse, they themselves were busted by the Montreal Urban Community (MUC) police.

Now they were really paranoid. When Cal phoned the next day, he was in trouble. Big trouble.

"I'm not going to talk to you right now," said Philippe, "because you and I have a serious problem. Don't call this place again."

Fuck.

What happened, he later found out, was that one of the Colombians or Cubans working back in the warehouse at Bosco had grabbed a container of stolen jeans, taken out a box, and was trying to peddle it downtown on Ste. Catherine. The victim of the hijack spotted him, took the barcode number from the box, and called the Montreal cops. They followed the Colombian back to the warehouse in Laval and busted | 263 everybody.

It took Philippe two weeks to discover that his employee was responsible for the arrests, not Cal. Broeker was a little paranoid now too. Neither the MUC nor the SQ was aware that he was an undercover agent. He'd find it awful hard to prove if his handlers decided to play hide-and-seek. He could easily get busted himself. If Philippe was suspicious, or more than suspicious, there was little to keep him from setting up Cal to either of them. A kilo of blow under the front seat of his car and a call by a friendly snitch to the MUC would be about all it took to get Cal ten years in the pen.

There followed a tiresome series of no-shows at meetings by the Colombians. A rendezvous with one of their representatives, a woman, was supposed to take place at the Sheraton Hotel. Inspector Demaine had a whole surveillance crew outside. It fizzled when she never made it past the border at Plattsburgh, New York. No visa! Someone able to do a $50-million dope deal ought also to be capable of obtaining themselves a valid visa for the country where the deal is to take place. You'd think. There was another no-show by a money man, one of the old-time Jewish racketeers in Montreal. It was getting to be a historical tableau around the warehouse duo: Buddy Then and Now. Philippe's heart attack must have shaken loose some chips upstairs. Where did they find these relics? A newspaper ad? Pretty soon, Philippe was asking Cal to mastermind the whole deal himself, go down to Colombia, supervise the loading, and put up $20,000 in front money. It was like *The Illustrated Book of Police Entrapment*. Cal would have to arrest himself — no one else was involved.

In the end, Inspector Demaine put Falcon on hold. Hung it up with mothballs in the cover-bag. Then, after three months, Serge Colombe shit-canned KGB too. The Crown could not persuade any Bulgarian official to come to Canada to testify against the counterfeit tax-stamp operation. Why wasn't Cal surprised?

Simone Vega was learning just how erratic life with an undercover agent could be, not to mention how unpredictable his income. While Cal had been paid a small salary during both these projects, there was no big bonus unless there were arrests, seizure, convictions. When the smoke cleared, there had to be something behind it to send to jail.

264 | It wasn't so easy to walk away from these operations either. Both the Bulgarians and Philippe were expecting deals to happen momentarily; they had to be carefully wound down. Rome wasn't destroyed in a day either. All the same, excuses weren't that hard to find; a missed phone call or meeting was enough reason for him to shut down things with the Bulgarians. They sulked, sure, but they always suspected themselves of not quite grasping the ways of the West, of not getting with the new program, which had much to do with being on time, showing up. Or he could say he had found somebody else. That started them all worrying about competition instead of thinking about him. Buddy's competition was fairly worrying, of course. With Philippe, he just said: "I came into this fucking deal as the middle man. Now you expect me to pull the entire goddamn wagon all by myself? Get real!"

All the same, he had put five or six months into the projects, heart and soul, and he couldn't help feeling let down.

He took these things very personally, mainly because he injected so much of his actual self into launching them that when they were shot down, he barely crawled out of the burning wreckage.

NOTHING MORE HAPPENED for almost a year. Cal had moved with Simone to Toronto on another project when Philippe next got back in touch. He apologized for the waste of time and money on the aborted cocaine deal. But he still wanted to do business with Cal. Pick a crime . . . How about counterfeit hundreds? About $20 million worth?

Cal called Demaine. The LOA was still active. He grabbed the train from Toronto and put up at the President Hotel in Laval. Philippe came up to his room and showed him a sample. They were good-quality hundreds too. Canadian dollars. One more time, he used the Bulgarian ploy. Not only did the Bulgarians, his clients, want to buy $10 million, half of the counterfeit from Philippe, but they also wanted to buy the presses, the plates, and hire his printer too. They were going to move the whole money mill over to Bulgaria and operate it from there.

Everything was going along just fine until the Mounties got clumsy. Again. As he walked through the lobby of the President, briefcase in hand, Cal saw a cop from the Falcon team emerge from the coffee shop. Coincidence? Not in his world. Then the man passed by, saying, "Hi, | 265 Cal."

"I don't know who the fuck you are, man," Cal replied, trying to minimize the damage.

But it was too late. Isn't it always? Philippe had a man watching the lobby. He had overheard the exchange. Cal ate breakfast, went to his room, and phoned the handlers, told them what had happened. As if they didn't already know. Don't worry about it, they told him. Who's gonna notice that? When Cal finally got Philippe on the phone, he could have answered that question. Philippe was gonna notice, that's who.

"We have a problem," he said. He sounded a lot less frail and weary.

"What problem?" Cal sounded innocence itself.

"I can't tell you on the phone."

"Aw, Jesus Christ! Did somebody pick up heat? Who picked up heat? Tell me."

"We don't have any problems with you," Philippe reassured him. "We have problems another place, know what I mean?"

"Is there anything on me?" asked Cal, starting to sound alarmed.

"I don't think so. But I'm not so sure about that. The people checked you."

"How they gonna check if there's anything on me?"

"Something's wrong, Cal. It's not me."

"I'm not coming back, then. I can't come back into that, Philippe. If I walk back in there and I have a problem waiting for me when I arrive, then I have a problem with three or four other clients. I'm not going to discuss anything but shipping and transportation, you understand, but since the first time I met Zeppo, this guy's been talking heat, this guy's been talking problems. I don't know what's cooking with you guys, but I can't jeopardize the cash and the connections I have there for a fouled deal. I don't know what to tell you, Philippe. But as far as going any further, I guess it's your call."

*The best way to end a prolonged siege is to set the enemy against himself, turning one against the other by spreading rumours to each of his untrustworthiness.*

"Cal, I know you're not happy about that, but I don't have a choice."

"Who's closin' it down, then?" inquired Cal.

"It's not me."

"Is it the storage place? Can you move it to a different location?"

"That's not the problem. I can't talk on the phone, Cal. Meet me right away."

"Something wrong with cops? Somebody see a car?"

"Yes. And the same car is at the hotel too."

"Mine? Is it my car at the President?"

"That's right."

"Well, it's on me, I guess. That's why I don't like having meetings at those fucking places."

"Yeah."

"I've got everything on me, though, everything in my pockets. But this has to be worked out." And finally: "I'm just going to walk away, Philippe. It's not worth doing time for, and there's not enough money in it for us."

"It's hard to move now. The place is wrong."

"I think we should walk away now. I don't think we should finish this deal."

"The verdict is yours."

"If your information is correct, I don't want any part of it. You have to take your own best guess. I don't know how I'm going to explain this on my side. I'm gonna start walking away from things here."

"We need some answers."

"I don't know what to do; I'm scared shitless right now."

He was too. He trembled.

FINALLY, THEY MET at a Second Cup in a mall across from the hotel. Philippe was not looking friendly. He looked as if some entity had shoved a drinking straw into his flesh and then sucked all the life and joy out of it. Cal tried to persuade him that the incident hadn't been quite the way it was related.

"The guy called me 'pal,' not 'Cal.' Just some guy being friendly is all it was, nothing more."

Philippe allowed that his francophone spy might not have been able to decipher American slang that well. Then Cal got all huffy and told him the deal was off — it's a heat score! He turned and left. The moment he walked into his hotel room, the phone started ringing. He ignored it. It rang and rang, knowing he was there. Finally, he picked up.

"Calvin," said Philippe, "you should not do that. We're just trying to be careful."

"You're trying to set me up, motherfucker! I'm going back to Toronto, and I don't wanna hear from you."

"It's not on my side, it's on your side."

"It's better if I don't come there. I'll arrange something that'll make it safer for you guys."

Once again, Cal had big bucks in his bank account, $20 million. He told Philippe that he was too terrified now about the deal. He was going to hand it over to a lowly subordinate: if they also thought he was being followed, then maybe he *was* being followed.

Demaine picked an undercover RCMP officer named Richard, who worked the docks, to pose as Cal's money man. With his broken nose, scars, and ponytail, Richard couldn't have looked more Richardly.

They took Richard up north of the city to the printer's house. Everybody was there to close the deal — Philippe, Zeppo, everybody. Except for Cal Broeker, that is. Richard badged them. Enter the SWAT team. One takedown is like another: noisy, violent, over before you know it has begun. Philippe and Zeppo went back to jail. Cal went back to Toronto.

AROUND THAT TIME, he began to have second thoughts about this under-cover life. The Mounties were always assuring him that his safety was their paramount concern, but he sometimes had a hard job believing them. They employed many agents, informants. Their attitude towards them was, quite simply, ruthless. Hard-hearted, cold-blooded, callous. If Cal Broeker took a few lead marbles in the head, his handlers would go home just like they did every day, say hi to the wife, feed the cat, take the kid to hockey. At times, operating between the bad guys and the Mounties, Cal felt like a rag caught between two mad dogs. He knew what such dogs did if they actually managed to tear the rag in half: shake the torn piece a bit, let it fall from their jaws, and glance down at it with scant interest.

*To state a lie firmly, categorically and with great authority,*
*undeterred by the fact that all concerned know it to be a lie,*
*is one of the principal activities defined by the term "practising law."*
— STEPHEN VIZINCZEY, *AN INNOCENT MILLIONAIRE*

In the mid-1980s, Yves Raic was a bilingual lawyer in Montreal, prominent in federal Liberal politics. Ironically enough, considering what was to follow, he was the chairman of the party's prestigious Judicial Affairs Committee, and he was active in then prime minister John Turner's election campaign in the city. He was part of a political-legal culture that had produced important Canadian leaders like Pierre Trudeau, Jean Chrétien, and Paul Martin. But by 1993, Raic was disbarred and Cal Broeker had to lend him US$4,500 so that biker loan sharks wouldn't break his legs.

Cal had met first met Raic while they were both at Arroway Ltd. in 1992. Raic was then working as a "legal consultant," negotiating trade contracts for the Leroys under the table, as well as making deals with the boys on the rez. He was an educated man from a Croatian background, with a lawyer's polished manner and a politician's ability to stonewall. He was definitely Cabinet material, this guy. No matter who he screwed, Raic always presented a front of injured innocence, never in the wrong. He could lie with some of the all-time champs on Parliament Hill, could even produce Olympic whoppers — giant lies of Washingtonian scope, Nixonian falsehoods that were brazen as well as audacious. Raic knew this

to be so, because there was one man who believed every word that came tripping off that silver tongue of his, a man of unimpeachable integrity: Raic himself.

Yves Raic shared Cal's interest in military history and strategy, and he could tell you every single detail of Patton's campaign in Germany, Napoleon's march into Russia, and many other less-than-legendary operations. Problem was, Yves Raic was an avid seeker of what he was pleased to call "a shitload of fun." He liked strippers and he liked drugs — all kinds of drugs — and these two foibles had turned his whole life into a disaster of epic proportions. He was a walking cautionary tale, living in a giddy welter of bad debts owed to even worse people. He was desperate for money all the hours of every day, all the days of the week. Consequently, he had furtive dealings with the Hell's Angels and with an especially terrifying enforcer with the Rizzuto crime family known as Little John.

Eventually, even the Leroys began to distance themselves, particularly when they learned Raic was working out of strip joints like Le Club Super Sex and Chez Paris. It doesn't do much for your confidence in a legal adviser when you have to consult with him through a wall of splayed, thrusting flesh and Spandex while his nose drips like a leaky faucet all over the contracts.

Raic, somewhat recklessly, had taken to borrowing money from the strip-club managers, saying it was for Little John. Even if he'd repaid the loans, this wouldn't have been a good idea. On Planet Buddy, it was the same as pleading to have your head blown off. Or at least begging for a good, disjointing, multiple-fracturing, never-forgotten kind of beating.

Yves Raic had to be the single most crooked guy that Cal had ever met, not excepting Ron Ong. Raic rat-fucked everybody. He would borrow $800 on a weekend and give Cal a check. On Monday, he would ask Cal not to redeem the check but to accept a partial cash payment of $200 instead. By Wednesday, he would be asking to borrow more.

Cal learned, unsurprisingly, to turn a deaf ear to his pleading.

"If you don't give it to me," Raic would say, "I'll probably end up being killed."

Raic's worrying about being killed was such a quotidian occurrence that it made Cal laugh.

"Yves," Cal would say, "can I have my money back if they're gonna kill you now? What's that watch you're wearing? Cartier?" | 273

No matter what desperate trouble he was battling, Yves Raic always managed to look slick, like the prosperous attorney he had once been. He was a hip guy in his late thirties, with dark, styled, shoulder-length hair and tinted glasses. He favoured professorial tweeds, and he was always trying to set Cal up with women. His own wife reportedly had taken a hike when some of the buddies broke down the door of their elegant apartment on Sherbrooke, looking to be repaid. Victor Leroy had urged Cal to lend Raic the $4,500, telling him it was a good deed. Cal agreed, thinking it was also probably a nice hook into Raic's underworld connections for his RCMP handlers.

Needless to say, just as night follows day, Raic left Cal hanging for the money, which amounted to almost $7,000 Canadian. It wasn't until April 1997, when he was working both the KGB file and Operation Falcon, that Cal caught another glimpse of the man. Raic was walking towards him on Bernard Avenue, in Outremont.

Cal was on the way back to Simone Vega's place with some ice cream. He had been going to Simone's stage shows and talk shows, hanging with her friends. As far as they were concerned, he was just an antiques dealer with money, a big entrepreneur. Big.

In reality, he was leading a mind-boggling kind of triple existence. He was posing as an international businessman for Philippe and Zeppo; he'd wear dark suits, shirts with elaborate French cuffs, even red or blue power suspenders to reinforce the impression. Around Pierre Maille and the Bulgarians, he would wear a lot of black to encourage the perception that he was a dangerous psycho-biker criminal. Son of Réal Dupont. And with the Indian smugglers, he'd go for an L. L. Bean/Outward Bound, rugged but casual look, since they would have killed anyone wearing a suit and tie. At other times, Cal looked so much like a cop that detectives in town for a convention would stop him in restaurants and ask what outfit he was with. He would carry changes of costume around in the back of his Mercedes in order to make these drastic transformations of identity. It could be quite exhausting.

However he was dressed, though, Cal Broeker was the last guy in the world Yves Raic wanted to run into. Or definitely one of them.

"Yves Raic," Cal said, laughing. "You sonofabitch."

At the sight of Cal Broeker, Raic was falling all over himself, he was almost shitting his pants. Big Cal wasn't the kind of dude you could stiff for seven large. All Gallic charm, Raic started acting like Cal was his dearest friend on the face of the earth.

"Calvin. It is sooo good to see you again. How are you?"

"I'm waitin' for my $7,000. How about that?"

Cal blew some smoke Raic's way — naturally he did — casually letting on that he'd had some of his Bulgarian ogres out hunting down the insolvent lawyer, that this "accidental" encounter was no fluke.

Raic invited Cal to his office in Old Montreal, on Place d'Armes. There, he would make everything right. When Cal arrived at the joint, they caught up with each other. Cal blew some more smoke about money laundering for the Bulgarians. Naturally he did. For his part, Raic related sorrowfully that he'd gone through bankruptcy and had married a stripper. Yes. Somehow, when a lawyer took a fall, one of the inevitable hallmark steps to perdition was the stripper wife. She stood there, *shakin' that thing* like it was the signpost to rack and ruin. A lawyer marrying a stripper, Cal reflected, was like him admitting, "The thing about me is that there is nothing whatsoever more important to me in this life than sex and drugs."

Cal wondered whether Raic had introduced Misty — or whatever her name was — to John and Geills Turner. This might have been a little challenging even for Raic, though, since the new Mme. Raic was presently in detox, fighting off that old coke Jones. Oh, and yes, the landlord was trying to evict Raic from his office too, for — surprise, surprise! — nonpayment of rent. Raic was living in a one-room apartment furnished with junk, trash, chintz from the Sally Ann, and whatever he could find on the streets during his nocturnal prowls. But call no man a fuck-up till he's dead — Yves Raic showed no signs of recognizing that he'd bottomed out, that there couldn't be a hell of a lot lower to go for a man who'd begun as well as he had. It was all a temporary embarrassment, this life he was currently living. Hardly his fault, of course. There were extenuating circumstances: clients who did not pay their bills; women who did pay theirs, but with his money. And of course, there was "the economy." When the economy was in its current state — whatever state that was — how could one expect to remain buoyant?

In the office, he had a number of strategy board games set up and was playing himself in three challenging matches simultaneously.

Raic believed he was winning.

Instead of paying Cal the $7,000 he owed, he offered him something better: a deal on counterfeit thousand-dollar bills, pinkies. They could make a millions on it, Raic said. Just millions! But first things first, he desperately needed a thousand-dollar loan till Monday. There was some minor pecuniary "embarrassment." Cal, seeing Raic as a kind of upscale Tom Habib and wanting to discover where this criminal trail might lead, lent him the money, peeling from his fat show-roll a thousand dollars in twenties. In return, Raic had to give him $8,000 in counterfeit. Samples.

Raic had heard rumours that Cal had set himself up as a crime kingpin in Bulgaria. Cal did nothing to correct this impression. He told Raic he was travelling all the time — Europe, the U.S., you know, doing big deals. Money laundering, drugs, name it. Raic bought it all, hook, line, and kitchen sink. He thought, the optimistic Raic, that he could make some money with Cal, or at least touch him up for further loans and a few gourmet dinners.

Who's zoomin' who?

You might ask.

Yves Raic might have been broke himself, but for others he was juggling millions. Typical buddy.

One of Raic's clients had been arrested the previous month with $1.2 million in Canadian counterfeit, Cal learned. The guy was out on bail and awaiting sentencing in October. He had also, Raic said, spent a year in Russia printing American and Canadian counterfeit for the Mafiya. He was good — he had to be — and he'd been very busy. There was a million on hand and another $13 million ready to go as soon as the presses could roll. Cal the expert wanted to know the price and whether the quality was good enough to be passed in banks. With rare candour, Raic admitted the counterfeit wasn't good enough to be passed in Canadian banks. That's why he was working with a Chinese group able to bank the stuff in both Hong Kong and on the mainland. Maybe Cal could do the same thing with his banking connections in Bulgaria?

Raic had, of course, already tried to pass a couple of the notes himself, so he knew how the banks would view them. The teller had spotted the intruders instantly. Raic protested his innocence, telling her a client had paid him in these odd bills and he wasn't aware they were counterfeit. I'm a lawyer, ma'am — my card — so I can assure you, I would not be here if I knew they were counterfeit. It had worked.

Cal said that his people were more interested in the technology and would want the plates and the press, the means to print the money themselves.

The price, according to Raic, was fifteen cents on the dollar; he would have to negotiate a deal for the plates and the press. Cal said it was too much.

"That's what the Asians are paying," said Raic.

"Can I have some samples overnight?" asked Cal.

"Only until 7 p.m. Unless you want to take them in trade for the thousand dollars?"

"Forget it. It's lousy quality."

"We can negotiate once your people decide on a final price. . . . Cal," Raic then said in a low, urgent tone, "I need to make a commission on this deal."

"Who's your client?"

"I can't tell you."

"I want to meet him."

"He won't do that. You'll meet me and maybe one other guy. We'll start with $3 million and finish with the rest. It'll be cash for cash."

"As buyers," said Cal, "we'll state the terms. Once we've seen the goods, we'll pay by check or international wire. Once we get them to a safe location, that is."

Cal took the seven fake thousand-dollar bills. As soon as he hit the street, he went to the first pay phone he saw and called Gilles Chambertin at the RCMP Counterfeit Division on Greene Avenue. Chambertin had a crew pick him up in ten minutes. They took Cal in and grilled him for hours. How do you know Raic? Where did you meet him? Why did you loan him the money?

In the end, Chambertin authorized Cal to probe Raic, agreeing to pick up a modest amount of expenses.

Cal set up a buy at the McDonald's in Old Montreal. Chambertin had a photo team nearby to record it all. The counterfeiter's thousand-dollar bill, the pinkie, was perfect, but they had messed up the gold foil stamp; Cal could flick it off with his finger.

The bad guys move fast, the good guys move slow. It took Chambertin a month to set up a sting operation to nail Raic and the counterfeit. The lawyer, allegedly, had it all sold to the Asian gangs in Chinatown inside of a week.

All the same, Raic thought he had Cal, the money fish, back on the hook. They met at a coffee shop in Outremont, and Raic asked to borrow another $500. Cal hadn't been paid back his original loan, *and* he was out another $1,000. He exploded, just went nuclear on the former head of the Judicial Affairs Committee. He started pounding the table and shouting. He stood and grabbed a chair, holding it up by one leg. A vein throbbed in his temple. His eyes bulged, as if rage were swelling up within and had begun to overflow. Raic could really piss you off.

"I'm gonna take this chair," Cal told him, "and stick the legs right up your ass! Then I'm gonna shove you right through that fuckin' wall."

Raic was genuinely scared. So desperate was he to pacify Cal that, there and then, he offered to introduce him to Little John, Vito Rizzuto's right-hand troll. To Raic, Little John was something approaching a tutelary deity. In the Montreal underworld, the Rizzutos were royalty. Little John, he knew, just as he knew day followed night, was the gatekeeper to worlds of lucrative business for Cal. If, of course, Raic could pick up another commission for his trouble.

Cal never learned Little John's surname. On the street, you just didn't inquire after such incriminating details.

IT HAD BEEN a long journey down into the labyrinthine caverns of the underworld for the grocer from small-town New York, and he had met some scary guys along the way — like Réal Dupont. But nobody could compare with the Rizzuto enforcer for sheer fright factor. According to his rep on the street, Little John did Satan's dirty work. The carnage, the violence, the cruelty, the danger were of mythological proportions. You were up against the Minotaur.

Little John, in reality, was a murderous dwarf. In his late forties, he was about five-foot-three and more than 300 pounds, most of it solid muscle above the waist. Just a massive chest. He had a scarred face, red-rimmed eyes, and a white moustache. His hands were huge sausage-fingered paws, just immense implements of bone-cracking, flesh-tearing terror. As far as Cal could see, however, the little mass of compacted trash was not so fearsome from a first impression. He dressed like a Wal-Mart shopper.

When he opened his mouth, though, what came out was chilling. The world was a far worse place thanks to his existence. Little John gave every impression of hating all humanity. After all, other people were breathing his oxygen.

Hollywood movies, no matter how "honest" and gritty, invariably flattered monsters like Little John. The reality was very different. He was never charming, never amusing; there was nothing whatsoever that was even vaguely attractive about the man. He was banal, a dull horror. Little John may have appeared to be human, but really he was a killing machine with instincts instead of thoughts. He had simplified life into two things: money and violence. The movies aren't ready for a gangster as brutal as Little John.

Cal was first introduced to Little John by Yves Raic at Le Moulerie, an upscale restaurant not far from the Manoir de Belmont. It was a fancy crowd: BMW drivers and soigné Westmount ladies who had just come from having their nails and hair done. Little John didn't care about his surroundings or the people in them. He didn't see such things; they weren't there. The enforcer was loud. He always looked like he was ready to go nuclear on the spot.

Cal offered to buy him a beer. He might as well have offered to rape his mother.

"JUST DON'T FUCK WITH ME!" said John. "THAT'S THE FIRST THING!"

Heads were turning at tables.

"I'm not gay," said Cal, "so you don't have to worry about that."

"IF YOU FUCK WITH ME, I'M GONNA CUT YOUR BALLS OFF AND STUFF THEM IN YOUR MOUTH!"

All around them, the elegant diners were freaking out. Who let those awful people in here?

"All due respect," said Cal quietly, "you can't come here and talk to me like this. I've gotta live here."

Even Cal was surprised to find that this worked. The enforcer looked ashamed of himself. He quietened down.

"Sorry, buddy," he mumbled. "I've had a tough day."

Cal began to worry that Little John was actually insane, out of control. They broached a few topics of mutual interest, but nothing concrete, and Yves Raic had a constant need to act as Cal's interpreter, explaining a remark here, a comment there as if another language was being spoken.

After one such interpretative sally, Little John turned to the former chairman of the judicial committee.

"Raic," he said, "you fuck off. You've got work to do."

Raic, it transpired, was muling drugs for Little John.

*Sic transit gloria mundi.*

Later, when Cal walked outside with him, Little John turned and said, "I'm the only reason Raic's still alive."

The Italian Mafia is a feudal organization. By virtue of his debts, Raic had become Little John's serf, his slave, his boy, his creature. His life literally depended on Little John's whim.

"Any deal we get into," said Little, referring to Raic, "I'll manage him like a monkey on a stick."

Awesome as it might have seemed, Little John's power to grant life or death was evidently not making the enforcer rich. He was driving the kind of car an unskilled labourer would resent, a rusting blue Pontiac GTO that had to be twenty years old.

"Let's you an' me go for a ride," he suggested. "Have a talk, you know."

As he always did, Cal presented himself as a big butter-and-egg man with the Russians and the Bulgarians. He impressed Little John with his knowledge of banking and shipping, debentures, seventy-five tens, MT100s, and other instruments of the new merchant. Little John was a simple guy, and this was some fancy shit. Cal was painting pictures of a world he couldn't imagine, opening up a lucrative space age of global enterprise to a battling survivor of Montreal's mean streets, a man whose trade was violence. He had no other skills.

They talked money laundering, they talked drugs, they talked arms, they talked counterfeit. Cal, naturally, talked big volume, just immense fucking deals. But so did Little John. To hear him tell it, rivers of contraband, vast inland seas of illegal commodities, were backed up in Rizzuto warehouses. Name it — smack, blow, weed, blue jeans — they had it on

hand. While it's easy to sell the odd ounce or few dozen pairs, though, selling a hundred or a thousand tons, five or fifty million pairs, is less simply achieved. Such deals are usually middled to a single customer. If you lose him, you have a problem. And the Rizzutos had a big problem in the form of Russian Mafiya poaching both their sources and their customers. Their only option was to make their own alliances among the Russian mobsters, setting one gang against another, and doing on their turf what the intruders were doing in Montreal. Little John badly needed a buyer, a trading saviour, somebody exactly like Cal. He might have had a couple of vague contacts with the local Bulgarians in Montreal, but Cal was counting on the fact that to Little John, the big-time players in Sofia, from the president down, were as remote as both the man in the moon and the men on the moon.

Little John affected great concern for Cal's European connections. The bikers and the Italians ran all the drug deals on the Ile de Montréal, he claimed. If the Russians turfed in, they would get their asses pounded into burger meat. But he, Little John, had all the right connections to deal the East Europeans in and make sure everything ran smoothly. He was the Man here, he tried to explain; he was Cal's best chance. This, it was implied, should be the start of a beautiful friendship.

An hour after Cal had left Little John, Yves Raic phoned him and said they were in business. As far as Little was concerned, it was a go. No doubt about it, Cal could impress with his line of Euro-jive. Now, however, he had talked his way into the biggest single criminal organization in the country. With any luck, he could see them all behind bars, just as he'd done with Larry Miller. Mission accomplished. His whole life would be vindicated.

After the Rizzutos, everyone was a minnow. At least, that's the way they liked to paint it. In reality, they were having a hard time hanging on to their turf with the Russians pouring into Montreal. Indeed, they'd recognized the need to extend themselves into Ontario, since one of these days they might be forced to relocate to somewhere like Toronto. The West End Mob had already moved out to Vancouver. It was a sign of the times. This continental drift in crime was rubbing everyone the wrong way, and it was clear to anyone who read the newspapers for more than entertainment that a series of gang wars was in progress. Slayings and executions, with known organized crime figures found dead in their cars and no killer ever apprehended, were increasingly common. The Italians blamed the Russians; the Russians blamed the bikers; the bikers blamed the Colombians or the Jamaicans. But everyone knew it was the Russians who were responsible. No one trusted them, and everyone feared them. Instead of standing up to them, however, buddy was in a mad scramble to take out what he could while he could. What did you expect? Heroics?

In the days that followed, Raic was phoning Cal several times a day and offering him deals on Little John's behalf. He used a code that could have been figured out by a six-year-old and seemed to draw more attention than if he'd used the proper terms. "Chocolate" was hashish, "sterling" was counterfeit, "hardware" was weaponry.

"We've got to do one good deal, " Raic told him. "Then the cash pot will be open."

It was clear that Raic had a lot riding on this one good deal himself.

The RCMP handlers were like kids on Christmas morning with this stuff; Cal had brought them an embarrassment of criminal riches. But because of the enormity of the fish potentially on the end of the line — the Rizzutos — they were also nervous. At first, they could offer no clear instructions beyond the caution to play everything on this one by the book. Any deviation would backfire if or when the case came to court. Because these guys could afford the very best legal minds, a platoon of juniors, assistants, and researchers would be combing through every single aspect, every word of every statement, every comma of every notebook, every step in any procedure — everything to do with the case that could be used to overturn it or, failing that, beat it.

At an early meeting, Little John offered a sample of counterfeit. Cal had to find a really good excuse to turn it down or else he'd be creating a potential problem. If he accepted any of the deals offered to him out of the blue without proper RCMP authorization, he was quite simply a criminal, liable to arrest and prosecution. He had no general mandate to fight crime in any way he saw fit, in whatever form it appeared. There was no such mandate. He could do a deal only if it was specified in an LOA — and even then he had to be very careful not to help move the targets along towards the crime, because *that* was entrapment. Even offer-

ing someone a lift in his car could be interpreted as entrapment.

For an LOA to work as structured, Cal had to know the kind of crime that would be committed in advance, otherwise the task force involved might not have the necessary clearance — or manpower, or jurisdiction, or equipment — to follow through. So to make things run as smoothly as possible, he needed Little John and Raic to take his deal, not the other way around. This was the only possible way for him to keep control. If Little John, Raic, or any other of the Rizzutos took his deal, they would find the inevitable RCMP SWAT team at the end of it, waiting to take them down, and no matter what, Cal could stay out of court. If they did-n't, there was probably no project. No project, no paycheck. Thus the only way Cal Broeker could survive was to do it *his way.* If he veered too much one way or too much the other, he was either dead or penniless.

YVES RAIC WAS NOT keeping all of his eggs in Little John's basket, however, no matter what his lord and master thought. His situation was too dire to permit the curtailing of opportunities when they arose.

A few days after the intro to Little, Raic set up a meeting between Cal and an Indian named Irwin Convoy. It was at a breakfast place called Eggsasperations on Mountain at Maisonneuve. If anybody had ever been aptly named, it was Irwin Convoy. He was the Rizzutos' rez connection, a conduit to the Mohawks and the tobacco-smuggling business on Kahnawake. Now in his seventies, Convoy had blue eyes, was tall and thin. With his white hair, deck loafers, and Yankees cap, he looked more like a corporate CEO out trophy fishing than he did an Indian cigarette smuggler for the Mafia.

And much to his horror, Cal immediately realized he had in fact met Convoy two years earlier, when he was seeing Elizabeth Dumas and doing some work with the Mohawk council on Kahnawake. At first, Cal suspected that his cover had been blown, that the meeting was a Rizzuto set-up.

"Cal used to live on the rez," said Raic helpfully.

"Oh, yeah?" said Convoy. "Where?"

So it wasn't a set-up, but it sure was a toe-curling, sweaty moment. Convoy had talked with Cal back then, called him by name. But luckily, at his age, Convoy had a memory shot with holes the size of moon craters. It was miraculous — and Cal was reluctant to believe in miracles — but Irwin Convoy didn't recognize C. Calvin Broeker at all. | 283

It got even more hair-raising, though, despite this.

"There was another big guy like you on the rez," Convoy said suddenly. "Yeah. He used to live with Elizabeth Dumas. He got arrested and sent to prison."

"No shit," said Cal. "I heard about that guy."

Silently praising God, Cal then said he wasn't interested in tobacco at this time and got up to leave before Irwin Convoy's memory could improve.

It was nice to know the smoke he'd spread around the rez in the wake of Dupont's takedown had not been wasted. Now it was clearly his version of what had gone on, not Dupont's, that was being told.

Pierre Maille, who was Justinian Sabot's partner at Kestrel Investments during the Dupont takedown, was still with Sabot and at Kestrel. Their office was just around the corner from Eggsasperations, on Maisonneuve. Halfway between the two locations, Cal ran into Little John standing in a corner doorway. It was no coincidence. The man was waiting for him. He pulled Cal abruptly into the shadowed recess, holding him by the necktie so close that Cal had to bend double and his nose touched Little's sandpaper jaw.

"See this?" said Little, pointing to his cheek. In broad daylight and an inch away, the details of Little John's face were horrible. It was a mess, his face — a big, knotty ball of tortured muscles, the raw skin pocked and pitted like an old dartboard. "Know how I got these scars?" he asked.

Cal shook his head.

"I was standing too close to a guy when I blew his skull apart, and the little chips of bone flew out and stuck right in my fucking face! We had to pull them out, one by one, with fucking tweezers, hundreds of 'em. Whaddaya think of that?"

What could one say? The face was Little John's badge of honour, the evidence of all he'd been through, all he'd survived. Those who passed him in the street didn't know the half of it. He'd seen things ordinary men and women couldn't even imagine. Forget the blood and gore, the amateur surgery and human chainsaw art. How many people know what it's like to tie a man to a chair and force a fully grown live rattlesnake down his throat, then look him in the eye? How many know how a man reacts when his penis and testicles are handed to him, detached from their usual, familiar spot and placed between fingers used to feeling them? All these secrets Little John would take to his grave with him.

Cal could spin war stories with the best of them, of course. And he now had to show this throwback Cro-Magnon that no matter how ferocious he got, he couldn't intimidate C. Calvin Broeker, who didn't care and didn't scare. So Cal brandished a scar of his own, on the hand.

"See that? Know how I got it?"

Little John shook his head. He liked this game.

"I shoved a butcher knife right through, bone and all. Pinned the hand to a door. Had to pull it out myself, then sewed up the wound myself. Whaddaya think of that?"

Little John was suitably impressed. Changing the subject abruptly, he told Cal he was going to the U.S. for a while.

Since Little had a criminal record, he couldn't enter the country legally, so he had to go on the boats, through the rez. It cost only around fifty dollars each way. Kahnawake and Akwesasne were a buddies' freedom road. And the world's longest undefended border looked it. It was a sieve. At any given moment, day or night, something that shouldn't have been was going across it to or from one of the reservations. Moreover, many perfectly law-abiding Indians felt it was symbolically appropriate to make a business of showing contempt for a border that they didn't recognize, and that itself symbolized their own humiliation.

"You have yourself a fabulous time, John," said Cal.

Little nodded, oddly introspective for a moment.

Cal walked on to the Kestrel offices. Maille had two steel suitcases there with the equivalent of US$5 million in pesos. There was, supposedly, another $500 million in a warehouse in San Francisco. He wanted Cal to launder it. All of it. Although he was now in the clear with regard to his role in Dupont's arrest, Cal was still never sure whether Maille was setting him up with this kind of shit, or perhaps just keeping him on the hook until Réal Dupont got out of jail. This aura of suspicion was either just a part of Maille's personality — he could be cautious or paranoid — or it had a more tangible explanation. And Maille would give him a strange look occasionally, as if something incriminating about Cal had been brought to his attention.

Bearing in mind the mandate of his LOA, Cal was hard-pressed to find an excuse not to launder the pesos. The best one he could come up with was that he wasn't certain how much of the cash was counterfeit. And he wanted his own counting machine, not Maille's.

As usual, Cal was juggling too many balls in the air at once. Just like he had at the IGA back in Chateaugay. Just like he had in Bulgaria. But he couldn't turn away from an opportunity if one arose — couldn't understand why he should when it came to buddy — and after all, was it his fault that shit happened when he was around?

AFTER THE DEBACLE at the McDonald's in Old Montreal, the counterfeit section wasn't interested in Raic any more. Cal was already running an LOA with the Falcon Task Force; they weren't about to issue a second. And he was probing Pierre Maille and Kestrel Investments for Proceeds in Montreal, so this was their call. When he told Sgt. Antoine Chambertin of Proceeds about the extent of his penetration of the Rizzutos, the Mountie was alarmed. This was more than a question of procedure, of going by the book, of sticking to the LOA. Cal was simply going too damn fast. He couldn't go after Little John without a task force the size of Orienter behind him. As Chambertin saw it, one way or another, somebody was bound to rat him out, and Cal would end up in a bag in the St. Lawrence River.

Cal's imagination was fertile when it came to the octopus of organized crime, and he wondered just how powerful the Rizzutos actually were. Show me a big fortune, he was prone to quote, and I'll show you a big crime behind it. It was a fact that some criminals had become powerful enough to put their sons in the White House. So how far-fetched was it to worry that the Rizzutos had a few highly placed friends in Ottawa? You can be sure, Cal told himself, that they have friends in high places somewhere. If they didn't, they'd be the first big mobsters in history not to have found anyone powerful to blackmail or bribe.

Raic was phoning him with criminal deals every day now. He couldn't keep walking away from them. Not morally and not credibly. Then there was a bad meeting with Little John at a coffee shop in Westmount where Cal had once met Justinian Sabot. Little John was under a lot of pressure himself. He had to produce his monthly tribute to the family, and he was having trouble coming up with the cash. Things were tight; no one wanted to play or pay.

Cal had arrived a few minutes late. Little John didn't like that. When Cal walked into the coffee shop, the enforcer immediately offered to take a few inches off his height by breaking his legs into powder with a base-ball bat. People of average height cannot imagine how bitterly they are resented by some smaller men, how cruel a blow the lack of a few inches can be, how disproportionately extreme the compensation factor can become. And Cal was not of average height. He was a giant beside whom Little John looked . . . well, little. It's unlikely that he had initially welcomed, let alone encouraged, people to call him Little, but it had stuck. Being Little John was nothing like being Big John — even if you worked for Robin Hood. All this occurred to Cal in the moments after he was greeted with this snarling threat.

Then Little John offered him all the money laundering for the Hell's Angels and the Rizzutos — if Cal could come up with the right rate. They were going to start off with $1 million. A lot more, $20 million, would follow. It was bewildering. When Raic phoned later that evening, Cal was upset. Ever since he had been threatened with arrest during Orienter, he had begun taping all his calls with both the bad boys and the police. Just in case it all wound up in a courtroom one day. He assumed that the cops were doing the same to him. The result, however, was that we have, preserved intact, almost every conversation he ever had from that time on.

"I appreciate John saying we'll have all the business from the H.A. and the family and everything," he told Raic.

"Yeah, yeah. You'll have no problem with that," said the lawyer. "But the rate is way too much."

"I'll never go through the grovelling I had to go through with John again," said Cal. "I'm so ashamed. I'll never do it again."

"It's nothing against you," Raic assured him. "He totally understands your position."

"I know he was a little angry at first. I know he calmed down towards the end. I understand his frustration."

But Cal didn't understand it as well as Little John's monkey did.

"He was angry for different reasons," said Raic. "It was nothing to do with you. When he walked into my place, he was angry with his general situation. The family is saying, 'Look, you're not making any money.' Then this thing was added on. We've been talking for months now, and we haven't done a thing. It was his own personal situation. He told me, 'At the end of the month I've got to produce, and if I don't produce, I have to look somewhere else.'"

"It's there," Cal told him. "It's right on the edge. And I'm not going to pull away for anybody. And tomorrow I'll have your money for you. I'll pull it out of my sock if I have to. I'm glad I have the confidence of John. He was so angry to start with."

"He wasn't angry with you," said Raic.

"But when he says he's going to break my legs and take a piece of my ass and chew it up, I worry about that," replied Cal.

"What?"

"He said he was going to take a baseball bat and trim my legs down to size."

"He was joking."

"He's a serious motherfucker when he jokes," said Cal.

"Didn't you see his smile? He was smiling."

It had been a tiny smile, scarcely visible.

Raic insisted that John meant no harm. "It was the first time I saw him smile that day. Your appearance made him smile."

"You know," confided Cal, "I think I'd have trouble dealing with John on a daily basis."

"Oh, no. I've known him for years," said the former chairman of the judicial committee. "It's easy. No problem. They're beginning to laugh at him in the family. He tells me, 'The end of the month is next week. I've got to produce a deal or go somewhere else.' I said, 'Little, relax.' He said, 'Relax? You know my problems. I was at your wedding. Things have been available for months, and we can't get a handle on it.' I took all this before you even arrived. When you arrived, he smiled. There's no problem between him and you. He's already on a natural basis quite assertive. But he likes you. 'Calvin is a likeable guy.' He told me that. Please, the next time have a look. He has a funny moustache, but it's easy to see when he smiles."

Cal wasn't so sure John was smiling at him.

It was very hard to tell.

All he knew for sure was that Little John wasn't someone to fuck around for long. He did that, he'd be dead. And "long" was what he faced the way things were set up. Cal had to find someone willing to pick this thing up and run with it, and do it quickly, because the thought of stalling Little for much longer made him sick to his stomach.

He had to do something now, so Cal decided to approach the Cornwall Regional Task Force, even though he had had his problems in the past with Ted Phano, who was now the boss of the operation. The tall, thin Phano had been promoted to detective sergeant with the OPP as a result of Orienter. Some cops were good on the street; Phano had developed a reputation as a virtuoso of office politics. In some ways, that was more important. After he heard what Cal had to offer this time, he agreed to a probe. No more. Const. Keith Tasque was assigned to be his handler. Tasque was kind of anonymous, a clerkly presence. CYA was his religion. Const. Ron Harlow was young, dark, in his twenties. He was the cover. These two resignedly referred to themselves as "grunts." Staff Sgt. Craig Owens was going to be the lead investigator.

The plainclothes crew with the Cornwall RTF were doughty small-town Canuck types, real Labatt's 50 drinkers. Cal would never visit HQ in Cornwall. He would call collect, under the name Tony Montreal. When they visited Cal at his apartment at the Manoir de Belmont, the Mounties were appalled that he would spend twenty dollars on a bottle of wine; they couldn't understand the fridge full of Veuve-Cliquot. Their standard operating procedure with agents and informants was the carrot and the stick. In this case, the carrot was a huge reward, maybe as much as $500,000. The Rizzutos had to be worth that much.

As for the stick, all they had to do was walk away and leave Cal to Little John. . . .

The enforcer troll was always checking up on him, testing. He would turn up at the Manoir de Belmont unannounced, just to see if Cal was there. Finally, Cal rented another apartment on rue Durocher, told Little that he was travelling in the States, and just holed up there. The pressure of having a psychopath on his case was beginning to rattle Cal's cage. Bad enough that Réal Dupont would be getting out soon, but the addition of the Little factor made "paranoid" too mild a term. Besides, he didn't *think* there were people out there who wanted to kill him — he *knew* they were out there. In his case, a paranoid *was* someone who knew all the facts. He was also starting to worry about Simone's safety. Elizabeth's too. And Doris. And his kids.

He was getting jumpy, real jumpy.

ALTHOUGH THE MOUNTIES had never come this close to penetrating the country's biggest crime family, Phano was encountering bureaucratic and jurisdictional roadblocks among the brass in Ottawa. As in many other aspects of Canadian life, there were problems between Ontario and Quebec. The Cornwall RTF had no authority to operate in Quebec. When officers came to visit Cal in Montreal, they talked about "going over to the dark side." If the Cornwall RTF was going after Little John and Vito Rizzuto, Montreal RCMP toes would get stepped on. If Little John wasn't a Hollywood hoodlum, the boys from Cornwall RTF were not movie cops, for sure. They weren't about to disregard orders from higher-ups; they were too professional for that. They wanted to keep their jobs and their pensions. Only in fiction did cops get so obsessive about justice that they disobeyed their superiors. In real life, if you busted one buddy, another always popped up to take his place.

Phano was pushing the project upstream in Ottawa. There were doubters. Ten street guys came to the Mounties every week and told them they could get Rizzuto. But Cal had credibility from Orienter and Dupont. Why, Janet Reno herself, the attorney general of the United States, had mentioned Cal (not by name, of course) in the Dupont case, the biggest counterfeit bust in history, and in Orienter, when she came to Toronto to give a speech. Calvin Broeker was a living example of Can-Am co-operation at its finest. You didn't doubt what he brought to your attention.

All the same, budgets had to be estimated and approved. After all, mounting a big project like this costs money. Phano had to prove it would be productive. A plan was being generated.

290 |     In August, Cal went to Ottawa and met an RCMP undercover man named Ronald Desbarats. Desbarats, another clerkly, bland type, was, appropriately, a specialist in white-collar crime. He would generally pose as a wealthy Bay Street banker who was way up into illegal financial transactions.

The role was eminently believable. While he was with the Leroys, Cal had encountered senior bank officials willing to do transactions off the books, to help out their institution's cash float. Of course, there was also a little bonus in it for them.

The idea in this case was that Cal would bring Raic, Little John, and a key member of the Rizzutos face to face with the UC. He would rent a limo and bring the Mafia don over the border from Quebec into Ontario. Then Desbarats would set in motion the money-laundering deal for the $20 million. Not too far down the line were a SWAT squad, a takedown, and ultimately jail for Raic, Little John, Vito Rizzuto, and his family.

But first, the brass hats in Ottawa had to give the thumbs-up.


EVERY DAY, CORNWALL RTF would get a call from Cal Broeker. Little John was climbing up his ass, desperate to deal. Raic too was getting more desperate, if that were possible, wandering around the city by metro, bumming meals from Cal at his favourite watering hole, Chez Vito on Cotes-des-Neiges, hitting him up for more loans. Things were getting so bad that Raic was even considering getting a job. All the while, Cal waited for the cops to move ahead, and the cops waited for clearance from the brass. Who the brass was waiting for is anyone's guess, but the whole process drove home the fact that this was no way to fight crime.

Then Yves Raic phoned to offer something extraordinary.

The Rizzutos had a man on the inside at an American arms manufacturer, in much the same way as Larry Miller had had a man on the inside at R.J. Reynolds. They wanted to do a big weapons deal. Very big.

Raic left a phone message for Cal.

"I've talked to our Little friend," said Raic, "and price will depend on where you want it delivered. The hardware is available in unlimited quantities. Prices are extremely good. They're direct from the manufacturer. And on a more kidding note, I hope you're not dead. If you resurrect, call me back. In the name of the Father, the Son, and the Holy Ghost. Have a shitload of fun."

The possibility of sudden death was real in Raic's world, and in Cal's too. They liked to kid about it. Maybe it would keep the reality away.

Cal met Raic at the Alexis Nehon food court. First thing, Raic asked for a loan, money to live on. Little John wouldn't loan him any more. And these deals with Cal Broeker seemed to be going nowhere. Cal told him about the banker in Toronto.

"This guy will do a big laundering deal. But only if you and Little meet him face to face."

"You said you met him in London?"

"Yeah, we made a shitload of money on an LC."

"Look, Little is getting worried about you and why everything is taking so long. What's this guy's name, anyhow?"

"Ronald Desbarats. He has a guy works with him. He'll probably be there too."

"Just so long as the group is small."

"I'm gonna intro you as the lawyer for John and his group. You gotta play that part."

"What do you mean? I am a lawyer."

"*Were*, you mean."

Raic frowned at this. "Little will have to talk to you today."

"Fine."

"No, listen. Either you meet him today or he'll come get you."

Cal didn't want that to happen.

"How about here at six o'clock?"

"Fine."

"I can accept no less than $500 today."

Cal reached for his show-roll wearily.

At six o'clock, Little John was enraged, as usual. He was pissed at a deal for grenades and C-4s that Cal had let go by because the Mounties were still waiting for an answer. And he needed Cal's help on a Hell's Angels telemarketing scam. Cal asked him to calm down. The whole world wanted Little John to calm down.

"YOU FUCKIN' OWE ME ALL THE TIME YOU WASTED."

"Okay, Little, okay."

"SOME BIG FUCKIN' PLAYER YOU ARE! THAT WAS A LOT OF BULLSHIT!"

"Look, John, I've spent a lot of my own money bringing this deal to the table."

"I OWN YOUR ASS! DON'T FORGET IT."

Was Little John now telling people he worked Cal like a monkey on a stick, Cal wondered? Was that what he'd become?

IN CORNWALL, MEANWHILE, Ron Harlow still had no news from Ottawa. Sometimes it seemed like his sole job was to humour Cal Broeker.

"I'm out of excuses," he said. "I can't instruct you because we don't know what we're doing here."

"I need orders," said Cal.

"Try to maintain your credibility."

"Any suggestions?"

"We leave it up to you," said Constable Harlow. "But of course, we can't direct you. If it's a yes, we meet with the investigators, make a plan of attack, and the LOA comes into play. We don't think there's any reason why it shouldn't, but you never know. We're just grunts here at the bottom of the ladder. Hold on tight. Keep on checkin' in. You'll be the first guy we call."

Then Cal phoned Ted Phano.

"We are working our asses off to get this done," said Phano. "After the meeting we had this afternoon, plus the meeting we had this week, it looks very good. The play's going to change a little bit because the guys who have a little bit more cash are coming into play, but that's good. That's excellent."

"That's what I set up here to do since last January," said Cal. "To penetrate into this group as far as I can and blow it up."

"I'll tell you something that's coming up the line," said Phano. "I'm just giving it to you. Food for thought. This is between you and I, so I thought I'd give you a heads-up on it. There's a concern here about the association between Raic and Little John. The concern is they want to go ahead with this, but they don't want the two together when we're dealing. They'd like to do Raic and Raic alone."

"Oh, that's easy," said Cal.

"We were trying to rack our brains today. How do we separate the two and still keep you into position?"

"Always remember," Cal told him, "I try to put the players where you want them to be without coercion, without entrapment. They come to me. If I tell Raic, 'Let's just do a deal between you and I,' he'll be totally agreeable to it."

"Just between you and I," continued Phano, "the only reason I'm telling you this is because I trust you. We're trying to get hold of a helicopter. Just to make it look like a big deal."

"That would be great. That would be super."

Why the hell was he going on about helicopters when he couldn't even get an okay on the project? Cal began to wonder if there was something he *wasn't* being told. And the more just-between-you-and-I's he heard, the more he wondered it.

"I think we're on the right track here," added Phano. "It's just that we have to be very careful with the brass. Be patient, follow the directions, and I'll tell you, it'll pay off."

"It would be such a travesty of justice and a disgrace if they get off," said Cal blankly.

"When they were reporting to me today, they said you thought that the guy supplying Raic with arms could be inside at the manufacturer?"

"Yes."

"I just about had a hard-on," said Phano.

"Yesterday, Raic told me on the phone, 'You'll be getting market price because John told me you'll be dealing with the manufacturer himself.'"

"We need to stay away from John. Somehow."

What was this stay-away-from-John stuff? Cal's anxiety increased.

"Well, you tell me how to place myself," he told Phano. "Because if the phone call comes and it's no go, I gotta bail. John has already given me too much on him and his organization."

"It looks like Tuesday noon we'll have a yea from both sides of the fence here."

When he got off the phone, Cal wondered why it was so important that Rizzuto and Raic be kept separate. The powers that be in Ottawa seemed eager to nail both individuals, but not together. Was it possible that an arrest of a formerly prominent party organizer in the company of one of the country's leading mobsters might be too embarrassing for the RCMP's political masters in the Liberal government? If it was possible, just how embarrassing could it potentially be? And just how undesirable was this potential embarrassment, and to whom? No one was going to tell Cal, though. Of that he was certain. He wasn't a member of the club. Hell, he wasn't even a landed immigrant.

A COUPLE OF DAYS LATER, Cal got Keith Tasque on the phone. As Phano had mentioned, the key meeting would take place the following Tuesday. Then they would all know whether the project was going forward or not.

"We're lookin' for a really good meeting Tuesday with the mucky-mucks," said Tasque. "But don't you tell me anything till it's signed. I don't want to know anything."

"I've been stalling for four months," said Cal. "It's important that senior management gets on the stick."

"We're moving very fast considering what's going on. You know what, you didn't meet the right guys there. You're in touch with the right guys there now, the ones who are particularly interested in the Italians."

"Yeah, but if John hears another excuse, I'm in big trouble."

"We have to smooth these guys from Ottawa over. 'You guys missed the boat, we're goin' with it.' But these other guys, they want to jump on now. They're goin', 'We've never been this close.' So they're very impressed. These are people with their own budget, and they're very interested."

"This is the highest level I've ever worked with," said Cal. "Larry Miller was nothing compared to these people."

"We've already attached a lot of things to impress these arseholes."

Arseholes. All the cops at Cornwall RTF sounded very clipped and crusty-Canuck to the American Cal Broeker.

Later, he talked again to Const. Ron Harlow.

Said Harlow: "The brass have to look at why the people in Montreal weren't doing anything and their reasons for not doing anything with you at the time. Once their position is explained and our position is explained, we'll be fine. This is a unique opportunity, there is no doubt."

"I don't want the thing to stagnate just because somebody's going to be embarrassed," Cal told him.

"Well, I think they believe you'd create too much heat in Montreal."

"Create too much heat?" Cal was incredulous.

"Yeah. You were talking about the articles in the papers about the Bulgarian trucking company?"

Articles in the paper?

Heat for whom? Cal wondered.

"Heat for me, you mean?"

"Yeah, absolutely. And the operators."

"That's why I want to move into Ontario," Cal announced.

"That's why the brass have to meet with the upper level and make sure we're not stepping on anybody's toes."

Yes, Cal thought when he got off the phone, a Rizzuto/Raic arrest would cause a great deal of heat, especially in the media. There would be calls for further investigations, maybe questions in the House of Commons. How many other Liberals in Montreal were connected to the Rizzuto family? How many campaigns had Rizzuto money financed?

THE NEXT DAY, he got Harlow on the phone again. He was pushing hard, maybe too hard.

"I can't believe the RCMP can't work together on the biggest fuckin' deal in a long time," he said. "I mean, they're giving me all the money laundering with the H.A. and the Rizzutos."

"We're on a good line, eh?" Harlow was unusually concerned about security. Just like the bad guys, the good guys were occasionally concerned about being overheard too.

If they only knew, thought Cal.

"John was pretty hot tonight," Cal told Harlow. "He said, 'I pretty much own your ass because I put people on hold waiting for you.'"

"Can I just put you on speaker? So everybody can hear and I don't have to fuckin' repeat everything?"

Everybody came to talk to Cal: Tasque, Phano, Owens.

"Where are you?"

"Back home at the apartment."

"Who drove you there?"

"Chambertin and Richard."

These were Cal's handlers from Proceeds in Montreal.

"There was no debriefing?"

"No. They said that was your responsibility and they're not going to do your work for you. I'm playing with my life and I'm into some childish games. I'm dealing with a mobster and killer who says he owns me. He's saying, 'I want to deal with you, the family has plans. We need somebody with your nuts and intelligence. But you're makin' it hard for me.' This is the last meeting unless I come up with something."

Keith Tasque, however, was more interested in what the Montreal RCMP were saying about Cornwall RTF.

"Have you heard about all the pissing in the division? This thing has gotten so big, everybody wants on."

"We don't need to establish a relationship between Raic and Ronald," said Cal almost desperately. "We need to do a deal. That's the main focus. They're ready to roll, ready to deal."

Nobody was going to leave Cal dangling in the cold, he was reassured. They weren't going to let Little John take him for a ride on the rez and have a talk, maybe with four or five big Mohawks. But the more Harlow reassured him, the less reassured he felt.

NEXT DAY, HE PHONED Cornwall again. He did it every day now. He got one of the women telephone operators. She had a sexy voice, with that distinctive Franco-Ontarian accent so prevalent in Cornwall.

"It's Tony in Montreal."

"Good morning, Tony."

"Is Ron there?"

The telephone operator sounded as blandly pleasant as ever. "He's out today."

"How about Keith?"

"He's out too."

Cal laughed nervously. In his mind's eye he could see them all in the | 297 office, signalling from their cubicles to the receptionist: none of them was in to C. Calvin Broeker.

"Can I speak to Ted Phano, then?"

"Sorry, he's in Ottawa today."

"How about Craig Owens?"

"He's not here."

Fu-uck.

Cal hung up in a sweat. The RCMP had disappeared on him. In the days that followed, he could not reach them by phone, by pager, by dogsled. He was soon in a panic. A 500-pound stress gorilla was clambering all over his back. Little John believed Cal was a millionaire international businessman. He was promising him a $20-million deal. The guy was so psycho and so desperate for money that Cal was even afraid he would maybe kidnap him and torture him until he handed over all his cash.

Fuck. Fuck. Fuck.

Cal paced back and forth in the Manoir de Belmont, fretting. He drank every inch of alcohol in the place. All the Scotch, vodka, wine, Veuve-Cliquot. He watched his tape of *Glory*, with Denzel Washington, then his tape of *Gettysburg*, all four hours of the miniseries.

Then he just threw Hendrix on the stereo system. LOUD.

And got totally hammered.

When all the booze was gone, he thought about drinking hair tonic.

Big, brave Cal Broeker was scared out of his wits.

Finally, finally, he reached Keith Tasque on the phone. Cal almost wept with relief. He turned down his stereo.

"We're not dead," said his handler.

"I'm scared to death," blurted Cal. "I paged so many times over the past few days. Last night till four in the morning."

That big monkey had just climbed off Cal's back. He let out a sigh. The

500-pound stress gorilla was gone. His body flooded with relief. The effect was almost orgasmic.

"My battery must've died," said Keith lamely. "We're coming up to see you this afternoon. Everything's fine."

"Keith, I'm gonna cry."

"We had a scare. We had a scare. We couldn't come to debrief you. We couldn't come till we worked this out with these . . . I'm not going to say arseholes."

"I'm not goin' anywhere," Cal told him. "I'm afraid to stick my head out the door."

"Everything's fine, everything's a go. We're gonna have you down to meet with the operators on Tuesday. Everything's fine."

"Thank you so much, my friend."

He had to stop himself from sobbing with gratitude. The only trouble was that the Mounties were becoming more unpredictable than the Mafia.


LATER ON, he talked to Ted Phano.

Cal had regained some of his confidence by then. Enough to get mad.

"I won't accept blatant stupidity in the face of success in a venture like this," he said. "'Cause there's only one time you go in."

"We'll overcome this shit, and we'll be very, very successful here," said Phano. "Nothing's more annoying than these little glitches, just a miscommunication on some level. The powers that be will resolve this over doughnuts and fuckin' coffee. Let's not forget our function in fuckin' life here. That is to kick the livin' shit outta these cocksuckers and do it in an agreeable fashion, where everybody's paid, everybody's content, and we've done the right thing for the fuckin' queen. I have to show my superiors that we're on-line with the plan. But believe me, we're policemen; we're not going to look the other way. But you know we have to satisfy a lot of masters."

"They're movin' product on Friday," Cal told him. "They're movin' in a million on Friday, a test run."

"That's great stuff. I don't want you to think for a minute I'm an old lady when it comes to these plans. Right now I'm up to my arse in fuckin' alligators tryin' to get this Raic thing goin'. If it comes off the way we anticipate it, there'll be high-fives at all kinds of levels. People will be saying this particular source is doing things nobody thought he could do. We believe it can be done as you say. Hang in with the boys here. I don't know what to tell ya. I'm not a fuckin' cheerleader."

Next, Cal talked over his plans with Phano. Keith and Ron were listening in.

Phano said, "You paint a picture. You know a prominent business-man, Ronald Desbarats, for whom you have the greatest respect. He's agreed to meet with a lawyer called Yves Raic. Desbarats is a careful per-son, prudent person. He doesn't make any moves without thinking; he just wants to meet Mr. Raic. Raic will go to dinner and Desbarats will have a sidekick, his gay younger brother or whoever the fuck. Remember, we have tremendous faith in you, getting to the top echelons of that particular family. Ronald Desbarats has got his shit together. His attitude will be 'I know where I'm going. Things are very lucrative for me now. I'm meeting a possible business contact.' Raic will report to Little John; *he's* going to report to Rocco Solosito or Mr. R., or somebody like that. Some people think we'll never get that far, but people here think we have a tremendous opportunity to impact on this group. That's what I sold our bosses on. We have to come in carefully, prudently. I have the confidence it's gonna go real smooth, real good, and say, 'Hey, this is great.' And believe me, nobody's as pissed as Keith and Ron, the grunts here."

"That's why I want to talk to some senior people," said Cal. "I think I deserve it. I'm in an extremely delicate position. Little is saying, 'I'm beginning to have the feeling that you're not who you say you are. You can't close deals; you have to run back to somebody for permission.' They've offered me carte blanche money laundering; I have it on tape, I have it on written notes, that the Mafia and the Hell's and the West End gang will give me 100 percent of their laundering."

"Listen, my friend, you're doing a hell of a job."

"Just tell the brass they gotta wake the fuck up," Cal said. "'Cause they're playin' with my life. When you guys go home, I hide. It sucks. I want to talk to these motherfuckers."

"Jeez, if you heard what we were saying about our outfit," said Phano, "you would have been proud of us. The bottom line is beyond our controls. I don't give a fuck. I've worked every police force in this country, you've got fuck-ups wherever you go. FBI, same thing. The paramount thing is, your name keeps coming up continually. How can we make it better for you?"

"Well," said Cal, "I just want senior management to get on the stick, instead of worrying about what merlot they're going to drink with dinner."

"Who knows at what level this gets buggered? All I know is that when I came out of that meeting the other day, we went to dinner, me and Keith and Ron, and we all felt really good. Just hang in with the fuckin' program, and we'll be havin' high-fives and drinkin' 50 and have a laugh or two. Because you're doing a tremendous job at a level most police only dream about."

CAL PHONED RAIC and told him to tell Little John the meeting with Ronald Desbarats was on. He had rented a 1988 white Lincoln limo for the evening, with a driver.

What he didn't tell Raic was that he himself was going to be wearing a wire. Cornwall RTF had a tail set up for the car as soon as it crossed over from the "dark side" into Ontario.

Cal phoned Keith Tasque to tell him about the arrangements.

"My pickup is at 3:15 with limo. We're gonna swing by and pick up Raic. The driver says we'll be in Ottawa at 5:30, maybe 5:45."

"Okay." Tasque paused, then asked, "Does Raic know where he's goin'?"

"No idea. Ontario. That's all he knows."

THE NEXT TIME Tony Montreal called Cornwall RTF, the white limo was fifteen minutes away. Keith Tasque took a long time coming to the phone. Cal could hear an excitement in his voice, as well as a certain wary distance.

He had awful news.

"We just talked to Ronald," said Tasque, meaning the UC, Desbarats. "Ronald must return to Toronto immediately. He won't be at the meeting tonight. There won't be a meeting."

"Don't tell me this," said Cal. "You jerkin' me?"

He felt certain it was a joke. They wouldn't do this to him, would they?

"I just got the word," said Tasque. "Just now."

Cal thought he heard the sound of background laughter on the other end of the line. He was suddenly chilled to the bone. "Don't tell me this," he said.

What the hell would he do now?

"Tell them that the meeting is just postponed. Ronald will get back to you."

"Fuck, Keith."

"Make your call. Get back and tell me what happened."

"My driver's gonna be here in ten minutes. What do I do about this guy?"

"Phone and cancel him. Get a receipt. We'll take care of it all."

"Ahh," said Cal. "Fuck me."

He was lost for words, numbed. It was a disaster. Little John was on his way, expecting to do a million-dollar deal. He had been furious the last time Cal had stalled him. His reaction to a cancellation was bound to be violent, maybe terminal.

"I know, bub," said Tasque. "Make your calls and get back to me. I need to know what's happenin'."

"The whole fuckin' family's up on this fuckin' meeting," said Cal. "I gotta show them something today. I'm not comfortable about my position in closing the meeting down. I gotta put them in front of somebody."

"We can't put you in front of anybody. We have to delay."

"Got a reason, Keith?"

"Ronald had to leave town," repeated Tasque, blank. He wasn't giving anything away.

"Is that the real reason, Keith? Or is that the smoke-and-mirrors reason?"

"That's the reason."

It was a stonewall from the RCMP. They weren't about to tell him a hair more than they wanted him to know.

"Yeah. I got it," said Cal stoically. Then, as much to himself as to Tasque, he stated, "Holy shit."

"It's out of our hands and out of our control."

"Do we have a project?" asked Cal.

"It's just been postponed."

"It's got to be more of a decision than that. Because the internal Cal can't take it. I'm just breaking down. I'm not playin' with a business deal, I'm playin' with tigers and sharks, y'know?"

"We're aware of the position you're in right now," said Tasque. "We're aware of it. Make your phone call and get back to us."

"I'm at a loss. I need some instructions. I don't know what to tell them."

"Ronald has returned immediately to Toronto."

"We understand the predicament you're in," said Ron Harlow on the other phone.

"I don't want John here kickin' the door down," said Cal. "I don't want John here screamin' and foamin' blood. He's off the fuckin' wall."

"Say it's nothin' to do with you," Ron advised. That's what he'd do.

That was a big help. Really good.

"I can't disappear," Cal told him. "John will be fuckin' hunting me."

"It stinks big time," admitted Keith Tasque.

"I know I'm not a member," Cal said helplessly, "but it's completely unfair to keep me blind and ignorant."

Cal was always made aware that he was nothing compared to an RCMP officer. They would make a bust on a project he initiated, then never invite him to the obligatory post-bust party. That sort of thing.

"Just tell 'em that," Tasque advised, as if he'd given an immense amount of thought to the problem of what Cal could say. "Tell 'em he's gone back to Toronto."

"You know what I'm gonna do," said Cal, thinking out loud. "I'm gonna take Raic out to dinner. Because the car's gonna be here any minute. Take him out to fuckin' dinner. I'm sick about this. If I don't do something to massage this guy, I'm gonna fuck myself big time."

"Hang on," he was told.

They talked to somebody out of earshot. Ron Harlow returned to the phone. "I just looked into that issue about the dinner?" he said, with an up-talk inflection that made it seem as if they were discussing what colour napkins to buy. "It can't be done. Too short notice. There'll be nobody there to cover."

"I got to do a face to face," said Cal. "I can't hide. They're gonna find me if I walk out to the movies with my lady or buy groceries. My whole ability to go on living in Montreal is at risk. I just got to do it. It's not committing a crime."

Ron went away for more orders.

"Stay on the line," said Tasque. "Keep talking to us. Ted Phano popped in. He's giving us wisdom."

Then Harlow returned.

"So how do you like us now?" he asked.

The Mounties' ruthlessness with agents and informants was out on the table, plain for Cal to see.

"I like you guys," replied Cal. "If I was a gay man . . . you know." He didn't even have the spirit to crack a joke.

Then Keith Tasque said something Cal would always remember: "We are agents of the government."

Cal could only wonder what level of the federal government had taken the decision to abort the operation against the Rizzutos. He started laughing hysterically. No other reaction was possible in the circumstances.

"Nice to hear you laughin' again."

"I'm not," said Cal.

He was laughing to keep from crying.

"I'm not either," replied the Mountie.

"Okay, let me go."

"You can't go. Stay on the line. We're not finished."

"Tasque, you're a little prick, you know that?"

"Actually, I'm quite a nice person," said Keith. "Look, we can't provide protection for you. And we don't want you to have dinner with him tonight."

Cal didn't know what to say.

What the fuck was going on now?

"You understand what I'm sayin'?" demanded Tasque.

"Okey-dokey," said Cal. Like a monkey on a stick.

What the fuck was going on?

"Tell me you won't have dinner with Raic tonight."

"I gotta make arrangements for my own safety. What happens if those guys come over here or they peg me on the street?"

"I can't answer that," confessed Tasque. "But we absolutely don't want you to have dinner. As per our LOA, I do not want you to do that. You understand what I'm sayin'? And I'm sorry, that's my direction for you tonight."

Cal hung up and called Raic. When he next talked to the RCMP, the whole group had him on the speaker-phone.

"Raic said he's fucked," said Cal. "John will probably tear him apart. I told him to put off the meeting indefinitely, as you instructed. He said, 'We're both fucked.' He's gonna try to figure out how to talk to Little John. I understand there's forces that are beyond your control and are vibrating at a different level. I realize that I'm not 'need to know,' not a member. But now people are playing with other people's lives."

He hoped they were taping him. He wanted the invisible brass hats in Ottawa to hear what was on his mind.

"This is going to create a problem for senior management," he said.

They were worried about the media? He would give them something to worry about.

"It's going to rear up and bite 'em in the ass," he said. "This is going to come up when somebody is going to get their brainbox splattered all over the pavement, and senior management is worried about what wine to serve for dinner."

Cal was aware that he'd become an inarticulate wreck. It was like talking to zombies, though. Either they didn't give a shit about him, or they just didn't realize the danger they'd created for him.

When he hung up the phone, Cal could only speculate about what the RCMP higher-ups were trying to do. Possibly by provoking Little John in this fashion, they were hoping he would eliminate Raic himself, saving them the embarrassment of an arrest and a trial. He went against instructions and took Yves Raic out to dinner anyway. What the fuck?

He'd never seen the former lawyer so forlorn, though. It was as if all hope had finally been snatched away from the man. Cal spun a plausible yarn about his contact having business problems that required urgent attention, but it didn't seem to make any difference to Raic. He just knew Little John would blame him, and he didn't have the strength to take it any more. He was so tired. It made Cal think of Réal Dupont.

Curiously, though, he never heard another word from Little John or any of the Rizzutos ever again. It was as if some invisible but potent force had reached into the entire project and terminated it, along with anything connected to it.

Then the probe from Proceeds in Montreal regarding Pierre Maille was suddenly cancelled. As far as Cal understood these things, he was being sent a message by the cops to stop pursuing the investigation of a certain group because it bothered someone. Who exactly it bothered, he'd never know. He wasn't a member.

The boys at Cornwall RTF also became, once again, hard to reach for C. Calvin Broeker.

"Is Ted Phano there?"

"He is not here this morning."

"Craig Owens?

"Not here"

"Keith?"

"Not here."

"Ron?"

"Not here."

There was nothing but silence. Except for Keith Tasque's voice in Cal's mind, saying, "We are agents of the government . . . agents of the government . . . of the government . . . the government . . ."

10

A Plough-horse
Hobbled

*The dream of a crook is a man with a dream.*

— STEPHEN VIZINCZEY, *AN INNOCENT MILLIONAIRE*

### September 1997

Bob Osler was in when Cal called — in fact, it was he who first had telephoned Cal. A staff sergeant who headed up the RCMP's Proceeds unit in Toronto (although their offices were in Newmarket), Osler had followed the Orienter project closely and wanted to lure Cal down to Toronto with a view to doing something equally prestigious.

The latest gimmick in crime-fighting was asset seizure. It's not clear why it had taken so long to work out that criminals are attached to their stuff and their money — what are they after, prestige? — but it had, and the Proceeds unit, freshly hatched, was badly in need of a big score to justify its existence. Cal figured he'd introduce Bob and the boys to Richard Aran, who had $100 million cash to launder for the mob.

You'd think, with the enormous amount of free time they have on their hands, the buddies would sign up for all kinds of courses in job-related skills. But they don't. They're lazy. And mostly stupid (the notion of a criminal genius is oxymoronic). A good many are illiterate, or at least have learning disabilities — severe ones. That's why someone like Richard Aran was so indispensable. Richard was a pilot, and he knew about boats too. He didn't look like a bad guy either. In his early forties, a finger under six feet, he weighed only about 140 pounds and had thinning, mousy hair. He looked like an unsuccessful bank teller. Yet there was more to him than met the eye. The word was that he'd been arrested once and jailed but had escaped along a live electric cable, dropping onto barbed wire and then bouncing to freedom. You had to know electricity to do that, and you had to have balls. Richard also had the reputation of being someone you could hand $5 million worth of cocaine and who'd hand you back $5 million in cash a month later. Practical skills and trustworthiness were rare commodities indeed in the underworld, and therefore Richard enjoyed a unique position among the gangs operating out of Montreal. He worked for all of them without anyone ever questioning his loyalty, yet his closest affiliation was with the West End Gang, or Irish Mob, headed up by Richard Casey. Aran was of Irish descent himself.

Thanks largely to the boisterous business practices of the Hell's Angels, Montreal had attracted a lot of heat during the nineties, so Richard Casey had decided to relocate his gang to Vancouver. Since his main business, as was true of all gangs, was now smuggling, he needed a port and he needed Indian reservations. So Vancouver wasn't a difficult choice — it was the only choice. This meant that Richard Aran, who still lived in Montreal, was doing a lot more flying than he usually did. Private flying isn't cheap, and crime doesn't pay like other businesses — there's no monthly check — so Richard the pilot was often saddled with bills he was expected to take care of himself until payoff time.

Cal met him through another man familiar with debt, the ubiquitous Yves Raic.

"I know you two guys are going to hit it off," said the former head of the Judicial Affairs Committee, as if it was a blind date.

Of course, Raic wasn't precisely disinterested in the result of this meeting either, and that meant his incessant phone calls to Cal soon included queries about the status of business with Richard. Richard got calls from him too, but there was nothing to tell Raic. The fact was that he and Cal had not found anything they could yet agree on doing together. Cal, however, suspected that Richard was feeling him out, stringing him along so he could get comfortable enough with him to broach a deal. Buddies like to reach a comfort level before they'll stick their necks out, and they find much comfort in borrowing money.

"Here," said Richard Aran, shoving a plastic bag at Cal in the antiques store on Greene Avenue. "Take it."

"What the fuck is it?" Cal asked him.

"Look, it's all I got."

Cal pulled a Montreal Canadiens hockey sweater out of the bag. It was covered in felt-tip scribbles.

"They all signed it," said George. "Rocket Richard . . . everyone." He looked Cal in the eyes, manly, supplicant yet threatening too. "I figure it's got to be worth four hundred."

"Bound to be," Cal agreed. "But I don't sell hockey memorabilia."

"It's not to sell — it's collateral. For a loan."

After that human sponge, Yves Raic, the idea of collateral for a loan was novel, so Cal plucked out his show-roll and peeled off four hundreds. George was genuinely grateful and promised earnestly to redeem the sweater very soon. Cal still has it.

But in his experience, a loan like this presaged a deal of some sort. Because they're often broke, buddies need to borrow, but they never repay loans. The loan is always tangled up with the deal that's about to go down, and the idea is that you're soon to make a pile through this guy, so what do you care about a few hundred bucks? A cop, of course, would have had to fill out a requisition and wait until it had cleared before agreeing to hand over any cash. Cal could try to claim it as a project expense — although only later, when there *was* a project — but he knew the chances of recouping it were slim to nil.

His hunch was right, though. A few days later, George said his people had $100 million they wanted to clean. Did Cal have any ideas for them?

Did he? Hell!

He called Bob Osler in Toronto and set up a meeting.

It was exactly what Bob was looking for, and an LOA was drawn up naming Richard Casey as the target.

CAL HAD EXHAUSTED MONTREAL — although he still had dormant LOAs going there — and his list of enemies was hitting critical mass. He still worried about that troll, Little John, popping out of a doorway and coming at him with a hammer. It was time for a change. So he and Simone moved to Toronto, taking an apartment in North York. It would make her career much harder to pursue. The French and the English in Canada aren't called two solitudes for nothing. The possibility of a French singer finding work in Toronto is about the same as a transvestite being asked to address the Empire Club. But she loved her man more than she loved her job. Without him, what reason would there be to sing anyway?

Before long, Cal had devised an extremely cunning idea for relieving both Richards of the $100 million. When Bob Osler heard it, he liked it too. In fact, he liked it a lot. But he had to get approval from upstairs before they could proceed with the scheme. It isn't prudent to say precisely what the plan was, since it's still in operation, reeling in millions of another gang's dollars at this very moment, but suffice it to say that it enabled those with too much unbankable cash to make investments that, theoretically, they could later recoup, with profits, through a legitimate bank account. If deployed in a more imaginative fashion across North America, such a scheme would have organized crime unwittingly funding everything from public housing to new schools — something that undoubtedly would count in their favour when those responsible stood before a judge.

With a new city to sniff out, Cal, while he waited yet again for the go-ahead from on high, made the most of it. In no time at all, he'd located the main biker hangouts and selected a bar on Front Street for his cold approach.

While we think of the biker bar as somewhere between a strip club and a pool hall, wreathed in smoke, awash in beer, the Front Street bar was actually a quite pleasant family restaurant that gradually became a biker spot as the night wore on. It's probably safe to say that this experiment in clientele contributed to the bar's eventual demise: although a lot of people enjoy slumming it, they don't want to feel unsafe. When you look up from your steak au poivre and your conversation with Granny to find the bar now thronged by scarred, tattooed, leather-jacketed Cro-Magnons waggling their tongues at your wife, you know it's time to get the bill.

As he usually did, Cal targeted the barman, Tommy, a personable young Jamaican. He would go in three or four nights running, dropping three or four hundred a pop, plus a hefty tip. Then he'd stay away for a while — absence sometimes being the highest form of presence. When Cal returned, Tommy — whose income probably doubled when Cal was in — would be overjoyed. Cal dropped all the usual hints too — Bulgaria, | 313 import-export, big show-roll, bigger bank balance — and soon he was being introduced to the late-night customers: Benny the Pig, Meathook, Shark, Billy Goat, Big John Bat — it was *Animal Farm* in there after nine o'clock.

The owner wanted to meet him as well, but Cal played hard to get. He came there for pleasure, not business. The more he insisted on this, the more interested everyone became in doing business with him. When Richard Aran flew down from Montreal to discuss progress on the $100-million laundering job, it was good for Cal to be able to take him to the bar, where he now appeared to have tight friends — some of whom Richard, naturally enough, knew himself. Because no one wants to introduce an undercover agent into their criminal circle, there's a great emphasis on the longevity of acquaintanceships. People Cal had known for only a few months introduced him as if they known him for years — and some even came to believe they *had* known him for years. When you've been drinking a bottle of Jack Daniels and snorting a gram or two of blow every day for a decade straight, a month and a year aren't so different anyway.

THE MAIN ONTARIO BIKER GANG Cal worked with has since merged with the Hell's Angels — although you can take it for granted that they originally applied for an Angels charter but were rejected (conditions for charter membership are fairly rigorous; many are called, though still not a few chosen). Shark and John the Bat were their main enforcers. If you were among the bike gang's network of pushers and had failed to pay for your weekly ounce or pound, Shark or John — and sometimes, if the debt merited it, both of them — would show up unannounced and remind you of it. They were very polite. The first time. If they had to come back and remind you again, however, they probably wouldn't speak at all. But just the sight of them was enough to make most people find the money, even if it meant selling their children for medical experiments.

Shark looked as if he'd been beamed down from 100,000 B.C., where he'd lived in a damp cave on a diet of raw hedgehog and toadstools. His teeth alone were terrifying, and he rattled as he walked, as if laden with metal implements to use on your debt. John the Bat was far more contemporary in appearance, a good 98,000 years ahead of Shark. He had actually been one of the Visigoths in the film *Gladiator* and was flown over to England with other bikers from North America (since Europe no longer breeds a convincing barbarian). He wasn't named after the flying rodent, however, but rather after — originally, at least — the baseball bat he kept clamped to his bike winter and summer. Although the only pitcher he'd ever faced held a gallon of beer. The nickname had evolved into Batty, the way these things do, and there was now speculation that its origins lay in insanity rather than mere violence.

The story was that Batty had found his girl with another man, and before dealing with her, he'd tied the man's testicles to a radiator with a length of piano wire. Then he threw the man clean through a second-storey window. The girl merely had her nose cut off. It was joked that Batty still had the testicles — which was why some people called him Four Ball. No one ever called him John — not to his face, at least. He'd mutilate you — that was how bitterly he resented being named after a penis, a can, a mark. He stood around six-foot-six and weighed a good 400 pounds; a great deal of this flesh was covered in jailhouse tattoos (achieved by making ink from burnt matches, cigarette ash, and saliva, then using a red-hot pin to work the ink into the skin — the result invariably becomes a blurred mess after a few years, so don't try it at home). On the Macedonian-sausage fingers of his left hand was L-O-V-E, and on the right H-A-. Cal wondered whether he'd meant to add T-E but had run out of ink or been interrupted. Or had the intention been to write H-A-H-A, but the joke wore off? Now, of course, it would be presumed to stand for "Hell's Angels" and viewed as evidence of supernatural prescience. But as with anyone whose legend is writ large, Batty kept the details of his life vague. He was touchy about these things, so you didn't ask. You didn't ask about his beard either. It was falling out in great clumps, and he was always smearing strands over the gaps and trying to glue them down with saliva. Maybe he was on chemo? Or maybe the toxins in his body were having the same effect? It was hard to imagine tumours daring to grow in there.

Cal became tight with Shark and Batty, mainly because he bought them thousands of drinks, but partly because his own legend was writ far larger than theirs. He'd mastered the art of the smokescreen, which, not unlike the silver screen, is about myth, not reality. And here big *is* better. The same story, when dipped in the wax of the myth-making subconscious of successive listeners, becomes at once grander and more basic. By making his yarns suitably short on detail and long on innuendo, Cal knew that human nature would elevate them to mythological epics before a week was out. This engendered in the two bikers a thirst for Cal's companionship that could not be slaked, as well as a ravenous hunger for his thoughts on business, his take on life.

Shark, who'd never left Ontario in forty years, yearned for information about other countries — especially Bulgaria, which Cal painted as bandit heaven. Shark couldn't hear enough about hunting wild pigs and ambushing trucks in the mountains. He wanted to go there so bad. You could tell he imagined himself arriving at the airport in Sofia, where he'd be greeted by customs officials and immigration inspectors who looked just like him: "Velcome 'ome, brother!" they'd say, waving him through the formalities and indignity that lesser mortals could not avoid.

Shark was very proud of his enforcing skills, and the members of the bike gang were clearly grateful for his services. In fact, to show their appreciation, they had purchased for him a monstrous $25,000 diamond ring, which Shark always wore. Owing to the state of the rest of him, however, strangers must have assumed he'd found the ring in a Christmas cracker. It looked incongruous, like a bison with a wristwatch or a crocodile with shoes.

Much pomp and ceremony had, it seems, accompanied the presentation of the ring, and Shark would often fondly recall this, his finest hour. It had taken place in a strip club on Gerrard Street and was by invite only. Everyone had worn tuxedoes — not your boring black tuxedoes, but ones in powder blue and chocolate brown, with velvet trim. The most stellar dancer in all the bike gang's vast stable had emerged from a huge cake and given Shark his own personal lap dance, followed by a blow job.

Everyone was drunk and stoned; the cocaine flowed like champagne and the champagne flowed like water. They all went for breakfast at Fran's on College Street at dawn. It was magical.

"I never paid for a single fucking drink," Shark would say in awe.

This was just as well, Cal mused, because Shark never seemed to have two cents to rub together. One night, after an exceptionally punishing attack on Cal's show-roll, Shark suggested that Cal might like to do a little business with the bikers.

"I keep my business separate from my pleasure," replied Cal, ever coy.

He did agree, however, to go back to Shark's place for further discussions. It was 3 a.m. Shark lived way out in the east end of Toronto, in an area that time had forgotten. It looked like the set from *Our Mutual Friend:* blacking factories, smokestacks, choking tenements, ancient hand-painted signs for Pear's Soap. You wondered if this part of town had a member to represent it in Parliament. Even the hookers were old and shrivelled.

Shark lived off a brick-surfaced alley in what appeared from the outside to be a garage. It appeared that way from the inside too. In fact, it was a garage. Dark, cold, lit by a single hanging bare bulb, it housed a good deal of garbage, many tools, and a spectacular, gleaming, customized 1996 black-and-platinum Harley Dyna Wide Glide 80ciEvo.

"CV carb with Dynojet thunderslide and Screamin' Eagle hi-flow air cleaner. . . . Here," Shark said, handing Cal a beer he'd taken from a ledge outside the window. "They chill on the sill." He laughed. Well, he made a guttural sound in the back of his throat, kicking an up-turned oil drum across the floor to Cal and adding, "Have a seat."

They sat on oil drums.

Some people, thought Cal, apologize for living in filth and squalor when they actually live in surgically sanitized, spotless environments; others live in filth and squalor and feel like kings. He kept thinking Shark would soon show him into a house via the rear door, but as he found when he went for a piss, the rear door opened onto another alley. It was a free-standing garage.

"So this is where you live?" Cal ventured.

"Yeah," said Shark, looking around himself expansively. "Got all me stuff here."

"Where'd you sleep?"

"In me bed," Shark replied, pointing to a small rectangle of what appeared to be oily rags just behind them. "I don't need much."

"I can see."

It was embarrassing. Shark offered Cal cornflakes. Cal politely declined. Shark poured himself some in a dirty mug, then tipped his beer over them, commenting that they tasted far better with beer than with milk. As there were no spoons — there were a good many wrenches — Shark slurped his cereal from the mug, and then began talking business. He mentioned millions of dollars, tons of dope, and the desire to get into real estate in a big way. | 317

"We need to clean up some cash," he said.

Cal wondered if Shark ever felt like cleaning up himself or the garage. A lot of folks less attuned to the criminal milieu might have found it hard to believe that a man who lived in a garage and slept on a pile of rags even knew what money laundering was, but Cal had seen worse. It's not called the underworld for nothing. Besides, it was kind of peaceful in Shark's garage; there was even an odd charm about the place when you viewed it through its occupant's eyes. No doubt Shark had the mandatory nightmare of a childhood — the dozen siblings, the succession of brutal stepfathers, Children's Aid, the foster homes, the diddling vicars, young offenders, then older offenders — and all he'd ever wanted was a room of his own, a (sliding) door with which to shut out the cruel world. What was it, though, that made the brutalized want to be brutal? You'd think they'd know better than anyone the horrors of brutality, and want to spare others from them. But they don't. They want to inflict others with their own pain. They want to perpetuate the cycle, not end it. Cal had experienced his own share of brutality as a child, yet harsh as it was, that brutality still had love behind it. It instilled a belief in the sanctity of toil, and in a man's infinite ability to rise out of the ashes, no matter how often he goes down in flames. To be men, not destroyers.

You couldn't have this kind of discussion with Shark, though. He'd think you were fucking with him. There was no still, small voice in there telling him what was right and what was wrong — and if you tried to insert one, you'd be fucking with him. "Don't fuck with me" — it was the most common thing some of these buddies said, and it meant "Don't make me look at myself." Shark had no introspection. He just reacted instinctively. Like an animal.

Cal played coy during this first meeting, saying he didn't do this and he wasn't into that. But he knew Shark was hooked.

Once the others saw Shark hanging with Cal, they too got interested. No one wanted to be left out — of what, they weren't sure, but they wanted in on it anyway. It was always suspected that people were doing private deals, and since Cal was good at feeding the rumour mill about himself, the late-night crew at the bar soon saw him as Big Money, Russians, Big Time. They saw Réal Dupont's Caribbean fantasy, because they all wanted out in their own way, wanted to be far from the rips and the beatings and the detention cells, in some feudal fiefdom of their own. Where no one would fuck with them. Failing this, however, they'd stay in the gang. There was safety in numbers, and these boys were hopeless on their own. They never looked for trouble by themselves, Cal found, and they were unusually easy to intimidate.

"I'm not gonna introduce you to my people dressed like that!" Cal once told Batty, whom he'd promised to fix up with some Russian mob contacts.

"Like what?" Batty asked, theatrically opening up his denim vest and leather jacket to peer down at his stained, filthy jeans and beat-up cowboy boots, as if he was the acme of sartorial splendour. "What's wrong with what I'm wearing?"

"For a start," Cal told him, "you look like shit. You smell like shit too. *And* you're a fucking heat score, man! Jeeeezus! You look like a fucking biker! I don't wanna be seen dead with you on the street. A cop looks and thinks, Oh, fuck. There's a biker . . . and who's that with him? You gotta show some respect, man. You bring heat around my people, you won't even have time to kiss your ass goodbye. You understand what I'm saying? And get a fucking shave — you look like a fat spider!"

Batty had beaten people into blood pudding for less. Much less. But he just stood there and took it. Next day, he appeared in a suit and tie, clean-shaven, face *and* head.

"How d'I look?" he asked.

He looked like an over-inflated Mussolini, but he did get an A for effort. He felt good about himself too, you could tell. He wasn't even fazed when the cream of Russian thuggery failed to show. Trouble was, the next time Cal saw him, Batty had reverted to fat spiderhood. Obviously, feeling good about himself didn't make him feel good. He needed to feel bad about himself. "Don't fuck with me" means low self-esteem too. But when all you've done in life is steal, peddle dope, and beat people into blood pudding, you have no reason to experience anything but low self-esteem. Bad is good. | 319

Good is bad sometimes, also. When bad things start happening to good people, they get pissed off. They feel the times are out of joint. Around now, this is what Cal was starting to feel.

You know that old cinematic device where dates start peeling off a calendar, faster and faster, to get blown in the wind, whirled into a tangle? Well, imagine it here.


### October 1999

It was hard to believe so much time had passed. But that's all it can do — pass. You can't hold on to it. You need to feel it falling through you like rain, like sunshine, like snowflakes to enjoy it. Cal had been working his butt off as usual, but things were different in Toronto. One of the Montreal LOAs was still active, yet it didn't seem to be panning out. Sometimes Cal drove the 401 east to Quebec and back three or four times a week. But either the cops didn't like his plans or they were too slow in moving to seize the day. In Toronto, Bob Osler had got the go-ahead for Cal's scheme and the Richard Casey LOA was activated, but Cal couldn't work the way he was used to working: alone. Protocol was more formal. Shark and Batty were constantly offering opportunities to get in on a dope deal, a smuggling racket, a cleaning job, but Cal could no longer just jump in and go with the flow. He'd had intimations of this before, in Montreal, especially with the Raic project, but it was nothing like as bad. He had to attend meetings, file reports, requisitions, justifications. He sympathized with the cops, but he couldn't work like that. In reality, neither could they. Policework was an immensely complicated, round-about, by-the-book process. If he'd said, "There's a ton of heroin being parachuted onto the Skydome roof at midnight," they'd have asked for more proof, said it was too fast, and ultimately not been able to respond. The buddies knew this too, knew that swift, unannounced operations would usually get by the bureaucracy.

They seemed geared to catch only the medium-level guys, the guys who weren't well connected and simply worked a particular angle and all sides of it. These guys'd import cocaine via the Dominican Republic, say, and be involved from the purchase in Colombia or Peru right through to the sale to fairly small dealers in Ontario. They knew shit about how to stay out of jail while making money. The bikers and the Italians in Ontario didn't get involved until the product had landed. When you're buying $50 million worth of blow, the Colombians will bring it to you. Wherever you are. It's up to you to make sure they don't take your money and keep the blow, of course, but that's what enforcers are for. A few apes with machine guns and low self-esteem make it clear to anyone that you can't be fucked with. That's what a gang is all about. It's a private army that works cheap.

The whole world's seen too many movies, and the bikers are no exception. They took few risks with product. They'd let it sit in a warehouse or garage for months if necessary, if they didn't feel good about it, if they didn't feel *comfortable*. The Colombians know it's not going to be easy to find another customer for 40,000 metric tonnes of cocaine, so they're also willing to wait. You don't see bargain sales on dope either; there's no two-for-one offer down on the mean streets, no Cartel Surplus stores, no Honest Head's Discount Emporium. The principles of supply and demand are well understood by the main players. They don't want their blow going out on the streets pure either — people might get used to it. Because a good-quality substance with which to cut the blow costs more than the blow itself in Colombia — and because there's no sense in bringing in 20,000 metric tonnes of perfectly legal baby laxative mixed with the coke — they leave the cutting to the customer. It ensures profits all the way down to the last coconut, who's probably selling pure laxative because he's pumped all the blow into his own arm but doesn't remember doing it. In fact, the market in illegal substances is a model of free-market virtues: self-regulating, better controlled than oil, and offering a fair profit to all concerned. It's very straightforward too.

Let's say the buy happens in a big hotel. The Colombians are in one room with the blow, the customer is in another with the money. All the middleman does is visit the Colombians, pay them $50 million, take the blow to his customer on the floor below, and with any luck, walk out with $100 million. It's taken an hour at the most — and the bulk of that time is spent watching money be counted and weighing blow, then counting money and watching blow be weighed. If you called the police and told them that such a deal was going down at eight o'clock tonight, they probably wouldn't be able to respond. It would be . . .

"Too fast, Cal. You gotta slow it down."

When you take into account all the money — the billions and billions — that's been spent on to so-called war against drugs over the past twenty years, you realize it would be far cheaper for the government to go down to Peru and Colombia, buy each year's entire cocaine production from the cartels, then burn it. And as the Taliban in Afghanistan recently proved, wiping out the narcotics industry is relatively simple, *if* that's what you really want to do.

How do you slow down time? Because time is on the buddies' side, and they can get away with anything as long as they do it quickly enough. If you can rob a bank at gunpoint in forty seconds or less — and people at gunpoint move quite fast when asked — no one will ever catch you, unless you're unlucky.

Cal became more and more conscious of the different clocks everyone was on as the final year of the millennium wound down. All those great American certainties had been torn from him now. He believed only what was in his own heart and soul. The rest was someone else's smoke. A season in hell does that to you: you lose faith, and everything else, after seeing what festers beneath the foundations. But you do gain something too: your self.

But now Cal wanted to work. He *needed* to work — he was nearly out of money. Yet everything that came up was too fast for the process at Proceeds. It had taken ages to set up the scheme that would relieve Richard Aran and Richard Casey of their money, and Cal had been forced to make Aran think it was his fault there were so many delays. It was a very delicate process.

"I think we're ready for you, Richard," he told him.

"Fucking finally."

"You just don't get back to me quick enough, Richard."

"Now I gotta get my people together on this."

"See, Richard! You're doing it again. When are you gonna get off the fucking pot?"

Richard got off surprisingly fast, though, and soon announced that his people were flying in for a meeting in four days. Now Cal had to request permission to attend that meeting. He had also acquired a new handler for some reason, one of Bob Osler's subordinates, Sgt. Dale Trotter.

Yes, life must have been hell for the younger Trotter, but now he was making it hell for everyone else. The police force is not the best place for a control freak, yet nonetheless it's one of their prime destinations. The possibility of exerting total control, of controlling everyone's lives, is probably irresistible for them. They'd be better off trying to empty the ocean with sieves, though, because the people they're serving and protecting won't co-operate — and neither will the criminals, no matter what you do to them. All Dale Trotter knew was that things should be done the way they should be done, and that way was, coincidentally, also his way. Like someone directing traffic on the Los Angeles freeway, he knew better than to be open to suggestions. If everything he said sounded like an order, it's because it usually was.

"I'm listening to the wire tape," he told Cal early in their relationship, "and you say, 'Listen, man, I gotta know how pure that white is.'"

"Yeah?" Cal said. "That's what you told me to say."

"No," barked Trotter, "I told you to say, 'Listen, motherfucker, I need to know that the cocaine is pure.'"

"What's the diff?"

"I gave you an *order,* and you disobeyed it — *that's* the diff!"

"I thought th—"

Trotter cut him off. "I didn't ask you to think, asshole! I *told* you what to do and you didn't do it."

"He's supposed to be a friend," Cal protested. "I wouldn't call him motherfucker. . . . And no one uses the term 'cocaine.'"

"Oh, *no one uses the term 'cocaine,'* do they?" Trotter put on a squeaky little voice, then changed back into his own bullying tone. "Well, *I* use the term 'cocaine,' the judge uses the term 'cocaine,' the arrest warrant will use the term 'cocaine,' the evidence tag will use the term 'cocaine.' It fucking *is* cocaine — I wouldn't say that was *no one,* would you?"

"Buddy doesn't use it."

"I see. And we're gonna let buddy fucking dictate us his terms, are we?"

"Why don't you just let me do my job?" Cal said.

*"Because I tell you what your job is; you don't tell me!"*

Cal bit his tongue. He'd complain about this asshole to Bob Osler when the time was right. But this waiting around to get on with the work that just pullulated out there, writhed off the newspaper every morning, spewed from the TV every evening, piled up in charts, reports, and in the very psyche of the city-dweller — it was driving him nuts. When you're ready and able to work yet they won't let you work, something festers. He felt like a plough-horse hobbled by the side of the field, watching the ravens pick worms from the flat, dusty, untended soil. Part of him understood, yet another part of him didn't. It made no sense. Here he was handing them crime after crime on a plate, and all they said was, "Hold on! Whoa, Nelly!" He could feel that old and unhealthy rage building up in him again. The same way he'd felt back in Chateaugay a lifetime ago. He wasn't built for inaction, and he wasn't built to be messed around like a schmuck — because *that* was happening too. Little things. Like he'd receive his expense money months late and it would be all cash, small bills, and a design that had gone out of circulation thirty years earlier. Proceeds of some primeval dope sting in the sixties, he was told. It was still legal tender, but it made the bank teller uneasy and it drew attention to him. It was a nuisance, something Cal didn't need. Why would they do this?

Cal was applying for Canadian citizenship now too, was going to make his life in the land he'd served so well and come to love. Because of the nature of his "job," however, the handlers would have to speak directly with immigration regarding employment issues. They had his whole dossier and were going to take care of it for him. But as Cal learned later, they did nothing with it and he was forced to restart the entire process. Since the Canadian immigration ministry makes Kafka's castle look like a studio apartment, this was cruel and unusual punishment indeed. Why would they do that? They questioned him constantly about his relationship with Simone too. They hadn't banked on her. He was supposed to be a one-man show, the guy in black who arrives on his horse alone, cleans up the town, has a fling with the purtiest widow, then leaves alone.

Except he hadn't left and he wasn't alone. And since Cal wasn't a Canadian citizen, they couldn't request funds to lay on a little security. Or so they said. They worried about Simone. Or so they said, but they also kept prodding Cal to dive deeper into the abyss and tell them what was down there.

WHEN THE DAY CAME for the meeting with Richard's people, Cal was told he'd have to wear a wire. He was also reminded that because everything would be taped, he'd have to go by the book: and that meant no accepting gifts paid for by the proceeds of crime. Including meals. The meeting was lunch.

In keeping with buddy's gourmet sensibilities, it was set for that shrine to haute cuisine, the Red Lobster on Keele Street. Five seafood lovers had flown in from Vancouver, including Richard Casey. Big, dangerous guys. The only way to deal with them was the way Cal had been instructed to deal: tough. Fucking tough.

"I'll have a glass of water," Cal told the waitress. "I'm not eating." He handed back his menu.

"Come on, man," Richard Aran said, coaxing him. "It's lunch."

"I'm here to do business," Cal replied bluntly, "not fucking eat. So let's talk business. I'm not hungry."

It had the same effect on the gangsters as it would have had on any group of businessmen who'd flown almost 5,000 kilometres to meet someone who could help make them richer: they tried to ignore it. But few things are more disconcerting than dining with someone who doesn't eat. If the buddies — who looked more like men energetically turning soil in a tiny garden than refined diners — felt uneasy, you can be sure it was a major faux pas. And Cal felt like an asshole doing it, even if they also serve and protect who only sit and watch. He had to use every ounce of his talents at bonhomie to steer the situation away from disaster.

"Who the fuck are you, anyway?" asked Richard Casey. "We hear different stories . . . and some of 'em ain't very nice."

Cal was certain Casey knew nothing concrete — he wouldn't have been there if he did — but nonetheless he'd heard things through the grapevine. But what things?

"Who fucking said I was nice?" Cal told him. "My people don't like bullshit because it walks. They like business. It talks to them. But if anyone tries to butt in on the conversation, they'll be wearing their butt as a hat — know what I'm saying?"

Richard Casey, a big, sandy-haired Viking of a man with pale greenish eyes, simply stared at him.

Cal decided on a gamble.

"A little rat like Réal Dupont tries to rip me," he said, "he's lucky to go to fucking jail, man. 'Cause when he gets out, I'm gonna be waiting." He paused to see if he'd guessed correctly — he had — before adding, "You wanna believe that piece of human shit, then I don't wanna do any business with you."

He got up to leave.

"Dupont is a fucking head case," Casey said. "But you can't blame us for listening to rumours, can you? Sit down, Cal. People I trust more say you're okay. I think we can do business."

"I don't need any more bullshit," Cal announced. "Threats, intimidation — it's fucking Mickey Mouse shit. My people are serious motherfuckers too, but we don't brag about it. You wanna do business, *that's* what we'll do. But you wanna jerk off, you do it alone, man."

"Sit," Casey said. "It's not our style either."

Cal ordered a coffee. It would be one of the only benefits he ever received from the proceeds of crime. He liked to imagine a defence lawyer asking him if he'd ever accepted bribes: "Is it not true, Mr. Broeker, that you accepted a cup of coffee, which you knew to have been paid for by the proceeds of crime, thereby enriching yourself from them? And you expect this court to believe you're an honourable man? Your honour, I request that this witness's testimony be struck from the records of this trial. . . ." Stranger things had happened. What are criminal lawyers for, after all?

THE MEETING WITH Richard Casey's people went off fairly well in the end. But Dale Trotter was far from happy with it.

"You didn't get what I *told* you to get," he yelled at Cal. "Maybe I should just get Carlos in on this to do it properly."

Carlos was Trotter's pet UC operative. He was constantly held up to Cal as a paragon of UC work, an undercover god. Carlos *delivered*. Carlos did what he was *told* to do. Carlos never fucked up. Carlos, it was implied, had a far bigger cock than Cal and balls the size of the Skydome. So how come, Cal wondered, Carlos didn't start this job himself? Indeed, how come he didn't have any memorable takedowns to his credit at all? How come no one but Trotter even mentioned him? Maybe he was just Trotter's imaginary friend?

Cal was as sick of Carlos, however, as he'd ever been of someone who might not exist. And he was sick of Dale Trotter's bullying rudeness. He was going to bring the problem to Bob Osler's attention now, not later. Cal knew how to take abuse from senior officers, like anyone who's been in the services, but this was starting to harm the project — and that was different, in his eyes. A severe character flaw was only a problem, an issue, when it got in the way of what everyone was really there to do. He had no problem serving a higher authority, but that authority was the common good, not Dale Trotter. Although it too could dish out abuse when it wished.

"Bob," he said, "I need to discuss something with you."

"I can't meet with you now," Osler told him, "I've got too many things on my plate."

"It's important, Bob. It relates to the project."

"Then bring it up with Dale."

"That's gonna be difficult."

"Why?" Osler seemed incredulous. "He's your new boss."

"What?"

"Didn't I tell you I'm retiring from the force next week?"

"Retiring?"

"Yep. I reckon forty years is long enough. My watch is over."

"I'm happy for you, Bob. You deserve it."

"Gonna go after some different fish, I guess."

"Great."

"Didn't you get an invite to my farewell party?"

"No, I didn't get that, Bob."

"Really?"

"Never saw it."

"I'm surprised."

As surprised as he was, Bob Osler didn't tell Cal where and when the party was to be, and no invitation ever came. Cal did know when Dale Trotter officially took over, though, because Dale made a point of telling him.

"This is going to be done differently from now on," said Trotter, "because *I'm* doing it and it'll be done *my way*. Otherwise it's the fucking 401 east, understand?" | 327

Dale Trotter was the kind of guy who hit you with a wet towel in the school locker room. The kind who made the training worse than the playing. The kind who often becomes a cop so that he never has to leave the locker room.

"I want you to call Richard Aran," he told Cal at their first meeting under the new regime, "and be fucking *tough* with him. Like Carlos would. I want him on tape saying they're moving heroin and cocaine, is that clear? I want to hear the words 'heroin' and 'cocaine' too. No more pussyfooting around with these fuckers."

"That isn't the kind of relationship I have with Richard," Cal protested once more. "I wouldn't talk to him like that."

"Like what?"

"The way you just suggested."

"Suggested? That wasn't a *suggestion*, Calvin," said the new head of Proceeds. "That was an order. . . . You do know what an order is, don't you?"

"Everything is going along just fine," Cal persisted, "and they're ready to bring us the hundred mill. Why mess with it now?"

But it was Dale Trotter who was being messed with. The man erupted like a junkyard dog, just one apoplectic torrent of barking abuse. It came naturally to him, yet the moment it stopped his features recomposed themselves and he was once more merely overbearing.

Although he didn't crave it and it wasn't essential, Cal didn't mind a little appreciation from time to time. Everyone needs the little pat on the shoulder that shows they're noticed, that their efforts, their toil, their pearls of dedication are not being cast before swine. What they don't need is a boss who doesn't want subordinates so much as obsequious, obedient, and grateful clones of himself. Only Trotter could satisfy Trotter, however, but — and this was probably the heart of the matter — even Trotter didn't come through in the end.

Unlike a cult or an ersatz religion, though, the RCMP's Toronto Proceeds Unit didn't exist simply for Trotter or anyone else to run it. It was on the cutting edge of modern law enforcement, the edge that would cut away buddy from his loot, and that was the deepest cut of all. When the pricey criminal lawyers began to howl, "Unfair! Unconstitutional! Violation of human rights!" you knew you'd hit a nerve, and even though the limb might not drop off, it would still never function that well again. Where all else had failed, Proceeds stood a good chance of succeeding. The trick was not to try to cut off all the Hydra's heads (because they just grew back again), but to separate its neck from its body. No one wants to realize his work is futile. Even those guys who spend their lives painting the same bridge have a sense of achievement. But so much policework has become little more than an exercise in futility, with a cop watching on while the very law he thought he was upholding is used to undo his work. It's bad enough trying to catch buddy *in flagrante delicto* to begin with, but when he's back on the streets in no time because of some procedural blunder you made inadvertently while arresting him . . . well, *this* was another dimension of futility altogether. You couldn't paint a bridge without any paint, after all. And you couldn't serve a law that resisted its own enforcement. This had ceased to be fun, Cal told himself as he left Proceeds HQ, after agreeing to call Richard Aran that night.

"WHAT'S THE MATTER, my beautiful love?" asked Simone.

You have to own a purring, musical French accent to get away with calling someone your beautiful love.

"Nothing," replied Cal. "Just work."

"You seem down."

"Yeah."

Simone, a ray of sunshine, was never down. She'd been up so long that what was up for most people was about as far down as she went. Cal had been brooding for some time, though. In their small apartment, the big, brooding man made it feel as if the weather outside was perpetually overcast and rainy. He carried his own micro-climate around with him.

Simone also carried a change of atmosphere with her wherever she went, but people don't notice an improvement in their mood nearly as keenly as they register a downturn.

Cal identified with Napoleon on St. Helena, but anyone stepping from the developer's Eden of North York into the Broeker home would probably have been more reminded of Martin Luther in his anguished cell at Worms. Cal's collection of military memorabilia and ecclesiastical bric-a-brac from the Middle Ages, his vast gothic chests and the kind of dark oak furniture that looks as if it lumbers around on its own feet when everyone's asleep, and the cases of antique leather-bound tomes and Simone's own collection of French first editions — all this had seemed part of the Montreal landscape, but in Toronto it made you feel as if you'd been beamed down into thirteenth-century Regensburg or Reims. Had he leaned upon a spear, C. Calvin Broeker could not have looked any more like the life model for Dürer's *Melancholia*.

But being called "my beautiful love" does wonders for a sad man. Besides, Cal didn't believe in being down. Not really. He might not have noticed that he *was* down, but once it got brought to his attention, he did something about it. He faced it head on and told it to shape up or ship out.

"You shouldn't do it if it make you uneasy," Simone advised when he told her in vague terms about his call with Trotter. "I don't like to see you un'appy, my beautiful love."

"Then you won't," Cal told her, leaping to his huge feet. "'Cause I ain't."

He went into the bedroom to make the call to Richard Aran. Simone could hear the volume but not the words.

"My people think you're being too vague, Richard," Cal was saying. "They suspect you're fucking bullshitting. So do I. You gotta be clear with us on what you're doing. We don't like being fucked around."

"You okay?" inquired Richard Aran.

"I'm fucking *great,* and I'd be better if you weren't fucking my people around."

"I didn't think I was."

"Well, you fucking are! Now let's be clear on this, Richard. Are you guys bringing in cocaine? Is that part of this deal?"

"You got heat or something, Cal?" Richard clearly couldn't believe his ears.

"No, I don't have fucking heat . . . unless it's on you."

"You just don't sound like yourself, Cal. . . . Is everything okay?"

"It's coming up fucking roses, man. And there'd be daffodils and tulips too if you people would stop fucking with us. Either you're straight with me or there's no fucking deal. Got it?"

"I don't understand what's bringing this on. Are you on your cell?"

"No," Cal lied. "It's a secure land-line."

"That's a relief."

"Now, is there cocaine involved, Richard? Stop giving me smoke!"

"Yeah, well, you know there is."

"I don't know fucking nothin', man. I need you to be totally fucking straight with me. *Is there cocaine involved? Are your people bringing in cocaine?*"

"You know they are."

"And heroin?"

"Same."

"Richard, you're not fucking listening to me. You are not being straight. Just fucking answer the questions. Are you bringing in heroin and cocaine?"

"That's part of the deal."

"Richard!" Cal was screaming into the phone now, spittle dripping from the mouthpiece.

"Okay! Yes, we are. Satisfied?"

"You can't fuck with my people, Richard. You do that, you're gonna be hanging from your own lungs, man."

"My people aren't choirboys either," Richard reminded him. "You're frightening me, Cal. You just sound so . . . so *strained*, you know?"

"I gotta lot of pressure on me. Let's do this fucking deal and we'll have a beer together, eh?"

"A lotta beers, my friend. You sound like you need a drink bad."

"Don't fucking worry about me. Worry about your people coming through on this."

"They're ready to go next week. Just say where and when."

"I'll tell you later today. But if you're fucking with me, Richard . . ."

"I wouldn't do it, Cal. I think of you as a friend, man."

"I don't need any friends. I need you not to fuck me around."

When he hung up, Cal was trembling with rage and sorrow. He'd never be able to look Richard Aran in the eyes again. He should never have gone against his own instincts on this matter. Never. He'd just screwed a relationship it had taken years to build.

As he blurted all this out to Simone, not the names or the people, just the gist, he was on the verge of tears.

"Maybe it's time for you to get out of this, my beautiful love," she told him.

He'd told her often that he wouldn't be doing the work for much longer. Crime wasn't rocket science, but there was only so long you could go on being a man in shark's clothing while picking off the real sharks one by one. They turned on each other without warning, so what could he expect? And Cal knew that when his turn came, it wouldn't be like it is in the movies. No one was going to phone in threats before backing them up. They'd just appear — on the street, when he was collecting his mail, in the supermarket, at the gym, somewhere and sometime — and — *whack* — he'd either be dead or wishing he was. If he survived, it would be only because that's what they wanted — and it wouldn't be a life worth the name. Just one beating rearranges a man's face permanently. He never resumes being Mel Gibson after the wounds have healed. The slightest interference with nature's proportions always leaves shades of the monstrous, the signature of demons.

"And do what?" Cal asked her. "Go back to cutting up meat? Because that's all I'm trained for."

When those we love lose confidence in themselves, it is like an elevator plunging in our own heart. We have all been taken down to that floor at one time or another — the floor of small horizons, of bleak prospects, of inchoate failure — thus we know it is a sign of one's humanity rather than a flaw. It is confidence that we should fear in others, not doubt. When a man looks at the horror of this world, the brevity of this life, and the prospect that no matter what he manages to accomplish it will all come to an end within a few decades anyway, when he looks at this and feels confident, we should turn and run. Confidence is about the most inappropriate response there can be to life, and those who tell you they are confident are either lying or dangerously insane. Or just extravagantly stupid. No man (or woman) should fear confiding his (or her) insecurities. They are a badge of honour.

"Don't be silly," Simone told him. "You know you can do anything you want to do. You know it is true."

"Do I?"

The problem with emotions is that they don't co-operate with us a lot of the time; they don't work with us on the project. When you're riding high and everything's coming up roses, you feel as if you could eat the world for breakfast and be at Mars by lunchtime. Yet when you need a little of that chutzpah — when everything's coming up poison ivy and you can't even shave without recarving your face — where the hell is it? It has gone over to where the grass is greener. That's confidence for you — a rat that leaves the ship not when it's sinking but when it looks as if it might sink. Yet when the storm clouds clear and happy faces reappear, when the imminent is postponed, that same rat is back, strutting up and down the poop deck in its admiral's uniform telling everyone, "I told you so, told you so . . ."

"Yes, but you can do it only for someone else, not yourself. You can do it for your god or your children or your country, but not for you."

"So what good is that?"

"That's all the good in the world, my beautiful love. Don't you see? That's how it's supposed to be. And that's what made me fall in love with you."

"That I'm a failure?"

"That you're a good man."

"No, I'm not. You have no idea."

"A good man never knows he's good. You don't think about yourself long enough to notice. But others do. And I do. There's so little goodness in this world that I wasn't going to let you go. Whatever you do, it will turn out all right. I know it will."

She reminded him of a Buddhist axiom he'd once quoted to her: "He who knows that enough is enough will always have enough."

"You're that man," said Simone. "You're happy with next to nothing because you know what enough is. That's why we'll always have enough."

"I've always thought that too much was enough," Cal told her.

He was never comfortable receiving compliments, although he gave them out the way Little John or Réal Dupont uttered threats. No man was ever more content than Cal when he was being of service to others, nor less content when he felt idle, unuseful. The lapsed Christian was a better Christian than he knew, the same kind of rough diamond as the men whom Jesus chose for disciples. Good men who were too busy being good men to know what they were, too busy serving to sit down at the meal.     | 333

"I just feel I've let everyone down," Cal told Simone. "Doris, my kids, Elizabeth, now you. Shit, I'm even letting the cops down."

"Or are you the one who's been let down? Hmm? All you've done is work your beautiful butt off for others, and they aren't even grateful."

"I don't want gratitude. I just want to do what's right."

"But you don't want abuse, do you? That's not right. I'll tell you what is right, though," Simone said, her eyes sparkling, "that you get out now and build a wonderful life for yourself. . . . No, not for yourself. For us!"

"For you, I could do it."

"Then do it for me. Just let the world get on with its own misery and let's build ourselves a place where it cannot come. Please!"

"Okay," Cal told her. "When this LOA is done, I'm out."

"No, my beautiful love. I think it should be now. . . . Right now."

Then the phone rang. Cal thought it would be Richard Aran phoning back to say that now he'd thought some more, Cal sounded far too weird for comfort, and so the deal was off. Indeed, he almost wished it was going to be this. But it wasn't. It was Dale Trotter.

"Well, I did it," Cal told him.

"I know. We were listening in."

"And?"

"You're gonna have to call him back, Calvin. You didn't do what I told you to do."

"What the fuck are you talking about, Dale? I did exactly what you told me — and against my better judgement. Now Aran thinks I'm off my fucking rocker and I'll never be able to look him in the eyes again. Nice going, boys!"

"You weren't tough enough with him. I told you I wanted the words 'cocaine' and 'heroin.' Now call him back and get me what I want!"

"Fuck you, Dale. Short of telling him I wanted him to be explicit for the court evidence transcripts, I think I did pretty much to the letter what you said. And I did use 'cocaine' and 'heroin.' Should I have asked him to confirm he was a felon and sign the statement or what?"

"I want him to say 'cocaine' and 'heroin,' not you, asshole. Maybe I should just move Carlos in and get this done right."

"You can move in Susannah of the fucking Mounties for all I care, Dale. But it ain't gonna happen. Richard Aran is not going to say 'cocaine' and 'heroin' because he don't use those words. It's as simple as that."

"Blow is what the wind does," Trotter sneered. "And smack is what your mother did to your ass. That's what some rich asshole lawyer is gonna say in court — after he's demolished your credibility as a witness by proving you dined with known felons in order to entrap them."

The buddies treated Cal better than this. It was unjust, and most of all, it was ungrateful. He changed the topic by telling Trotter that Aran was ready to bring in the $100 million next week.

"Too soon," Trotter said instantly. "We won't be ready. You've got to delay them."

"After what I just said, that's gonna be pretty fucking difficult, don't you think?"

"Just do what you're ordered to do," snapped Trotter. "And I'm ordering you to phone him back right now and delay the money. Are we clear?"

"With all respect, Dale," Cal replied, "you do it!" Then he hung up.

Simone applauded wildly.

"See," she said, "everything works out in the end, doesn't it, my beautiful love?"

"Yeah, but it's also not over till it's over."

"But it is over! It's over."


### September 2000

And it was. More or less. Over. Cal didn't need Simone to make up his mind for him, since he knew he couldn't continue much longer in such an atmosphere of frustration. While he knew that the job he did was the key to dismantling organized crime, it wasn't going to be that effective until a new kind of police unit, one specifically designed to fight organized crime, was established. Such a unit would be capable of swift actions and reactions, unhampered by red tape and a mistrustful public. It would fight fire with a raging inferno. Buddy wouldn't know what had hit him. And men like Cal would be able to work the way they needed to work, either alone or in groups, without having to worry about entrapment or accepting the proceeds of crime or getting buddy to spell out his criminal intentions or deeds for the wire. Such a unit would have only organized criminals as targets, and would prove to those concerned that the police could tell the difference between professional crime and the other manifestations. The results would speak for themselves. Right now, however, such a unit was just a dream. The reality was that Trotter and his men would miss the chance to seize Richard Aran's $100 million because of red tape and restrictions from above. This meant that Cal's work would amount to nothing in the end, and thus he'd receive no bonus. He could lead them to water, but he couldn't make them sink their tongues into it. For similar reasons, a shipment of hashish in Vancouver had slipped through RCMP fingers. Again, thanks to the way the LOA was written, Cal wouldn't be paid if the result wasn't what the cops wanted. It didn't matter that he'd done everything asked of him, and that the failure was not in any way his fault. Either they refused to pay or they shorted the bonus, handing over $3,000 instead of $30,000. It was standard procedure with informants to keep them nervous and ignorant, and there was no provision for someone as useful as he'd been to enter the ranks. Rather than see all his work brushed aside or messed up at the last moment, he decided to quit. There was no alternative.

But Cal couldn't just walk away. It wasn't in his nature. He had too much respect for the RCMP not to follow through a little longer. Yet it was over because Cal had decided it should be over. He wasn't about to blame anyone. Even Dale Trotter merited some admiration. Sure, Cal would tell you the truth of the situation, but the moment he suspected you'd formed a poor opinion of Trotter, he'd come to the man's defence. It was a hard job, and it took a certain temperament to do it. Trotter might be a tightass, but he was also a courageous man who put service to his country before himself and stood in the line of fire every day of his life in order to do it. The people who talked of peace and love and made wind chimes weren't prepared to die for peace and love, were they? Or wind chimes. They just preached it and let others do the work. But every day of the week and every week of their working lives, the men in blue stand guard over the rest of us while we sleep or go about our lives in relative safety.

"Nothing's gonna hurt you, they say," Cal once said. "Not on my fucking watch."

"Are you going to be okay?" we asked him.

"I'm gonna be just fine."

The leaves were just beginning to turn, and squirrels were busy gathering in their supplies. Here a nanny played with a truculent child; there two young lovers sat on a park bench drowning in each other's eyes. The air was high and blue, and the city spread out below us, with its patchwork of well-planned parks and its stacks of opulent office towers, looking very pleased with itself in the way Toronto can.

"This place is a paradise," Cal said, gesturing around himself. "I just hope and pray no one screws it up for you."

"We hope you and Simone are going to be . . . you know, safe."

"All that worries me," Cal told us, "is that when I stand before my Maker, I can give a good account of myself. That's all that matters to me. I hope I can say, 'Listen, pal, it's hell down there, but I did the best I could.'"

His giant laughter echoed back from buildings on three sides, as if there was a legion of disembodied Cals watching over us in the ether.

### January 11, 2001

Réal Dupont was released from prison during the first week of January. High up on his list of old friends to reacquaint himself with was C. Calvin Broeker. Cal still had his cellphone then, and it would ring as we worked on this book. People he knew to be associates of Dupont's urgently wanted to see him about a deal. It was never Dupont who called — perhaps he didn't trust himself not to tell Cal about all the crunchy, meaty things he was going to do to him at their reunion.

Tragically, however, this reunion was not to be. On the night of January 11, Réal Dupont was driving on the south shore of Montreal when — model citizen that he was — he stopped at a red light. He didn't notice someone slip out of the van behind him; all he heard was a tap on his side window. He turned to see a man he recognized, and he could just about make out what the man was saying: "*Au revoir,* motherfucker!"

When the lights turned green again, Dupont didn't move. He just sat there. He'd been shot five times in the head and died instantly.

Cal was told by his old handlers that the Banditos, a rival biker gang, had done the deed. But it could have been almost anyone. You didn't come across many people *là-bas* who wanted Réal Dupont alive. You probably couldn't find many who want Cal Broeker alive either. But he's nowhere to be found.

He calls from time to time, usually from the road, heading to another joint, but we don't know where he is. It always sounds peaceful, though, wherever it is. And so does he. He sounds like a man who, after his season in hell, has finally found himself.

# Appendix of Documents

## Mohawk Council of Kahnawake

P.O.Box 720,
Kahnawake, Quebec. J0L 1B0
(OFFICE OF THE COUNCIL OF CHIEFS)

Tel. (514) 632-7500
Fax. (514) 638-5958

| 343

08 Ohiarihkó:wa/July, 1994

TO WHOM IT MAY CONCERN:

Mr. Calvin Broeker is assisting the Mohawk Council of Kahnawake with respect to obtaining financing for a Commercial Center within the Territory of Kahnawake, Quebec (the "project"). In this regard, Mr. Broeker is authorized to discuss the project with potential lenders and to receive, for transmittal to the Mohawk Council of Kahnawake, information and proposals relating to financing the project.

Mr. Broeker has not been authorized to make any binding commitments on behalf of the Mohawk Council of Kahnawake.

Yours very truly,

**MOHAWK COUNCIL OF KAHNAWAKE**

Per: _Joseph Tokwiro Norton_
Grand Chief Joseph Tokwiro Norton

P.2

71

**DEPARTMENT OF THE TREASURY**
UNITED STATES SECRET SERVICE

344 I

SYRACUSE RESIDENT OFFICE
POST OFFICE BOX 7006
SYRACUSE, NEW YORK 13261
(315) 423-5338

August 22, 1994

File: 114-711-19007-1

Inspector ᙭᙭᙭᙭᙭᙭᙭᙭
Counterfeit Section
Royal Canadian Mounted Police
4280 Dorchester West
West Mount, Quebec

Dear Inspector ᙭᙭᙭᙭᙭᙭

Please consider this an official request to bring an individual
to Canada for the purpose of becoming a confidential informant
and/or agent of the RCMP.

We believe this individual can provide assistance to your agency
in our joint investigation of the C.19007 counterfeit case.

This individual has agreed to testify in any court proceeding
relevant to the conclusion of this case. Further, in as much as
the individual is a United States citizen and lives there, the
United States Secret Service will assume responsibility to
relocate this individual should it become necessary.

This individual is described as a white/male, 6'4", 260 lbs,
brown hair, blue eyes, date of birth 11/17/53, place of birth
Niagara Falls, New York, SSN ᙭᙭᙭᙭᙭᙭᙭᙭᙭ and has no know
criminal record.

Your assistance in this matter is deeply appreciated.

Sincerely

᙭᙭᙭᙭᙭᙭᙭᙭᙭

᙭᙭᙭᙭᙭᙭᙭
Special Agent
U.S. Secret Service

### LETTER OF ACKNOWLEDGEMENT

I, Calvin Clarence BROEKER hereby understand and acknowledge the following:

1345

1.      This letter of acknowledgement complements the letter of acknowledgement signed on October 14th 1994 with respect to my assistance to the Royal Canadian Mounted Police.

2.      I have been specifically informed and agree that the Royal Canadian Mounted Police will open a bank account in my name. The said bank account will be opened in a Canadian bank, at the sole discretion of the Royal Canadian Mounted Police. I also understand and agree that the Royal Canadian Mounted Police will deposit 12 million dollars into this bank account. I understand and agree that I have no right over this money and/or any part of it and that this money will only be in this bank account for the purpose of this investigation. I understand and agree that the Royal Canadian Mounted Police is the sole owner of this money.

3.      I hereby confirm that I have read and fully understand every paragraph of this letter of acknowledgement.

Dated at the City of _Montreal_ in the province of _Quebec_
this _6th_ day of _September_ 1995.

~~XXXXX~~
Witness

~~XXXXXX~~
(Signature)

~~XXXXXXX~~
Witness

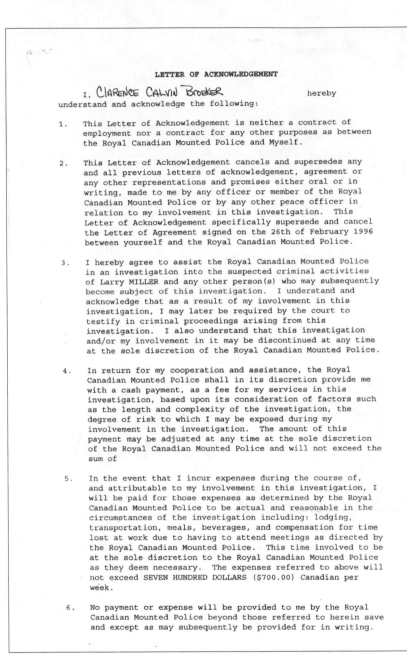

**LETTER OF ACKNOWLEDGEMENT**

I, CLARENCE CALVIN BROEKER                    hereby
understand and acknowledge the following:

346 |

1.  This Letter of Acknowledgement is neither a contract of
    employment nor a contract for any other purposes as between
    the Royal Canadian Mounted Police and Myself.

2.  This Letter of Acknowledgement cancels and supersedes any
    and all previous letters of acknowledgement, agreement or
    any other representations and promises either oral or in
    writing, made to me by any officer or member of the Royal
    Canadian Mounted Police or by any other peace officer in
    relation to my involvement in this investigation.  This
    Letter of Acknowledgement specifically supersede and cancel
    the Letter of Agreement signed on the 26th of February 1996
    between yourself and the Royal Canadian Mounted Police.

3.  I hereby agree to assist the Royal Canadian Mounted Police
    in an investigation into the suspected criminal activities
    of Larry MILLER and any other person(s) who may subsequently
    become subject of this investigation.  I understand and
    acknowledge that as a result of my involvement in this
    investigation, I may later be required by the court to
    testify in criminal proceedings arising from this
    investigation.  I also understand that this investigation
    and/or my involvement in it may be discontinued at any time
    at the sole discretion of the Royal Canadian Mounted Police.

4.  In return for my cooperation and assistance, the Royal
    Canadian Mounted Police shall in its discretion provide me
    with a cash payment, as a fee for my services in this
    investigation, based upon its consideration of factors such
    as the length and complexity of the investigation, the
    degree of risk to which I may be exposed during my
    involvement in the investigation.  The amount of this
    payment may be adjusted at any time at the sole discretion
    of the Royal Canadian Mounted Police and will not exceed the
    sum of

5.  In the event that I incur expenses during the course of,
    and attributable to my involvement in this investigation, I
    will be paid for those expenses as determined by the Royal
    Canadian Mounted Police to be actual and reasonable in the
    circumstances of the investigation including: lodging,
    transportation, meals, beverages, and compensation for time
    lost at work due to having to attend meetings as directed by
    the Royal Canadian Mounted Police.  This time involved to be
    at the sole discretion to the Royal Canadian Mounted Police
    as they deem necessary.  The expenses referred to above will
    not exceed SEVEN HUNDRED DOLLARS ($700.00) Canadian per
    week.

6.  No payment or expense will be provided to me by the Royal
    Canadian Mounted Police beyond those referred to herein save
    and except as may subsequently be provided for in writing.

- 2 -

7. I have been specifically informed and agree that any monies advanced to me by the person(s) previously mentioned in paragraph three (3) above, during this criminal investigation in Canada may be considered proceeds of crime and must be turned over to the Royal Canadian Mounted Police.

8. Upon the conclusion of this investigation the Royal Canadian Mounted Police shall in its discretion provide me with a one time financial assistance fee of fifteen thousand dollars, ($15,000.00) in Canadian funds in order that I may re-establish myself to an area of my choosing where I will be solely responsible for now and in the future, my physical and finacial security.

9. I have informed the Royal Canadian Mounted Police and hereby confirm that at no time during my association with the persons involved in this investigation, have I knowingly made threats or promises, or taken any other action that would induce those persons previously mentioned to commit any act that they would not commit of their own free will.

10. I have been specifically informed that my assistance to the Royal Canadian Mounted Police in this investigation does not at any time exempt me from criminal and civil responsibilities.

11. The Royal Canadian Mounted Police, its members and agents, will not be liable for any injuries or damages caused by, resulting from or suffered by me, as a result of my involvement in this investigation.

12. I hereby confirm that I have read and fully understand every paragraph of this Letter of Acknowledgement.


Dated at the City of Montreal, in the Province of ~~Ontario~~ Quebec

this 24th day of April , 1996.

XXXXX
Witness

XXXXXXX
(Signature)

XXXXX
Witness

348 |

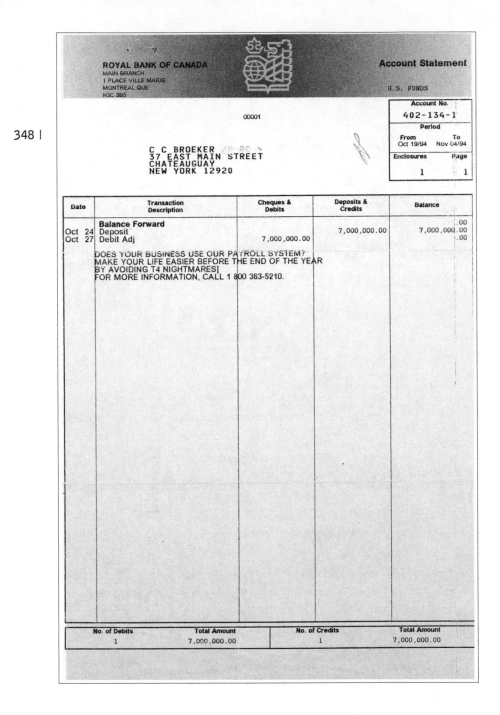

**ROYAL BANK OF CANADA**
MAIN BRANCH
1 PLACE VILLE MARIE
MONTREAL QUE
H3C 3B5

**Account Statement**

U.S. FUNDS

00001

| Account No. |
| 402-134-1 |

Period

| From | To |
| Oct 19/94 | Nov 04/94 |

| Enclosures | Page |
| 1 | 1 |

C C BROEKER
37 EAST MAIN STREET
CHATEAUGUAY
NEW YORK 12920

| Date | Transaction Description | Cheques & Debits | Deposits & Credits | Balance |
|------|------------------------|------------------|--------------------|---------|
| | **Balance Forward** | | | .00 |
| Oct 24 | Deposit | | 7,000,000.00 | 7,000,000.00 |
| Oct 27 | Debit Adj | 7,000,000.00 | | .00 |

DOES YOUR BUSINESS USE OUR PAYROLL SYSTEM?
MAKE YOUR LIFE EASIER BEFORE THE END OF THE YEAR
BY AVOIDING T4 NIGHTMARES]
FOR MORE INFORMATION, CALL 1 800 363-5210.

| No. of Debits | Total Amount | No. of Credits | Total Amount |
|---------------|--------------|----------------|--------------|
| 1 | 7,000,000.00 | 1 | 7,000,000.00 |

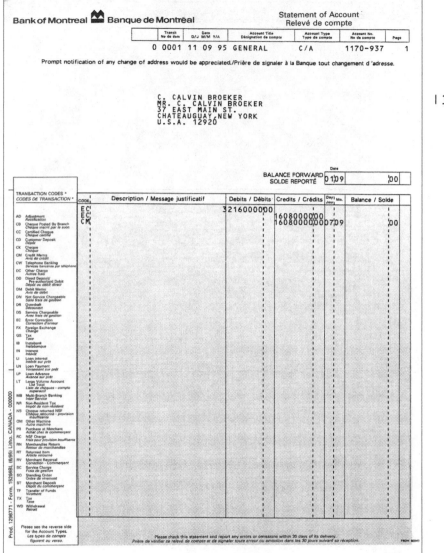

# 120 MILLIONS DE FAUX

PHOTO MICHEL GRAVEL, *La Presse*

Le surintendant Jean-Pierre Witty de la GRC et l'agent Edward Lamb des services secrets américains montrent une partie des faux billets qu'ils ont saisis à Candiac.

## Citoyen de Chambly sous les verrous

**ANDRÉ NOËL**

La Gendarmerie royale du Canada a effectué la plus importante saisie ...

avaient permis à la Sûreté du Québec de faire des perquisitions chez les policiers de Chambly, l'année derni...

...ue, selon une sour... le financier d'une ...la vente des stupé...bly. Un mandat in...contacts avec Ge...igeant du célèbre ...l.

...s Régates interna

**VOIR FAUX EN A2**

ČANADA
PROVINCE DE QUÉBEC

**ASSIGNATION À UN TÉMOIN**

| | | |
|---|---|---|
| District | : LONGUEUIL | Cause : 505-01-03693-955 |
| Localité | : LONGUEUIL | Officier enquêteur: GR38203 |
| Corps policier | : Gendarmerie Royale du Canada | Génier Jean-Pierre |
| No. d'événement | : grc95MCOM5115 | Tél : 939-8314 |

**NOUS ENJOIGNONS À**

| 351

Calvin Broeker

, Québec

Tél. dom.:
Tél. aff.:

DE COMPARAITRE personnellement devant
        la Cour du Québec, chambre criminelle et pénale

au Palais de Justice, 1111, Boul.Jacques-Cartier Est, Longueuil
à  9.15 heures, le 11 mars 1996          Salle : 1.18
pour rendre témoignage pour la poursuite dans la cause de :

            Réal Dupont

inculpé de : 465(1)c)      C.cr. Complot

            452a)        C.cr. Mise en circulation de monnaie contrefaite

Apportez avec vous

    a\s: de l'enquêteur audience:11-12-13-14-15 mars 1996

Nous avons signé à LONGUEUIL
            Le 19 décembre 1995

_____
Personne autorisée

**AVIS AU TÉMOIN**

Vous avez l'obligation de vous présenter à la cour pour témoigner dans cette affaire. Si vous refusez de vous présenter, des mesures plus contraignantes seront prises contre vous. Pour des renseignements additionnels, adressez-vous au Service aux témoins et victimes.

Toute personne comparaissant devant le tribunal doit être convenablement vêtue.

Apportez avec vous ce document et conservez vos reçus afin d'obtenir les indemnités de déplacement. Vous avez droit au remboursement de vos frais réels de transport (autobus, automobile, train, etc.) SELON LE MODE LE PLUS ÉCONOMIQUE, compte tenu de l'ensemble des frais et indemnités accordés conformément à la réglementation.

Si vous êtes assigné comme témoin de la poursuite, vous pouvez produire votre demande de paiement au Service d'indemnisation des témoins avant de quitter le palais de justice.

Si vous êtes assigné comme témoin de la défense, vous devez produire votre demande de paiement au procureur qui vous a assigné (nom, adresse, numéro de téléphone du procureur de la partie qui doit indemniser le témoin):

• SJ-249CPQ (95-02)                                                                                                      2.

352 |

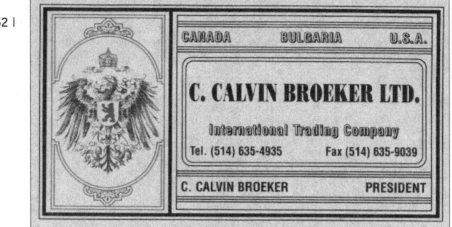

**REPUBLIC OF BULGARIA**

OFFICE OF THE PRESIDENT

I 353

3 February 1995

To whom it may concern:

During a recent meeting with Dr. Zhelyu Zhelev, President of
the Republic of Bulgaria, Mr. Calvin Broker received full
moral and political support for his project designed to
facilitate relations with reliable international business
and investment groups in the USA and Canada.

Mr. Broker's activities can prove beneficial for helping
Bulgaria's economic growth and attracting investments by
creating reliable links with representatives of the political
and business elite.


Dr. Boyan Slavenkov
Economic Advisor
to the President
of the Republic of Bulgaria

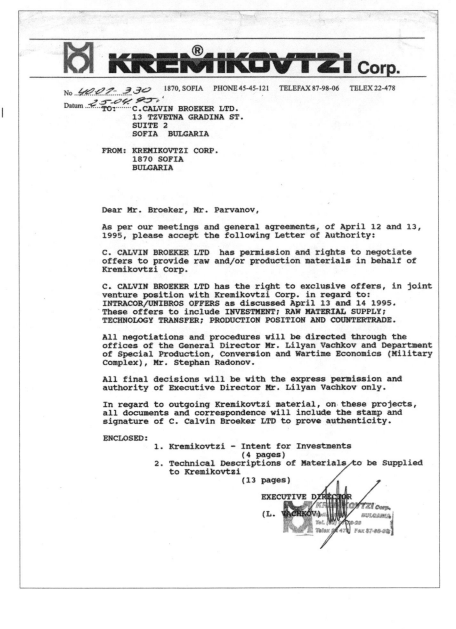

354 |

# KREMIKOVTZI Corp.

No _40.02.330_   1870, SOFIA   PHONE 45-45-121   TELEFAX 87-98-06   TELEX 22-478

Datum _25-04-95_
TO:   C.CALVIN BROEKER LTD.
      13 TZVETNA GRADINA ST.
      SUITE 2
      SOFIA  BULGARIA

FROM: KREMIKOVTZI CORP.
      1870 SOFIA
      BULGARIA


Dear Mr. Broeker, Mr. Parvanov,

As per our meetings and general agreements, of April 12 and 13,
1995, please accept the following Letter of Authority:

C. CALVIN BROEKER LTD  has permission and rights to negotiate
offers to provide raw and/or production materials in behalf of
Kremikovtzi Corp.

C. CALVIN BROEKER LTD has the right to exclusive offers, in joint
venture position with Kremikovtzi Corp. in regard to:
INTRACOR/UNIBROS OFFERS as discussed April 13 and 14 1995.
These offers to include INVESTMENT; RAW MATERIAL SUPPLY;
TECHNOLOGY TRANSFER; PRODUCTION POSITION AND COUNTERTRADE.

All negotiations and procedures will be directed through the
offices of the General Director Mr. Lilyan Vachkov and Department
of Special Production, Conversion and Wartime Economics (Military
Complex), Mr. Stephan Radonov.

All final decisions will be with the express permission and
authority of Executive Director Mr. Lilyan Vachkov only.

In regard to outgoing Kremikovtzi material, on these projects,
all documents and correspondence will include the stamp and
signature of C. Calvin Broeker LTD to prove authenticity.

ENCLOSED:
          1. Kremikovtzi - Intent for Investments
               (4 pages)
          2. Technical Descriptions of Materials to be Supplied
             to Kremikovtzi
                    (13 pages)

                    EXECUTIVE DIRECTOR

                    (L. VACHKOV)

*Embassy of the United States of America*

January 19, 1994

| 355

To:        C. Calvin Broeker
           President
           C. Calvin Broeker Ltd.

From:      John J. Fogarasi
           Commercial Attache
           U.S. Embassy Sofia

Subject:   Expression of Support for Your Activities on Behalf of
           Hummer Corp.

Having met and reviewed your plans for the promtion of U.S.
products to Bulgaria, I would like to express my encouragement
and support for the promotion of Hummer vehicles for civilian
usage in Bulgaria.  U.S. products and specifically U.S. vehicles
have already made a strong impact in Bulgaria and I anticipate
that the Hummer will reach equal success.

Moreover, your strategy of long-term commitments to the market,
willingness to make serious investments and to provide technolgy
to Bulgaria will significantly promote your objectives.  In line
with our activities, the U.S. & F.C.S. offices looks forward to
assisting you in your promotion of Hummer vehicles and other U.S.
exports.

Sincerely yours,

356 |

JOHN M. McHUGH
24TH DISTRICT, NEW YORK

416 CANNON HOUSE OFFICE BUILDING
WASHINGTON, DC 20515-3224

TELEPHONE
202-225-4611

**Congress of the United States**
**House of Representatives**

February 6, 1995

COMMITTEE ON
ARMED SERVICES

Subcommittee on Military
Installations and Facilities
Subcommittee on Oversight
and Investigations

COMMITTEE ON
GOVERNMENT OPERATIONS

Subcommittee on Environment,
Energy and Natural Resources
Subcommittee on Employment,
Housing and Aviation

Mr. Calvin Broeker
37 East Main Street
Chateaugay, New York 12920

Dear Mr. Broeker:

This will follow up your recent telephone conversations with my Washington office and acknowledge receipt of the information your provided concerning your recent business trip to Bulgaria and the Bulgarian government's interest in utilizing your services to facilitate the establishment of diplomatic relations between Bulgaria and Saudi Arabia, as well as the establishment of an air corridor over Bulgaria between the United States and Saudi Arabia.

I am initiating an inquiry to officials at the State Department to express my interest in these matters and to request I be furnished with a detailed report addressing these initiatives. I will be in further contact with you upon receipt of the State Department's response.

Sincerely yours,

John M. McHugh
Member of Congress

JMM/jfk

**United States Department of State**

*Washington, D.C. 20520*

MAR 30 1995

357

Dear Congressman McHugh:

Thank you for your letter of February 6, 1995 concerning the inquiry from your constituent, Mr. Calvin Broeker, on the Bulgarian government's reported interest in using Mr. Broeker as an intermediary in establishing a Saudi Arabia-United States air corridor via Bulgaria, and in establishing diplomatic relations between Bulgaria and Saudi Arabia.

We are pleased with Mr. Broeker's positive business assessment of his trip to Bulgaria. However, Mr. Broeker is also correct in his assessment that a private businessman would be an unusual channel through which to discuss normal government-to-government issues, and it is not a channel we would pursue. Aviation issues should be broached by government officials through our Embassies in Sofia and Riyadh. In fact, the United States communicates regularly with both Saudia Arabia and Bulgaria on aviation issues. As for diplomatic relations between Saudi Arabia and Bulgaria, that is still a matter for those two countries to determine.

I hope that you find this information useful in responding to your constituent. Please do not hesitate to contact this office again if we can be of further assistance.

Sincerely,

*Wendy R. Sherman*

Wendy R. Sherman
Assistant Secretary
Legislative Affairs


Enclosure:
      Correspondence returned.


The Honorable
     John M. McHugh,
          United States House of Representatives.

358 |

**SUBPOENA TO A WITNESS**
*ASSIGNATION À UN TÉMOIN*

Form / Formule 16
Section / Article 699

CANADA
PROVINCE OF ONTARIO
*PROVINCE DE L'ONTARIO*

To / à: .... Calvin BROEKER ............

EAST REGION EST
.................. (Region / Région)

Of / de: ...............................

WHEREAS ......... Nicholas MILLER et al .......................... of ...........
*ATTENDU QUE* .......... de
.................................................... has been charged that he/she, on or about
                                                 *a été inculpé d'avoir le ou vers*
~~the~~ xxxxxxx ~~day of~~ xxxxxxxxxxxxxxxxxxxxxxxxx ~~19~~ xxxx ~~at~~ xxxxxxxxxxxxxxxxxxxxxxxxxxxxxxxxxx
~~le~~ xxxxxxxxxxx ~~jour de~~ xxxxxxxxxxxxxxxxxxxxxxxxxxx ~~à~~ xxx
xxxxxxxxxxxxxxxxxxxxxxxxxxxxxxxxxxxxxxxxxxxxxxxxxxxxxxxxx ~~did commit the offence of~~
xxx                                                      ~~commis l'infraction consistant à~~ x
Between the 1st day of January, 1996 and the 23rd day of October, 1996, at the City of
Cornwall and elsewhere in Canada and in the State of New York and elsewhere in the United
States of America, unlawfully did conspire together the one with the other or others of the
and with a person or persons unknown to commit the indictable offence of selling goods that
had been unlawfully imported into Canada, to wit: spirits, contrary to Section 155 of the
Customs Act R.S.C., 1985 Chapter 52.6 as amended, thereby committing an offence under Secti
160(b) of the Customs Act and the Section 465(1)(c) of the Criminal Code of Canada.

and it has been made to appear that you are likely to give material evidence for the prosecution or defence
*et qu'on a donné à entendre que vous êtes probablement en état de rendre un témoignage essentiel pour la poursuite
ou la défense*

THEREFORE, this is to command you to attend before the presiding judge or justice on the
*À CES CAUSES, les présentes ont pour objet de vous enjoindre de comparaître devant le juge ou le juge de paix présidant
à l'audience le* January 12-23 and until completion of the trial
......... ~~day of~~ ................... , 19 98 ....., at 09:00 A. M, at .Main St., ..............
        *jour de*                            , à              *heures, à*
Alexandria, Ont. .......................courtroom ...................................
                                      *à la salle d'audience*

☑ to give evidence concerning the above charge;
   *pour rendre témoignage au sujet de ladite inculpation;*
(ignore if
not completed)
☐ and to bring with you anything in your possession or under your control that relates to the
   *et d'apporter avec vous toute chose en votre possession ou sous votre contrôle qui se*
(ne s'applique
que si rempli) said charge, and more particularly the following: *(specify any documents, objects or other things required).*
               *rattache à ladite inculpation, et en particulier les suivantes: (indiquer les documents, les objets ou autres
               choses requises).*

.........................................................

.........................................................

Dated the .....24.... day of .. Nov. , 19 97 . at . Cornwall ..........
*Fait le*          *jour de*              *à*

.................................................
Justice of the peace in and for Ontario or Clerk of the Court
*Juge de paix dans et pour l'Ontario ou greffier du tribunal*

CC 1700 (rev. 02/94) (formerly CC 0163)

# Index

| 361